e-Business and e-Commerce Infrastructure: Technologies Supporting the e-Business Initiative

e-BUSINESS AND e-COMMERCE INFRASTRUCTURE: TECHNOLOGIES SUPPORTING THE e-BUSINESS INITIATIVE

Abhijit Chaudhury
Bryant College

Jean-Pierre Kuilboer
University of Massachusetts Boston

McGraw-Hill Irwin

Boston   Burr Ridge, IL   Dubuque, IA   Madison, WI   New York   San Francisco   St. Louis
Bangkok   Bogotá   Caracas   Kuala Lumpur   Lisbon   London   Madrid   Mexico City
Milan   Montreal   New Delhi   Santiago   Seoul   Singapore   Sydney   Taipei   Toronto

McGraw-Hill Higher Education

*A Division of The **McGraw-Hill** Companies*

E-BUSINESS AND E-COMMERCE INFRASTRUCTURE:
TECHNOLOGIES SUPPORTING THE E-BUSINESS INITIATIVE
Published by McGraw-Hill, an imprint of The McGraw-Hill Companies, Inc. 1221
Avenue of the Americas, New York, NY, 10020. Copyright © 2002 by The McGraw-Hill
Companies, Inc. All rights reserved. No part of this publication may be reproduced or
distributed in any form or by any means, or stored in a data base or retrieval system,
without the prior written consent of The McGraw-Hill Companies, Inc., including, but
not limited to, in any network or other electronic storage or transmission, or broadcast for
distance learning.
Some ancillaries, including electronic and print components, may not be available to
customers outside the United States.

This book is printed on acid-free paper.

domestic   1 2 3 4 5 6 7 8 9 0 FGR/FGR 0 9 8 7 6 5 4 3 2 1
international 1 2 3 4 5 6 7 8 9 0 FGR/FGR 0 9 8 7 6 5 4 3 2 1

ISBN 0-07-247875-6

Publisher: *George Werthman*
Senior sponsoring editor: *Rick Williamson*
Senior marketing manager: *Jeff Parr*
Project manager: *Jill Howell*
Production supervisor: *Gina Hangos*
Media producer: *Greg Bates*
Coordinator freelance design: *Artemio Ortiz Jr.*
Senior digital content specialist: *Brian Nacik*
Cover design: *JoAnne Schopler*
Typeface: *10/12 Bembo*
Compositor: *TechBooks*
Printer: *Quebecor World Fairfield Inc.*

Library of Congress Cataloging-in-Publication Data

Chaudhury, Abhijit, 1951-
   E-business and e-commerce infrastructure: technologies supporting the e-business
initiative / Abhijit Chaudhury, Jean-Pierre Kuilboer.
     p. cm.
   Includes index.
   ISBN 0-07-247875-6 (alk. paper)
   1. Electronic commerce—Technological innovations. 2. Business
enterprises—Computer networks. I. Kuilboer, Jean-Pierre. II. Title.
HF5548.32.C4725 2002
658.8′4—dc21   2001034504

INTERNATIONAL EDITION ISBN 0-07-112313-X
Copyright © 2002. Exclusive rights by The McGraw-Hill Companies, Inc. for
manufacture and export.
This book cannot be re-exported from the country to which it is sold by McGraw-Hill.
The International Edition is not available in North America.

CONTENTS

PART 2
NETWORKING TECHNOLOGY

Chapter   2   Networking Fundamentals   39

Chapter 3   Communication Protocols for E-Business   81

PART 4
SOFTWARE SOLUTIONS FOR E-BUSINESS

Chapter   8   Searching Mechanisms   310

Chapter 9   Software Agents for E-Commerce   335

Chapter 11   Packaged Solutions for E-Business   406

PREFACE

The need for this book

The world of e-commerce is undergoing a major consolidation. Most of the pure-play companies failed to come up with a viable revenue model but the fascination of consumers to buy online and to surf the web for information continues unabated. More than 100 million Americans visit the web every month and popular portals such as Yahoo and MSN continue to attract over thirty million visitors a month. The volume of sales in business-to-consumer sector continues to grow at more than 50% a year. This is reflected by the growing participation in e-retailing by conventional brick-and-mortar companies. WalMart, K-Mart and Dell have launched major initiatives. Companies such as Dell and Cisco do business on the web that runs into millions of dollars a day.

In the business-to-business sector, the growth in volume is even more phenomenal. Most consulting firms such as Forrester, Gartner and AMR forecast worldwide business-to-business e-commerce to exceed $6 trillion by the year 2004. Companies such as GE and CISCO are reputed to be saving billions of dollars and the payback period of many such projects are in months. Major Fortune 100 companies such as GM, Ford and General Mills have launched major projects in this area. They are reorganizing their internal business processes and setting up an appropriate technology platform so as to reap the maximum benefits—an activity identified as e-business.

The effect of e-business on firms is multidimensional. It saves costs by permitting a much cheaper mode of communication. Since communication is a pervasive activity in business, e-business is impacting companies in multiple ways—much of which is still to be invented. It allows firms to sell their wares on the web, to develop close and coordinated relationship with suppliers, to promote customer service, to enable firms in the same industry to exchange goods and services on electronic trading exchanges, to improve customer relationships, and to promote self-service by customers in the area of procurement and by employees in the area of knowledge management. Companies, such as GE that are reorganizing themselves so that their core business processes are aligned with e-business activities, are reaping the maximum benefits.

The phenomenon of e-business needs to be understood by all professions in the areas of accounting, marketing, operations, human resources, and finance. They need to be capable of identifying newer opportunities arising in their own areas as a result of the e-business phenomenon. The underlying technology platform makes this possible. To appreciate the linkage between the new technology and the new opportunity space that it creates, business people need to have a general understanding of what this technological platform is all about. They need to understand how the power and characteristics of the platform is getting enhanced over time. They should be able to visualize the business opportunities that will become feasible as most residences in America get connected to broadband networks and as wireless gets increasingly powerful and economical so that the theme of anytime, anywhere pervasive business becomes a reality.

The goal of this book is to promote a general understanding by nontechnical professionals of the technology platform and its components. The objective is that these professionals should be able to understand from the business perspective the developments in the technology field. They should have a clear grasp of the important concepts and jargons that are used to describe the technology and its capabilities.

The Intended Audience

The book is meant for senior undergraduates in business schools, graduate students in MBA programs, and students specializing in the fields of accounting information systems, management information systems and computer information systems. The book is also intended for practicing professionals in the area of marketing, accounting, information systems and operations. No technical background is assumed but it helps if students are familiar with the World Wide Web. The book can be used as a standalone text for a semester or a quarter course with a title such as: Technologies for E-Business. It can be used as a supplementary text for courses on e-commerce, e-business, e-retailing, direct marketing, supply-chain management and accounting information systems.

Book Structure and Organization

The book consists of four parts. The first part consists of one chapter, which describes the business aspects of e-business. Different types of e-commerce such as business-to-business and business-to-consumer are identified and their drivers and business models are discussed. The other three parts describe the e-business technology platform. The platform consists of three layers—the network layer, the servers that are connected by the network, and the software that runs over the servers. The second part, which focuses on the network layer, consists of chapters 2-5. The basic technology of networks and the issue of security are discussed in this part. The third part focuses on servers and consists of chapter 6. Finally, part four contains chapters 7 to 11 to describe the software technologies that enable e-business.

Part 1: The Business Aspect

- Chapter 1: E-Commerce and E-Business
  This chapter discusses the business aspect of e-commerce and e-business. The two forms of e-commerce, business-to-consumer and business-to-business and the social and technological factors that are leading to their growth are studied. Various activities that make up an e-commerce transaction are highlighted. E-governance is also touched upon in this chapter.

Part 2: Networking Technology

- Chapter 2: Networking Fundamentals
  The goal of this chapter is to introduce the basics of networking technology. The following concepts and technology elements are reviewed: Digital and Analog, pulse code modulation, and data compression. The different media are discussed and the telephone network, on which the Internet and the Web runs, is described in detail.
- Chapter 3: Communication Protocols for E-Business
  This chapter introduces the concept of a protocol, which is a system of rules that permit communication. It shows how protocols used in the World Wide Web such as HTTP are members of a family or architecture. Networks known as intranet and extranet are described. New web-based wireless application protocols are reviewed.
- Chapter 4: Network Security and E-Commerce
  This chapter supports the idea that the commercial Internet cannot survive without protection for buyers and sellers. It assesses diverse threats to e-business and associated remedies. Internal security aspects including Virus epidemics and the tools used to avoid them are covered in depth. Active protection of the organization perimeter and the use of firewalls are also reviewed.
- Chapter 5: Authentication, Encryption, Digital Payments, and Digital Money
  E-business opens the enterprise to the external world. Associated with this trend, the visibility of business processes and their

access by a range of entities is changing the security landscape. In this chapter we survey the concepts of authentication, secure communication through encryption, and address questions of electronic payment.

Part 3: Servers for E-Business

- Chapter 6: Server Platform in E-commerce
  The chapter introduces extension to the traditional computing platform concept. Whereas a traditional platform entails hardware and operating system, an e-commerce operational platform encompasses additional servers including the web servers, application servers, and database servers. The chapter uses a layered approach covering the path of a typical transaction from client browser to the back-end processing linking to legacy systems.

Part 4: Software Solutions for E-Business

- Chapter 7: Languages for the Web: HTML, XML, and beyond.
  The chapter discusses programming languages and the necessary building block for the World Wide Web. It surveys languages, tools, and techniques from HTML to XML illustrating the dynamism of the underlying technology. It provides short examples and a brief tutorial illustrating the use of HTML and the promising applications of XML.
- Chapter 8: Searching Mechanisms
  The focus of this chapter is on search engines, their various types and how they operate. The chapter reviews historical search mechanisms on the Internet such as Archie and Veronica and software variously termed "spiders," "crawlers," "agents," and "softbots." Subject and topic directories such as Yahoo, and full-text search mechanisms such as Alta Vista are described.
- Chapter 9: Software Agents for E-Commerce
  This chapter develops an understanding about software agents in general and in the field of e-commerce in particular. Basic technologies such as artificial intelligence and statistical methods used in building software agents are discussed. Various types of software agents and a variety of agents actually in use in e-commerce activities are considered.
- Chapter 10: Multi-Media and Web-casting on the Web
  With improvements in both hardware and software widely available, users' expectations are reaching new highs. This chapter introduces tools and techniques associated with multi-media that web developers will use to enhance the visuals

of their sites. The chapter covers a range of practices including audio, graphics, and video that enable more active e-business interactions.

- Chapter 11: Packaged Solutions for E-Business
  The focus of this chapter is on software packages that help in the implementation of e-business. E-business requires a platform that enables integration among business applications within a single company and across different companies. The chapter discusses the back-end systems that are necessary to execute the orders received, which is a key e-business activity. It reviews packaged software solutions that integrate web-based order processing with associated business processes such as payment systems, customer support, and shipment.

THE KEY PEDAGOGICAL COMPONENTS OF THIS TEXT

Learning Objectives

Each chapter opens with a set of learning objectives for which the focus is on knowledge and skills the students acquire while studying the chapter.

Overviews

The chapter overviews provide the quick snapshots and a preview of chapter contents.

Opening Vignette

Each chapter begins with a vignette that covers many of the topics introduced in the chapter. These opening stories provide the reader with a mechanism for addressing the practical and business use of the chapter material.

Closing Case Study

Most chapters include a closing case study, which will help your students apply what they just learned. These case studies profile an actual business and then require your students to use the chapter material to answer a variety of questions.

End of Chapter Review

Each chapter concludes with the following items to help your students better understand and research the dynamic area of e-Business.

- Key Terms
- Problems or Projects for further practice
- References and Further Readings

The Web Site

(http://www.mhhe.com/business/mis/chaudhury)
To help keep the text as up-to-date as possible and create interactivity among you, your students, and the upcoming technology, we've created a Web site that both you and your students will find invaluable. The Website provides links to tools for developing simple e-commerce shop fronts, and for developing XML code and its validation. The Website also provides updated links to web addresses discussed in the book.

TEACHER SUPPORT

An Instructor's CD ROM has been created to help with course organization, lesson planning, and lecture presentation.

Instructor's Manual

The Instructor's manual contains answers and solutions to all end of chapter questions.

PowerPoint Slide Presentations

A core PowerPoint Slide Presentation of approximately 30 slides per chapter is available for distribution to students for note taking purposes as needed.

Web Site

At http://www.mhhe.com/business/mis/chaudhury. All Instructor Support materials are available on a password protected page of the Website.

Acknowledgments

I very much appreciate the helpful comments I have received from my colleagues Professors H. Raghav Rao from SUNY Buffalo, Luvai Motiwala from University of Massachusetts and Hee-Dong Yang from Ewha University, South Korea and Abdul Ali from Babson College and Dr. Abhijit Sanyal from Mercer Consulting. I am also grateful to my family for their continued support. I am thankful to my wife Banani for providing the time and freedom to pursue this project and my children Sidhartha, Ruspa and Aurelia for their assistance relating to diagrams and proof-reading.

Abhijit Chaudhury

More than any other group I would like to dedicate this book to the hard working students at the University of Massachusetts Boston. Through their contagious hard work, they have provided valuable feedback and have helped formulate material for the next generation. Along the way many people, too numerous to list from industry, have provided helpful information to help mold the material included in this project. To all of them I offer sincere gratitude. To my family and friends who have helped me through the years I extend many thanks.

Jean-Pierre Kuilboer

Our gratitude is also extended to the fine reviewers of the manuscript who provided feedback on the drafts of this textbook. They are:

- Sulin Ba, *University of Southern California*
- Reza Barkhi, *Virginia Tech*
- Kaushal Chari, *University of South Florida*
- Debabroto "Dave" Chatterjee, *Washington State University*
- Vidyanand Choudhary, *Carnegie Mellon University*

- Charles Davis, *University of New Brunswick, Saint John*
- Richard Johnson, *Southwest Missouri State University*
- Luvai Motiwalla, *University of Massachusetts, Lowell*

Your comments, especially the critical ones, have helped us tremendously in refining the book.

From both of us, it has been our privilege once again to work with a host of talented individuals, all of whom wanted this book to be as successful as possible. We would like specifically to mention a few people. They include; Rick Williamson, Senior Sponsoring Editor, and Jill Howell, Project Manager, at McGraw-Hill.

THE BUSINESS ASPECT

E-COMMERCE AND E-BUSINESS

Chapter Outline

Learning Objectives

By the end of this chapter, you should be able to:

- Differentiate between two kinds of e-commerce.
- List the social, technological, and business drivers fueling the growth of e-commerce.
- Identify various channels and activities in e-commerce.
- Explain the nature of business values created by e-commerce.
- Understand the various business models underlying e-commerce.
- Appreciate how an Internet company such as eBay is employing business principles discussed in this chapter.

Chapter Overview

This chapter discusses the business side of e-commerce. Subsequent chapters focus on technologies that make this possible. In Chapter 1 we study the two forms of e-commerce and the social and technological factors leading to their growth. The various activities that make up an e-commerce transaction and the business models that are driving the commercial world to adopt e-commerce are discussed. We also consider some technological building blocks that these business models employ. Finally, we detail how a successful e-business company, eBay, has employed many of the business principles discussed in this chapter.

A Business Vignette

Instead of struggling with traffic and crowds of anxious holiday shoppers, Yvonne Abraham of the *Boston Globe*,[1] decided to do her Christmas shopping on the Internet. She discovered a huge world of online shopping: electronics, wine, toys, drugs, books, clothes, groceries, music, more. She was among some 40 million people shopping on the World Wide Web during the Christmas season. According to Forrester Research, Internet revenues from household customers were expected to jump from $32 billion in 1999 to $93 billion by 2002.[2]

Figure 1–1

Estimated Global and U.S. E-Commerce

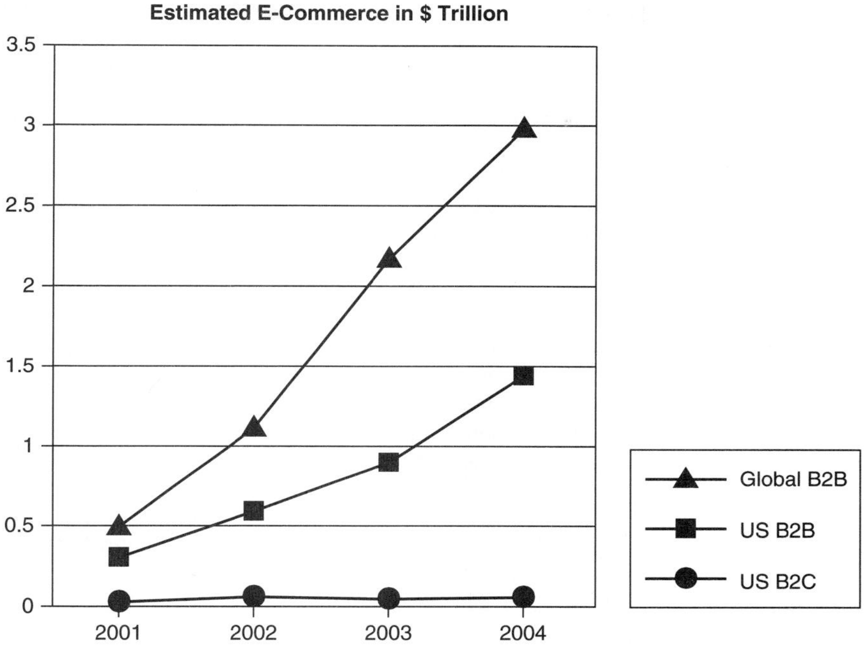

Estimated E-Commerce in $ Trillion

Source: "Riding the Storm," *The Economist*, November 6, 1999.

Revenues from Internet transactions between businesses also are showing dramatic growth. According to Forrester Research, business-to-business e-commerce will grow to $1.3 trillion by 2003 (Figure 1–1).[2] Large corporations such as Ford Motor Co. and General Motors Corp. are moving procurement operations to the Web. These Web-based systems connect suppliers, business partners, and customers, resulting in a huge online market. Ford formed a joint venture with Oracle to establish AutoXchange.[3] GM collaborated with Commerce One, a supplier of Web-based procurement systems, to build TradeXchange, a business-to-business e-commerce portal.

More recently, GM, Ford, and DaimlerChrysler announced they would merge their separate e-commerce initiatives into a single product, Covisint. The three companies have equal ownership in the new venture, and Oracle and Commerce One are collaborating to run the new enterprise. It debuted with more than $350 million in sales in the last three months of 2000. More than 200 suppliers have signed on, and Renault SA and Nissan of Japan have joined as partners. The new venture is expected to eventually have over 30,000 suppliers in the auto industry connected to a single platform. The biggest gainer will be the consumer; e-commerce on the new platform is expected to trim a few hundred dollars from the price of a car.

These ventures indicate the significant scale of operations that business-to-business e-commerce may eventually achieve. For instance, the AutoXchange part of the new venture will accommodate Ford's few thousand suppliers providing $80 billion worth of components, spare parts, and materials. This is the first step in expanding the system to the extended supply chain of about $300 billion. Ford expects to save about 20 percent on procurement and inventory costs alone, besides reducing ordering cycle times. GM's goal is to make the new venture the world's largest virtual marketplace in the manufacturing industry. This will allow GM, Ford, and DaimlerChrysler to grow as the center of a worldwide Web-based system that is likely to transform how business is conducted between business partners all over the world.

The new e-commerce platform will eventually provide a platform where manufacturers, suppliers, and customers can collaborate. It will allow automobile manufacturers to build cars just as Dell Computer Corp. manufactures computers—built one at a time to customer specifications. Consumers will log on to the Web, configure an automobile from various available choices, and place their orders. Cars will be made to order and delivered within a few days.

What Is E-Commerce?

The term **e-commerce** is used as a catchall phrase to describe several interrelated concepts and business phenomena. Buying books, executing stock trades, and checking your bank account on the Web are all described as e-commerce. These activities share two commonalities. First, they are all related to business and commercial activities. Second, the systems are running over the Internet platform and are using the World Wide Web. A working definition of e-commerce would describe it as the conducting of business activities using the Internet platform and in particular the Web. The Web runs over the Internet platform and uses the hypertext transfer protocol.

The use of a toll-free telephone call to place an order does not involve e-commerce. While it is a business-related activity, it does not use the Internet. Retailing activities, such as the Home Shopping Network, that use media such as satellite television or the telephone do not constitute e-commerce based on the above definition. This restrictive definition helps us to focus on the business consequences arising solely out of the Internet platform and the Web.

This definition of e-commerce also does not include electronic data interchange (EDI), which is the technology many industries use to allow their computers to exchange data. While these activities are business-related and are being conducted over a telecommunications platform, they are not using the Internet. Later in this chapter, we elaborate on how the EDI initiative of the 1980s is being extended by e-commerce.

Types of E-Commerce

There are two types of e-commerce: business-to-consumer and business-to-business. In business-to-consumer e-commerce, the two parties involved are a business and an end consumer. An end consumer is also known as a direct consumer. Business-to-consumer e-commerce involves *shopping* and activities such as promotion, ordering, and payment.

In business-to-business e-commerce, activities are often related to *procurement.* As consumers, we shop for apparel, groceries, automobiles, and toys. As businesses, we procure office supplies, raw materials, manufacturing equipment, and power plants. Procurement involves multiple individuals. The people who consume the items are different from those that authorize the purchase and they are different from the people who negotiate the price, and they all follow formal office processes. The forces that drive these Web-based procurement activities are different from those that fuel business-to-consumer e-commerce. Consumers are subject to different factors than businesses (e.g., business competition). The technologies used in the two types of e-commerce also differ. These differences are discussed in the next chapter. We differentiate between these two types of e-commerce whenever it is appropriate.

Business-to-Consumer E-Commerce

In **business-to-consumer e-commerce,** a direct consumer uses the Internet platform, particularly the Web, to conduct activities such as browsing, ordering, and making a payment. The Internet is not the first platform that has provided consumers with the ability to shop from home using a telecommunications medium. Most of these efforts did not succeed. A study of these failures will make us sensitive to how social factors interact with technology.

History of Business-to-Consumer E-Commerce

Since the early 1980s, businesses have been trying to provide customers with an electronic alternative to visiting a "brick-and-mortar" store. It began with information services that could be accessed from home. One early effort was Boston's Citinet,[4] which offered a variety of services such as real estate listings, electronic mail, concert schedules, and employment opportunities. Prodigy,[4] another popular service of the time, provided home shopping, stock trading, home banking, and airline reservations.

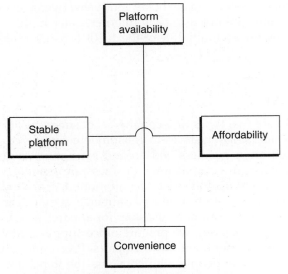

Figure 1–2

*Factors determining a
technology's
acceptance*

Source: Stephen P. Bradley and Richard L. Nolan, eds., *Sense and
Respond* (Boston: Harvard Business School Press, 1999).

    In 1984, Chase Manhattan launched a home banking system in col-
laboration with AT&T.[5] Consumers could link to their bank and display
their accounts on a television using a device provided by AT&T. Personal
computers were not yet popular, and AT&T developed a device that re-
sembled a keyboard with a card reader. Customers would insert their
cards and the keyboard would make a telephone connection to the bank.
The television would display the data and customers would execute their
transactions using the keyboard. Consumers reacted enthusiastically to
the technology in laboratory tests, so management ordered a major roll-
out. But the venture failed because consumers were turned off by the
bulky wires on the floor of their living room required to make connections between their television, the telephone, the power outlet, and the
keyboard. This kind of change in their home environment was not
acceptable.
    Mercer Consulting provides a framework to predict the acceptance
or a rejection of a new technological platform.[5] We will adapt the framework (see Figure 1–2), which consists of four elements:

- Affordability. Currently available substitutes determine the
  affordability of the new alternative. Factors such as switching
  costs are included.
- Convenience. This is measured not only as savings in time and
  labor, but also as a change from existing habits. The ease of

switching to the new technology in terms of existing habits and the extent of training required determine the convenience.

- Stability and the power of the technological platform. If a technology is powerful for the task for which it is intended and the technology is mature and stable, then it is more likely to find acceptance.
- Availability of the technological platform. Consumers are more likely to turn toward technologies that are available in a variety of settings than those that are restricted to special places.

Each of these dimensions can be plotted against a four-dimensional system with the zero rating as "poor" and one as "excellent." Different technologies can be plotted as shown in Figure 1–3 on a four-dimensional system. The closer a technology is to the outer limits of the diamond, the more likely it is to succeed in the marketplace. The e-mail system in the early 90s was close to the diamond's perimeter and grew rapidly in popularity. In contrast, online training for computer programming suffers from many drawbacks. There is no universal and stable platform that

FIGURE 1–3

Acceptability profile of various technologies

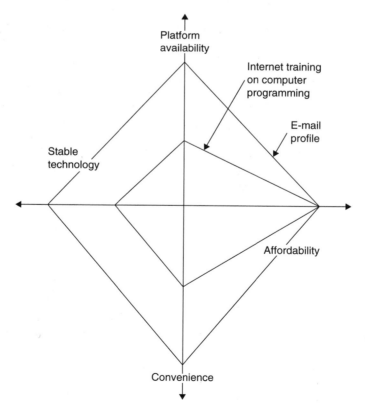

provides high bandwidth delivery of course material. For the student, it implies a considerable change of habit from attending a classroom with face-to-face interaction to online interaction through e-mail.

The framework makes it easy to comprehend why most of the attempts at e-commerce in the early 80s did not succeed. Few people had access to computers, shopping using a computer required a major shift in individual habit, and the computer was an expensive and unstable platform. No wonder these attempts failed to get off the ground.

Demographic and Technological Drivers

The four elements of the Mercer framework can be classed into two categories—social (affordability and convenience) and technological (stability and availability). Changes in these two areas have been an impetus for the increasing popularity of e-commerce among consumers.

Society has gradually become more familiar with technology and better educated. The proportion of college-educated Americans has progressively increased from 11 percent of the total population in 1970 to 24 percent in 1998.[6] Computers are in an all-time high of 60 percent of households, and 20 percent of homes have more than one (see Figure 1–4).

FIGURE 1–4

Estimated percent of U.S. households with one or more PCs

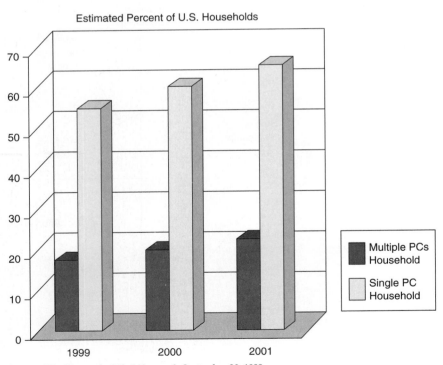

Estimated Percent of U.S. Households

Source: "The Dawn of e-Life," *Newsweek*, September 20, 1999.

From using a spreadsheet to tracking home finances to banking from home is not a major change.

Several factors support a move toward a simpler home-based life, which can be achieved through technology. Most families now consist of dual-income couples, so a technology that saves time and labor has a strong appeal. The convenience of shopping or banking at home is increasingly more attractive to harried consumers, who are growing into more demanding customers. Increasing quality at a decreasing price is the norm in many consumer markets. Reduced prices over the Web attract many consumers.

While habits and culture are undergoing a gradual evolution, technology is moving by leaps and bounds. In the mid-80s, a $2,500 PC came with a 9600 bps modem, a 10 MHz chip, and a 520 MB hard drive. At half the price today, consumers can have a 56 kbps modem, a 1GHz chip, and a 20 GB hard drive. (Figure 1–5 shows the estimated average price of a PC from 1995 to 2003.) Plus, PCs are now ubiquitous. One can, for example, log onto the Internet from practically anywhere—the home, the hotel, the airport. High-bandwidth connection is increasingly available in many residential areas. Cable companies provide Internet connections at close to a million bits per second. Telephone companies offer digital subscriber line (DSL) service with a communication capacity

FIGURE 1–5

Estimated average price of a PC

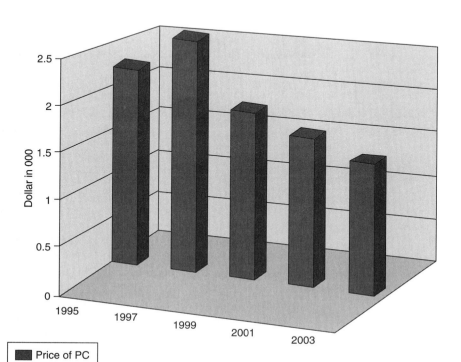

FIGURE **1–6**

Activities in business-to-consumer e-commerce

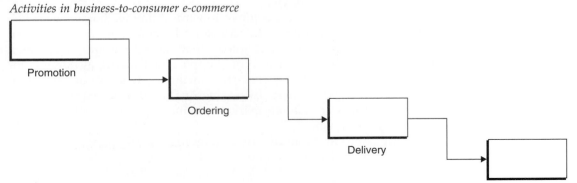

close to nearly a million bits per second. (Chapter 3 considers these communication platforms.) Compression technologies are helping convert the Web into a multimedia environment. Cellular phones are used to receive e-mails and palm-held computers to download Web pages from the Internet.

Activities in Business-to-Consumer E-Commerce

The interaction between a business and a consumer consists of the following activities (see Figure 1–6):

- Promotion
- Ordering
- Product delivery
- After-sales support

In each of these areas, the e-commerce platform is beginning to play an important role. Advertisements appear on portal sites such as Yahoo!, just as they do on TV, radio, and newspapers. Books, apparel, furniture, and CDs can be ordered over the Internet. A digital product such as music or software can be downloaded, and after-sales service can be rendered through e-mails and frequently asked questions (FAQs).

Promotion.   Advertising expenditures on the Internet are expected to increase from $3.3 billion in 1999 to $33 billion by 2004.[7] By 2004, about 8 percent of all advertising dollars are expected to be spent over the Internet. The following is a small sample of techniques used:

- Banners. These are found at the top of Web pages, mostly at portal sites such as Yahoo! and Alta Vista. They can carry a company's name, logo, and product description. Clicking on the banner connects the user to the advertiser's website.
- Buttons. These are less intrusive than banners and are placed in more relevant positions. For instance, if you are reading about Cisco at an online trading website, clicking the button might transfer you to a page where you could trade its stock or learn more about the company's stock performance.
- Superstitials. These pop up on their own page between content pages. They typically download while the user is reading the main page, and thus they do not make the user wait.
- Rich-media banners. These use technologies such as Flash, Shockwave, and Java to combine video, audio, and animation. In the future, they may rival the television for building brands.

Limitations of the Web.   Despite these emerging technologies, the Web as an advertising tool suffers from several drawbacks. First, only small banners can be shown. This compares unfavorably to the impact that is possible with television or through full-page newspaper advertisements. Second, the Web surfer is "out of control," still a mouse click away from your site. Third, the cost per thousand (CPM) exposure values used by advertisers to evaluate the effectiveness of a medium are not well established for the Web.

However, there have been many success stories, including a successful website for Saturn Corp. Instead of focusing only on the car, the site features a lease-price calculator, an interactive design shop for choosing options, and an online order form. The site for Lipton, Inc.'s Ragu sauce has garnered numerous awards. In addition to providing basic advertising information about sauces, Ragu focuses on developing a relationship with the consumer through its interactive website, which includes coupons, market research surveys, online contests, recipes, a virtual guide to Little Italy in New York, fun for kids, and Mama's guide to romance. The fundamental goal of the website is to create consumer loyalty.

Advantages of the Web.   As a promotional channel, the Web enjoys several advantages over a passive medium such as television, print, and radio. First, the Web is interactive and thus gets the individual more involved with the medium. Web surfers often say that they feel they are "in control" in contrast to other interactive experiences, such as reading a catalog and placing an order using a toll-free telephone number. The power of the Web comes from its almost instantaneous nature.

Second, the Web is much more focused than television or newspapers. The Web experience can be tailored to each user. It can be converted to a micromarketing tool, with advertising designed for each consumer. The challenge is to capture the buying habits of customers. This is often done by bribing the user to part with personal information, including details about purchases, in exchange for free goodies. Examples are sites such as Amazon.com and products such as FireFly that use old music purchases to predict the CDs a consumer is likely to enjoy (discussed further in Chapter 9).

Third, the Web is a participatory tool; that is, many people can communicate with each other in an online community. Producers of products with low information content can promote such community-based sites focusing on a related social goal. For instance, pharmaceutical companies can help establish online breast cancer or diabetes societies, and Procter & Gamble could set up sites related to children's hygiene and care. These societies often invite both experts and novice users (potential buyers) to interact about relevant issues.

The challenge in Web-based advertising is to effectively employ the focus, interactivity, and participation. Some good possibilities are playing a snippet of music before buying, browsing a book, virtually visiting a house and its neighborhood on the screen before actually visiting the house, configuring a PC at the producer's website before ordering (Dell.com), or tracking the progress of overnight packages (Fedex.com).

Ordering.   Internet sites have been classified into three Cs: content-oriented, commerce-oriented, and community-oriented. University sites are content-oriented, and Amazon.com is an example of a commerce-oriented site. IVillage.com provides a community-oriented site that is focused on females. While the focus of a content-oriented site is to provide information, a commerce-oriented site provides the facility to place an order. Such a site needs to be able to access databases of products, orders, customers, payment information, and shipping alternatives. Connection to a database server is an essential element of the platform that is required here. (Chapter 6 will discuss the variety of such platforms and their requirements.) There are also transaction sites that provide competing prices from other websites. These sites use the technology of agents to identify the best bargain. (Agents are discussed in Chapter 9.)

Several examples of interesting Web-based ordering initiatives were launched in the late 90s, though most of these firms do not expect online ordering to exceed the physical storefront. Estee Lauder, a cosmetics company, has set up Clinique.com as an online gift-referral and ordering program. Women can register for Clinique products and e-mail gift requests to friends and family who can order without ever setting foot in a store. GM has unveiled a program, GM Buy Power (GMbuypower.com), in which prospective buyers can order a car electronically. The orders are delivered from the dealer's, not the manufacturer's, inventory. The goal is to supplement the dealer, since tire-kicking is an essential part of the car-buying experience that cannot be duplicated online. The critical aspects of most marketers' businesses will continue to be through their physical storefronts, but as more manufacturers begin to experiment with virtual storefronts, an increase in direct online sales seems inevitable.

Delivery.   Digital products, such as software, news, and music, are ideally suited for delivery over the Internet, saving time and money compared to the alternative of shipping the product. (Chapters 2 and 3 discuss the communication technologies that make transport of digital content over the Internet platform possible.)

After-Sales Service.   Customer support is the final link in the chain between the producer and the consumer. The Internet allows delivery of after-sales service to customers through the use of e-mail, search engines, and bulletin boards. Companies are developing knowledge-based systems so that customers can find the answers to their questions. (Search engines are discussed in Chapter 8.) Firms use various technologies such as customer relationship management software, data mining tools, and personalization tools to develop long-lasting relationships with customers. These customer-related services are characterized as e-service.

A good customer support system adds value to products and services and is an integral part of any successful business. Several industry studies have assessed the differences between telephone and electronic support. Over 90 percent of software companies surveyed report that they offer Web-based and e-mail services, and electronic support has been found to be a good complement to telephone-based support.

Fostering the development of communities on the Web is becoming a popular way of providing support in e-commerce environments. The potential of deepening customer relationships through electronic communities excites many businesses.

Establishing an E-Community

Many companies now host virtual communities to assist their customers. A successful example is that of Cisco, which is reportedly saving over $500 million a year by providing customer assistance over the Web. Cisco encourages its users to interact over its website and meet each other's needs (www.cisco.com). The use of Web-based arrangements to allow customers to support each other is not only a good public relations move, but it also takes a considerable load off the company's support staff. By providing users and developers with information and contacts, it builds loyalty to its brand name and promotes collaboration between its customers.

GeoCities and Tripod are good examples of the virtual community model. Both claim a membership of over a million each, and both allow members to set up their own Web pages and their own virtual communities. Their websites supply the tools necessary for such virtual communities to run. Similar popular websites are run by businesses to exploit the concept of the virtual community. For example, Diabetes.com, which is funded by Sun Microsystems and Bayer Pharmaceuticals, achieves good public relations for the companies.

Establishing a popular **e-community** involves several formidable tasks. The challenge is to develop a meaningful community composed of relationships that engender not only personal involvement but also loyalty to the hosting company and its products. Done successfully, the benefit to the company of a virtual community of users is several times the costs of hosting the Web site. There are broadly three types of online communities: communities for intimacy, communities for interests, and communities for transactions.

In communities for intimacy, members engage in one-to-one conversation and have strong attachment to each other. The relationship is their primary focus, and participants are likely to engage in synchronous message exchanges. Websites for dating are examples of an intimacy-oriented community. For example, Cupidtouch.com encourages individuals to engage others on a one-to-one basis and provides personal chat rooms, virtual postcards, and e-mail. Members generate much of the content that is exchanged, and the conversation can proceed in an atmosphere of autonomy and confidentiality.

The virtual communities for interests fulfill human needs for tertiary social groups such as clubs and neighborhoods. The goal is to engage with several members in a community. Members have fun exchanging opinions and thoughts on a range of matters. The interactive nature is that of many conversing with many. Shared interests are also the focus of these groupings. Conversational systems, rather than one-to-one chat rooms, better serve the needs of this type of community. Much of the interaction is asynchronous, and threaded discussions allow members to track responses from several people. It also allows members to join or leave the discussion at various stages. Because large groups are involved, the discussion needs to be moderated. The host needs to clarify the rules of conversation and ensure their compliance. The WELL community and the GeoCities and Tripod sites are examples of interest-oriented communities.

In the third type, communities for transactions, members log on to receive information from the host and execute commercial transactions. Their primary interests are to get information or indulge in business-related activities that serve their goals. Even if they engage in conversation with other members, they are primarily task driven. The host generates virtually all the Web content. The nature of interactions is one-to-many, with the host communicating with the members. The sense of a community is

TABLE 1–1   Three Types of Virtual Communities

	Intimacy	Interests	Transactions
Motive	Relationship	Shared interests	Information and transaction
Interaction	One-to-one	Many-to-many	One-to-many
Web content	Member-generated documents and messages	Discussion groups and member-supplied contents	Host-supplied documents
Autonomy	Member driven	Moderated discussion groups	Host driven
Technology	E-mail, telephone, chat sessions, virtual postcards, virtual greeting cards	Bulletin boards, threaded discussion, forums	Web display of documents and multimedia contents; facility to conduct commercial transactions

weak. It is similar to mass media-generated communities, such as a community interested in a popular TV series or a sports event. Most company websites are inadvertently of this type.

Table 1–1 summarizes the features of the three types of virtual communities. It enumerates their distinctive features as well as the technologies that are necessary to develop such virtual communities.

Creating Business Value

The goal of all businesses is to survive and maximize shareholder value. This is made possible by reaching intermediate goals, which are often described as **business values.** Three types, or dimensions, of business values are:

- Operational excellence, under which businesses emphasize low costs, low overhead, quick response, and streamlined processes.
- Customer intimacy, where the focus is on establishing lifelong relationships with customers and meeting their individual needs.
- Product and service leadership, with continuous innovation in product and service lines and investment in research and development.

Successful companies develop strategies that emphasize a combination of the above business values, with the combination defining their competitive profile. E-commerce platforms enable businesses to obtain values in all the above dimensions. It helps reduce costs involved in the delivery of digital products, such as software, and of customer support. Websites are a major source of data relating to consumer buying habits. Such data provide the possibility of developing a more intimate relationship with customers. For example, BN.com and Amazon.com use data related to purchases to offer customized advice about books and records that may be of interest to individual customers. The potential of providing innovative services over the Web is limited only by one's imagination. The Web can furnish perpetually fresh content and allow access to vast and specialized databases. It can provide a visual appeal that will eventually match that of television. Finally, it permits a closer relationship between desire, ordering, and delivery than any other competing channel.

In their efforts to obtain business values, businesses often follow a phased life-cycle pattern in establishing websites (see Figure 1–7). Companies usually start by providing general information or content on the Web. The content not only informs customers but also serves as a promotional avenue for products. Annual reports and product catalogs are available. Information is targeted to customers as well as to other stakeholders of the firm including shareholders, employees, and suppliers. Later, the website adds more specialized content that helps to reduce labor costs

FIGURE 1–7

Evolution of Web initiatives

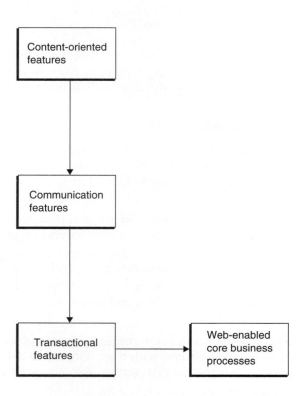

incurred in supporting prospective and actual customers over the phone. Two-way communication is emphasized. Customers are encouraged to contact the company over the Web platform through e-mail and by completing forms and sending comments and advice about the company's products.

Commerce or transaction is usually the next step. Websites act as online stores and malls. In a Web-based transaction, the customer interfaces directly with the ordering system of the company, obviating the need for an expensive human intermediary. Companies such as Dell have leveraged their websites into major ordering channels that operate at a fraction of the cost of those that are human-based. The last stage in the development cycle of a website is the improvement and transformation of key internal business processes. Companies such as Dell and Cisco have led the way. Their Web-enabled core business processes strengthen customer service and streamline the supply chain. Using the Web creatively creates business value in terms of operational efficiency and enhanced customer relationships, as well as development of innovative services and products.

Creating Consumer Value

Consumers shop on the Web because they find value there. Just as business value has dimensions, so does **customer value.** While all customers are looking for a satisfactory experience, several aspects contribute to making that experience satisfactory. These dimensions of customer value can be captured as four Cs: cost, choice, convenience, and customization.

Cost.   Cost savings is a major reason consumers go online. A survey of textbook costs reveals that books bought online are routinely cheaper than those purchased at brick-and-mortar alternatives. Auction sites such as eBay also help consumers achieve the best value for their money. Web shopping agents can compare prices for the same item. (Chapter 9 details the role of agents and various auction methods used on the Web.)

Choice.   Users are only a click away from a variety of websites. The strength of virtual companies lies in their ability to provide a vast selection without incurring storage costs for all that is offered on the Web. The wide choice available at Amazon.com makes that site popular.

Convenience.   The Web provides unmatched convenience for purchasing products. Shoppers can review product details, compare prices, place an order, make payment, and arrange delivery, all without leaving home.

Customization.   Websites can create and filter information and news to make it pertinent to the user. Subscribers to *The Wall Street Journal* Interactive Edition get their news filtered according to their preferences. Amazon.com welcomes buyers by name and suggests books that reflect previous buying habits. Boeing customizes websites to the buyer, offering spare parts and technologies that are relevant to the aircraft the buyer has already purchased.

Models in Business-to-Consumer E-Commerce

A business model describes the basic framework of a business. It tells what market segment is being served, the service that is being provided, and the means by which the service is produced. In short, it tells the *who*, *what*, and *how* of a business. For Amazon.com in 1998, *who* referred to the entire book-buyer segment, *what* referred to the books, and *how* referred to the use of a Web platform to advertise, sell, and coordinate with the publishers to deliver the books to customers. At the end of 1999, Amazon.com began representing other companies, through zShops, selling products such as apparel, software, and toys. It started acting as a Web-based mall, gathering a variety of merchants under a single portal site. Thus, the *what* and the *who* parts of the business model changed. Amazon.com was now not only serving consumers but also other sellers. In other words, the company had substantially changed its business model.

By providing a new communication and processing platform, the Web allows for a variety of combinations of who, what, and how. The channels of promotion, ordering, delivery, and customer support previously discussed have an alternative platform. This alternative provides novel ways of creating customer and business value through an array of business models.

The bewildering variety of business models coming into existence can be categorized into two groups: primarily Internet-based or pure-play companies and brick-and-mortar companies. For example, eBay.com is pure-play while Toyota is brick-and-mortar type. Of course, no company can be totally disembodied; eBay has offices, but most of its action is found on the Web. For Web-based companies, business models can be further subdivided into those that act as the more traditional retail merchants and those that act as portals (see Figure 1–8). Amazon.com acts as a traditional

FIGURE 1–8

Business models for business-to-consumer e-commerce: pure-play

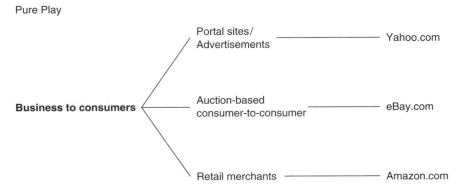

Pure Play

Business to consumers
- Portal sites/Advertisements ——————— Yahoo.com
- Auction-based consumer-to-consumer ——————— eBay.com
- Retail merchants ——————— Amazon.com

retailer on the Web. It sells books, CDs, and electronic items. Retailing activities such as these are sometimes described as e-retailing. EBay provides an online forum for individuals to engage in auctions. Because it facilitates transactions between buyers and sellers, who are both customers of eBay, its activity is characterized as customer-to-customer e-commerce. Portal sites such as Yahoo.com and Lycos.com provide search and shopping facilities. They attract visitors and earn revenue by selling advertising targeted to those visitors. Few pure-play companies have survived to this point. Their business models did not prove viable. The strategy of "getting customers at any cost" did not work. The expenses required to establish a brand name proved too high and there was no commensurate revenue stream because of the excessive number of players in any market segment. But the failed pure-play companies have provided useful information to traditional brick-and-mortar firms as they go ahead with their online initiatives.

For brick-and-mortar companies, the challenge is to incorporate Web-based channels into existing operations so as to maximize synergy. The alternative of e-commerce is both an opportunity and a threat for brick-and-mortar companies. They can either creatively use the alternative to provide more value to their customers and thereby strengthen their market position, or they can sit back and watch their competitors do the same, to their detriment. They face a dilemma: strengthen an existing channel relating to the customer or establish a competing channel. A new channel can conflict with existing ones. For instance, by selling directly on the Web, Gateway.com is now competing with retail stores, such as CompUSA, that sell Gateway's products.

Business models for primarily brick-and-mortar companies expanding to the Web can include several goals (see Figure 1–9):

- Establish new channels, which may lead to existing channels or parts of channels becoming unnecessary. This is often known as **disintermediation.**

FIGURE 1–9

Business models for business-to-consumer e-commerce: primarily brick-and-mortar

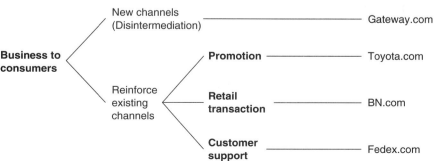

Primarily Brick and Mortar

TABLE 1–2   Websites and Business Models for Business-to-Consumer E-Commerce

Site	Who	What	How	Business Value	Customer Value
EBay.com	Everybody	Any product	Allow individuals to trade goods among themselves through auctions	• Efficient execution • Customer relationship	• Good price • Access to uncommon items • Shopping convenience
MySimon.com	Everybody	Any product	Provide comparative prices for goods sold on the Web	• Customer service and relationship	• Best price • Shopping convenience
Toyota.com	Potential Toyota car buyers	Only Toyota automobiles	Provide an alternative channel for promotion	• Customer relationship and customer support	• Easy access to relevant information
WSJ.com	Individuals too busy to read their newspaper	Business information	Provide news on the Web and through e-mails	• Additional source of revenue through subscription	• Convenience of having news tailored to one's needs

- Reinforce existing promotion efforts, which most companies do when they get on the Web.
- Provide an alternative channel for ordering, such as Barnes & Noble, which provides the facility to order books on the Web.
- Assist in customer support, as Federal Express does through its website, www.Fedex.com, where customers can track parcels.

These models can be studied by answering questions such as: What is the who, what, and how logic of the business model? What kind of business value is being created for the company? What kind of consumer value is being created for the consumer? Table 1–2 outlines various business models for several websites. Subsequent chapters, particularly Chapter 6, discuss the technological platforms necessary for implementing these business models.

Business-to-Business E-Commerce

Business-to-business e-commerce is experiencing phenomenal growth. Businesses have realized the potential of the Internet to dramatically reduce costs across the supply chain. It is allowing them to reshape relationships with suppliers by integrating production and shipment plans. In a recent survey conducted by Booz, Allen & Hamilton, 90 percent of top managers of the 500 largest companies in the world reported that they believe the Internet will have a major impact on the marketplace. Forrester Research, a high-tech consulting firm, predicts that business-to-business e-commerce in the United States will reach $1.3 trillion by 2003.

History of Business-to-Business E-Commerce

The concept of business-to-business informational systems originated in inter-organizational systems (IOS), where computer systems of companies exchange information. Companies such as American Airlines and American Hospital Supply and Products (AHSP) pioneered this concept in the 1960s. By getting its customers, the hospitals, to directly interface via computers with AHSP's in-house ordering system, the company saved labor costs. Customers were keying in the order, not AHSP employees. It also saved time and postage. Customers could even track their orders online. In addition, AHSP's ordering system was building relationships; customer who used its system were reluctant to migrate to a competitor's system. By having AHSP's terminals on the customers' premises and encouraging them to fill their orders directly, AHSP was creating several business values: operational efficiency, innovative service, and enhanced customer relationships. In return, customers obtained better prices and a more responsive ordering system.

Business and Technology Drivers

The current business environment is sometimes characterized as hyper-competitive. An ever-increasing number of suppliers for a product or service leads to greater choice for customers who become more demanding. The suppliers may be local or foreign. Local competition has increased because of deregulation in industries such as airlines, telecommunications, banking, and finance. New foreign trade rules, as imposed by the World Trade Organization (WTO), are opening local economies around the world to international suppliers.

A demanding clientele is forcing suppliers to reduce prices and provide superior service. As businesses are squeezed on price, they seek opportunities to reduce costs, not only within the company but also across the whole supply or value chain (see Figure 1–10). Each step in a supply chain may add a markup amounting to 20 to 30 percent of the value. Across the whole chain, a customer may pay as much as 100 percent over the basic manufacturing price. Every participant in the supply chain must justify its existence and the markup it imposes on its suppliers. Businesses need to ask themselves, "Can others in the industry do without me?" If a business's contribution is not justified, other participants in the value chain bypass it and the business becomes disintermediated, that is, its presence in the value-chain is no longer welcome.

FIGURE 1–10

A typical value chain

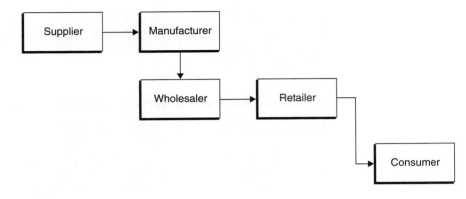

Advances in communication and processing technologies are enabling reconfiguration of value chains. If customers can contact manufacturers directly, why would they need retailers and wholesalers? The Web provides a platform where all the participants in an industry, such as banks, insurers, shippers, wholesalers, retailers, and manufacturers, can now collaborate. The platform can promote the growth of an entire ecology in which all participants can engage in many-to-many communication and coordination.

Traditionally, every member company in the value chain has been running its own business processes on computers that were isolated from each other. Output from one information system in one company to another information system in another company was made through paper and rekeying of data. In the 1980s, electronic data interchange (EDI) emerged to allow computers to talk to each other across company boundaries. The Internet has added to that capacity by permitting not just simple textual data to be exchanged, but also more complex data such as catalogs, drawings, and specifications.

Activities in Business-to-Business E-Commerce

The relationship between a supplier and a direct consumer can be described by the term *shopping;* the relationship between two businesses can best be described as *procurement.* Procurement can run from a few dollars to billions. Many individuals are involved in the procurement process, which is formal and recorded. Legal, business, and decision-making aspects of procurement are very different from those of direct consumers buying products for their own personal consumption.

Just as the relationship between a direct consumer and a seller was described earlier in terms of various activities, the relationship between two businesses selling to each other can also be described in terms of

FIGURE 1–11

Activities in business-to-business relationships

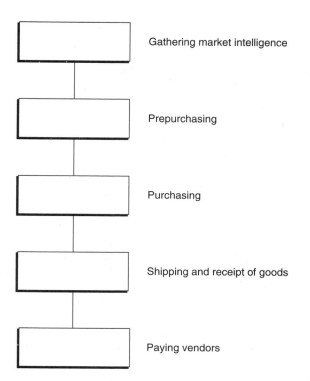

Gathering market intelligence

Prepurchasing

Purchasing

Shipping and receipt of goods

Paying vendors

activities that form a transaction cycle, as shown in Figure 1–11. These activities are:

- Gathering of market intelligence. Companies buy complex products and need to obtain, for example, specifications of products and services offered, their quality, and warranties. Imagine the complexity of selecting a vendor for a nuclear power plant and the information that is required to make such a selection.
- Prepurchasing. This consists of steps preceding an order. Important activities include making a request for proposal (RFP), seeking a request for quotation (RFQ), providing specifications to vendors, and negotiating contract conditions.
- Purchasing. This step consists of all activities that are required in placing an order. The deliveries have to be agreed on and purchase orders must be acknowledged.
- Shipping and receipt of goods. Buyers have to be informed about shipment schedules and proper receipt of goods needs to be obtained. Many shipments are preceded by advance shipment notices.

• Paying. The vendors have to be paid according to the contract, and payment instructions must be issued to banks.

EDI and E-Commerce

Electronic data interchange has played an important role in the automation of activities between vendors and suppliers. EDI allows two computers in two different businesses to exchange textual data in machine-readable format. In the absence of EDI, when a buyer issues a purchase order, the order document must be posted. At the vendor's end, the order data then need to be rekeyed into the ordering system of the supplier (see Figure 1–12). Considerable labor and time is saved if the computer that issues the order can communicate directly with the computer that processes the order.

While the communication channel easily can be established between two computers, it does not mean they will understand each other. Companies adhere to different descriptions and codes for their products.

FIGURE 1–12

Paper-based transaction between a vendor and a buyer

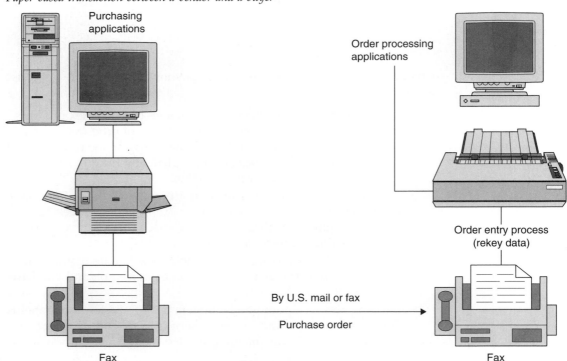

The information provided in purchase orders is not identical across companies. Before the two computers can communicate, the companies need to standardize product information, product codes, and purchase order and shipping notice formats. EDI provides such standardization in a variety of industries. Third-party service providers sell hardware and software that establish EDI linkages between parties in a particular industry (see Figure 1–13).

EDI differs from business-to-business e-commerce. A buyer of routers can visit Cisco's website to find information and place an order, thereby engaging in business-to-business e-commerce. The buyer is not engaged in EDI because EDI is limited to the computer-to-computer automated exchange of data. It does not include the interactive way data are filled in on a Web form. Also, much of EDI is conducted over valued-added networks (VAN), not over the Internet. A Web-based site offers the user media-rich documents such as electronic catalogs, whereas in EDI the computers exchange only textual data. EDI is a complementary technology to Web-based transactions between suppliers. Where the data

FIGURE 1–13

The EDI mode of transaction between a vendor and a buyer

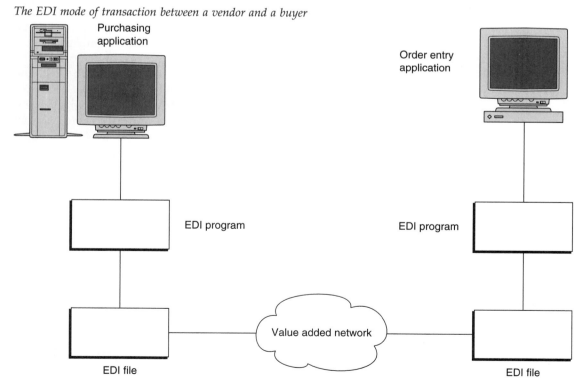

FIGURE 1–14

Business models for business-to-business e-commerce: primarily Internet

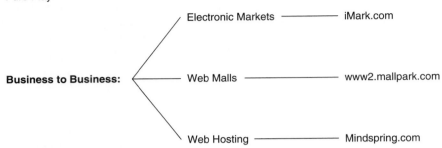

Business Models for Business-to-Business E-Commerce

Pure Play

Business to Business:
- Electronic Markets ——————— iMark.com
- Web Malls ——————— www2.mallpark.com
- Web Hosting ——————— Mindspring.com

exchange is done directly between computers and does not require human intervention, EDI will continue to play a major role. Newer forms of EDI that use the Internet platform are emerging, and EDI will remain an important module in the technological platform that links buyers and sellers electronically.

Models in Business-to-Business E-Commerce

As in business-to-consumer e-commerce, various business models can be categorized into those that are relevant to pure-play companies (see Figure 1–14) and those that are more relevant to brick-and-mortar businesses (see Figure 1–15). Many companies have emerged to meet the needs of those pursuing various business models on the Web. Some provide Web-based electronic markets, such as iMark.com, where the website serves as a forum for buyers, sellers, shippers, and bankers to conduct business transactions. Web malls are becoming popular. Amazon.com through its zShops is attempting to become the biggest Web mall.

FIGURE 1–15

Business models for business-to-business e-commerce: primarily brick and mortar

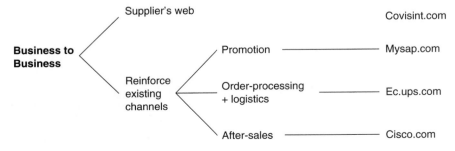

Business Models for Business-to-Business E-Commerce

Primarily Brick and Mortar

Business to Business
- Supplier's web ——————— Covisint.com
- Reinforce existing channels
  - Promotion ——————— Mysap.com
  - Order-processing + logistics ——————— Ec.ups.com
  - After-sales ——————— Cisco.com

TABLE 1–3   Websites and Business Models for Business-to-Business E-Commerce

Site	Who	What	How	Business Value	Customer Value
MySap.com	Customers and consultants for SAP products	Provide details about SAP products and available consulting services	Users and prospective users can get information from the website and communicate with each other	Customer relationship	Access to information about products and consultants
Fedex.com	Companies having account with or individuals using Fedex's services	Any product	Customers can access Fedex's information systems to retrieve data relevant to them	Customer service and relationship Efficiency and cost savings in providing customer support	Convenience and access to operational information

Businesses do not need to procure their own Web domain addresses and run their own servers. Companies, such as EarthLink.com, will host your website on their servers and provide many banking services such as credit card processing and payment.

Brick-and-mortar companies need to develop a synergistic role between their existing channels and their new Web-based channels. Good examples of Web-based channels that support and enhance existing channels include MySAP.com, where visitors can find information about SAP products and the nearest reseller and the services they offer. Similarly, Fedex.com lets customers track their parcels online, reducing Federal Express's human-based telephone support system costs. Cisco has developed a customer-support system on its website where users exchange information about Cisco products. Table 1–3 analyzes business models for two websites.

E-Government

Governments in Europe, the United States, and Japan are building websites and portals that facilitate interaction with their citizens (see Figure 1–16). India, for example, is in the forefront in providing service to taxpayers over the Web. In the United States, all the state governments and most cities are running their own websites. Providing service to

Figure 1–16

Portal website belonging to the State of North Carolina

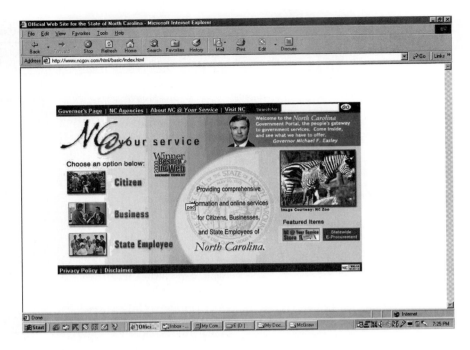

citizens through websites is characterized as **e-government.** These websites are called portals because they provide links to various services offered by the government. The portals are usually directed to three classes of users: citizens, businesses, and state employees. Through these portals, a user can find information about rules and regulations, download forms, and even conduct transactions. For instance, in Massachusetts, residents can file income tax returns over the Web (www.state.ma.us/dor/dorpg.htm) and check on the status of their refund. California runs one of the more advanced government portals in the United States (www.my.ca.gov). The site can be personalized by the user, has very comprehensive search facilities, and allows site administrators to track and analyze visits to the site to identify user interests.

The portals are not only convenient to taxpayers but are also economical to the governments. Citizens can avoid traveling to government offices and standing in long lines, and the governments save on employee time providing forms and answering questions.

E-Business

IBM popularized the term **e-business** when it launched an ad campaign in 1997 to differentiate its product offering from products of other e-commerce vendors. While e-commerce, both business-to-consumer and business-to-business, focuses on conducting basic transactions with

Figure 1–17

E-business activities

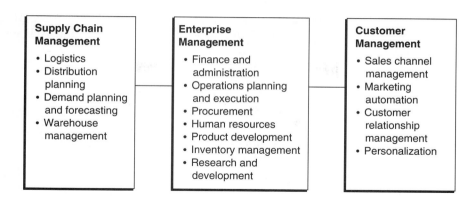

customers and suppliers online, e-business encompasses all the activities of a company that make e-commerce possible. Kalakota defines *e-business* as a "complex fusion of business processes, enterprise applications, and organizational structures necessary to create a high-performance business model."[8] In a more restricted vein, IBM defines *e-business* as the "use of Internet technologies to improve and transform key business processes." Because transactions with suppliers and customers are key business processes in a company, e-commerce activities are a subset of e-business activities. Web-enabled individual business processes and integrated application platforms, such as enterprise resource planning systems from SAP, are important building blocks of the technology platform that enables e-business.

AMR Research describes e-business in terms of three sets of activities: supply chain management, enterprise management, and customer management (see Figure 1–17). Supply chain management consists of processes related to logistics, distribution planning, demand planning and forecasting, and warehouse and transportation management. Enterprise management consists of business processes that implement finance and administration, operations planning and execution, procurement, human resource management, product development, inventory management, and research and development. Finally, customer management consists of activities related to sales channel management, marketing automation, customer relationship management, and personalization. All the processes that implement the above functions constitute e-business.

Business-to-Employee Applications

Business-to-employee applications are a growing subset of e-business. With the advent of globalization and the formation of a value chain where companies come together to provide an economical and responsive service to customers, the need has grown for a universal platform that facilitates employee collaboration. The Internet and the Web provide such a platform. It is available nearly everywhere and at all times. E-mail and discussion groups allow employees distributed around the world to collaborate on joint projects. It allows a company chief executive to communicate directly with her employees on a regular basis.

Telecommuting is increasing as more and more employees work away from their offices. For instance, large companies, such as IBM, have at least a quarter of their workforce away from their desks 80 percent of the time. Web **portals** allow firms to keep in touch with their off-site employees. The portals, centralized Web pages, provide links to personnel policies, product specifications, prices, and order entry systems. As more of the critical business processes such as inventory management and ordering systems becoming Web-enabled, portals are becoming a focal point for employees to log into and perform their tasks while away from their office. Portals also deliver training, advertise internal job openings, and promote the company's products to its own employees. Plumtree (www.plumtree.com) is a popular supplier of portal software; companies such as Ford, British Petroleum, and Procter & Gamble are using its products.

Information Technology Platform for E-Business

The basic framework that motivates this book is the enabling relationship between a technology platform and the business models it makes feasible. The nature of the platform determines what can be made or delivered and how it is delivered, promoted, and serviced. As platforms change, newer business models become possible. A world that is limited only to physical postal communications cannot sustain large, integrated multiplant enterprises. Multisite firms became feasible only with the advent of railroads and telegraphs.

The Internet provides a new technological platform. It is more productive than a telephone, more interactive than a television, and more current than a newspaper. Businesses are still working out new business models that this platform makes profitable. This process is inherently experimental, as seen by the failures of many business-to-consumer e-commerce ventures in 2000. Envisaging the potential of a new platform requires a deep understanding of the technological platform, its capabilities, and its limits. This book focuses on the various components and layers of the Internet platform, which consists of three layers (see Figure 1–18):

- Networking infrastructure.
- Server platforms connected by this network.
- Software solutions that run over the server platforms.

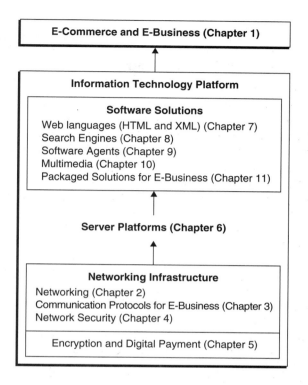

FIGURE 1–18

*Technology platform
for e-business*

This book, organized in the above order, presents the subcomponents that make up the three layers of the Internet platform. The next four chapters, which are part of the networking section, focus on networking fundamentals, communication protocols in e-business, security, and digital payment over the Web, respectively. The section on server platforms consists of Chapter 6. The last section focuses on software solutions for e-business. It has chapters on Web languages such as HTML (hypertext markup language) and XML (extensible markup language), search engines, software agents, multimedia, and packaged solutions for e-business.

Case: eBay Inc.

Do you like to buy on a fixed-price basis or do you love to negotiate? Most of us prefer to shop on a fixed-price basis. But eBay adopted a contrarian approach and pursued auction-based shopping. Surprisingly, consumers have flocked to this shopping mode, and eBay today connects some 5 million buyers and sellers worldwide. More than 63 million adults in the United States recognize the eBay name, according to a study by Brad Institute, in comparison to 101 million adults who recognize the Amazon.com name.

EBay Inc.'s founder, Pierre Omidyar, conceived of putting a flea market on the Web that permitted haggling among buyers and sellers. He realized that not all products have a fixed and stable price. If an item is unique, such as a painting, or if the supply and demand fluctuates, as in the case of shares and commodities, then the items are unlikely to have a stable price. The only way to determine the price in such a case is to let the buyers and sellers get together and settle it among themselves.

The management savvy of eBay CEO Meg Whitman turned Omidyar's quirky idea into a success. She made eBay into an electronic form of a global bazaar where visitors can enjoy the fluid give-and-take on a friendly and funky website. She also piloted eBay's successful initial public offering (IPO) in September 1998 and guided the company in growing into an e-commerce giant. Whitman is a rare woman CEO in the fast-moving world of e-commerce. She has an MBA from Harvard University and has extensive brand management experience at companies such as Disney's Consumer Products Unit, Stride Rite Corp. and Hasbro, Inc.

Pricing was not the only novel feature of eBay's business model. Most e-commerce sites have yet to make a profit, including mighty Amazon.com. But eBay is a major exception. It made money right from the start. The company's business model avoids all costs associated with physical logistics. It does not take physical possession of the goods and therefore does not incur shipping, warehousing, and tracking costs that a company such as Amazon.com must bear. It acts as a broker and charges sellers a commission and a listing fee. Despite sales of over $1 billion, eBay employs only a few hundred people. Investors like an Internet company that, for a change, is profitable. EBay has boosted its stock valuation over $8 billion.

EBay also has been successful in creating a community among its visitors. According to *Business Week*,[9] eBay's members are intensely loyal and spend an average of 130 minutes on the site—double that of any other website. Whitman describes it as a "community-commerce" model where people hang out not only to deal but also to communicate. Some of these repeat visitors have become small dealers who represent brick-and-mortar establishments. EBay is fast becoming a storefront for small businesses throughout the nation. The company is planning to branch out into auctioning items that cannot be mailed, such as antique cars, furniture, and properties. Whitman is confident that eBay is "going to change retail forever."

Summary

This chapter discussed the business side of e-commerce. We examined the two forms of e-commerce—business-to-consumer and business-to-business—and the social and technological factors leading to their growth. The activities that make up an e-commerce transaction and the business models that are driving the commercial world to adopt e-commerce were covered. Finally, we discussed eBay, which has employed in its e-business initiative business principles discussed in this chapter.

Key Terms

Business value   17

Business-to-business
  e-commerce   22

Business-to-consumer
  e-commerce   7

Business-to-employee
  applications   31

Customer value   19

Disintermediation   21

E-business   30

E-commerce   6

E-community   16

E-government   30

Portals   32

Review Questions

1. What type of business model has eBay adopted? Compare it to the model adopted by Amazon.com.

2. Why do consumers flock to eBay's site? What kind of consumer value does the site offer?

3. Use the Mercer Consulting framework (affordability, availability, stability, and convenience) to analyze consumer acceptance of the following new e-commerce related technologies:

   a. Watching television on a personal computer. A PC brings in interactivity; users can click on part of an advertisement to obtain more information and go to a different TV channel or website.

   Clarify your assumptions about the demographic sector you have in mind. Select a demographic group that is most likely to embrace the new technology.

4. Visit www.unicast.com. Write a short note on the use of superstitial in Web-based advertisement. Describe what it is and how it works. How does it compare with banners as an advertising vehicle?

5. How does business-to-business e-commerce differ from business-to-consumer e-commerce? What are the prospects of business-to-business e-commerce?

6. Describe the drivers of growth for business-to-business e-commerce.

7. Describe some of the business models employed in business-to-business e-commerce.

8. What role is the Internet platform playing in e-governance?

9. What is business-to-employee application? What role is portal software playing in the development of these sites?

Projects

1. Visit websites belonging to student-developed businesses such as www.digimo.com, www.startemup.com, www.centrata.com, and www.priorityflowers.com. Write a short note on these businesses.

2. Assume your school wants to start an e-commerce initiative. Develop a business plan as to how it may implement the venture.

References, Readings, and Hyperlinks

1. "Diary of an On-line Shopping Trip." *Bostan Globe,* November 4, 1999.
2. "The Storefront: Enterprise-Strength E-Business." *DB2 Magazine,* Fall 1999.
3. "Riding the Storm." *The Economist,* November 6, 1999.
4. "Equivalent of Cable TV Coming for Computer Users." *Boston Globe,* February 13, 1989.
5. Bradley, Stephen P., and Richard L. Nolan. *Sense and Respond: Capturing Value in the Network Era.* Boston: Harvard Business School Press, 1999.
6. Haylock, Christina Ford, and Len Muscarella. *Net Success.* Holbrook, MA: Adams Media Corporation, 1999.
7. "Advertising That Clicks." *The Economist,* October 9, 1999.
8. www-3.ibm.com/e-business/overview/28212.html
9. "In the Ring: eBay versus Amazon.com." *Business Week,* May 31, 1999.
10. Kalakota, Ravi, and Marcia Robinson. *E-Business: Roadmap for Success.* Reading, MA: Addison-Wesley, 1999.
11. Martin, Chuck. *Net Future: The 7 Trends That Will Drive Your Business, Create New Wealth, and Define Your Future.* New York: McGraw-Hill, 1999.
12. Seybold, Patricia B. *Customers.Com.* New York: Times Business, 1998.
13. Sokol, Phyllis K. *From EDI to Electronic Commerce: A Business Initiative.* New York: McGraw-Hill, 1995.
14. "The Dawn of e-Life." *Newsweek,* September 20, 1999.
15. "E-Management Survey." *The Economist,* November 11, 2000.
16. "The eBiz 25." *Business Week,* September 27, 1999.
17. Chaudhury, A.; D. Mallick; and H. Raghav Rao. "Web Channels in Electronic Commerce," *Communications of ACM* (expected in year 2001).
18. www.amrresearch.com/services/modelcopy.asp
19. www.state.ma.us/dor/dorpg.htm
20. Weill, Peter, and Marianne Broadbent. *Leveraging the New Infrastructure.* Boston: Harvard Business School Press, 1998.

NETWORKING TECHNOLOGY

CHAPTER

2

NETWORKING
FUNDAMENTALS

Chapter Outline

Learning Objectives

By the end of this chapter, you should be able to:

- Differentiate between analog and digital signals and between analog and digital messages.
- Explain how an analog signal is converted to a digital signal and vice versa.
- Understand how multiplexing technologies allow multiple signal streams to be sent through the same media simultaneously.

- List the various media choices such as copper wire, coaxial cable, fiber optic, and wireless transmission.
- Describe the bandwidths of various transmission media and the "last mile problem."
- Explain various types of wireless transmission and their different generations.
- Understand new protocols in wireless transmission such as Bluetooth.

Chapter Overview

You are traveling to your office in a car. On the AM radio, you hear about a forthcoming initial public offering (IPO). You think it is a good investment opportunity, so you take out your Web-enabled personal digital assistant (PDA), connect to your broker's website, and place an order. This mobile commerce, or m-commerce, is a type of e-commerce where the wireless platform is used to conduct business. What are the current prospects of this technology? Wireless telephony currently is using generations one and two. What applications will wireless technology enable when generation four is implemented in 2005?

To make an informed guess about the nature of e-commerce in the future, a businessperson needs to understand the basics of the networking platform that enables interaction between buyers and sellers. This chapter introduces the fundamentals of the networking technology. The following concepts and technology elements are reviewed:

- Digital and analog. This chapter discusses the difference between the two and why digital systems are preferable to analog systems. Most technologies are migrating toward the digital version.
- Pulse code modulation (PCM). Signals in nature, such as our voice, arise as analog signals, so it is necessary to transform them to digital through PCM. PCM makes it possible for voice and video to be transmitted over telephone lines.
- Modulation. The wireless, whether it is the satellite or the cellular transmission, is an analog medium. Digital messages are carried

over the wireless through a process of modulation, amplitude modulation (AM) and frequency modulation (FM).

- Multiplexing. Just as multiple conversations can be held in the same room, multiple signals can be transported over the same medium through a process of multiplexing, time division multiplexing and frequency division multiplexing.
- Data compression. The current generation of wireless phones has a limited capacity. Data need to be compressed so that Web pages can be transported to mobile devices and displayed.
- Communication media. A variety of media is being used in our homes and offices such as satellite transmission, coaxial cable, local area network cables, and telephone lines.
- Telephone networks. The Internet runs over the telephone networks and its power and limitations constrain the kinds of business interactions that are possible over this platform.

A Technical Vignette

Bandwidth-intensive applications, such as video, broadcast-quality voice, and collaborative engineering, are creating enormous demands for data communication capacity over the Internet. To meet these increasing demands, the public data networks need major upgrading. Improvements in three areas are visible. The capacity of the networks used by the Internet service providers (ISPs) is being augmented, the routers connecting the networks are being replaced by high-speed optical routers, and massive Web server farms are being developed to host data-intensive applications.

Telephone companies are racing to provide high-capacity synchronous optical network (SONET) lines to ISPs. Most of the long-distance carriers are upgrading their fiber optic networks to OC-192 10 gbps lines. These lines use dense wave division multiplexing (DWDM) techniques to increase the data capacity of fiber lines. In DWDM, lights of various wavelengths are sent simultaneously through the same fiber to increase the capacity multiple times. Qwest is at the forefront in employing the latest optical technologies. The company is converting its 18,500-mile backbone to OC-192. Williams, another long-distance carrier, is laying 20,000 miles of fiber that will run OC-192 lines. Similarly, Level 2, an emerging global carrier with many international locations, is laying high-capacity cables linking the international sites with 50 cities in the United States. An OC-192 line running at 10 gbps can download a three-hour movie in just one second. Such high capacities are required for collaborative work on large CAD/CAM files. OC-192 lines make feasible real-time collaboration between virtual engineering design groups spread across the country. Manufacturers and their suppliers' design teams can co-develop products in a concurrent fashion, thus significantly reducing product development lead times.

Use of terabit (1,000 gigabits per second) routers is also augmenting the data capacities of the ISPs. A terabit router is like a high-speed interchange from one state highway to another one. These routers provide links between high-speed backbones run by telephone companies and ISPs; data traveling on one company's backbone switch to another company's backbone. Terabit routers have the capacity to transmit high-definition television (HDTV) signals with a quality that is natural to the eye. These optical routers have built-in management functions that help operators maintain a trouble-free network.

Massive Web farms, being developed by Intel and other companies, will connect to these high-capacity backbones. The first such server farm, from Intel, employs 10,000 servers. Eventually, Intel plans to have more than a dozen such farms in Tokyo, London, and the United States. These server farms, linked to high-capacity lines, will provide Web-hosting service and end-to-end e-commerce service to companies that do not wish to develop their own systems. Companies such as Citigroup and Excite@Home Corp. are migrating their Web services to these Intel server farms. Eventually, these farms will provide customized service, application hosting, data storage, and broadcast-quality audio and video. With OC-192 SONET lines, terabit routers, and server farms, help appears to be on the way for businesses confronting an ever-increasing demand for data communication.

Digital and Analog

Familiar technologies such as radio, videocassette recorders, and telephones are or were originally analog in nature. However, the Internet is a digital system. A major transformation of the e-commerce technological platform is under way, forcing familiar analog technologies to give way to their digital counterparts.

The word *digital* stands for discrete. For instance, written words and alphabets are discrete, as are the traffic signals and the alphabetical grades on a report card. There only a few fixed values. In the case of the English language, there are 26 letters. On the other hand, the word *analog* stands for continuously varying values. Most phenomena in nature are analog (e.g., temperature, humidity, and pressure). Both sound waves and light waves are analog. Human communication can be both digital and analog. Our language is digital, but music and gestures are analog.

When the signal value can be one of only a few discrete values, it is called a **digital signal.** Often, signals in communication are in the nature

FIGURE 2–1

Analog and digital signals

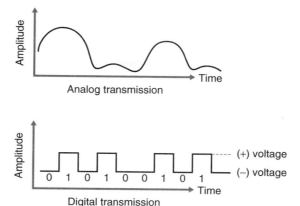

of electric current. Digital signals often have just two voltage values (e.g., plus and minus 15 volts) and the value changes abruptly from one to another. But for **analog signals,** the value changes in a smooth fashion. Figure 2–1 compares digital to analog signals.

It is important to differentiate between signals and messages. The human voice is analog because it varies in a continuous fashion. But if you are reading the alphabet grades, your message is digital. It is common to use analog signals to send digital messages and, conversely, to use digital signals to send analog messages. Transmitting a text file over the telephone (which is analog in most homes) involves using analog signal transmission for a digital message. Similarly, the CD-ROM encodes music, which is an analog message, in a digital format. Table 2–1 presents combinations of digital and analog signals and digital and analog messages.

Digital versus Analog

Digital transmission is preferred over analog transmission for a number of reasons. First, digital signals are easier to recover after distortion.

TABLE 2–1   Digital and Analog Signals and Messages

	Digital Message	Analog Message
Digital Signal	Computer hard drive reads a text file	CD-ROM plays music
Analog Signal	Modem transmits a text file	Stereo speaker transmits music from a cassette

FIGURE 2–2

Signal regeneration in digital transmission

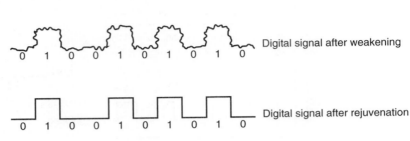

Original digital signal

0 1 0 0 1 0 1 0 1 0

Digital signal after weakening

0 1 0 0 1 0 1 0 1 0

Digital signal after rejuvenation

0 1 0 0 1 0 1 0 1 0

Over time, a signal weakens due to resistance in the medium, and its shape gets distorted. If the signal is digital, it is easy to recover the original shape because there are only two possible shapes (see Figure 2–2). That is not the case with analog signals, where the waveform may be any continuous shape. After distortion, there is no way to know what the original shape was. There are ways to remove noise, but not all noise can be removed, and when the signal is amplified so too is the noise.

Second, a digital sequence can be converted to a decimal number using binary arithmetic. This number can then be used for encryption and for error correction. For instance, the number may be divided by a large value and the remainder sent along with the digital signal. At the other end, the receiver may use the signal received to repeat the same calculation. If the receiver gets the same remainder, then there is a high likelihood that the message has been received without error. These calculations are not possible if the signal is in an analog form.

Finally, much of new technology is digital. Most equipment uses computer chips that recognize only two values: 1 and 0. Much of the current traffic over networks is computer data which are digital in nature. When the platform is digital, unnecessary conversion and reconversion between digital and analog signals can be avoided.

Conversion of Analog to Digital

Because much of nature is analog, most signaling and media technologies initially appear in analog form. Television, radio, and the telephone all developed first as analog systems. The cassette recorder is also analog; the magnetic material distribution on the surface of the tape is analog to the sound waves that are recorded. The microphone attached to personal computers is analog, as are the speakers.

However, much of human communication consists of digital messages such as text. Computers are digital and the only data they use are binary data: 1s and 0s. In fiber optic transmission, light or laser is sent as pulses in which on and off correspond to 1 and 0. Part of the telephone network that connects our homes to telephone central offices is analog. Because the network is designed to accept continuously varying signals, it is often necessary to convert digital signals into analog signals and vice versa. That also happens in computers. The CD-ROM reads and encodes music in a digital format. However, the signals sent to the speakers are analog. Similarly, the microphone generates analog signals, but the voice that is recorded on the hard drive is digital.

Converting an analog signal to digital is conceptually similar to describing a continuous curve to someone over the phone. For example, the variation in share price for a stock in a day can be described over the phone by reading out values of the share price at, say, 15-minute intervals. The listener could graph these values, yielding an approximation as to how the share price may have varied throughout the day. The same logic is used in technology and is called **pulse code modulation** (PCM).

To convert analog phone signals to digital pulses, PCM measures the signal at a certain frequency and reports the height of the signal. It takes measurements every 1/8,000 of a second and uses 8 bits to report the height of the wave (see Figure 2–3); that is, it takes 8,000 * 8 = 64,000 bits, or 64 kilobits per second, to provide an approximation of the analog signal. The value 64 kbps is an important unit in telephony—it represents in the digital world a single voice line. Capacities in digital transmission systems are often represented as multiples of this unit.

FIGURE 2–3

Pulse code modulation

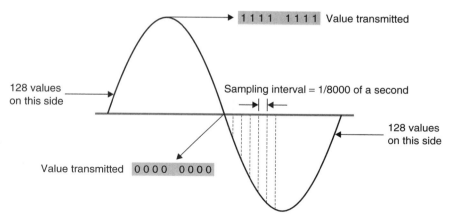

1 1 1 1 1 1 1 1 Value transmitted

128 values on this side

Sampling interval = 1/8000 of a second

128 values on this side

Value transmitted 0 0 0 0 0 0 0 0

A CD is another device that has analog signals (music) encoded as digital. A laser reads the presence and absence of crevices burned into the surface. A crevice represents the bit 0, and its absence, the bit 1. It uses 16 bits to measure the height of an analog signal, and it measures it 44,100 times per second for each of the two channels of a stereo system. Therefore, it uses 44,100 * 16 * 2 bits to record music for each second. That equals 176 kilobytes (a byte is 8 bits) per second, or 3,600 * 0.176 = 633 megabytes for each hour of music.

PCM techniques are also used in digital cellular phones and in Internet telephony. The sampling rate in digital cellular phone is lower at 8 kbps. PCM is also used for recording video analog signals in digital format. It uses 10 bits to measure the amplitude of the light wave and does it 9.2 million times per second. That is, a live video can be digitized at 92 mbps (million bits per second).

Modulation

We often need to send a digital signal stream of 1s and 0s using analog transmission; that is, with continuously varying signals. A smooth varying signal (see Figure 2–4) has four characteristics: amplitude, frequency, wavelength, and phase. The amplitude is the measure of the intensity of the wave. In Figure 2–4, it is represented as the height. This height varies continuously; it rises, falls, and rises again. Frequency measures the number of times it cycles through this rise and fall every second. Hertz (Hz) is a measure of frequency; 1 Hz equals 1 cycle per second. Wavelength is the physical distance between comparable points on the adjacent waves. The phase of the wave at a point measures the relative state of the amplitude in the rise and fall cycle.

When an e-mail is being transferred over the analog phone line, it is necessary to represent the text message (which is digital 1s and 0s) using

FIGURE 2–4

A smooth wave

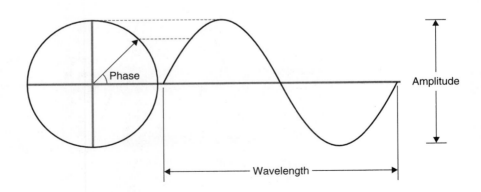

FIGURE 2–5

*Using AM to
transmit letter A*

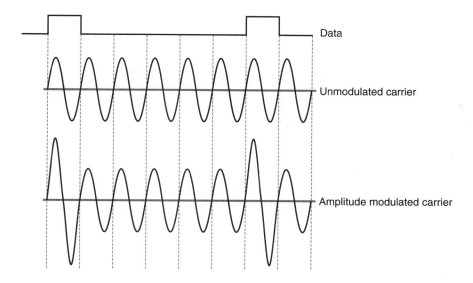

a continuously varying current. There are several ways to use a regular wave to accomplish that.

Amplitude Modulation (AM)

In **amplitude modulation,** 1s and 0s are represented as waves of two different amplitudes. For example, 1s may be represented as waves of high amplitude for a certain duration, and 0s as waves of low amplitude for the same duration. In the world of sound, this would correspond to talking loudly and softly. Assume that the time duration is equal to a single cycle. The letter A is represented as 1000001 in the computer. To transmit it, we would send a wave of high amplitude, followed by five waves of low amplitude, and finally a wave of high amplitude (see Figure 2–5).

Frequency Modulation (FM)

In **frequency modulation,** 1s and 0s are represented as waves of two different frequencies. For example, 1s may be represented as waves of high frequency for a certain duration, and 0s as waves of low frequency for the same duration. In the world of sound, this would correspond to talking at high pitch and low pitch. The letter A is represented as 1000001 in the computer. To transmit it, we would send a signal of high frequency, followed by five signals of low frequency, and finally a signal of high frequency again (see Figure 2–6).

Figure 2–6

Using FM to transmit letter A

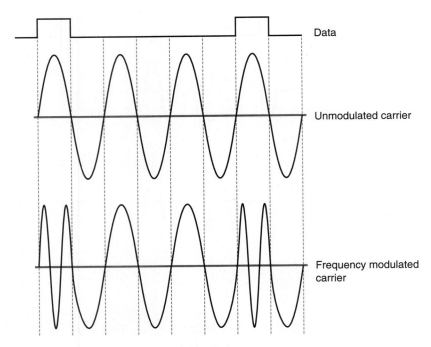

Multiplexing

Often multiple signals need to be sent over the same medium at the same time. This allows for more intensive use of the telecommunications media. The technology that achieves this is known as **multiplexing.** Two popular modes of multiplexing are **frequency division multiplexing** (FDM) and **time division multiplexing** (TDM).

FDM was introduced so that multiple voice signals could be placed on the same telephone wire that connected our residences to the telephone network central office. With FDM, multiple analog signals are superimposed on the same medium, but each signal occupies a different frequency spectrum (see Figure 2–7). This is similar to what happens in a musical chorus when vocalists sing different notes at the same time. The equipment used for FDM is called a multiplexer, and it works in pairs. At one end, the multiplexer unit places different signals over the same wire, while at the other end the signals are separated by the other multiplexer.

In time division multiplexing, each signal is allotted a time slot (see Figure 2–8). Time is sliced and shared among different signal senders. Here, too, multiplexers operate in pairs. At one end, the signals are put

FIGURE 2–7

Frequency division multiplexing

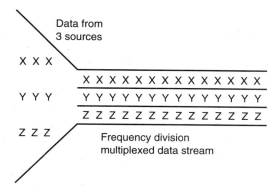

FIGURE 2–8

Time division multiplexing

together and, at the other end, they are separated. TDM works with digital signals in which bits or bytes are taken in from different data streams and put on the medium. At the other end, the composite data stream is then split into the constituent data streams. With TDM, time is allocated to all data sources irrespective of whether they have data to send or not. This can lead to unused time slots when the data sources are down.

A more efficient scheme is *statistical TDM* in which the statistical multiplexer allocates time slots dynamically on demand. When there are more data sources than time slots available in a transmission frame, the data sources are furnished with buffers, and the multiplexer continuously scans these buffers and multiplexes the data when available.

Digital cellular systems depend on the application of the various technologies discussed here—PCM, AM, FM, FDM, and TDM.

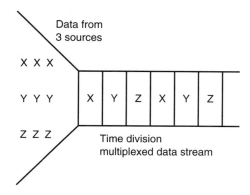

Data Compression

Without **data compression,** the limited bandwidth of the current communication platforms would be insufficient to transmit audio, images, and video. Data compression techniques help by sending a similar amount of information using fewer bits. Modems, multiplexers, and various storage devices use data compression. These techniques are based on finding redundant or repeating bit patterns and then substituting them with a smaller bit pattern. For example, letters such as *E, A,* and *I* appear very often. Substituting the seven-bit codes for these letters with special two-bit codes reduces the number of bits that need to be transmitted.

There are two types of data compression techniques: lossless and lossy. No information is lost with lossless compression. Business applications such as payroll cannot tolerate a loss of data. With lossy compression, some of the information is lost. In video transmission, it may not be perceptible to the viewer if some data bits are not transmitted. Data transmission for video can be reduced considerably by reducing picture resolution as well as the number of colors used.

A few methods can be used in data compression. A text document can have many blank spaces, usually occurring around diagrams and tables and between paragraphs. A blank space takes seven bits like any other character. A sequence of such blank spaces can be replaced by sending three bytes of information (see Figure 2–9). The first byte is a nonprintable character that signals that the next two bytes refer to information on compressed data. The second byte refers to the character being replaced, and the third byte refers to the number of characters in the repeating sequence. A byte of eight bits could refer to any number from 0 to 255 instances. If we had a sequence of 100 consecutive blank spaces, we would require only three bytes to replace the same information provided by the hundred bytes.

Similarly, graphical user interfaces often have a uniform color background such as blue. A graphical display showing 64K (65,526) types of colors would require two bytes (2^{16} = 65,526) for each pixel to represent the background color. A method of compression that employs a special

FIGURE 2–9

A data compression scheme

S = Special Character

R = Repeated Data Character

C = Character Count

character to signify the start of data compression information, two bytes for the color, and say four bytes for representing the number of pixels that have the same color would provide significant savings in data bit transmission.

Digitized video signals in videoconferencing employ a different technique. For a room-based videoconference, much of the room background and the foreground table remains unchanged from one moment to the next. Therefore, it is not necessary to send the same information over and over again. Only that part of the frame that has changed is sent from one frame transmission to another in videoconferencing. This results in high data compression. Video also permits the use of lossy compression techniques. The resolution level and the variety of color seen can be sacrificed to achieve a reasonably speedy transmission.

Media

Media are the substance through which the signals flow. Communication media are ubiquitous. Many popular media forms are available right in the living room: twisted-pair copper wiring used for telephone wires, coaxial cables to bring television signals from cable providers, and electromagnetic radiation picked up by cellular phones or radios. Media can be described in terms of four characteristics:

- Cost.
- Transmission capacity.
- Maximum length of the media before the signals need to be regenerated.
- Protection against electrical and magnetic interference.

The physical material out of which a medium is constructed and the method of construction and form dictate the amount of data the medium can carry. Interference from the environment also affects the actual data-carrying capacity of a medium. A signal cannot travel forever. It starts losing its energy and integrity in terms of shape and other characteristics. Most media have a well-defined maximum length, called segment length, beyond which the signal needs to be amplified and the distortions removed. All electric signals are subject to interference arising from the environment. These sources may be power cables or other signal cables, machines, elevator motors, fluorescent lights, photocopiers, magnetic sources, or radio transmission equipment. Shielding is used to prevent interference.

Following are the four types of media commonly used in telecommunications: twisted-pair copper wire, coaxial cable, fiber optics, and wireless transmission.

Figure 2–10

Copper wiring

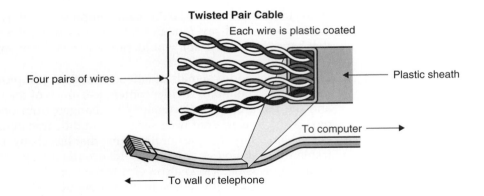

Twisted-Pair Copper Wiring

Four pairs of wires

Each wire is plastic coated

Plastic sheath

To computer

To wall or telephone

Twisted-Pair Copper Wiring

This popular cable type is used for standard telephone wiring. It is low cost and easy to cut, lay, and crimp. It consists of pairs of wire twisted around each other to reduce any electrical interference. Each wire is insulated, and the wire pairs are enclosed in overall casing (see Figure 2–10). Ordinary telephone wire is not provided with any special shielding, but varieties are available that use a foil or a copper-braided shield.

The unshielded twisted pair (UTP) is rapidly becoming the medium of choice for local area networks (LAN). It was originally designed for voice, but it is now popular for data as well. Twisted-pair cabling is rated by the Electronics Industry Association/Telecommunication Industry Association (EIA/TIA). The most popular ones are rated category three (CAT3) or category five (CAT5). Category three is used for voice and category five is used for data transmission. It is common to lay CAT5 cables for both telephone and LAN connections. CAT5 cables can support data transmission up to 100 million bits per second, but they have severe distance limitations in terms of segment length. Usually, the signal needs to be regenerated every 100 meters.

Coaxial Cable

The television industry helped develop **coaxial cable.** At its core is a central conductor wire that is covered by a layer of insulation, a conductive mesh sleeve, and an outer shielded insulator (see Figure 2–11). Because of its shielded construction, coaxial cable is much less susceptible to interference and permits longer segment lengths. It is used for long-distance telephone transmission and local area networks.

With coaxial cable, data transmission rates of over 100 mbps are possible, and it can carry both analog and digital signals. It is most commonly

FIGURE 2–11

Coaxial cable

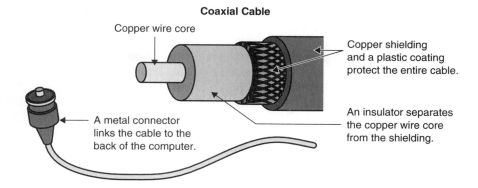

used in homes to transmit cable television. Its popularity as a medium for LAN has waned because it is much more difficult to work with than UTP cables. Using frequency division multiplexing, a coaxial cable can transmit thousands of voice channels or hundreds of cable television channels.

Fiber Optic

Fiber optics (see Figure 2–12) uses light rather than electric current to transmit a signal. A laser or light source at one end sends laser pulses at more than a billion times per second to a detector at the other end. The light is switched on and off, which represents 1s and 0s of a digital stream. An optical fiber has a cylindrical shape and consists of three concentric

FIGURE 2–12

Fiber optic cable

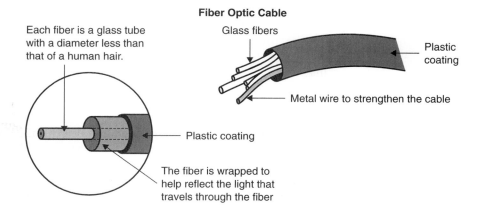

sections. At the center is a fiber comprised of glass or plastic with a diameter smaller than a human hair. This inner core, which carries the signal, is surrounded by glass, called cladding, with a different refractive index.

Glass fiber is available in two forms: single-mode fiber and multimode fiber. Single-mode fiber is more expensive, has a larger carrying capacity, and can send signals over a thousand miles before using a repeater. The multimode fiber is cheaper and has a lower data carrying capacity. The two cores, the inner core and the cladding, are represented as a pair of numbers. For instance, a popular multimode fiber has the specification of 62.5/125, which means the inner core has a diameter of 62.5 microns (a millionth of a meter) and the outer has a diameter of 125 microns. The commonly used single-mode fiber has the specification of 8/125. The two concentric cores are, in turn, covered by a protective cladding. Many such fibers are grouped together to form a fiber optic cable.

Fiber optic has many advantages. It does not use electric signals and is therefore immune to electrical interference. It is very light and thin and a needs low duct space. The light signals experience less weakening as compared to electric signals and, therefore, can be sent over much longer distances before they need to regenerated. It has enormous capacity, which is rated in gigabits (thousand million) per second. Most trunk lines in telephone networks are now fiber. More efficient schemes are being developed to enhance the data-carrying capacity of the fiber. In dense wave division multiplexing (DWDM), for example, lights of different wavelengths or color are sent simultaneously through the fiber, thus increasing the data capacity multiple times. DWDM is being used to develop fiber backbones with capacities as high as 10 gigabits per second.

However, there are disadvantages to fiber optic as well. It is expensive because electric signals need to be converted to light and vice versa. It is difficult with which to work and demands a higher degree of skilled effort in laying and maintenance of fiber cables. For these reasons, the use of fiber optic in the LAN environment is still limited. While it is not popular to use fiber as media carrying signals to individual desktops or servers, they are sometimes used as riser cables between floors of buildings and for cable runs across the campus.

Wireless Transmission

There are two types of configuration for wireless transmission: directional and omnidirectional. In directional transmission, a transmitting antenna focuses electromagnetic waves in the direction of a receiver. With an omnidirectional configuration, the antenna spreads out the electromagnetic signal in all directions, and many antennas can receive the signal. Homes have both configurations. Broadcast radio, whether AM or FM, uses an omnidirectional broadcast system; there is no need to orient sets in the direction of the sending antenna. But to receive direct broadcast satellite signals, satellite dishes need to be oriented to a precise direction toward the satellite.

Terrestrial Microwave.   Microwave transmission is an example of directional wireless transmission. Two types of applications for microwave transmission are terrestrial (ground-based) and satellite-based systems. In **terrestrial microwave,** a parabolic dish antenna is usually directed toward a receiving antenna in a line-of-sight configuration. These antennas are mounted on towers to avoid obstacles between the pair of antennas receiving and sending. Frequencies are in the range of gigahertz (10^9 Hz). Long-distance transmission requires a series of towers. Such a system is often used as a backup for fiber-based lines. Terrestrial microwave can be used for both voice and television.

Satellite Microwave.   Satellites are actually microwave relay stations in space to link two ground-based stations on Earth. The satellite receives a signal from one ground station and, after amplification, relays it to another ground-based station. A transponder receives a signal, amplifies it, and transmits it downward. The transponder receives the signal at one frequency and transmits at another. **Satellite microwave** systems are usually described as 12/14 GHz—the first number specifies the downlink frequency and the second number is the uplink frequency. A satellite houses a dozen to two dozen transponders and each transponder has a transmission rate of about 50 mbps. The 12/14 GHz band is called K band. In this band, the uplink frequencies are from 14 to 14.5 GHz, while the downlink is from 11.7 to 12.2 GHz. Previously, most satellites used 4/6 GHz, called the C band. With the C band, the uplink frequency is between 5.925 and 6.425 GHz and the downlink is between 4.7 and 4.2 GHz. Because satellites are parked above the equator, they are separated by at least four degrees so as to avoid interference of signals, but this limits the number of satellites and existing bands are becoming saturated. An expected new band will use 19/29 GHz, where uplink will be 27.5 to 31.0 GHz and downlink will be 17.7 to 21.2 GHz.

Satellites are usually placed in a geosynchronous orbit (i.e., the position of the satellite with respect to the Earth remains unchanged) and are often referred to as geosynchronous earth orbits (GEO) satellites (see Figure 2–13). They orbit at a height of 22,200 miles above the equator. At that height, it takes only two satellites to cover the entire planet. GEOs suffer from some disadvantages, one of which is latency. Because the satellites are so distant, it takes a fraction of a second for the signal to reach a satellite and bounce back, and this delay can be annoying on a phone call.

FIGURE 2–13

*Geosynchronous
satellites*

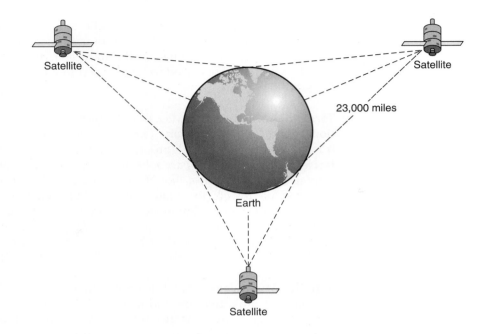

Also, the huge distances require more energy for transmission and, as a consequence, systems are bulky.

Satellite systems for telephony without latency can be achieved by bringing the satellites closer to Earth. **Low earth orbits** (LEO) systems that have satellites within 1,000 miles of the Earth have been developed. However, they require many more satellites to achieve the same coverage as a GEO system. Iridium has a system of 66 LEO satellites. While the company recently went bankrupt, Globalstar and Teledesic have other LEO systems in the works. The goal of Teledesic is to create an "Internet in the sky." It is designed to have 288 small satellites that would cover most of the Earth and would offer Internet and video-conferencing facilities starting in 2002. Between LEO and GEO is middle earth orbit (MEO), which requires 10 to 12 satellites at about 6,000 miles up.

Satellites are used in two types of configuration: point-to-point and point-to-multipoint. With point-to-point, two ground stations communicate via a transponder on a satellite (see Figure 2–14). With point-to-multipoint, a satellite provides communication between a sending station and multiple receiving stations (see Figure 2–15). A satellite is inherently a broadcast system in which a single station can broadcast to multiple stations, making satellites popular for television broadcasting.

Satellites are also used for business applications. A transponder's capacity can be divided into multiple channels, and businesses can lease

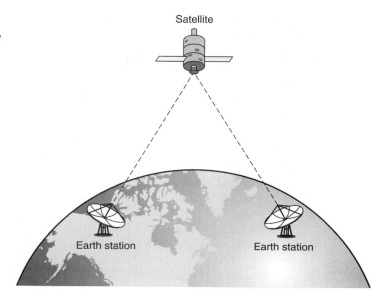

FIGURE 2–14

Point-to-point satellite configuration

these individual channels to communicate between offices. The very small aperture terminal (VSAT) is becoming popular as a way for a number of sites to communicate with a hub station via a satellite station. In this configuration, outlying stations cannot communicate with one another directly; they need to relay their signals via the hub station.

Alternatives to satellites are being considered. One proposal involves an airship flying at 50,000 feet above a metropolitan area. Laslink is

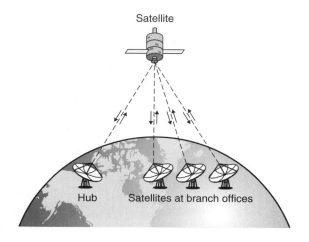

FIGURE 2–15

VSAT configuration

TABLE 2–2   Frequency Spectrum for Various Transmissions (Hz)

AM Radio	VHF TV and Shortwave Radio	VHF TV and FM Radio	VHF TV	UHF TV	Microwaves	Infrared Light	Visible Light
10^6	10^7	10^8	10^8–10^9	10^{10}	10^{11}	10^{12}	10^{14}

proposing to employ such an high-altitude airship. Services would include videoconferencing and high-speed Internet access. The company is planning to build a fleet of 100 planes at a cost of $700 million and utilize two planes in a metropolitan market.

Satellite Broadcast Radio and Television.   Several distinctions can be made between microwave satellite transmission and radio/television broadcasting. Whereas satellite transmission is unidirectional, radio broadcasting is omnidirectional. Radio broadcasting does not require dish-shaped antennas, and they need not be precisely aligned. The broadcast frequencies are also different. The radio broadcasting system encompasses frequencies from 20 MHz to 1 GHz. The broadcast range covers AM radio, FM radio, and UHF and VHF television. Table 2–2 describes the frequency range for various radio and television broadcast services.

Telephone Network

The telephone network is over 100 years old. Called the **public switched telephone network** (PSTN), it provides a point-to-point connection between two telephones. During the early part of the 20th century, a telephone operator working at a switchboard manually connected two telephones. Once the connection was established, it was held open between the two telephones until they disconnected.

Manually operated switchboards were replaced by automatic switches, which were arranged in a simple hierarchy before the AT&T breakup in 1984 (see Figure 2–16). The central office (CO), also known as the local exchange, houses a level 5 switch and may serve anywhere from a few hundred to about 100,000 subscribers in a business district.

Level 4 switches are housed in toll centers. All long-distance calls go through these switches. The circuits connecting level 5 switches to those of level 4 are mostly digital and employ fiber optics, coaxial cable, microwave, and copper cables. About 20 level 5 switches feed to a level 4 switch. There are close to 25,000 COs and about 1,500 level 4 switches in the United States. A dozen level 4 switches feed into a level 3 switch.

FIGURE 2–16

Telephone switching network hierarchy

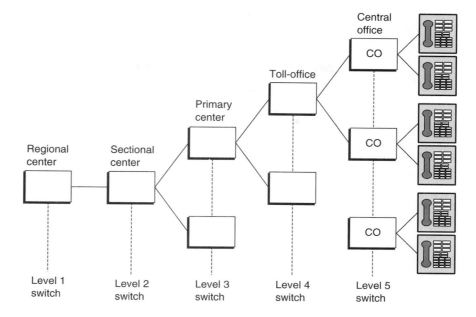

Before divestiture, switches at all levels belonged to AT&T. After divestiture, the switch hierarchy was no longer simple.

Most lines connecting telephones to the COs are still old copper wire cables that were laid decades earlier. The circuit connecting subscribers to the CO is still mainly analog. The lines have limited capacity, and the analog system delivering digital data through modulation techniques can, at best, provide 56 kbps. However, these same cables working as digital systems, where the signal is sent as digital pulses, can accommodate as much as 6 mbps, depending on the state of the wiring and the distance from the CO to the subscriber's premise. Digital subscriber line (DSL) technology is discussed later in this chapter.

The limited capacity of the analog system that connects residential telephones to COs is often characterized as the "last-mile problem." It is the biggest hurdle to supplying high-bandwidth services to homes. Beyond the lines connecting homes to the COs, the telephone lines are all fiber-based. In research laboratories and in actual implementations, the capacities of these fiber-based trunk lines are increasing by leaps and bounds. With dense wave division multiplexing, fiber capacities are doubling every 9 months, in contrast to the 18-month cycle for doubling of processor capacities. In 10 years, the data capacity of the fiber is expected to jump 10,000 times in the range of terabits per second. A fiber connection to a home in the future will allow users to download a whole movie in a few seconds. Unfortunately, fiber connection to all residences is not economically feasible. It is estimated it would cost about \$100 billion to lay fiber to all homes. Later in the chapter, we discuss different solutions for this last-mile problem.

Wireless Local Loop

This technology is still being developed and rolled out. With **wireless local loop** (WLL), the wires connecting the home to the telephone company's CO are replaced by wireless communication. A wireless switch box with an antenna replaces the telephone company's network interface in the home. The antenna in the home communicates with a neighborhood antenna operated by a wireless company. With channel and frequency reuse patterns, the systems are expected to provide high-speed digital service. By avoiding the low-capacity analog connection to the CO, the service is expected to be a popular solution to the last-mile problem.

Packet Switching Networks

The telephone network discussed earlier is a circuit switched network. In such a network, a connection is established from the sender to the destination and the connection is kept alive for the duration of the session during which all resources on the circuit are unavailable to other users. The U.S. telephone system uses circuit switching technology where a call establishes a circuit from the originating phone through the local central office through the switching offices at various levels to the destination telephone. In a digital phone system, the telephone equipment samples the voice signal using PCM technology and converts it into a digital data stream. These signals are then multiplexed using TDM and FDM over the trunk lines.

With a circuit switching system, even though signals from many conversations travel over the same trunk line, a 64 kilobits per second capacity is reserved for each conversation during the call duration. Once a call is under way, no other network traffic decreases this reserved capacity.

In contrast, no such continuous physical connection is established in a **packet switching** network. For a file to be sent from one node to another, the file is broken into small units of data, called packets, that are multiplexed over trunk lines. Software at either end of the network disassembles and assembles the packets in the right sequence into files. The packets are like envelopes in the U.S. postal system. They bear the address of the destination node and carry a small amount of data. These packets move independently through the network system, where routers direct the packets to the right links by reading the addresses on the packets. The packets are independent of one another and they all share the network capacity. Breaking communication into packets allows the same data links to be shared among multiple users of the network.

The packet switching network was designed for data communication. It allows for more efficient use of network capacity. For low-capacity packet switching networks, voice transmission is not feasible because the packets that make up the voice may arrive out of sequence. The Internet is a packet switching network. Another common type of packet switching network is the X.25 network, commercial wide area network for data transmission. Internet protocol packets can also be carried on an X.25 network. Most EDI systems are currently implemented over X.25 networks.

Digital Transmission Services

The telephone network uses three popular digital transmission systems —the T-1 carrier, the optical carrier (OC) system, and the integrated service digital network (ISDN).

The T-1 Carrier System

The T-1 services (see Figure 2–17) were developed in the 1960s to allow higher transmission rates over copper cables connecting telephone company switches. T-1 is a digital service and its higher capacities allowed telephone companies to send more data through existing lines. The service was extended to subscribers in the 1980s. Two pairs of copper cables were laid to the subscriber's premises, one pair for sending and the other for receiving. Currently, T-1 services also use fiber optic cables. T-1 services require the use of several technologies.

FIGURE 2–17

A T-1 connection

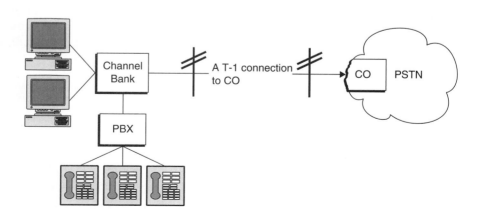

- Because T-1 is a digital system, it is necessary to convert analog signals at the customer's premises to digital pulses (1s and 0s). This is accomplished by using pulse code modulation technology (PCM), and equipment called a channel bank is used to convert analog to digital.
- The digital signal stream carries 24 channels of 64 kbps of data (24 * 64 = 1.536 mbps). The various channels are multiplexed using time division multiplexing. The multiplexing occurs at the channel bank on the customer's premises. The T-1 line also has an overhead of 8,000 bits and, thus, the total bits carried on a T-1 line are 1.544 mbps (1.536 mbps + .008 mbps).

The T-1 carrier system is associated with a hierarchy called digital standards (DS), which are independent of the transmission systems, such as T-1. T-1 delivers the bandwidth necessary for the DS-1 standard. While T-1 and DS-1 are not equivalent terms, they are often used interchangeably. There is a hierarchy based on the DS system. The DS-2 system is carried by a T-2 carrier. The T-2 carrier is constituted by 28 T-1 lines, that is, by multiplexing of 672 (28 * 24) 64 kbps services. Similarly, the DS-4 system uses the corresponding transmission service of the T-4 line, which is an aggregate of 4,032 (6 * 28 * 24) multiplexed 64 kbps channels. The hierarchy is as shown in Table 2–3.

Companies lease the T-1 or T-2 connection to the telephone company's CO or to their own branch offices. They may lease a T-1 line connection to their Internet service provider (ISP). ISPs, in turn, may lease T-2 lines from telephone companies to set up a regional or a national backbone. Lines can be leased as multiples of T-1 lines and also as fractions of a line.

The SONET System

Synchronous optical network (SONET) is a transmission service that uses optical fiber. The difference between T-1 and SONET transmission services lies primarily in data speed and how the various channels are constituted into one digital stream. Just as there is a digital service

TABLE 2–3   North American DS Carrier Hierarchy

T-n	DS-n	Number of Voice Channels	Mbps
T-1	DS-1	24	1.544
T-2	DS-2	672	44.726
T-4	DS-4	4,032	274.176

OC level	OC-1	OC-2	OC-9	OC-24	OC-48	OC-96	OC-192
Mbps	52	155	466	1,244	2,488	4,976	10,000

TABLE 2–4 Part of the Optical Carrier Level

hierarchy, there is an **optical carrier hierarchy** categorized by optical carrier (OC) levels (see Table 2–4). SONET services, as provided by telephone companies, have extensive performance monitoring and fault detection capacities. For instance, it takes less than 1/1,000th of a second to sense a problem and switch traffic to an alternate route. SONET circuits are implemented as rings, in which one side of the ring is used as a spare line when the other line ceases to work. Internet service providers lease SONET lines to run their national-level backbones. Large companies use SONET lines to establish private networks.

The Integrated Service Digital Network

An **integrated service digital network** (ISDN) is a digital service that runs over the public switched telephone network and on existing copper cables. It is a switched service; that is, a number is dialed to set up a connection and subscribers are billed local or long-distance rates for the time. Two standards of ISDN are a basic rate interface (BRI) and a primary rate interface (PRI). The basic rate provides for three channels, two for data at 64 kbps and one for signaling at 16 kbps. The two channels at 64 kbps can be used in any combination for voice and data. Thus, BRI allows connection to the Internet at 128 kbps. PRI ISDN allows for a speed of 1.526 mbps. PRI is similar to T-1, but unlike T-1, it offers only 22 data channels at 64 kbps and one control channel at 64 kbps.

Unfortunately, ISDN lacks widespread availability in the United States. While ISDN is popular in Europe, it has not been popularized by the telephone companies in the United States. To be able to subscribe to ISDN service, the local telephone company needs to offer it, and the subscriber's premise has to be within 18,000 feet of the telephone company central office.

Wireless Telephony

Wireless transmission can be categorized into three groups, depending on its range of operations:

- Wide area systems are targeted to mobile subscribers who could be communicating from any location.
- Local area systems are targeted to users whose movement is limited to an area such as a building or a campus.

Table 2–5   Wireless Telephony Technologies for Voice and Data Communication

Wide Area Communication	Local Area Communication	Personal Area Network
• Cellular telephones (voice and data)	• Wireless local loop systems (voice only)	• Small networks consisting of devices such as headphones, cell phones, PCs, and printers
• Satellite systems (voice and data)	• Wireless LAN (data only)	
• Pagers (data)		
• Specialized packet systems such as CPDP (data)		

- Personal area networks are small networks less than 10 meters in diameter and connect equipment such as laptops, PCs, printers, and cellular devices.

The three groups of wireless system are shown in Table 2–5.

In this section, we will consider cellular telephones, pagers, and specialized data systems such as CPDP. Satellite systems were discussed earlier, and wireless LANs will be discussed later in this chapter.

Analog Cellular Systems

The technology has evolved from earlier radio and telephone systems that worked with a single transmitter for the entire city, sharing the few frequencies that were available. The breakthrough of cellular technology involved a technique for reusing the same frequencies over and over again in different cells.

In North America, the popular analog system is called the **advanced mobile phone system** (AMPS). AMPS uses a pair of FM analog channels for two-way communication. There are several such channels in each cell, few of which are dedicated to control. Since the channels are separated by frequencies, the technology is called frequency division multiple access (FDMA). The entire territory of coverage is divided into hexagonal cells, with each cell having a few hundred to a few thousand subscribers. Each cell has a base station with a transmitter, and all cellular phones in the cell communicate with the transmitter. Two companies are allowed to run an AMPS cellular system in one area. One of the companies is the local terrestrial telephone company, and the other is a cellular operator. The frequencies allocated to the two operators are presented in Table 2–6.

Each cellular operator has about 400 channels in the frequency allocated to it. Since the frequencies in adjacent cells have to be different,

TABLE 2–6   Frequencies for AMPS System

Band	Cell Phone Transmit	Cell Phone Receive
Local telephone company	824–835, 845–846.5 MHz	869–880, 890–891.5 MHz
Cellular operator	835–845, 846.5–849 MHz	880–890, 891.5–894 MHz

about 100 channels are available to each operator in each cell. The cells are connected to a mobile telephone switching office (MTSO), where all the calls from the cells arrive and are then, if required, transferred to the local terrestrial telephone company's public switched telephone network (see Figure 2–18).

The MTSO manages all call activities. When a cellular phone is switched on, it starts communicating with the MTSO on one of the control channels. The phone informs the MTSO about its number and the MTSO notes its cell location. When a call is made to a cellular phone, the MTSO uses this knowledge to initiate the connection to the cellular phone. The MTSO also informs the phone about the services to which it is entitled. For example, a phone may be in its home territory or roaming territory and, therefore, can access services at various rates.

A cellular phone initiates a call by sending a request on the control channel for a pair of channels, which the MTSO assigns. The MTSO also tracks the call as it moves from one cell to another and manages the transfer from one base station to another at another channel pair frequency. The transfer involves a loss of communication for a fraction of a second.

FIGURE 2–18

Cellular transmission system

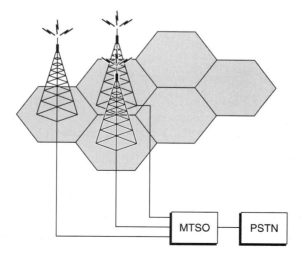

The AMPS allows the use of a modem. Modems are available with laptop computers that connect to cellular phones, but the communication permits usually low data capacities, such as 9,600 bps.

Digital Cellular Systems

With the increasing popularity of cellular phones, cellular operators experienced pressure to increase capacity. Consequently, some operators decided to use time division multiplexing access (TDMA) methods to offer digital service over the same frequencies they were using for their analog cellular systems. They designated part of their channels to carry digital signals. TDMA splits each 20 KHz channel into three channels that carry an 8 kbps digital stream each for voice. The technology is called D-AMPS, 'D' for digital. Although the service is not suitable for data transmission, it allows for multiple digital channels in place of a single analog channel.

A digital cellular system uses a variety of technologies discussed earlier in the chapter. For instance:

- Pulse code modulation (PCM) is used to convert the user's voice to a digital data stream.
- Modulation technologies such as amplitude modulation (AM) and frequency modulation (FM) are used to transport the digital data over the wireless network, which is an analog medium.
- The wireless system uses different frequencies for different conversations, which is an instance of frequency division multiplexing (FDM).
- Sometimes a single frequency channel is used to serve as many as three users using time division multiplexing (TDM).
- Finally, some of the digital cellular systems are implemented on the principle of packet switching technology.

Personal Communication Service

Personal communication service (PCS) is a digital service that operates at a different frequency than AMPS. It is assigned the frequency ranges of 1,850 to 1,910 MHz and 1,930 to 1,990 MHz, 120 MHz total (see Table 2–7). While the AMPS system had two operators to share the frequency allocated, PCS has six unequal blocks shared among multiple operators. Half the blocks, designated A, B, and C, are assigned 20 MHz of spectrum, and the blocks D, E, and F are assigned 10 MHz of spectrum each. Compared to digital cellular, PCS cells are smaller and have weaker antennas, but it can be used for data communication.

TABLE 2–7   **Wireless Phone Systems and Frequencies**

Service	Frequencies
800 MHz Cellular	824–849 MHz, 869–894 MHz Total = 50 MHz
Personal communication service	1850–1910 MHz, 1930–1990 MHz Total = 120 MHz
Nextel	806–821 MHz, 851–866 MHz Total = 20 MHz

PCS uses digital technologies such as TDMA or **code division multiple access** (CDMA), invented by Qualcomm Inc. (see the case at the end of the chapter). The technology involves code to provide separation. CDMA uses a spread spectrum to place 64 channels in a 1.25 MHz radio spectrum. All 64 channels use the same spectrum with a frequency-hopping coding scheme that is unique to each conversation. Because of the unique codes, these conversations can be separated at the receiving end. CDMA is sometimes likened to a dozen couples talking simultaneously over the same phone with each couple talking in a different language.

Nextel

The Nextel network is operated by Nextel Communications. The network is an enhancement of the old technology of specialized mobile radio (SMR). In SMR, one powerful transmitter covers a large area with few frequencies. It provides two-way radio dispatch service that is used by taxis and public safety personnel, and it allows voice, data broadcast, and mobile telephone service. The enhanced SMR (ESMR) is similar to cellular service with regard to cells and the reuse of frequencies in nonadjacent cells. The total spectrum allocated to Nextel is 20 MHz (see Table 2–7).

Cellular Digital Packet Data

IBM developed **cellular digital packet data** (CPDP) to use the spare capacity in 800 MHz analog cellular networks to send short, burst messages such as e-mails and credit card authorizations. The service, which is available in most metropolitan areas, takes advantage of the unused airtime at the start and end of a cellular phone conversation. The information is transmitted at 19,200 bps in the form of packets. CPDP provides Internet connectivity to laptop computers.

Paging

Paging is a cheaper and simpler service than cellular phone service. Most pagers are one-directional, point-to-point service. A paging system uses several antennas to serve a metropolitan area. The antennas send short messages to the pager, typically a one-line message display limited to 20 characters. Most pagers can display only numbers. Pagers are small and consume low power. They are often used in conjunction with cellular phones. A pager alerts a person about an incoming call by displaying the telephone number. The cellular phone is used to dial back the number. Some paging services have a nationwide reach of services, such as SkyTel Communications, which has a network of towers and satellites that beam signals all over the country.

I-mode

A packet-based wireless phone service called **i-mode** is offered by NTT DoCoMo in Japan. Introduced in 1999, by January 2001, it had over 15 million subscribers. It allows services that require color and video to be delivered over handheld devices. Subscribers can browse specially formatted Web pages, make airline reservations, conduct stock transactions, and send and receive e-mails. It is a popular hit with teenagers in Japan. For many of them, i-mode is their only portal to the World Wide Web. The service is based on a packet switching network and does not use the WAP protocol and its associated Wireless Markup Language. Instead it uses a simplified version of HTML called Compact Wireless Markup Language (CWML). NTT has said that eventually it will support the WAP-based standards and specifications.

Wireless Personal Area Network

A **personal area network** (PAN) is comprised of electronic devices within a single room and around a single user. A PC connected to a local printer and a DVD player attached to a music system are common instances of a PAN. The media often used are cables and infrared. A new technology, called **Bluetooth,** facilitates connection of domestic devices via wireless transmission. Named after the 10th-century Danish king Harald Blatand (Bluetooth), who conquered and integrated much of Scandinavia, this new technology has been developed by all the important players in the field of wireless technology. It originated in efforts to link home audio and video systems via wireless. The technology is being developed to connect both portable systems, such as headphones and mobile phones, and embedded systems, such as television, audio, and video systems at home. It relies on a passive system of devices communicating to each other within a 10-meter radius to constitute a small network called a pico net. Several pico nets can then communicate with each other within the confines of a home to make up a larger network called a scatter net.

The technology as it is being developed has several distinctive features. First, it is based on packet switching network technology. The wireless medium can thus be shared by multiple devices. It is a low-power system and can therefore be embedded in small devices such as a headphone. A Bluetooth chip containing a small antenna is expected to cost only a few dollars, so it can affordably be installed on all electronic devices from a PC to a printer, stereo system, television, DVD player, terrestrial phone, and cellular phone.

Because of the communication protocols being developed, a cellular phone can be used in multiple ways in the personal area network. It can be used at home to dial up the land-based line system through the standard phone. Two cellular phones can communicate as a pair of walkie-talkies within a residential environment. Similarly, a headphone can be used to hear music streaming from an MP3 player and can also be used to switch to a phone call. Because of interconnectivity between devices, the television remote could be used to store music and programs on the PC hard drive and replay the program on the audio-video system.

The Bluetooth technology employs the same spread-spectrum technology used in wireless LANs and discussed later in this chapter. Bluetooth devices can either connect point-to-point or connect to a server in a computer network, which is known as point-to-multipoint mode. The capacity of these Bluetooth PANs is expected to be 1 megabit per second, which is much lower than the current LAN standard 802.11b capacity of 11 megabits per second.

Generations in Wireless Telephony

The technologies for wireless telephony discussed in this chapter are often categorized as belonging to different generations. The first generation (**1G wireless telephony**) is the analog wireless phone system, discussed earlier, called advanced mobile phone system (AMPS). It continues to be a popular system in the United States and is well-suited to voice communication.

The second generation (**2G**) is the digital technology used in PCS discussed earlier. In 2G technology, the sound of the user's voice is converted to a digital stream using the PCM technology, previously mentioned. These digital streams are then sent over the wireless medium using code division multiple access (CDMA). Both the first and second generation suffer from the low capacity of 10 kilobits per second, which is a barely a fifth of what can be achieved from a modem at home. Also, they are both based on circuit switching technology. When a user communicates on a certain frequency with the cell tower, the same frequency is not available to any other user in the cell, even though human communication has frequent silent gaps.

The third generation (**3G**) is broadband digital. It will be based on packet switching technology and will support a data capacity of 2 megabits per second. A refinement of CDMA technology, called wideband-CDMA (w-CDMA), is expected to be used in some of the 3G implementations. The first implementation of this generation was expected to occur in Japan where the i-Mode cellular service operator, NTT DoCoMo, was to implement the first 3G wireless network in 2001. In addition to the current service of voice and e-mail transmission, the third generation i-Mode wireless networks will support audio and video transmission. The technology will allow a commuter in a train to have a video conversation on a small screen with somebody in the office.

While the third generation wireless systems are being implemented in Europe and Japan, the fourth generation (**4G**) networks are still on the drawing boards. The pioneer in this area is a consortium of NTT DoCoMo and Hewlett-Packard. Fourth generation mobile phones will provide CD quality sound and could be used to download MP3 music files. They will be equipped with global positioning system technology, which will help in locating the user and allowing websites to offer location-sensitive services, such as making reservations for nearby restaurants.

Modems

The word *modem* is derived from the terms: *mod*ulation and *dem*odulation. A **modem** converts a digital signal into an analog signal that carries a digital message. In this chapter, we discussed how amplitude and frequency modulation is used to send digital messages using analog signals. These techniques are used in modems. There are three types of modems: modems used with personal computers and voice lines; modems offered by cable TV companies providing Internet services; and modems used with digital subscriber line technology. The latter two technologies are popular methods for coping with the "last-mile problem."

Personal Computer Modem

A modem sits between a personal computer and the telephone jack at the wall (see Figure 2–19). It receives digital signals as output from the computer, which it converts into analog signals suitable for transmission over the analog telephone circuit. It also performs the reverse function—receiving analog signals over the phone line and converting them into digital signal pulses suitable for the computer. A modem serves several functions other than modulating and demodulating. It dials a telephone number; it responds to incoming telephone calls; it compresses data; and it checks for errors. The latest standard for modems is V.92, which was adopted in November 2000.

FIGURE 2–19

A PC modem

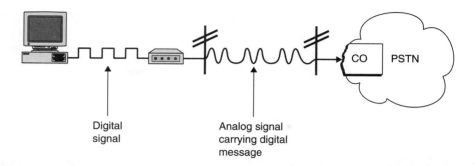

Digital
signal

Analog signal
carrying digital
message

Cable Modem

The **cable modem** is used to provide high-speed access to the Internet through the cable TV network. The modem connects to an Ethernet LAN card in the computer, and at the other end, it connects to a cable outlet that is split to separate signals meant for the television from signals meant for the computer (see Figure 2–20).

FIGURE 2–20

A cable modem

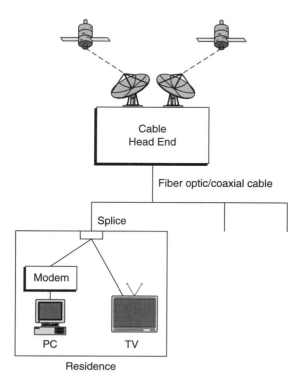

The cable TV system consists of a farm of satellite dishes that receive signals from various satellites (see Figure 2–20). This is known as the head end. From the head end, these signals are carried over fiber optic cables to a neighborhood concentrator. Coaxial cables are run from the concentrator to the subscriber's premises.

The cable modem carries data upstream and downstream from the computer to the cable head end. In the downstream direction from the cable head end, the digital data are modulated over the analog signals carried by coaxial cables. The data are placed on a single 6 MHz television carrier signal between the frequency range 42 MHz and 750 MHz. The upstream channel from the subscriber is between 5 and 42 MHz. These frequency ranges vary from one implementation to another. The upsteam and downstream data speeds are different as well. Upstream data speeds range from 200 kbps to 2 mbps, and downstream they go up to 10 mbps.

These speeds are shared by all the subscribers who are connected to the same coaxial cable concentrator in the neighborhood. All messages are broadcast and the Ethernet protocol is used to manage access to the shared media. The actual data rate that is available to an individual subscriber is a function of the number of other subscribers who are sharing the same line at the same time. When too many users in one neighborhood use the same line, performance can drop dramatically. Cable companies, therefore, restrict users from telecommuting, from hosting websites, and using their networks for videoconferencing. Internet connection, as offered by cable TV networks, is a popular solution to the last-mile problem.

Digital Subscriber Line (DSL) Modem

Digital subscriber line (DSL) technology uses ordinary copper telephone wires to transmit data at speeds around 6 mbps. It uses the same copper wires that are currently connecting homes to the telephone companies (see Figure 2–21). As with the cable modem, the DSL modem is an alternative solution to the last-mile problem.

DSL data rates are usually asymmetric with a lower upstream (from the subscriber to the telephone company) data rate than downstream (to the subscriber) data rate. That is why the term *a*DSL is often used to account for this asymmetric data transmission rate. The actual rate of data transmission depends on the distance from the subscriber's premise to the CO, as well as on the quality and state of the telephone line. For DSL to work, the CO should be within 18,000 feet of the subscriber. Smaller distances permit higher data transmission rates.

The DSL technology works with devices that perform the function of a modem at the CO and at the subscriber's site (see Figure 2–21). The modem creates several channels using frequency division multiplexing.

FIGURE 2–21

A DSL modem

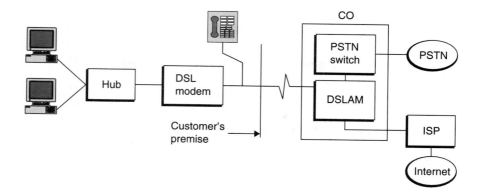

One of the channels is used for voice and others for data transmission. These channels are further divided by time division multiplexing to allow multiple data streams to flow through them. At the CO end, DSL technology requires a specialized router to separate the voice channel from the data channel. The router is called a digital subscriber line access module (DSLAM). The voice channel is routed to the existing public switched telephone network switches, and the data are routed to data circuits that take the data to an Internet service provider. A splitter at the subscriber's site separates the voice channel from the data channel. The data channel is then taken to a DSL modem, which modulates the signal into digital pulses so that it can be input into a computer.

Local Area Networks

Ethernet

Networks can be classified according to the distances they cover and the technologies they use. The networks previously discussed, such as the telephone network and the Internet, are called wide area networks (WAN). A WAN covers a large geographic area, such as a city or a country, and operates over a medium that is leased from telecommunications providers. In contrast, **local area networks** (LANs) are confined to a small area such as a building or a campus. A LAN is owned by a single organization and the organization owns everything about the LAN, including the media.

Ethernet is one of the most popular LAN architectures. The Ethernet technology was the brainchild of Robert Metcalfe, who invented the concept in the early 70s while working for Xerox. The first Ethernet specification was published in 1980 by a consortium of companies—Digital (now Compaq), Intel, and Xerox. The technology was later adopted by the

Institute of Electrical and Electronic Engineers (IEEE), which published its own specification in 1985.

The following are the important features of Ethernet:

1. Ethernet uses a variety of media. It employs coaxial cable of two varieties and twisted-pair copper wire, as is used in the telephone wire. The twisted-pair copper wire of a particular specification, called category 5, is currently the popular choice for Ethernet networks.

2. Ethernet uses a bus topology; that is, all the nodes on the network connect to a single transmission line. Conceptually, if not physically, the nodes are connected to a medium whose ends are not connected. It is a broadcast system where the data frames flow to all the nodes in the network. Physically, the network may look like a bus or a star network. Figure 2–22 presents a hierarchy of star networks in which the center of each star is a hub. Within each hub, the nodes are connected to a bus resident in the hub that encases the bus. The hub is connected to each computer by a twisted pair of wires that terminate at a network interface card (NIC) plugged into the computer.

3. Maximum data throughput capacity varies by Ethernet type. The most common and the standard is 10 mbps. The "fast" Ethernet is 100 mbps, and the gigabit Ethernet is 1 gigabit per second.

4. The Ethernet follows a simple method for nodes to access the shared media called carrier sense multiple access and collision detection (CSMA/CD). In CSMA/CD, nodes listen to the medium to determine whether data frames are traveling or not. If the medium is silent, the node starts to transmit the Ethernet data frames. Sometimes two nodes will start transmitting simultaneously, resulting in "collision." The

FIGURE 2–22

An Ethernet local area network

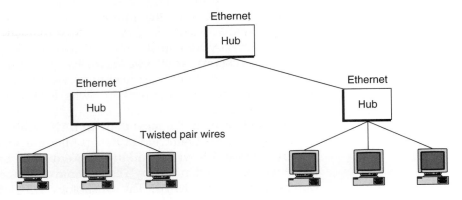

network interface cards can sense a collision and when they do, they stop transmitting and wait for random times before they start the process. All these activities are part of the data-link layer of the OSI model, and they are implemented by the NIC.

Wireless Local Area Networks

Wireless local area networks use radio frequency to transmit and receive data. The data being transmitted are modulated on a frequency carrier. Wireless LANs are becoming popular as a substitute for wired LANs or as an extension to an existing wired LAN, particularly in markets such as health care, retail, and warehousing. In these industries, mobile personnel need access to data wherever they may be. For instance, physicians and nurses work over a wide area in a hospital and need access to patient data. Similarly, retail and warehouse workers need access to product and delivery data. A wireless LAN has several advantages over a wired LAN:

- It supports mobility and provides access to servers and data over a wide area, such as a building or a campus.
- No installation or wire pulling is required. It is ideal for work environments where the layout changes.
- It is a scalable technology. A few wireless LAN portables can be extended later to wireless interconnections between large wired LANs.

A wide range of technologies is used for wireless connectivity in a LAN environment, some of which are:

- Narrow-band technology. A radio system transmits and receives information on a specific frequency. Varying frequency channels are provided for different pairs of conversation.
- Spread-spectrum technology. Instead of transmitting on a single frequency, the information is transmitted simultaneously over a spectrum of frequencies. The expanded frequency usage cuts reliability and security. The transmitter and the receiver are both tuned to the same parameters for the spread-spectrum signal. To a receiver that does not have access to the parameter, the transmission is similar to background noise.
- **Frequency-hopping spread-spectrum** technology (FHSS). The transmission is narrow-band, but the frequency of transmission is changed according to a pattern known both to the transmitter and the receiver. At any one time, the transmission uses a single frequency, but at different times varying frequencies are used. The frequencies are changed according to a fixed pattern.

Figure 2–23

*A peer-to-peer wireless
local area network*

Laptops with antennas

- **Direct-sequence spread-spectrum** technology (DSSS). As in spread-spectrum technology, a wide spectrum of frequencies is used to transmit and receive. However, with DSSS, redundant bits are transmitted over the same frequency spectrum. The system is more reliable due to the transmission of redundant bits.

Wireless LANs can use a variety of configurations. The simplest involves having a few portable computers equipped with wireless adapter cards communicating between themselves through an antenna system. This permits a peer-to-peer network where the portable computers have access to each other's hard drives (see Figure 2–23).

A more common configuration has multiple wireless laptop computers accessing a central server. The laptops are equipped with an antenna that comes as a PCMCIA add-on card. The wireless laptops use a "network access point" that is connected to a wired network on which the server resides. An access point can serve about 50 clients over an indoor area 500 feet in diameter (see Figure 2–24). Access points are distributed over the entire premise so that the whole area is blanketed by wireless coverage. Finally, wireless connections can also be used for interconnecting

Figure 2–24

*Extension of a
terrestrial LAN
through use of
network access points*

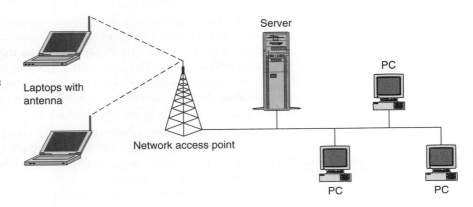

Laptops with
antenna

Server

PC

Network access point

PC

PC

LANs in separate buildings. Currently, the popular standard for wireless LANs is the wireless version of Ethernet, IEEE 802.11b. The standard permits a shared data capacity of 11 megabits per second.

Bandwidth

Bandwidth is a measure of data that can flow in a unit of time. Bandwidth has two different measures for analog and digital technologies. In the analog medium, data are usually sent as continuous signals at different frequencies. The analog bandwidth is calculated as the difference between the maximum and the minimum frequency of the signal that can be sent. For instance, in the case of twisted-pair copper wires used for telephone, the lowest and the highest frequencies are 300 Hz and 2,400 Hz respectively. The bandwidth for the medium is, therefore, the difference, which is 2,100 Hz.

The bandwidth for digital systems is measured in bits per second. For the same pair of wires, in case of digital pulses, data can be sent as much as 6 mbps. The digital bandwidth is, therefore, 6 mbps. In general, the higher the bandwidth, the higher the data-carrying capacity. The data networking infrastructure is, in some ways, like a road. It carries traffic, and there is a capacity and a need. When the need exceeds capacity, gridlock results, and the Web is characterized as "world wide wait."

Consider some voice and video applications to assess what data-carrying capacities are required and then compare these with what current network infrastructures can offer. The human voice, for example, has a frequency range from a few hundred Hz to about 20 KHz. The bandwidth required in analog systems is, therefore, about 20 KHz for the human voice. In practice, even 15 KHz for adults is sufficient, as the full range of 20 KHz is audible only to children.

Some analog phone lines have a bandwidth of only 2 KHz, making the voice over the phone different from the natural voice. Radio-based analog systems such as amplitude modulation (AM) allow 5 KHz. Actual transmission is sent as duplicate, so 10 KHz is allowed for each AM radio station. For public FM radio stations, 15 KHz is allowed for each channel, and with spare bandwidth in between, 100 KHz is allowed for each station. Not surprisingly, FM reception is much superior to its AM counterpart.

The highest fidelity voice reproduction occurs in digital music CDs. The voice is encoded by a sampling system that works at 44.1 KHz, using 16 bits for each channel. There are two channels and it all leads to about 1.41 mbps per second (44,100 * 2 * 16). Against this requirement, digital voice lines in telephones allow 64 kbps. Digital cellular phone systems allow 8 kbps, and PCS cell phone uses 9.6 kbps. Real audio transmission over the Internet requires at the minimum 14.4 kbps. The data capacity of connections to the Internet available to residences is gradually improving. Currently, the best modems can yield 56 kbps. With cable and DSL modems, this capacity is now a few hundred thousand to a few megabits per second. Compared to what is required for a high fidelity system, networks are far from providing broadcast quality audio over the phone lines and the Internet.

As for video, the bandwidth of a television channel is 6 MHz. Both UHF and VHF television channels are provided 6 MHz each. In cable television, where multiple channels are sent by frequency multiplexing, 6 MHz of bandwidth is allocated for each channel. The digital transmission of television signals requires about 6 mbps, and that is the capacity provided for digital satellite systems transmitting digital television signals. A videoconference requires much less. At 284 kbps, a data stream can fill a quarter of the screen and provide decent stereo sound as well. Barely acceptable full-screen video and stereo sound requires about 1.2 mbps. Considering the current limited data rates available for domestic consumers, broadcast television and video over the Internet is still many years away.

Case: Qualcomm

Irwin M. Jacobs, chairman and CEO of Qualcomm (Quality Communications) and a former professor at the Massachusetts Institute of Technology, savors proving his critics wrong. A decade ago, he invented a much more efficient wireless technology that few believed would be successful. But it was! Since then, Jacobs has grown his company into a $4 billion giant in wireless communication. Qualcomm has been involved in various facets of the wireless business including designing computer chips for wireless telephony, manufacturing wireless handsets, and running a wireless network.

Jacobs has now decided to focus more on the company's core strengths. Qualcomm is getting out of manufacturing chips for the wireless industry. As one of the most creative research and development laboratories in the wireless industry, Qualcomm holds patents on the basic technology building blocks, and most manufacturers of cellular technology products pay royalties to Qualcomm. About 15 percent of the world's wireless phones use Qualcomm technology. As the industry moves to better technologies and higher speeds, half of the world's cellular phones are expected to be using technology developed by Qualcomm.

Wireless technologies, like all other communication technologies, are evolving rapidly. Qualcomm is contributing to this revolutionary growth. It makes 90 percent of the chips that use code division multiple access (CDMA) technology. The company recently launched an appliance that is a cross between a handheld computer and a wireless phone. The device can be used to send and read e-mails, surf the Web, and place stock orders. Qualcomm developed a technology that allowed movies to be streamed to a computer on the back of a pickup on a highway. It achieved this by sending data over 30 times faster than what was previously feasible. Many believe that Qualcomm will grow into the exclusive club of wireless giants that includes Nokia, Motorola, and Ericsson.

Summary

This chapter focused on fundamentals of data communication and the basics of wireless communication. Basic concepts such as digital and analog, various modulation techniques, and different types of multiplexing were reviewed. A variety of transmission media were covered. The telephone network and various digital services were described. The "last-mile problem" was discussed along with various solutions, such as cable modems, DSL modems, and wireless local loops. Chapter 3 considers various Web protocols and how the Internet operates.

Key Terms

1G to 4G wireless telephony   69
Advanced mobile phone
  system   64
Amplitude modulation   47
Analog signal   43
Bluetooth   68
Cable modem   71
Cellular digital packet data   67
Coaxial cable   52
Code division multiple access   67
Data compression   50
Direct-sequence spread
  spectrum   76
Digital signal   42
Digital subscriber line   72
Ethernet   73
Fiber optics   53
Frequency division
  multiplexing   48
Frequency-hopping spread
  spectrum   75
Frequency modulation   47

I-mode   68
Integrated service digital
  network   63
Local area network   73
Low earth orbit   56
Modulation   46
Modem   70
Multiplexing   48
Optical carrier hierarchy   63
Packet switching   60
Personal area network   68
Personal communication
  service   66
Public switched telephone
  network   58
Pulse code modulation   45
Satellite microwave   55
Synchronous optical network   62
Time division multiplexing   48
Terrestrial microwave   55
Wireless local loop   60

Review Questions

1. Differentiate between a digital signal and an analog signal.
2. What are the important characteristics of a periodic signal?
3. Why is digital technology often preferred over analog technology?
4. Describe the various methods of multiplexing.

5. Compare media types such as twisted-pair copper wire, coaxial cable, and fiber optic cables.
6. Compare the three digital transmission systems: T-1 carrier, SONET, and ISDN.
7. Describe the different types of wireless telephony systems.
8. Show how technologies such as PCM, AM, FM, FDM, and TDM are combined to make a digital cellular system possible.
9. Describe digital subscriber line technology.
10. What is the "last-mile problem"? Describe some solutions discussed in this chapter.
11. Differentiate between a local area network and a wide area network.
12. What is Ethernet? How is CSMA/CD related to Ethernet?
13. Describe some wireless technologies used in wireless LANs.

Projects

1. Visit www.bluetooth.com. Write a short note on the technology and its applications. How is the computing environment at homes and offices likely to change as a result of this technology?
2. Visit a site such as Buy.Com to find out about networking products required to set up a small residential local area network that connects three personal computers so as to share a printer and a single high-speed connection to the Internet through a high-speed cable modem.

References, Readings, and Hyperlinks

1. Bates, Regis J. "Budd," and Donald Gregory. *Voice and Data Communications Handbook.* New York: McGraw-Hill, 1997.
2. Dodd, Annabel. *The Essential Guide to Telecommunications.* Upper Saddle River, NJ: Prentice Hall, 1998.
3. Harrington, Jan L. *Ethernet Networking Clearly Explained.* Boston: Morgan Kaufman, 1999.
4. Lu, Carry. *The Race for Bandwidth: Understanding Data Transmission.* Redmond, WA: Microsoft Press, 1998.
5. Schneiderman, Ron. *A Manager's Guide to Wireless Communications.* Boston: AMACOM, 1999.
6. Stallings, William, and Richard Van Slyke. *Business Data Communication.* Upper Saddle River, NJ: Prentice Hall, 1997.
7. Stetz, Penelope. *The Cell Phone Handbook.* Newport, RI: Aegis Publishing Group, 1999.
8. "Wireless Web: Special Report." *Scientific American,* October 2000, pp. 18–57.

COMMUNICATION PROTOCOLS FOR E-BUSINESS

Chapter Outline

Learning Objectives

By the end of this chapter, you should be able to:

- Explain the idea of protocol and the need for protocol layering for communication.
- Describe the OSI model of communication protocol.
- Point out the important features of the TCP/IP, the Internet protocol suite.

- Understand the protocols used in the World Wide Web such as HTTP and URL.
- Differentiate between *intranet* and *extranet*.
- Describe the new Web-based wireless application protocol (WAP).

Chapter Overview

This chapter begins with the concept of a protocol, which is a system of rules that permit communication. It shows how protocols are members of a family or architecture. The protocols used in the World Wide Web, such as HTTP, are discussed. The chapter also describes networks known as intranets and extranets and reviews the platforms on which extranets run, such as a virtual private network (VPN). Finally, a new Web-based wireless application protocol (WAP) is discussed.

A Technical Vignette

We are witnessing the end of an era of "pure products," or machines that perform only one function. The telephone can only be used to call some-body, the microwave can only be used for heating, and the refrigerator can only be used for cooling. In offices, though, we now have appliances that perform multiple tasks. A fax machine, for example, can be used to copy, and the copy machine can be used to scan. Both can be controlled and used with the aid of a personal computer.

The Internet and the Web revolution are about to reach our toasters, refrigerators, and microwave ovens. All these appliances can hold embedded communication chips, and they can all be connected to the Internet with their own network addresses. For instance, the family cook will be able to place a call from the car using the cellular phone to tell the microwave to heat dinner. The oven will be able to download recipes from the Web. The refrigerator will be able to read the bar code of an empty juice container and reorder it from the Web-based grocery store. Many of these "smart" appliances will be based on microelectromechanical systems (MEMS)—a technology based on smart sensors that communicate.

Ed Zanders, President and COO of Sun Microsystems, predicts[1] that "in the next few years cars, washing machines, dishwashers, microwave ovens, refrigerators, and toasters will have interface with the World Wide Web and not just the PCs." Appliances will become easier to use, even as they grow more versatile. While cooking, for example, the oven's console may enable users to conduct bank transactions from home. Andrew Lippman, Associate Director in Media Arts and Science at the Massachusetts Institute of Technology, predicts that within the next three to five years, Web and broadband connections from the home to the Web will become widespread. John Chambers, CEO of Cisco Systems, remarked in an Internet conference: "The next revolution will be connection to the home. Within the next five years, everything will be connected—voice, data, and video." New technologies are on the way in both the local area and wide area environments. In the local area setting, a new system called Bluetooth is being developed that will enable radio-based devices to talk to each other in a building. Bluetooth will allow a personal computer to control and monitor all the electronic devices in the home, from the television to the oven.

The world of wide area wireless networks is still limited by low capacities. The web and Internet services now accessed from the desktop are still some years away for wireless devices. But much is being accomplished on the technology front. For instance, in the area of wide area wireless communication, Nokia is helping Global Systems for Mobile Communications (GSM, a wireless standard used in Europe and by some carriers in the United States) networks evolve into being data-centric. High-speed circuit switched data (HSCSD) over wireless transmission currently enables data up to 56 kbps and is likely to improve up to 115 kbps in just a few years. HSCSD will become an excellent bearer for wireless application protocol (WAP), a creation of Ericsson. WAP is designed to provide Internet-type services and applications to handheld devices by facilitating the display of specially formatted Web pages on low-resolution and low-bandwidth devices such as a cellular phone. These devices will run a microbrowser that will display documents using Handheld Device Markup Language (HDML).

Nokia is also designing cellular phones that have innovative features such as a small mouse, a wheel, or other elements that allow the user to type e-mail. These technologies will allow a wireless device user to receive, for example, breaking news, stock prices, and weather reports and to send and receive e-mail. Nokia, Ericsson, and Qualcomm are the three wireless giants leading the way toward a mobile information society.

What Is a Protocol?

A protocol is communication rules that participants must follow for communication to occur. Our lives are full of such protocols. Every time we pick up the phone, say "hello," and identify ourselves, we are following a protocol. The word *hello* informs the listener that a telephone conversation is about to begin. The listener gets prepared to receive a request from the speaker. Similarly, the address on a letter follows a certain schema. All participants in this communication—the sender, the receiver, and the post office—follow the same schema. If they don't, the letter does not reach its destination.

Protocols do not live in isolation. Communication is a complex activity, and this activity could be viewed as consisting of simpler and more basic acts. Protocols are rules of communication that govern each of these basic actions, and they come as part of a family. In data communication, the activity is defined as a sequence of simpler actions and the rules that define them are described as protocol layers.

Protocol layers also exist in a paper-based communication. The content is usually organized into a certain structure. For instance, the various parts of an office memorandum include "from," "to," and "date." The sender and the receiver must agree on the language to be used in the correspondence and the data to be included in the fields. In an interoffice memo, the name of the sender and the office needs to be mentioned as part of the "From" field while in an intraoffice memo, name alone may be sufficient.

The envelope containing the letter must conform to the requirements of the U.S. Postal Service, as must the addressing schema. The envelope could be sent by certified mail to ensure delivery to its destination. The letter moves through various sorting centers, and the same sorting logic needs to be followed at these centers.

A simple protocol scheme for this communication exercise is as follows (see Figure 3–1):

- Reading and writing of messages.
- The registration method for ensuring delivery from the source to the destination.
- Forwarding of the letter from the source to the destination, through intermediate postal sorting centers.
- Delivery to and collection of letters from the postal system.
- Addressing of the envelope, the addressing scheme, and the size and shape of the envelope.

Each of these layers may be viewed as delivering different services. Each layer uses the service of the layer below and it communicates with it by passing data objects. For example, before a letter can be delivered to the

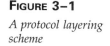

Figure 3–1

A protocol layering scheme

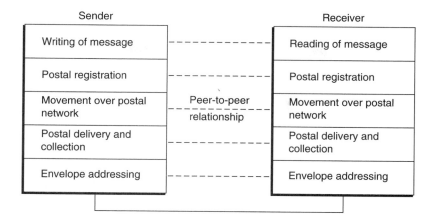

postal system, it must be addressed. For the letter to be forwarded through the postal sorting centers it needs to be delivered. Though often the terms are used interchangeably, *services* are not identical to *protocols*. Services are the functions and protocols are the rules for information exchange. Protocols are used in the delivery of the services.

The concept of peering needs to be understood as well. Identical layers at the sending and destination sites are related. This is referred to as a peer-to-peer relationship, a virtual relationship between identical layers across various sites. The scheme of registration followed at the sending end must be the same as the registration scheme at the destination end. They both have to participate in this activity for the registration scheme to work satisfactorily. Similarly, in the addressing of letters, the addressing scheme must be the same at both the ends.

The next section discusses a popular model for communication called **open systems interconnection** (OSI). The scheme is popular as a pedagogical tool. The protocol systems used in the real world have often developed independently of it, but they can be mapped to the OSI scheme with some stretching.

The Open Systems Interconnection (OSI) Model

OSI is a model of communication recognized by the International Standards Organization (ISO). Other models, such as transmission control protocol/Internet protocol (TCP/IP) for the Internet and the Web, are discussed later.

The OSI model grouped into two sets has seven layers. Layers 1 through 4 deal with the communication function, and layers 5 to 7 deal with user-oriented functions. Layer 0, which is usually not shown, includes the physical media (physical media were discussed in Chapter 2).

FIGURE 3–2

The OSI model

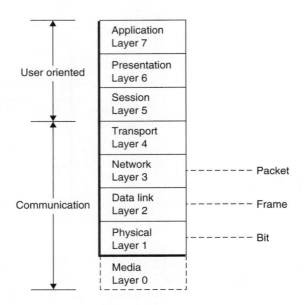

In the OSI model, each layer provides service to the layer above. Each layer is concerned only with the nature of the service provided and not the methods used for generating the service. This insulates a layer from concerns as to how the adjacent layer provides the functions. By defining each layer in terms of its functionality alone, it is possible to specify each layer as a set of operations that stand alone. The seven layers are illustrated in Figure 3–2.

Physical: Layer 1

This layer provides for the transfer of data bits. It includes specification for various modulation techniques, pin-out interfaces, voltages, and other similar issues. It provides for activities conducted by a modem (Chapter 2 discussed modulation techniques, such as amplitude modulation and the functions of a modem).

Data Link: Layer 2

While layer 1 focuses on the delivery of physical bits, the **data link** layer is concerned with the delivery of frames. The bits are arranged in a certain order to constitute a **frame.** In addition to data bits, a frame also carries information on, for example, addresses of the sender and the recipient, as

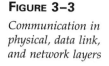

FIGURE 3–3

Communication in physical, data link, and network layers

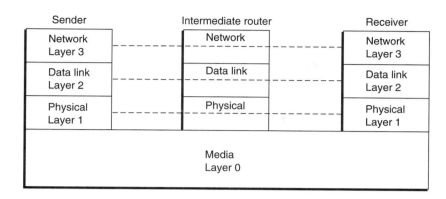

well as codes relating to error checking. The delivery that this layer specifies is on adjacent nodes. The data link layer specifies how a node gains access to the media, how it picks up the frames from the media, and the structure of the frame. The specifications related to the digital standard (DS) and optical carrier (OC) hierarchies, discussed in Chapter 2, are part of the data link layer.

Network: Layer 3

The network layer deals with data transmission from the sender to the destination, all across the network (see Figure 3–3). The data frame in layer 2 is now called a data **packet** in layer 3. The data packet bears the network addresses of the sender and the receiver. This layer deals with the entire path followed over the network (e.g., determination of the network route, reliable delivery, and collection of billing and accounting information). The primary task of this layer is to route messages through many segments in the network. In an Internet network, many paths are typically possible, and the network layer specifies the routing algorithm to be used for determining the route.

Transport: Layer 4

The transport layer is a source to the destination layer (see Figure 3–4). The activities of the transport layer are executed at the sender and the receiver ends. It is the first layer of the set of layers that perform the user-oriented functions. It is concerned with ensuring end-to-end delivery, or that the destination receives the message that has been sent, that no packet has been lost, and that the packets, when they are moved

FIGURE 3–4

Peer-to-peer communication between layers

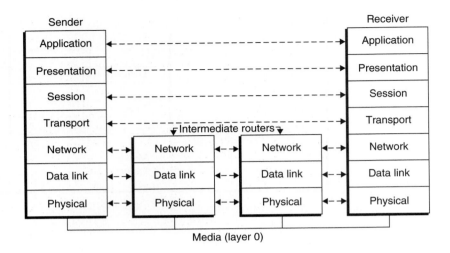

to the higher layers, are in the right order. It achieves this by affixing sequence numbers to the packets at the transmission end. The transport layers at the destination and transmission ends engage in a conversation to achieve the objectives of the transport layer. This type of conversation is a case of virtual communication at the peer-to-peer level.

The first four layers can be summarized as follows: Layer 1 settles matters at the level of electrical engineering. Layer 2 provides specifications of how nodes in the network take turns in sending messages over the media, as well as the structure of the message as it is sent to an adjacent node. Layer 3 is concerned with sending from the source to the destination, across the entire network, and layer 4 ensures that the messages are sent and received in an error-free manner.

Session: Layer 5

The session layer is concerned with the establishment and maintenance of the connection. If a connection fails, the session layer specifies the process of reestablishing the connection. The session rules specify the order of conversation, the topic for negotiation, the pace at which the data are sent, and the control on data flow to be exercised. An example is sending data to a printer. The computer and the printer must agree on the size of data that needs to be sent to fill the buffer and the process by which the buffers are emptied and new data are sent by the computer.

Presentation: Layer 6

The presentation layer specifies the format in which the data are transferred during the communication process. The types of services performed include changing of data codes, encryption, and data compression.

Application: Layer 7

This layer is the ultimate source and sink of data exchanged during communication. It provides for services that other applications may require from the data communication perspective. An example is X.400 protocol that is used by various e-mail applications.

The Internet

The Internet originated in the 1960s as a result of research supported by the Advanced Research Project Agency (ARPA) of the U.S. Department of Defense (DOD). The number of research sites around the country was increasing, and they often needed to exchange computer data between themselves and with the ARPA. They required a network that could exchange data and be sturdy and reliable in a warlike environment. The DOD initiated funding research activities to achieve this goal. While the federal government provided the funding, the research was carried out in a handful of universities throughout the country.

Basic Features of the Internet

The first version of the network that emerged was called ARPANET. Its features were adopted in what eventually became the Internet. This network had the following characteristics:

Data-Centric.   There were initially no plans to exchange voice. The telephone system operated by AT&T provided an excellent and reliable voice network. The Internet was designed exclusively for data communication.

Separation of Communication and Data Processing.   Architecturally, the processing task by a computer was separated from the communication task. The computers that were limited only to processing were called hosts. The communication task was assigned to a separate set of computers, called gateways or routers. Heterogeneous host systems would communicate through routers that followed the same protocols. This concept came to be known as internetwork. Under this scheme, most

FIGURE 3–5

*A packet switching
network*

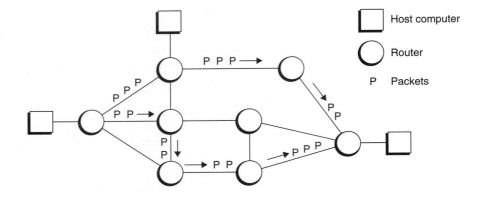

gateway computers were under the jurisdiction of the authority that managed the network, and the host computers were under the jurisdiction of the local sites.

Packet Switching.   The concept of packet switching (discussed in Chapter 2) was developed for ARPANET. Instead of a dedicated line from point A to point B, as used in telephone systems, the hosts in a packet switching network send packets that travel independently over the network. The telephone system is a circuit switched system where a link is established between two telephones and the link is held for the duration of the conversation. This network abandoned the notion of a fixed link.

For ARPANET the data traveled as small packets and the routers routed these packets from the sending nodes to the destination nodes via intermediate nodes (see Figure 3–5). The pieces of this network were made operational by Bolt, Beranek, and Newman of Cambridge, Massachusetts, in 1969. This packet switching network included the following features:

- The network consists of two types of nodes, hosts and routers (see Figure 3–5). The hosts are the originators and the destinations of the data packets. The routers are responsible for routing the packets from the originating host to the destination host via intermediate routers in the network.
- The routing over the Internet is a "connection-less" system; that is, no fixed routing is maintained between hosts across networks. The routers have their own routing tables that change according to the network state. Each packet, as it arrives at the router, is directed to another link according to the routing table in use at that moment. Therefore, as the network state changes due to congestion or link failures, routes followed by the packets change as well. Packets in the same session follow different routes and arrive at the destination host out of sequence. The destination

Figure 3–6

A simple version of the Internet

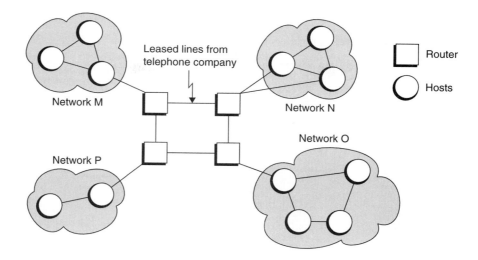

A simple form of the Internet is illustrated in Figure 3–6. It presents four (for illustration purpose only) islands of computing or physical networks. Each network has multiple hosts, and these networks are connected by another network, the Internet. The Internet is a network that connects other networks. In Figure 3–6, four routers that are connected to each other by point-to-point data circuits leased from telephone companies constitute the Internet. Gradually, the Internet consisting of routers connected over leased lines grew larger than ARPANET, as more physical networks came into existence and connected themselves to the Internet.

host has to get the packets in the right sequence before passing them on to the application running at the host.
 • The Internet is a "best-effort" delivery network, meaning the network attempts to deliver the packets to the destination host, but if trouble develops, such as congestion or link failure, the packets are discarded. It is up to the host computers to recognize the communication failure and to take corrective action. This approach allowed the network protocols to be simple.

Connection to the Internet

To connect a computer to the Internet, it must connect to a router that is part of the Internet. This router is usually sponsored by a university, a research center, or a commercial company (**Internet service provider,** ISP) providing Internet access. ISPs operate at many levels. Local ISPs lease connections from a national or a regional ISP, and then provide dial-up access to users. The national and regional ISPs have their own backbone

FIGURE 3-7

A national Internet service provider

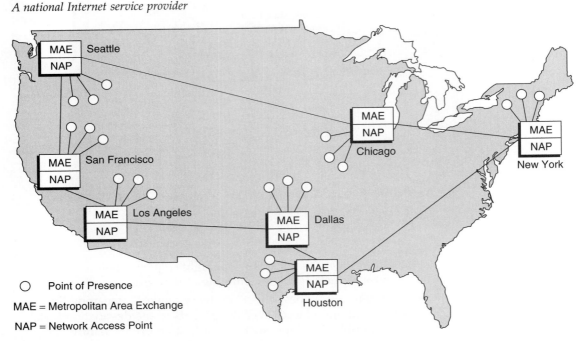

```
MAE   Seattle
NAP

MAE   San Francisco
NAP

MAE   Los Angeles
NAP

MAE
NAP   Chicago

MAE
NAP   New York

MAE   Dallas
NAP

MAE
NAP   Houston
```

○   Point of Presence

MAE = Metropolitan Area Exchange

NAP = Network Access Point

networks to carry Internet traffic. They charge local ISPs for their connection to their network.

The Internet consists of a complex set of networks that spans the world.
These networks belong to various governmental organizations and private
ISPs. The ISPs lease lines from telephone companies and microwave and
satellite operators to run their own backbone circuits. These circuits have
data capacities ranging from 45 mbps (T-3) to OC-192 (10 gbps) lines. In the
United States, these backbone circuits meet at several network access points
(NAPs), at many metropolitan area exchanges (MAEs), and at private peering points to exchange data packets among themselves (see Figure 3–7). The
backbone circuits belonging to the various ISPs use these meeting points to
exchange data packets among themselves. Local level ISPs connect to MAEs
in order to gain access to the Internet circuits owned by National ISPs.

The connection between a computer and the Internet is obtained
through:

1. A dial-up link between a computer and an ISP. Usually, ISPs have
   local phone numbers that subscribers can dial. The data traffic
   from these local phone numbers arrives at local exchange carrier
   telephone switches and is then carried over the phone lines, such

Figure 3–8

Connecting to the Internet

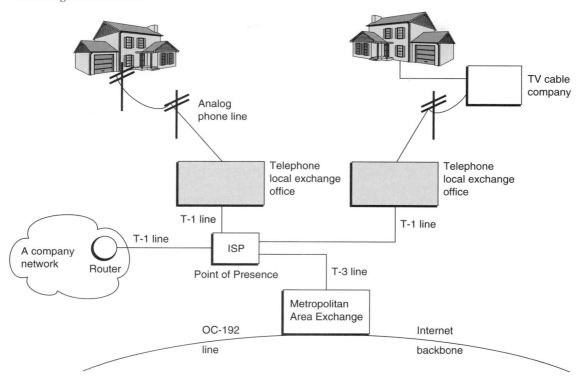

as a T-1 line (1.544 mbps), to an ISP (see Figure 3–8). At the other end, an ISP is connected to an Internet-backbone carrier. The ISP usually leases high-speed digital lines such as T-3 (45 mbps) to carry traffic to an Internet backbone carrier site, often an MAE.

2. A cable TV line. Data are transferred from the cable TV network to an ISP. In turn, this traffic is sent out over a high-speed digital line, such as a T-3 line, connecting it to an Internet backbone carrier site.

3. A router belonging to an ISP and a router that is part of the customer's network. Data packets travel from the subscriber's router to the ISP's router, which gets them to the Internet.

The Internet Protocol Suite

The Internet layering model developed independent of the OSI model discussed earlier. The Internet model is known as the TCP/IP protocol suite, or transmission control protocol and **Internet protocol.** The suite can be

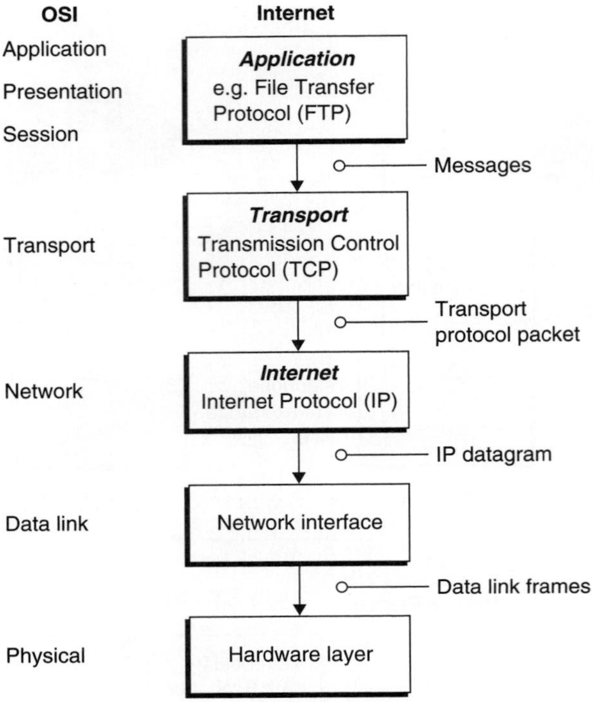

FIGURE 3–9

The Internet protocol suite

OSI	Internet
Application	**Application** e.g. File Transfer Protocol (FTP)
Presentation	
Session	
	— Messages
Transport	**Transport** Transmission Control Protocol (TCP)
	— Transport protocol packet
Network	**Internet** Internet Protocol (IP)
	— IP datagram
Data link	Network interface
	— Data link frames
Physical	Hardware layer

mapped to the OSI model with some stretching. Figure 3–9 depicts the TCP/IP model and its relationship to the OSI model.

The TCP/IP suite consists of four layers that run over a fifth layer, the hardware layer. The four layers are: application, transport, Internet, and network interface.

Network Interface Layer

This layer is responsible for accepting the data packets (IP packets) arriving from the network and transmitting them over the specific link on a network. If the network is a local area network, the functionality is implemented in a device driver that resides in a network interface card. In the case of a wide area network, such as a packet switching network, this layer implements the data link layer of the packet switching network.

Internet Layer

The following tasks are performed at the Internet layer:

- The Internet layer accepts a packet from the transport layer. It encapsulates the packet into another packet called an IP

FIGURE 3–10

Encapsulation of IP datagram in a data link frame

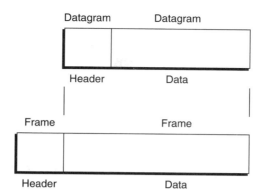

datagram, and fills the header of the IP datagram with details, such as the address of the destination computer (see Figure 3–10).

- A routing algorithm is used to find the next router to which the datagram must be sent, and then it passes it on to the appropriate router interface for transmission to the next router.

- It handles the incoming IP datagrams from other computers. It determines whether the datagram is meant for a local computer or if it needs to be forwarded to another router. For datagrams addressed to the local host, it deletes the datagram header and passes on the packet to the transport layer at the host computer.

- The layer also sends and receives error and control messages.

Internet Addressing.   The Internet, as with any network, consists of nodes and links. The links are usually terrestrial lines leased from telephone companies. The nodes are either computers or routers. The computers, called hosts, may be linked to each other locally, forming a separate island of computing. These islands of computing, in turn, are connected via routers that comprise the Internet. A host computer can be identified as a particular host in a specific network. IP addressing follows a two-level scheme: one part of the address specifies the network; the other part details the host in that particular network. This can be contrasted with the addressing scheme used by the U.S. Postal Service, where a multiple-level addressing scheme is used that identifies the state, the city, the street, the house number, and the individual in the house.

The IP address consists of 32 bits. It is written as a set of four bytes (a byte is eight bits) separated by periods. The bytes may be written as their decimal equivalents. Thus, a 32 bit Internet address:

10000001   00011111   10000001   00011111

is written as 129.31.129.31. One part of the IP address specifies the network and the other part specifies the host. Thus, conceptually each address is a

TABLE 3–1   IP Network Classes

IP Class Network (1)	Lowest Network Address (2)	Highest Network Address (3)	Network Part of the Address (4)	Number of Addresses Available	Number of Hosts Available in Each Network
A	0.1.0.0	126.0.0.0	First byte	128	16,777,214
B	128.0.0.0	191.255.0.0	First two bytes	16,384	16,382
C	192.0.1.0	223.255.255.0	First three bytes	2.1 million	253

pair consisting of network address and host address. The number of bits used for specifying the network depends on the class of the network. A simplified version of these network classes, and the way to identify the network and the host address from an IP address, is shown in Table 3–1.

According to Table 3–1, class A networks are the rarest, but these networks can accommodate a very large number of hosts, above 16 million each. These network addresses have been assigned to institutions such as AT&T, IBM, and MIT. There are more than 16,000 class B networks, and each can accommodate about 16,000 hosts. Class C networks are the most abundant. There can be 2.1 million of these, and each can accommodate 253 hosts. Other classes of networks are reserved for special purposes such as multicasting.

Table 3–1 specifies for each type of network the highest and the lowest network addresses. Knowing the IP address of a host, it is easy to identify the type of network in which the host resides. For instance, the IP address 158.121.112.91 refers to a type B network because the first number is between 128 and 191 (column 2, Table 3–1). Since, it is a type B network, the first two bytes identify the network address, which is 158.121 (according to column 4, Table 3–1, type B networks have the first two bytes as the network address). The last two bytes identify the host address, which is 112.91.

It is not so much the host as the network connection that is assigned an IP address. A host usually has one connection to the network and, therefore, it has one IP address. A router that is linked to two other routers has three connections—two to other routers and one to the network it is serving. It thus has three IP addresses. For example, consider Figure 3–11, which shows three local area networks: 192.28.1.0, 192.28.2.0, and 192.28.3.0 (Networks X, Y, and Z). The networks are connected by point-to-point T-1 links, which are themselves networks with addresses: 192.28.4.0, 192.28.5.0, and 192.28.6.0. There are three routers: A, B, and C. Router A has three connections, the addresses of which could be 198.28.1.1, 198.28.4.1, and 198.28.6.1. Similarly, routers B and C have three IP addresses each.

FIGURE 3–11

Routers with multiple IP addresses

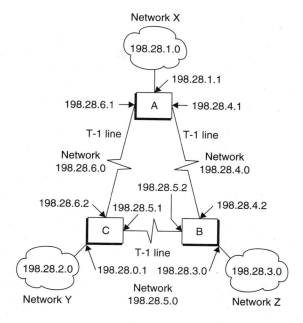

Domain Name Addressing.   The IP addressing scheme of 32 bits is not particularly user-friendly. It is difficult to remember and write such large numbers. Addresses need to be pronounceable and easy to remember. For instance, this author's website used to have the address www.chaudhury.mis.umb.edu, in which the actual IP address was 158.121.112.98. The readable IP address that is used has a hierarchic structure. At the top level, are domains such as edu, com, gov, or mil (see Table 3–2). Within each domain, are many networks, such as "umb" in this case, which stands for the University of Massachusetts, Boston.

TABLE 3–2   Internet Domain Names

Domain Name	Meaning
edu	Educational institutions in the United States
gov	Government institutions in the United States
com	Companies in the United States
mil	Military institutions in the United States
Country Codes such as fr, in, uk	For countries such as France, India, and the United Kingdom, respectively.

FIGURE 3–12

*Part of the domain
name server tree*

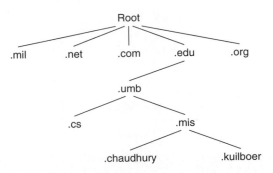

Further down, is a subnetwork of "mis," which stands for the management information systems department. Finally, the machine is identified as "chaudhury." (see Figure 3–12)

The use of such domain names requires a scheme that translates the user-friendly readable names to actual IP addresses. This is achieved through a system of servers called domain name servers (DNS). The DNS is usually a dedicated server that provides name-to-address translation. The translation is performed using a table that lists the host names and IP addresses. The DNS system is distributed and efficient. These servers communicate between themselves, and every network has at least one DNS. The computers on the network operate a program called name resolver that can call on at least one DNS to obtain the IP address. Frequently used names are cached by a DNS to provide efficient service to clients making requests.

Address Resolution Protocol.   While the DNS provides the address mapping between the name and IP address, that alone is not sufficient to get a packet to the destination. For instance, once the DNS has completed the mapping between this author's machine name "chaudhury.mis.umb.edu" to the IP address, 158.121.112.98, at the sending machine end, the packets will bear the IP address and arrive at the university's network. It still must reach this author's machine.

However, in the last leg of this travel, the packets run over a local area network, and they are encapsulated in Ethernet frames. The frames have to bear the hardware address of this author's machine. Thus, there needs to be a translation between the IP address and the hardware address. This translation is done according to address resolution protocol (ARP). ARP provides the means for locating the actual physical device when the IP address is known.

IP Routing

Routers are devices that connect various networks, without which the networks would remain separate. Figure 3–13 displays a simple example of routers in use.

Figure 3-13

An Internet with two routers and routing tables

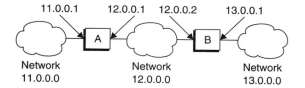

As previously described, the Internet is a packet switching network. In such a network, a packet can have multiple routes from one node to another. Routers choose one route over another. The routing operation is invisible to hosts that connect to the network, and the IP protocol defines how a route is selected. Routers determine how to route the packets by using a routing table. Consider the example depicted in Figure 3–13. Three networks, 11.0.0.0, 12.0.0.0, and 13.0.0.0, are connected by two routers, A and B. The IP packets or datagram bear the IP address that has the network identifier; in this case, it has one of the three numbers, 10, 11, or 12. Since the first byte number is less than 127 (refer to Table 3–1), they are all type A networks. The first byte specifies the network address. The routing tables at routers A and B are noted in Table 3–3.

A variety of routing algorithms are used in the IP environment. The IP protocol also specifies how routers exchange information to update routing tables.

Transport Control Protocol (TCP)

IP is an unreliable mechanism for datagram delivery because it has no scope to report lost or duplicate datagrams. The datagrams in an IP network may follow different routes and usually end up arriving at the destination host out of sequence. This mechanism was deliberately adopted to keep the routers' communication function as simple as possible.

Transmission control protocol (TCP), a transport layer protocol according to the OSI model, provides reliability on the Internet. The TCP is

Table 3-3 Routing Tables

Router	Packet Addresses to Network	Route to Address
A	11.0.0.0	Deliver directly
	12.0.0.0	Deliver directly
	13.0.0.0	12.0.0.2
B	11.0.0.0	12.0.0.1
	12.0.0.0	Deliver directly
	13.0.0.0	Deliver directly

implemented as software that runs on the sending and receiving hosts. It does the following:

1. TCP breaks the data stream it receives from the application layer into small packets, called segments, that can fit inside a datagram.
2. The IP datagrams are numbered, and TCP sends the datagram using a system of acknowledgment-with-retransmission paradigm. If a datagram is not acknowledged, the datagram is retransmitted.
3. At the destination end, TCP acknowledges the receipt of datagrams to the sender. It rearranges datagrams into the correct order and then passes them on to the application layers.

To understand the TCP operation, consider a simple form of transmission called the stop-and-wait protocol, in which the sender transmits a single datagram and then waits for acknowledgment. The overhead is very high in this protocol because an acknowledgment message is sent for every datagram. The transmission becomes unidirectional because at one time, the message is going in one direction only. The efficiency of such a protocol can be improved by having an acknowledgment at every, say, fourth datagram. There is now a bidirectional transmission with datagrams flowing in one direction and acknowledgments in the other direction at the same time. Also, for every four datagrams, there is only one acknowledgment. This is called a sliding window protocol. The number four defines the size of the sliding window, setting the number of data packets a sender is allowed to send simultaneously before awaiting acknowledgment. Sliding window protocol makes efficient use of the network because it limits the acknowledgment overhead. The size of the sliding window is a function of the network state, and TCP is an adaptive protocol that dynamically changes the sliding window size to accommodate the network condition.

World Wide Web Protocols

The Web and the protocols that make it possible are the invention of Tim Berners-Lee. His genius lay in combining the technology of Hypertext with that of the Internet. The Web system consists of servers and clients. The clients are referred to as browsers. Software such as Netscape and Internet Explorer are examples of browsers that operate on client machines. The browsers make requests to the servers and the servers fulfill the requests. Tim Berners-Lee wrote the **hypertext transfer protocol** (HTTP), which governs the interaction between the browser and the server. The servers are called Web servers or HTTP servers. His scheme required that all pieces of information on the Web be assigned an address called a **uniform resource locator** (URL). The response by the Web servers is sent in a universally accepted format called **Hypertext Markup**

FIGURE 3–14

Web protocol stacks

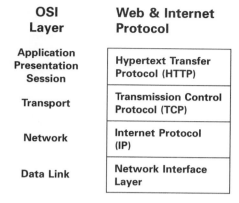

OSI Layer	Web & Internet Protocol
Application Presentation Session	Hypertext Transfer Protocol (HTTP)
Transport	Transmission Control Protocol (TCP)
Network	Internet Protocol (IP)
Data Link	Network Interface Layer

Language (HTML). Irrespective of the client machine, all browsers understand HTML. Because of the universality of URL and HTML, both designed by Tim Berners-Lee, documents can be accessed from any Web server and retrieved in a readable form by any browser in the world.

Web protocols such as HTTP run over the TCP/IP platform, which arranges reliable data delivery between the Web server and the browser (see Figure 3–14). To make the communication possible through TCP/IP, the Web server and the client both need to have their own IP addresses. When the browser is running on a computer located in a local area network, the network administrator assigns an IP address to the client machine. If the computer is connecting to the Internet through an ISP, the ISP assigns an IP address to the client for the duration of the session. The ISPs have a set of IP addresses assigned to them, which they dynamically allocate to subscribers as they log on to the Internet and remove as they log off.

Hypertext Transfer Protocol (HTTP)

The HTTP protocol specifies the type of request a browser can submit as well as the type of responses the Web server can make. It is built around a simple four-step interaction scheme (see Figure 3–15).

1. The browser makes a connection to the HTTP server using the TCP/IP protocol. The address of the server and the file requested are specified as part of the URL address.
2. The browser makes a GET request in which it specifies its nature, the type of the machine on which it is running, the operating system, and the types of files it can accept.
3. The Web server responds to the client by usually sending a file formatted according to HTML or in a format requested by the browser.
4. The connection between the server and the browser is closed.

FIGURE 3–15

Interaction between an HTTP server and a browser

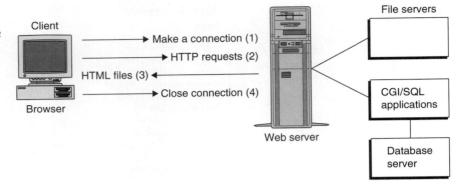

A typical GET request from a browser to a Web server appears as follows:

GET/HTTP/1.1
Accept: image/gif.
Accept-Language: en
UA-pixels: 1024*768
UA-color: color16
UA-OS: Windows 98

In turn, the server responds by sending the file requested, which is preceded by a header that describes the characteristics of the file being sent. A typical file header sent by an HTTP server looks as follows:

HTTP/1.1 200 OK
Server: Microsoft–IIS/4.0
Connection: keep-alive
Date: Mon, 01 Jan 2001 22:101:10 GMT
Content-Type: text/html
Accept-ranges: bytes
Content-Length: 5574

A browser can make other types of requests; a popular one is POST. With the POST request, a browser submits a form to an HTTP server with values for the various fields in the form. The POST method uses additional headers to transmit the names and values of the form fields in HTML form.

Uniform Resource Locator (URL)

The URL addressing scheme used on the Web follows this structure: [protocol]://[Web server address]:[port]/[directory]/[file name]. The following is a typical URL: http://chaudhury.mis.mgmt.umb.edu/aby/msis414.htm. The URL specifies the protocol as http, the domain name as chaudhury.mis.mgmt.umb.edu, the directory as aby, and the file name as msis414.htm. URLs are also used to send query strings and path information. The query string is used when the file requested is not an HTML file, but a program that executes. The program is provided with parameter values, which are sent along with the query string. The result of the execution is then sent by the HTTP server, suitably formatted as an HTML document. An example of a typical query string is http://www.web-technik.com/scripts/product.exe?category="drink" & availability="yes".

The HTTP is a stateless protocol; that is, once a session is started, no values relating to the state are carried along during the session. A browser requests the server for a page, the server provides a page, and all information about the request recently met is lost. Often, information through a session and information across sessions needs to be maintained. For instance, a website must maintain the list of items added to a shopping cart. Similarly, if the site requires a password, it must maintain the information about the legitimate entry as more requests are made on the site.

A popular method to maintain state information is through the use of "cookies." A cookie is a piece of information that a browser writes on the client machine and accesses before making a request to a website. The browser carries over the cookie information to the Web server. Shopping cart information can be maintained and updated in the form of a cookie. Also, a cookie can carry information about user name and password, which can then be passed over to the Web server every time a new Web page is requested.

Wireless Application Protocol (WAP)

The **wireless application protocol** (WAP) is a family of standards that specifies how cell phone users can access the World Wide Web. The standards facilitate a user of a cell phone or any handheld wireless device to pull up information from the Web and display it on a microbrowser and the tiny screen on the wireless device. The WAP standard is being implemented by all wireless carriers in Europe and by Sprint and Nextel Communications in the United States.

The major obstacle to displaying data from the Web on the screens of cellular phones is the small screen size. The screens are unable to display the images and graphics on the HTML pages. Also, the wireless bandwidth is limited to 10 kilobits per second. Phone.com, a California-based software company, created Handheld Device Markup Language (HDML) specifically for the wireless application. It serves the same purpose for the microbrowsers that HTML does for the regular browsers. It allows for formatting tags to properly display data on the tiny screens. The HDML evolved to a new language called Wireless Markup Language (WML), which is currently at the core of WAP.

The WAP standard also specifies how a standard HTML page on a website is translated to WML format for display on cell phones. Usually, when a cell phone user types the website address on a WAP-enabled phone using its keypad, the microbrowser sends the signal over the wireless to the cell phone transmission tower. The tower relays it to a special WAP server. The WAP server is a gateway that connects to the Internet. The server pulls down the Web page, converts it into a WML format, and sends it to the microbrowser. The cell phone receives the document in WML format and presents the information on the small screen. However, conversion from HTML to WML is trouble-prone. Many websites are creating separate versions of their Web pages written in WML so that they are specially targeted to WAP devices. For instance, MapQuest, Go2Online.com, and MSNBC.com have created WAP versions of their sites. More than 5,000 WAP-friendly sites are listed in www.cellmania.com.

Intranet and Extranet

The Internet protocol is an open standard. The specifications were developed with funding from the federal government, and they are available to anyone who wants them. Open standards often lead to many vendors producing according to the standards. This leads to market competition, resulting in lower prices and better quality. The same thing occurred to networking equipment and services built according to Internet protocols. Companies found it economical to develop networks for their own use, which used the Internet protocol suite.

An **intranet** is a network that uses protocols such as TCP/IP and HTTP but limits access to users from a single organization; unlike the Internet, an intranet is not open to the world. Often, the intranet runs over high-speed local area networks or high-capacity lines leased from telephone companies. Because of high data capacity, these networks tend to offer bandwidth-intensive applications, such as Web-based training; work flow applications, such as office supply requisitioning systems; and groupware applications, such as bulletin boards and discussion groups.

An **extranet** is a network where access is available not only to a company but also to its suppliers and customers. Like the intranet, the extranet is a network that employs Internet and Web protocols such as TCP/IP and HTTP. Because of connections to suppliers and customers, the extranet cannot be limited to a local area network. A major company that extends access to its extranet to suppliers usually develops it. Adding parts of intranets belonging to the company and its suppliers often constitutes the extranet (i.e., it is in the form of a shared space built from spaces belonging to individual companies). The Internet links the individual spaces to each other. The extranet is used for exchanging product specifications as well as bids and prices. It allows logistical links between customers and suppliers.

The main platform of an intranet is the LAN. The most popular architecture for a LAN is the Ethernet. Over 90 percent of new LANs conform to the Ethernet model. Ethernet LANs are also being extended by wireless LANs, another area of rapid growth in networking. Ethernet and wireless LANs were discussed in Chapter 2. A popular platform for extranets is the virtual private network (VPN).

Virtual Private Networks (VPN)

An extranet connects local area networks of a company and its suppliers by using the Internet. This leads to problems associated with security and confidentiality. Several companies, including Microsoft, 3Com, and Cisco, have jointly developed a protocol called layer 2 tunneling protocol (L2TP). The L2TP software runs on the servers and the clients. The software encrypts the message and encloses it in L2TP packets, which are wrapped in standard IP datagrams for transmission across the Internet. The L2TP software helps establish a virtual network between clients and servers that runs over the Internet (see Figure 3–16).

FIGURE 3–16

Virtual private network

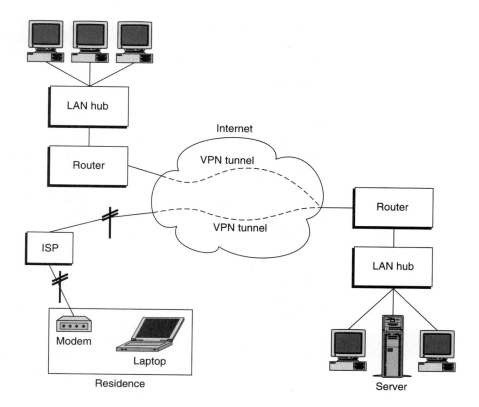

The L2TP software can control and manage user access to various parts of the information systems belonging to suppliers and customers. The system helps create a shared information space between many parties in an industry. Since the network operates over the Internet, it avoids the need for setting up expensive, private leased line channels between contractors, as is required for electronic data interchange. VPN-based transactions are becoming a substitute and sometimes a complementary system to EDI. They are used to facilitate just-in-time deliveries, an exchange of documents, the delivery of orders and shipment notices, and the joint development of production plans. An ambitious extranet project called Auto Network Exchange (ANX) is based on VPN. ANX enables the big three automakers, GM, Ford, and Chrysler, to interact with their 20,000 suppliers.

Profile: Tim Berners-Lee

Tim Berners-Lee invented the World Wide Web in 1990. The Oxford University physicist built the first Web server and the first browser as well as the protocols that allow conversation between them, such as HTTP, URL, and HTML. Berners-Lee's genius lay in combining two technologies, hypertext and the Internet, both of which had existed since the 1960s. Hypertext was the 1965 invention of Ted Nelson. Subsequently, Douglas Engelbert, inventor of the computer mouse, developed a collaborative workspace that used hypertext as a tool for group work. The Internet, while it rose to public prominence in the 1990s, has been popular with the university and the research community for the past 30 years. Michael L. Dertouzos, director of the MIT Laboratory for Computer Science, marvels that "thousands of computer scientists had been staring for two decades at the same two things—hypertext and computer networks. But only Tim conceived of how to put those two elements together to create the Web."

Tim Berners-Lee is the son of mathematicians who were part of the team that programmed Mark 1, the first commercial stored-program computer, at Manchester University in the 1950s. Berners-Lee's father had always been interested in ways to make computers intuitive and in ways to make connections between ideas, the way the brain does. He investigated ways to arrange data and concepts.

Berners-Lee's first attempt to develop the Web was called Enquire, after a book of the same name. To Berners-Lee, the book seemed like a "portal to a world of information, everything from how to remove clothing stains to tips on investing money. Not a perfect analogy for the Web, but a primitive starting point."

He developed the Web at CERN, the European Laboratory for Particle Physics in Geneva, Switzerland, as a means for keeping track of connections between people, projects, and computers. Many document management tools in use at CERN at that time attempted to do the same. All those tools required that the documents from various sources be brought under the control of one authority, in one format, and linked by some rigid structure such as a matrix or a tree. Researchers working on diverse projects did not welcome this. These projects were running on different computer systems using various documentation principles. Berners-Lee developed the novel idea that the documents were to reside wherever they were, only they were now to bear an address called a universal resource identifier, and related documents were to bear hyperlinks to one another. This system fostered a loose weblike relationship in which documents resided under the control of the authors on their computers, but they were now accessible to everybody participating on the Web.

Colleagues of Berners-Lee are not just impressed by his technical virtuosity, which is considerable, but also by his humanism. While the Web is in the midst of a frenzy of entrepreneurs and engineers trying to make their first million or billion, he has never wavered from his goal of making the Web a tool for all humanity. He has never confused technology with the goal that the technology is supposed to serve. Berners-Lee had the first Web server and browser working in CERN by Christmas Day 1990. He noted: "As significant an event as this was, I wasn't that keyed up, only because my wife and I were expecting our first child due Christmas Eve. As fate would have it, she waited a few extra days. We drove to the hospital during a New Year's Eve storm and our daughter was born the next day. As amazing as it would be to see the Web develop, it would never compare to seeing the development of our child."

Berners-Lee is currently the director of World Wide Web Consortium (W3C), which is the major driving force behind the development of technical specifications for the Web. W3C, which is based at MIT and has research centers in France and Japan, has recently developed the specification for XML, Extensible Markup Language.

Source: Tim Berners-Lee, *Weaving the Web: The Original Design and Ultimate Destiny of the World Wide Web* (San Francisco: HarperSanfrancisco, 1999).

Summary

This chapter began with the notion of a protocol as a system of rules that allows communication to occur. Protocols come as members of a family or architecture and make the Internet possible. The OSI model was reviewed. The seven layers of the model—application, presentation, session, transport, network, data link, and physical—were covered. The Internet protocols TCP and IP were mapped to the OSI model. Protocols used in the World Wide Web, such as HTTP, were discussed and the concepts of intranet and extranet were explored. Platforms on which extranets run, such as virtual private networks, were examined. The new protocol for Web-based wireless application, the wireless application protocol, was reviewed.

Key Terms

Application   89

Datagram   95

Data link   86

Extranet   104

Frame   86

Hypertext Markup
  Language   100

Hypertext transfer protocol   100

Internet protocol   93

Internet service provider   91

Intranet   104

Network   87

Open systems interconnection   85

Packet   87

Presentation   89

Session   88

Transport   87

Uniform resource locator   100

Wireless application protocol   103

World Wide Web   100

Review Questions

1. What is a protocol? Give some examples.
2. What are the various layers comprising the OSI model?
3. Relate the Internet protocol suite to the OSI model.
4. Describe the IP protocol. What is DNS?
5. Describe the TCP protocol. How is it related to the IP protocol?
6. Differentiate between intranets and extranets.
7. Describe the different elements of HTTP.
8. How is WAP related to HTML?
9. What is VPN? What role can it play in business-to-business e-commerce?

Projects

1. Visit the website www.w3c.org. Write a short note on the activities of the World Wide Web Consortium.
2. Visit the two sites www.phone.com and www.salesmountain.com. Write a short note on the convergence of wireless and Internet technologies. What do you think are the prospects for m-commerce (mobile commerce)?

References, Readings, and Hyperlinks

1. Informing Appliances, on www.economictimes.com on 11/28/1999.
2. Bates, Regis J. "Budd," and Donald Gregory. *Voice and Data Communications Handbook*. New York: McGraw-Hill, 1997.
3. Berners-Lee, Tim. *Weaving the Web: The Original Design and Ultimate Destiny of the World Wide Web*. San Francisco: HarperSanfrancisco, 1999.
4. Comer, Douglas C. *Internetworking with TCP/IP: Vol. 1*. Upper Saddle River, NJ: Prentice Hall, 1995.
5. Derfler, Frank J., and Les Freed. *How Networks Work*. Indianapolis: Que Publisher, 1998.
6. Naik, Dilip C. *Internet Platform and Protocols*. Redmond, WA: Microsoft Press, 1998.
7. Rybaczyk, Peter. *Novell's Internet Plumbing Handbook*. San Jose: Novell Press, 1998.
8. Schneiderman, Ron. *A Manager's Guide to Wireless Communications*. Boston: AMACOM, 1999.
9. Stallings, William, and Richard Van Slyke. *Business Data Communication*. Upper Saddle River, NJ: Prentice Hall, 1997.
10. "Wireless Web: Special Report," *Scientific American*, October 2000, pp. 18–57.
11. www.cellmania.com
12. www.phone.com
13. www.wireless.com
14. www.w3c.org

NETWORK SECURITY AND E-COMMERCE

Chapter Outline

Learning Objectives

By the end of this chapter, you should be able to:

- Estimate the technical security requirements for a network.
- Evaluate the business impact of security decisions.
- Conduct a security audit of a small network.
- Control access to the computing resources.
- Establish acceptable security solutions.
- Understand how viruses operate and how to protect systems from them.

Chapter Overview

Commerce transactions through the Internet require trust that both the seller and the buyer will be protected at many levels. Traditional sellers are concerned about the risk of not being paid for their products and services. Both sellers and buyer live in fear of hackers. Buyers have the fear of being overcharged, not receiving what they paid for, and divulging information that may not remain confidential. Brick-and-mortar operations have physical contact with their buyers and can check credit cards and signatures in a face-to-face encounter. While progress has been made in the area of electronic signatures, the equivalent to face-to-face interaction remains to be developed for the Web. In this chapter we assess a variety of threats to e-commerce, why it is important to consider this important facet of conducting business, and how a sound security policy will protect both seller and buyer. We also cover both the physical and logistical aspects of security relevant to the authentication of business transactions.

A Technical Vignette

One of the most dangerous threats to the security of e-commerce is the spread of viruses. In a computing environment, a virus is a program or piece of code loaded into other programming without the user's knowledge to cause some unexpected and usually undesirable event. It resides on the start-up portion of a disk or is attached to another legitimate program. When a user executes an infected disk or program, the virus is inadvertently propagated. Recently, the author of the Melissa Macro virus was sentenced to prison in an unprecedented case. Melissa was a harmless virus that caused no direct damage except that it propagated so quickly that it clogged mail servers, halting millions of transactions.

Since Melissa other viruses have gained notoriety. Recent ones include the Minizip, the BubbleBoy, and the Bolzano viruses. The security industry wages a constant battle against hackers who are making their viruses more and more sophisticated. Viruses that spread through the Internet can infect thousands of computers quickly, costing businesses time and money.

Internet Security Requirements (Secrecy, Integrity, and Availability)

Web security is a broad subject that could easily fill volumes. Security has been a concern in the computer industry since its infancy, but new challenges have appeared with the advent of the personal computer and the Internet. The sheer volume of computer use in a networked environment places considerable stress on the security of most organizations. Security issues can be classified according to a number of dimensions. A commerce site has to fulfill the following requirements:

- Secrecy: the category of computer security that deals with the protection of information due to unauthorized disclosure and the authentication of the data source. This important topic is covered in Chapter 5.

- Integrity: a cornerstone of secure Internet communications. The concept addresses the validity of the data and the guarantee that the data have not been tampered with during transfer. In this chapter we cover viruses and their potential nondiscriminate disruption of site integrity. Intrusion detection and other measures related to both secrecy and integrity will warn against hackers and their potential threats to a business. While no defense will ever be totally foolproof, some measures will be helpful.

- Availability: the insurance that the site will be reachable in a timely manner when the user is a legitimate stakeholder. Its absence can lead to high opportunity costs. Many of the remedies to security risks run counter to network performance because they add a layer of processing to the already burdened systems. In this chapter, we address the availability of service and its disruption though denial of service (DOS).

These three basic concepts are illustrated in the following example.

Two lawyers are working together on a corporate case. One of the lawyers is in Boston, and the other is in New York. The content of their correspondence must remain secret. The client informs the Boston lawyer that he should offer to settle for $10 million, but the client will negotiate a settlement up to $50 million if the offer is not accepted. If the adversary does not settle, the litigation will proceed to court, where the client knows he will likely lose after further court discovery about his business practices (new facts admitted to the lawyer in the same correspondence). It is very important that the discussion remain privileged. If the information is divulged to the opposing side, then the opponent can develop a strategy against it, either by pushing the settlement to the maximum amount or introducing the new facts in court. If the matter is urgent and the Boston lawyer decides to send the information through the computer network, secrecy has to be assured and the author of the document has to be legitimate, because the New York lawyer will base his work on these instructions.

After the message is sent, a process should insure that the content is not tampered with; that is, integrity is assured. Imagine that the message is hacked and the content replaced with instructions to initially offer $100 million but to go as high as $500 million. Or suppose a virus infects the file that was sent through insecure e-mail, so the New York lawyer cannot use it in a timely fashion or inadvertently infects all his other court documents.

In a last scenario, the New York office is disrupted by a "denial of service" attack. In this case, the lawyer never receives the new instructions and thus makes an erroneous decision to refuse settlement and pursue the case in court. In this case, the lack of availability is catastrophic for the client.

Threats can originate from outside or inside the company, and both physical and software protective measures should be taken to protect the perimeter of the network and the assets within the controlled local network.

Business Impact of Faulty Security

E-commerce is based on trust and limiting customer exposure to risks. Without these qualities, disaster could strike. As organizations become more dependent on online sales, they will encounter more threats. Internet distributors depend on high inventory turnover and low margin to generate positive cash flow from operations. A hacker's attack a few weeks before Christmas would jeopardize a toy distributor's entire season. Such disruptions could easily occur through denial of service (a condition where malicious requests overburden the server, thereby denying access to legitimate users) or the publicized fact that a hacker stole credit card data from the firm, triggering public mistrust. The incentive to manipulate the stock market through network hacking and business disruption could also spur the involvement of the underworld in hacking.

Malicious or nonintentional breach of security can cause havoc in a pure e-commerce business. Auction sites operating both in the business-to-consumer and the business-to-business arenas are potentially vulnerable. A hacker infiltrating the auction site through illegitimate access could disrupt the auction by resetting the auction to zero just before closing time, introducing erroneous bids, changing bids, or during the bid, examining the authorized ranges from other bidders. Absentee bidders often use automated agents to set their maximum bids. These amounts should be unknown to the other bidders and the seller. With a current bid of $2,000, for example, if bidder A was authorizing up to $10,000 for an item and this information was breached, then bidder B might give up and let A have the item at the current price, depriving the seller of an honest auction. Or if the limit amount were known to the seller, the seller could set up dummy bidder C, who would bid the item up to $9,999 and cheat bidder A. The Web auction process is highly sensitive to security breaches.

Security Threats

Loss, Damage, or Distortion of Data via Hackers

Once internal or external hackers enter the e-commerce system through a gap in the security defenses, opportunities abound to destroy, damage, or modify the system. Malicious acts include destroying Web pages, crashing the system, or changing its content. For example, a catalog could be modified such that prices are reduced, allowing the hacker to purchase items below market price. Since it would be difficult to distinguish between the hacker and honest buyers, the firm either delivers at a loss or subjects itself to the wrath of the customers and negative publicity.

Risks from Viruses

New viruses are created every month by the hundreds. Unfortunately, no one has any long-term solutions to combat this problem. Users should keep their anti-virus software up to date and always run the software to check a specific file before opening it. But even recently updated anti-virus software can fail to detect a new virus. That is why users should never open an attachment sent by e-mail unless they are expecting it. But those rules may not be sufficient anymore. Viruses now spread via Internet Relay Chat (IRC) channels. Software also can get infected from Word documents received from other users.

A dangerous example of a virus is Babylonia, which has many features of other recently released viruses:

- It spreads via e-mail (by patching Windows system files).
- It infects system files with copies of itself.

- It infects Windows help files (which makes it extremely difficult to find and remove because most virus scanners do not scan help files).
- It can spread via IRC, a popular tool on the Web (if the user is using the common mIRC program).

All these methods of replication are implementations of previous viruses, but the Babylonia virus combines them all and, as a consequence, reaches a huge amount of users. To help itself spread, Babylonia stirs the user's curiosity enough to open the attachment, which had been masquerading as a fix for the Y2K problem. But instead of fixing the computer, the virus contacts a website in Japan to download a plug-in module. This feature allows the virus to be updated remotely, making it easy for the author to alter the virus's behavior. Fortunately, the Babylonia virus infects only Windows 95 machines, until some hacker ports it to other platforms.

Other viruses expected to cause their share of problems include the Mypics virus, which also spreads by e-mail and which attacks on January 1, a date that could be easily changed. Mypics attempts to delete data from all the local hard drives, masquerading as the Y2K problem. The Chantal virus, also triggered on January 1, 2000, deleted all files from the root directory (C:\) and spreads via MS Word files. The Kriz virus triggers on December 29. The Fix2001 Trojan virus masquerades itself as a Y2K fix, but instead of fixing anything, it erases the entire hard drive immediately.

Unauthorized Access to the System

Unauthorized access to an e-commerce system can be perpetrated by insiders (current disgruntled employees or previous employees) or by sophisticated hackers. Hackers often will focus on an unsecured commerce server or on the underlying operating system itself. Once they have entered the system, they can steal valuable information. In December 2000, hackers broke into the commerce site of Egghead.com and were suspected of stealing more than 3 million credit card account numbers. Reports from credit card companies suggest that about 7,500 accounts have shown suspected fraudulent activity.

Financial Loss to Company or Customers

Any major disruption to a website by hackers can bring an Internet business to the brink of bankruptcy. Customers will end up paying for hackers' exploits as firms pass the losses on in the form of higher prices. To investigate the suspected breach, the business will have to stop trading, thus causing prejudice to buyers and sellers alike. As an example imagine an online broker who would stop transactions in the middle of a volatile stock market day. The clients would not have their transactions completed and the broker would fail to collect its commissions and would be subjected to a number of lawsuits.

Breaches of Personal Privacy

Often the back end of public websites contains information that is very hazardous to divulge. Individuals are very reluctant to furnish information that could become accessible online. Examples include a popular media event concerning the online publishing of U.S. personal earning and benefit estimate statements by the Social Security Administration. Although people were happy to have this information available to them, they were revolted to learn that their personal information was accessible to others, who could provide known information such as their names, social security numbers, mothers' maiden names, and places and dates of birth. These are public record and could easily be used to circumscribe personal data. Another well-known occurrence of privacy breach resulted from a probe in 1993/1994 where 1,300 IRS employees were suspected of using government computers to access individuals' tax records.

The preceding incidents all illustrate the potential for abuse triggered by a networked and distributed society. In the following sections we will outline some of the security issues with focus on what should be protected and what remedies are available to this effect.

Security Policy Development

Security requirements extend to the physical and software assets of the site. When a website is outsourced, the physical security is delegated to the third party, but similar measures should still be taken to prevent potential damage to the site content. A number of security hardware and software applications are widely available, and sound procedures for their deployment and maintenance are crucial. If the website is hosted by the website owner, then the security policies and their enforcement rest solely with the organization. Preventive security measures can be categorized as follows.

- Administrative security.
- Network security.

Administrative Security

While many security issues are related to technology, the administrative aspects should not be neglected. The administration of network security should include measures such as policies, procedures, training, and staff accountability. Before effective steps can be taken to secure a network, a framework should be established to guide the security implementation. Security management is an essential element of the security framework.

The first step of the planning process is to have a team determine the needs. The team should include people from various areas of the enterprise. The policies developed should be the result of a group effort, and all groups should accept policies before deployment. Business requirements should guide any security assessment. The security team should reach a consensus on questions such as the following:

- What services are required by the business and how can they be met securely? If the business uses a Web server, then the HTTP needs to be secured.
- How much do employees depend on the Internet and the use of e-mail? The heavy use of e-mail requires S/MIME.
- Do users rely on remote access to the internal network? Remote access requires the use of Telnet, which in turn needs a security measure.
- Is access to the Web required?
- Are customers supported through the Web?

In most cases, complexity is inversely related to security. The more services and the more complex the services, the less feasible it is to assure a secure network.

Threats can be classified in order of priority, emergency, and cost. Security procedures could be ranked as critical, need more assessment, need watching but are too costly, or nonsignificant. Based on the previous assessment, a root security policy should be adopted. The root policy will provide the framework on which the other policies will be built. High-level documents incorporating the root policy could include the following subsections:

1. Security architecture guide.
2. Incident-response procedures.
3. Acceptable use policies.
4. System administration procedures.
5. Other management procedures.

Assigning accountability for each policy is important. Hackers will exploit any flaw to breach the system. They can gain access to assets without being detected. Staff should be trained to react promptly and effectively to security incidents, applying relevant and proportionate responses to the threat. If suspicious activities are uncovered, the staff should trigger an organized prepared response and preserve the evidence of the attack for further remedies.

A major concern of an e-commerce business is the protection of its own data, but even more, the defense of customer information. Most e-commerce organizations store customer information online, where precautions should be taken to avoid any loss. If a site is hosted remotely, suspicions should be even more heightened. Not only should the ISP have policies and procedures in place, but the service level agreement also should stipulate serious remedies in case of a breach.

If the users are hosting their own site, or hosting it with a commerce service provider (CSP), it should sustain the same level of inquiry. Experience is an important factor in the implementation of a secure socket layer, which is a mechanism set to secure a site. As will be considered in Chapter 5, certificates issued by a responsible certificate authority should increase the level of trust in the site. Potential liability in the event of a breach of client information should be covered by insurance, either held by the company or by the host provider. When a company is dealing with an industry with specific security requirements, these should be addressed to the regulator's satisfaction.

Network Security

All systems and servers have their own weaknesses. Modern networked systems include many processes and applications that are not necessary for a standard installation. These additional services can expose the network through unknown security holes. In mainframe environments, security can be relatively strong because of centralization, limited access, and solutions such as resource access control facility (RACF). However, in a distributed computing environment, critical information (e.g., financial transactions, trade secrets, and customer records) resides on multiple servers in multiple locations. The need to protect this data is equally important, but it is more difficult because employees, contractors, partners, and customers have greater access.

While operating system vendors are attempting to improve their products, the complex mix of operating systems, utilities, and applications results in a continuous stream of security holes and patches. System vulnerabilities are caused by issues such as the UNIX superuser. With any UNIX system, a user is created with "root" privilege, that is, the authority to make changes to system files, applications, and security rights. On any system, there must be a way to kill a runaway program, purge corrupted files, reset passwords when users forget them, remove users' permission to use the system, and a myriad of other system management tasks. On the UNIX machine, this role is assigned to a superuser or root (not to be confused with the root directory). The superuser can override file security and do almost anything on the system. The superuser cannot see a password, since it is encrypted, but can change it. Any user with a user ID of 0 is a superuser. Such users should always have a password. The system administrator should not always log on as a superuser because it is too easy to make a trivial mistake and damage the system, perhaps by issuing the command "rm *" in an important directory (rm is the UNIX command used to erase files). Instead, the administrator should log on as a regular user, then switch to superuser with the "su" command when needed. The difficulty of setting the system correctly is an inherent weakness of any operating system. An unauthorized user could maliciously switch to superuser status and harm the system.

Trusted OS is one means of protecting the server, even though the restrictions of a Trusted OS environment are not practical in most business situations. A Trusted OS is an operating system that has been customized to close all potential security weaknesses. It is highly secure, but some of the otherwise available features of the operating system have been removed. Commercial operating systems have proved to better meet customer needs for flexible, compatible, and scalable systems on which to base enterprise applications. They have a clear upgrade path that is typically not available as soon as the level of customization of the OS diverges widely from the off-the-shelf product. To make an off-the-shelf system more secure, the administrator will have to keep track of a number of advisory messages informing the computing community of the inherent flaws in the operating system, the network, or the applications. Most default configurations create dummy users (such as "Guest" or "Anonymous") or services, which, left enabled, could lead to security flaws. For example, it is wise to delete the guest account by default on all corporate computers. Enabling it opens a door to the network and allows hackers to penetrate other resources. A knowledgeable administrator should also be aware of any harmful bugs and act to remove and disable them. A number of systems are classified as "hardened," also called *Bastion*, a synonym of "fort," which is supposed to be more resilient to hacker attacks. The securing process consists of disabling unnecessary accounts, unnecessary services, and unused communication ports and restricting access to common batch files and system utilities.

The installation process and the history of installed modules should be documented and verified to protect against employee turnover and to facilitate the application of future security patches. Most operating systems display the version level and the build level at start-up, giving important information to the administrator.

Vulnerabilities to systems and applications are announced frequently, and network administrators should consult often sites such as Bugnet (www.bugnet.com) and CERT advisories (www.CERT.org/). Many patches are published, but hackers are constantly monitoring the same lists to find tools to breach systems. Corrective actions in response to security alerts should be prompt, but not disproportionate or hastily implemented to avoid creating other side effects.

Desktop computers should be subject to the same level of caution as their respective servers. As internal clients, they could be breached in the same fashion as servers. Policies should be instituted regarding direct access through modems behind the firewall and the use of employee mandatory passwords. Passwords should be complex and no words found in common dictionaries should be used because hackers are likely to use them to attempt log-ins. Passwords should include mixed case, numbers, and punctuation and should be changed periodically. Choosing a sufficient length of at least 8 to 12 characters that is not easily breakable will retard any break-in. An internal check can be performed by running a password breaking utility for a test of the password and discarding it if it is too easily guessed. For servers, the passwords should be even more difficult to guess because hackers are more likely to persist in their efforts to break these accounts. Just a few people should know the root password of the server in order to provide timely responses if an account requires adjustment.

Assets access controls are of many types. The common approach is to physically secure rooms and equipment with locks. Computer room access should be limited to operating personnel, and entries should be logged in order to track anomalies. Smart cards or biometric tests such as fingerprints are increasingly used to control access. Equipment can be locked to tables so that it is not easily stolen.

Similarly, software and data should be protected with a number of security layers. User ID and passwords is the most common but the weakest means of protection. In the future, passwords could be used in conjunction with smart cards to access software and data. The second most common security measure is protection from viruses.

Virus Protection

Computer **viruses** are human made and self-replicating code that can affect operating systems, applications, and documents. The virus code is designed so that the infection occurs without the knowledge or permission of the computer user and propagates itself rapidly by infecting other files and passing itself inconspicuously to other computers. In the past, viruses were transferred through executable files, but new viruses have been devised to infect systems from regular e-mail and other electronic documents.

At some point, the virus is triggered to do its damage, called the payload, to the host computer. The payload can come in different forms, such as displaying a harmless message that appears on the screen, changing characters or words in document files, or deleting files from the host computer's hard drive. The nature of viruses varies significantly and more than 50,000 of them have been recorded over the past few years.

The first virus that received a great deal of publicity was the Morris worm, which in 1988 infected a large network used by the Defense

Department and many universities. The monetary damage was estimated at $98 million, but the real harm was that other hackers followed suit in hopes of getting similar publicity. Many anti-virus programs have become available and continuous battles occur between hackers and the anti-virus developers. These programs periodically check the computer system for the most popular viruses using virus signatures or monitoring for some uncommon program behavior. A virus signature consists of a sequence of bytes in the machine code of the virus. A good signature is one that is found in every object infected by the virus, but is unlikely to be found if the virus is not present, i.e., the likelihood of both false negatives and false positives must be minimized. Unfortunately, the accelerating influx of new computer viruses threatens to outpace the ability of experts to analyze and catalog signatures for them.

Aside from disconnecting the site from the Internet, not allowing file transfer, and not allowing the use of e-mail and diskette, there is no chance that one can avoid exposure to software viruses in a computerized environment.

Virus Categories

The basic virus principles are regularly recycled, allowing virus detection software to not only detect known viruses, but to try to derive patterns protecting against upcoming threats. Viruses are classified into three main categories:

- File infectors attach themselves to program files, usually selected .COM or .EXE files. They can infect any program for which execution is requested, including .SYS, .OVL, .PRG, .MNU and other common system files. The virus designers often choose to infect commonly triggered files so that the infection spreads faster before any detection can be developed. When the program is loaded, the virus is loaded as well.

- System or boot-record infectors infect executable code found in certain system areas on a disk. They attach to the boot sector on diskettes or the master boot record on hard disks. A typical scenario is to receive a diskette from an innocent source that contains a boot disk virus. When the operating system is running, files on the disk can be read without triggering the boot disk virus. However, if the disk is left in the drive and the computer is turned off or the operating system is reloaded, the computer will look first in the "A:" drive, find the disk with its boot disk virus, load it, and make it temporarily impossible to use the hard disk. This is why users should make certain they have a bootable floppy disk.

TABLE 4–1 Virus Groups

Boot sector	Macro
Worms	Companion
Link	Multipartite
Partition sector	Polymorphic
Trojan horses	Memory Resident (TSR)
Parasitic	IRC Worms

- Macro viruses are among the most common and virulent viruses. They are encoded as a script and embedded in a document. Many applications, including Microsoft Word and Excel, support powerful macro languages that are used as the transport for the virus. Macro viruses infect Microsoft Word applications and other programs using a script to set themselves up and typically insert unwanted words or phrases.

Other common forms of attack can originate from the virus types displayed in Table 4–1.

Macro viruses and e-mail viruses are becoming the most common because they evade the older types of virus checkers, which expect that any virus comes as an executable program. Newer viruses' attempts at evading protection software are often successful because of their polymorphic adaptation. They change their format between attacks or become inert after an attack to evade detection.

A worm is a type of virus or replicative code that situates itself in a computer system in a place where it can do harm. "ExploreZip" is an example of a worm. Like most computer viruses, worms usually come in as "Trojan horses." A Trojan horse is a program that contains malicious and harmful code and is apparently a harmless program or data. It can get control and do damage to the host system. Another example of a worm is the virus known as "BubbleBoy," which has been posted to public websites devoted to virus writing. BubbleBoy was the first e-mail-borne computer script that did not require a user to open an e-mail or e-mail attachment to infect its host. To date, there have been few reported victims of the virus, but since it is now available for download and imitation by virus writers, its release into the Internet as well as the appearance of destructive variants are highly likely.

Over the years, a large number of viruses have been written. Repertories of viruses exist in many organizations. A number of websites are maintained by security associations in order to fight the plague of computer viruses.

If you think you have a virus, want more information about viruses, or want to learn how to protect your site more effectively, the following sites will be instructive:

- Data Fellows Virus Information Center: http://www.datafellows.com/vir-info/
- International Computer Security Association: http://www.icsa.net/
- IBM Antivirus Online: http://www.av.ibm.com/
- Symantec AntiVirus Research Center: http://www.symantec.com/avcenter/
- Network Associates Virus Alerts: http://www.nai.com/asp_set/anti_virus/alerts/intro.asp
- Virus Bulletin: http://www.virusbtn.com/
- CERT at Carnegie-Mellon University: www.cert.org/
- CIAC (Computer Incident Advisory Capability): www.ciac.org/

In addition to considering viruses, these sites address many related security issues and are an asset in an e-commerce toolbox.

There are no ideal ways of protecting e-commerce sites against viruses. The best protection is to know the origin of each program and file loaded into the computer, but this is almost impossible in the case of e-mail. A number of products have been developed and targeted at the detection, protection, and eradication of viruses on both single-host and local networks. Among the most popular solutions are McAfee VirusScan, Norton AntiVirus, and CA Innoculan.

Because new viruses are released daily, a defense is most effective if the virus scanning software is loaded with the latest virus signature files and upgrades. Most leading virus software products provide some subscription with periodic updates, as well as other security services. Networked solutions can automatically scan the network for viruses and download the periodic updates.

A virus-scanning defense will always lag behind the skills of some hackers, so the organization should plan on being disrupted at some point. Sound recovery policies in the cases of security breaches will add additional protection to the knowledge and information assets of the organization.

Backup and Recovery

Organizations need to have clear procedures for backup and recovery. Disasters from hackers, hardware failure, or nature can strike even the most prepared organization. Backups should be conducted periodically. Procedures for short- and long-term backups address different needs. Daily backups should be kept close to where they will be needed in case of hardware failure. The static pages on the website should be backed up at least weekly and whenever revisions are made. If the e-commerce system shares the same hardware with the database containing the transactions, full and incremental backup should be implemented daily. In a round-the-clock operation the marginal computing capacity should be sufficient to proceed without halting the business.

While most organizations have published plans for backup and recovery, many are not enforcing them adequately. Recovery procedures should be rehearsed in a realistic environment. A number of questions should be asked. Can the business really count on the alternative sites? Do employees know the proper procedures? Does the alternative site have the necessary network connections to operate the business? Where is the backup stored and in what format?

Short-term backups should be available on site in case quick recovery is needed. Practical media for small backups include CD-RW or replicated hot hard drive. Weekly or long-term backups could be stored either on tape (a receding solution) or on disks in a remote network attached storage or storage area network. Network attached storage (NAS) is a device attached to the network like any node. NAS servers can access data directly from only the devices they control. A storage area network (SAN) is a discrete network of data-storage devices and servers that allows unrestricted exchange of information. SAN servers can access data directly from any device and do not transfer data over the LAN. In most new systems, both NAS and SAN are implemented using hard-drive technologies.

Storage of vast amounts of customer information complicates backup and recovery. While a few years ago it took a few thousand mainframes to store 75 terabytes, now the capacity of one Web portal uses as much. Organizations keep customer data for longer periods and have most of the information at their fingertips in order to reduce support costs. Often backup of such a large data set has to be done incrementally and stored in a readily available place. Remote backup also increases security concerns if data are transmitted to another location.

In addition to internal protection processes, a business needs to protect the perimeter of a network. Access to and from the Internet should be monitored and restricted to authorized users. Entering and exiting messages should be filtered for harmful content. Firewalls and proxy servers can provide a peripheral defense to the outside.

Firewalls

A firewall is designed to keep the fire from spreading. In a building, a firewall is a brick wall completely dividing sections of the structure. In a car, a firewall is the metal wall separating the engine and passenger compartments. In a computing environment, a firewall is a set of related

programs located at the boundary of the network that protects the resources of a private network from the users of other networks. With a
firewall in place, the organization allows its workers access to the Internet,
prevents outsiders from accessing the organization's data resources, and
controls what outside resources its own users can access.

The design goals of a firewall are:

- Control the traffic from the inside to the outside and vice versa.
  All traffic must travel through the firewall. All access to the
  network is blocked, except via the firewall.
- Establish local security policies to allow only authorized traffic to
  traverse the periphery of the network. Firewalls implement these
  policies in various ways as explained next.
- Avoid penetration through simplicity. A complex firewall can lead
  to parameters being omitted, thus allowing a backdoor to the
  system.

Firewalls can be classified into three distinct categories: packet filtering
router, circuit-level gateways, and application-level gateways.

Packet Filtering Router

A packet filtering router (see Figure 4–1) submits all incoming packets to
a filter applying a set of rules. The router can clean the data in both directions, forwarding or discarding packets as they are checked. The filtering rules are based on policies applied to the fields in the Internet
Protocol and the transport headers. The objects checked are the source
and destination addresses, the IP field, and the port number that determines which application will receive the packets (i.e., mail, TELNET, or
the Web server). The filters are typically set at matching field to patterns.

FIGURE 4–1

Packet filtering router

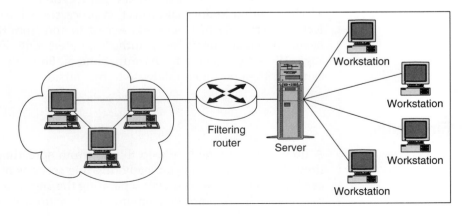

If a match exists, the rule is applied, either accepting or discarding the packet. Two default rules can apply, either discard or forward. Discarding by default is more secure but requires more administration. Forwarding by default allows all packets not explicitly prohibited to traverse the network. The most conservative policies are appropriate for e-commerce. Allowing just certain ports and certain directions limits exposure to hacking.

The following are popular attack mechanisms against packet filtering routers:

- In a source routing attack, the initiator lists the route taken by the packet to the destination, hoping security measures will be bypassed. The remedy is to insure that applied rules discard all packets using this method of routing.
- In tiny fragment attacks, the hacker divides the packet and forces different header fields into separate fragments. The method is intended to confuse rules analyzing TCP headers. The cure is to discard packets with TCP and a recognizable fragment offset of 1.
- IP address spooling involves using internal addresses for what are really external hosts. Another approach is to use legal external IP addresses, which will be positively recognized and allowed in. The solution is to discard the packets with the inside address source coming from the external port of the router.

Circuit-Level Gateway

Circuit-level gateway establishes connections between users on the outside and users on the inside (see Figure 4–2). It does not allow direct end-to-end links, but instead it establishes distinct TCP connections from the outside user to the gateway and from the gateway to the inside user. Once the connection is achieved, the packets travel through without checking

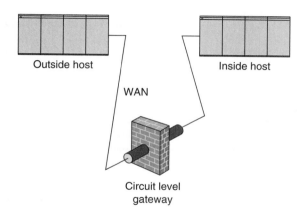

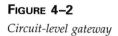

FIGURE 4–2

Circuit-level gateway

Outside host

Inside host

WAN

Circuit level
gateway

the content. The gateway can be set to act as a proxy service on inbound connections and as a circuit level on outbound connections.

The circuit-level gateway does not provide network-layer services and does not forward Internet control message protocol (ICMP) messages, by which hackers try to gather site-related data (or sneak access into the system). ICMP is an extension to the IP defined by RFC 792. It supports packets containing error, control, and informational messages. The PING command, for example, uses ICMP to test an Internet connection. An application of the circuit-level gateway is the SOCKS software, which provides layers between the application layer and the transport layer.

An organization with complex networks and resources at different levels of risk may devise more complex architecture. Internet firewalls are intended to keep unauthorized Internet users from accessing private LANs. Figure 4–3 illustrates multilayered firewalls that partition the network into segments that have direct access to the Internet and a more private segment (intranet) that has two levels of firewall protecting it from

FIGURE 4–3

Architecture with multilevel firewalls

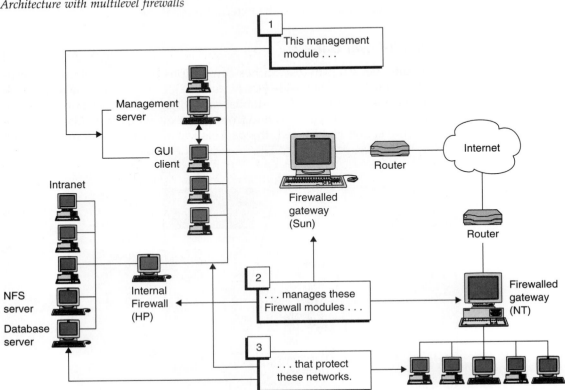

outside access. The two levels enable the business to apply a different set of rules to subnetworks.

The firewall can also keep members of the LAN from accessing Internet segments judged inappropriate for their work.

Firewalls offer four benefits to a security environment: service control, direction of transmission monitoring, user/profile monitoring, and usage/behavior monitoring. Service control was the original target of the firewall software. Service controls define the types of Internet services allowed for inbound and outbound traffic. They can filter communications based on IP addresses and TCP port numbers. Second, firewalls monitor the direction of particular service requests and the transmission through the firewall.

Third, users have a profile and are expected to use a restricted number of processes. This feature is available to users within the organization boundaries as well as to remote users. For remote connections, additional security compliance is required before access is granted. As will be explained in Chapter 5 authorization is granted only if the user can be authenticated and if the request seems justifiable.

Fourth, in the Internet environment, the firewall filters a request for a particular service through company policies for legitimate usage. For example, spam, an intrusive use of e-mail, is filtered in and out of the organization.

Application-Level Gateways

An application-level gateway allows the network administrator to control access at the application level. It implements stricter security than packet-filtering routers and is often easier to set up. Rather than depending on generic packet filtering tools to manage the information flow, the application-level gateway implements special-purpose code controlling the traffic to a particular application. For example mail gateways allow users to keep the same address, regardless of which machine they use at the time. The system administrator can configure the support only for those features of the application that the network administrator considers safe. This enhanced security comes with increased costs in term of purchasing dedicated gateway hardware and the need for a special gateway for each particular application.

OSI	TCP/IP
Application	**al-gw**
Presentation	
Session	
Transport	
Network	
Data Link	
Physical	

Protecting the network could also involve hiding it or its individual components from prying eyes. If a hacker has no knowledge of the assets within the network, it is unlikely the assets will become targets. One way to achieve this goal is to use proxy servers.

Proxy Server

A proxy server sits between a workstation user and the Internet so that the organization can ensure security, administrative control, and caching service. It intercepts all requests to the real server to determine if it can fulfill the requests itself. If not, it forwards the request to the real server. Application-level gateways are functionally similar to proxy servers. They operate as transfer agents for application-specific messages. If well implemented and configured, they are more secure than packet filtering systems. Instead of guessing at the range of threats derived from the allowed and forbidden patterns at the TCP and IP levels, they concentrate on the few permitted applications.

A proxy server is associated with, or part of, a gateway server that separates the enterprise network from the outside network and a firewall server that protects the enterprise network from outside intrusion. Proxy servers have two main functions, improving performance and security.

Proxy servers that also act as cache servers can dramatically improve performance for users because they save the results of all requests for a certain amount of time. Consider the case in which both the first user and second user access the Web through a proxy server. The first user requests a particular Web page. The second user later requests the same page. Instead of issuing a request to the Web server where the page resides, which can be time-consuming, the proxy server simply returns the cached page that it already fetched for the first user. Because the proxy server is often on the same network as the user, this is much faster. Proxy servers support hundreds or even thousands of users. Major online services, such as America Online and CompuServe, employ an array of proxy servers.

Proxy servers can also be used to filter requests. To the user, the proxy server is invisible. All Internet requests and returned responses appear to come directly from the addressed Internet server. For example, a firm might use a proxy server to prevent its employees from accessing a specific set of websites.

Even some combinations of the best practices still lead to a weak system. An internal demilitarized zone (DMZ) firewall translating IP addresses is used by organizations that want to host their own Internet services without forgoing unauthorized access to private networks. The DMZ usually contains devices that are not completely isolated from the Internet, such as FTP, Web (HTTP), and mail servers.

Security Audit

A computer and information security audit can be extremely difficult. The growing complexity of information systems requires a comprehensive and detailed review of existing security policies and procedures. The audit can be performed in-house or by an independent agency and can help administrators and security personnel identify key strong and weak points in a given system and assess the readiness of the network to repel hackers. Security audits, as in accounting, follow rigid, predetermined plans designed specifically for the system. They should be conducted by internal or external auditors with current real-world experience in the design and implementation of enterprise network security programs.

After the audit, the security experts identify areas of compliance and recommend improvements where required. A security audit service will deliver both an executive-level document that identifies critical security requirements and a detailed report that offers tangible approaches for action.

Security audits feature:

- Top-down interviews including the client's executive team, functional managers, and representative users.
- Identification of deviation from existing policies.
- Analysis using proven security practices methodology (SPM).

Firms benefit from a security audit in several ways, including enhancing trust from customers and insurance companies. By comparing currently implemented security to established policies and directives, the audit provides the client with a baseline understanding of the present security situation as well as guidelines for compliance to management standards.

Upon completion the auditing team should deliver the following:

- An overview of the security audit process.
- Documented management goals and priorities.
- Variations from management goals versus actual implementation.
- Recommendations based on best practices and SPM.
- Recommendation of security improvements consistent with management goals and expectations.
- Prioritized list of recommendations to meet management goals.
- Documented recommendations for improvement beyond current goals.
- A project summary from the security team.

A security audit offers a high-level assessment of the risks that may exist in externally visible systems. A remote scan can simulate how a hacker with no inside knowledge of a network configuration might try to penetrate the system. Using state-of-the-art tools, auditors will scan all the publicly accessible IP addresses and search for well-known vulnerabilities. The network will be scanned several times to ensure accuracy. The same scanning script can be delivered to network personnel and run periodically after any change to the network configuration. A report generated from the scans outlines what services are available on the network from the Internet and also lists all potential vulnerabilities and recommended corrective action.

Security Levels

Security of the Organization

Organizations are particularly sensitive to security issues. Intrusion to a company network can have extensive repercussions, so intrusion detection should be a vital part of any organizational measures to fight security breaches. Products and services related to intrusion detection abound, and an organization should construct a good fit between its requirements and the offerings available in the marketplace. To select the right solution, the vendor should answer a number of questions satisfactorily.

- How many types of attacks are detected?
- What is the incidence of false positives (intrusion is detected, but none has occurred)?
- Does the company employ hackers?
- Does the product require updates to its rules? And if so, who develops them?
- How does the vendor keep up to date with the latest attacks?
- Can the product be managed from off-site?
- What is the scalability? How many devices can be managed at a time?
- What is the impact of the product on the network/host performance?
- How is the product customized or configured to satisfy specific site policies and needs?

Intrusion detection can be either host- or network-based. Host-based intrusion detection monitors a single system, whereas network-based intrusion detection monitors all activities over a given network or segment. Host-based detection requires the use of the host system's resources such as disk space, RAM, and CPU time. As such, it affects system performance and is most appropriate when only a few critical servers need to be protected. Network-based intrusion detection performs rule-based or expert system policies set by the network administrator as well as loaded signatures that identify suspicious activities and attacks.

Network intrusion detection identifies and responds to misuse and policy violations. Sensors situated at determined points on the network monitor and compare traffic against patterns or "signatures" that represent suspicious activities, misuse, and attacks. The sensor can react and send alerts and commands to a security management system or directly to network equipment. Routers and firewalls will then be reconfigured to deny access to the attacker.

Security of the Client

Connections on the Internet are not anonymous. In e-commerce, the seller has a fiduciary role to guard information such as customer addresses, telephone numbers, and credit card information. (Chapter 5 details mechanisms that partition the information about the customer order, including demographic and credit information.) Any transaction may leave residual information, violating the privacy of the customer. Features aimed at improving e-commerce performance may hinder security. Page caching creates a weakness when transaction data are kept on the client machine, often in a clear-text format. The server should empty its cache when the transaction is complete, but this could still lead to aborted transaction data being stored on the client's disk. A partial solution is to disable the cache before the start of the transaction and then to reenable it after the transaction is completed.

At its inception, the Internet was standardized on stateless connections. Not remembering the location and the state of previous connections preserved anonymity as well as simplified the system. Using the Web's hypertext transfer protocol (HTTP), each request for a Web page is independent of all other requests. A client could link to the Internet and browse. On a subsequent visit, the browser on the client machine would not remember where it left off the last time it was browsing. Locations and data did not store on the client and the server did not track visited pages. On a transactional e-commerce environment, this is a serious handicap, so a device called a cookie was developed to maintain a limited amount of information on the client machine. A cookie is information (a small file) a website inserts on the hard disk so it can remember something about the user later. In e-commerce, cookies identify users and possibly prepare customized Web pages for them. When users enter a website using cookies, they may be asked to fill out a form providing information such as name and interests. Cookies provide virtual memory to store customer information, which can be recalled on every visit and used by the server to build personalized Web pages.

Cookies can be used in several ways. For example, an airline's website might create a cookie that contains a selected flight itinerary. Or it might only contain a record of those pages visited at the site. A cookie can help a website identify a repeat visitor and provide more personalized services. At Amazon.com, the bookstore's website uses a cookie to store information about a visitor's favorite subjects and later uses that information to recommend books.

While customizing to the individual customer can be rewarding, caching user IDs and passwords in the cookie should be avoided. A third party could use the data stored in the cookies for illegal transactions. Potential customers are increasingly avoiding cookies, fearing security flaws. In both Netscape Navigator and Microsoft Internet Explorer, the user has control over whether to accept cookies (see Figures 4–4 and 4–5).

In Navigator, to control computer behavior with respect to cookies:

1. From the Edit menu, choose "Preferences."
2. Click the "Advanced" category.

FIGURE 4–4

Setting cookie access in Netscape Navigator

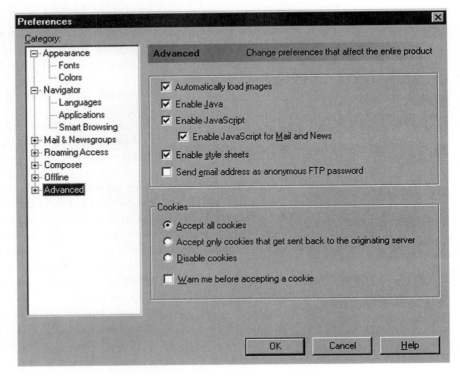

FIGURE 4–5

Cookies setting for Internet Explorer

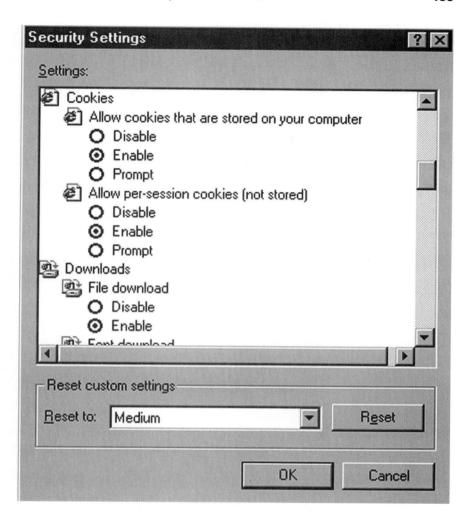

3. Click one of the radio buttons.
   - In most cases, "Accept all cookies" is the optimal choice.
   - Pressing the second button means the computer will not send a cookie to a server that did not originate it.
   - To be notified when Netscape Communicator accepts a cookie, check the third option, "Warn me before accepting a cookie."

In Internet Explorer, the security related to cookies is set as follows:

1. From the "Tools" menu, choose "Internet Options."
2. Click the security tab.

3. Click on Internet zone and choose the custom level. Under this alternative, set the level of security desired. As seen in Figure 4–5, the choice can be at the session level (not stored) or permanently stored on disk.

Security as a Third Party

Often hackers lack the computing power to break into secure sites and thus use collective multiple attacks from third parties to overwhelm a site. Businesses need to protect themselves from being used in such a manner.

Denial of service (DOS) is an increasingly common occurrence on corporate networks. One type occurs when, from a single point, the hacker floods the targeted network with meaningless messages intended to overcome the server's processing capacity. Requests cannot be processed on time and the system breaks down, denying legitimate users access. This type of attack is relatively easy to counter and can be traced back when the hacker is not too sophisticated and the network administrator has taken preventive measures.

A new, more powerful and troubling form of DOS is the distributed denial of service (DDOS). It is relatively impossible to counter, and some corporations are spending considerable resources trying to fight back. Any site could be an anonymous node in a devastating attack against a third party, exposing its owners to a legal and public relations nightmare. The DDOS attacks can be launched simultaneously from hundreds of remote-controlled attack servers, without the owners' knowledge.

Trinoo, Tribe FloodNet (TFN), TFN2K, or Stacheldraht ("barbed wire" in German) can be downloaded from hacker sites and used to start an attack. First, the hacker gains root access to a number of servers using tools such as SSCAN and SATAN to seek out vulnerabilities. Having established the list of weak servers, the hacker runs scripts on them and installs an agent for the future attack. Once the agent has been installed and started, it is ready to attack. Because the host server is an unknowing participant, the hacker does not attempt to spool the messages and instead optimizes the flood against the target.

With thousands of noncommercial entities such as universities, schools, and nonprofit organizations that cannot afford full-time security consultants, the hacker has a huge pool from which to choose for the attack. Currently, most e-commerce sites have firewalls that may prevent them from being the accomplice in the distribution of agents or act as agents themselves. But poorly configured firewalls make attractive targets and are no assurance of protection.

In the DDOS, there may be a single hacker, but the hacker uses the remotely controlled servers to multiply the effect of the flood. Once started, the DDOS is virtually impossible to stop and will disrupt the business. Packets arriving at the firewall can be blocked, but it is impossible to discern which could be legitimate messages. Contacting the third parties can be difficult because the hacker may choose international bases. The only real preventive measure is global education about security issues and better filtering of the packets at the edge of the network so that only packets with legal source addresses pass through the routers. Once detected, disks containing agents should be analyzed because they may store the remnants of addresses of hundreds of other compromised machines. DDOS represents a major threat to e-commerce.

Directory Services

Directory services have evolved from a purely functional piece of the enterprise's networking infrastructure to become more crucial to achieving success on the Web. Directories support strong security as they help the administrator control resources and their allocation to users across the network. A directory provides users with services enabling single sign-on and administrators with tools to manage security services for internal desktops, remote users, and e-commerce customers. Directory services identify all resources on a network and make them accessible to users and applications. Managed resources include websites, enterprise resource planning, e-mail addresses, firewalls, routers, computers, and peripheral devices such as printers. Most end users are not aware of the directory service and benefit transparently from its advantages. A good directory service makes the physical network topology and protocols invisible so that a user can access any resource without knowing where or how it is physically connected. Traditionally, the directory service was a repository for company passwords and user profiles. The e-commerce explosion has changed the landscape, and new directory services use dual repositories for internal and external users.

Currently, Novell dominates the market with its Novell Directory Services, a product running on Novell servers and NT servers and licensed to a number of other dominant companies. Microsoft recently developed Active Directory Service to address some of the same needs. Open source solutions have been proposed. Based on **X.500,** the standard for directories sponsored by the International Telecommunications Union (ITU) previously called **CCITT,** the open source solutions offer promises for large-scale directories, but X.500 is large and unwieldy. The X.500 approach calls for the open systems interconnection protocol, which is rapidly being replaced by the TCP/IP choice. Another solution, the lightweight directory access protocol (**LDAP**), is emerging that integrates various directories in a simpler manner.

LDAP is being actively developed by the Internet engineering task force and is currently in version 3. The ability to securely access (replicate and distribute) directory information throughout the network is necessary for successful deployment. LDAP's acceptance is driving the need to provide an access control model definition for LDAP directory content among servers within an enterprise and the Internet. Currently, LDAP does not define an access control model but is needed to ensure consistent, secure access across heterogeneous LDAP implementations. The requirements for access control are critical to the successful deployment and acceptance of LDAP in the marketplace and its use in secure environments.

As the boundaries blur and the need for integration arises, metadirectories have surfaced. They are assumed to unify disparate directory solutions. Both Microsoft and Novell, strong contenders with service directories, have recognized this new need and are promoting their solutions. Novell developed a metadirectory with XML support, DirXML. Microsoft obtained its metadirectory with its acquisition of Zoomit. IBM has developed metadirectory technology for its SecureWay. Given the functional importance of a metadirectory, it soon will be merged with existing directory services.

With a unified directory, for example, a network administrator will not have to change a user's ID and password for human resource applications, financial applications, and e-mail. The use of a metadirectory and the underlying directories will make single registration and single log-in a reality. Security will be much easier to administer and enforce.

Many organizations are working on making the use of enterprise directories a common practice. With a concerted effort and an open forum, such as the forum intended to rectify its potential interoperability difficulties, the LDAP has achieved good progress toward enterprise directory functionality. Other open standard technologies, such as XML and DEN (the directory enabled networks), will bring synergy to the initiatives.

Single Sign-On (SSO)

SSO is the policy-based way to increase security while decreasing the associated administrative costs. Single sign-on provides a global user authentication entry point to all IT resources. The complexity of Web security increases as Internet and intranet e-business grows. To protect each application, the proliferation of passwords results in complicated access routines for users. If a solid SSO system is not in place, the user will end up being the enemy of the security system by reusing passwords frequently or losing them.

SSO should enable the users to connect seamlessly to the Web applications they need through a unique password. When connecting, each user will perform a single and secure sign-on to a centralized SSO server. Once identified, the user is allowed seamless access to the multiple applications granted to that user. This enforced security not only simplifies navigation for users and extranet partners, but also dramatically improves productivity by reducing log-on time and help desk support.

Case: Express Search

Even firms with traditionally high public trust can fail when it comes to security. Nonmalicious violation of privacy can put the company goodwill at risk and trust can rapidly evaporate. One high-profile example is Go.com, the result of the 1999 merger of Infoseek Corporation and Walt Disney's online unit, Buena Vista Internet Group. Infoseek was a pioneer in search software. For users who search the Web frequently and want to use it more efficiently, Go.com developed Express Search, a desktop software that searches multiple search engines and websites simultaneously. Express Search is different from other search engines in that it runs within the Web browser and provides an easier to use, faster interface. Express Search has an open architecture that allows for mass distribution, easy updates, and extensive personal customization.

The Express Search software is downloaded and run on the client machine. As an open system, Go.com's Express Search operates a two-way (to and from the client machine) open HTTP server on port 1234 of the client. This server was set by default to not require proof of identity from users. As part of the scheme to obtain better performance, this feature left the server open to hacker attack.

An attacker could submit remote queries on Go.com servers and view queries and personal links left by previous legitimate users, who expected privacy. Hackers could also access the configuration interface, which revealed the e-mail addresses of users who registered the software. The configuration could also be changed remotely, making it possible to add, remove, and/or alter personal links. In hacker's terms, the means to subvert system security is often called an exploit. In this case, the exploit worked as follows:

- If a user on an independent service provider server (e.g., with Internet address of user.dialup.isp.com.) is running Express Search, the hacker can access its Go Express HTTP server by visiting http://user.dialup.isp.com:1234/.
- The hacker can then observe the user's search history, obtain the user's e-mail address, and even reconfigure the search server.

Many such examples of security lapses exist, emanating from organizations believed to be experienced in the industry. While some instances can be considered only annoyances, they reflect companies' poor preparation for this new mode of communication. Often, no remedy exists and the user is left with poor choices. Currently, the only solution to prevent attacks at Go.com is to disable Express Search on your computer and wait for the company to develop a patch.

Note: Go.com is the search engine used by Disney, ABC, and their affiliates.

Summary

Security issues are important and numerous. Figure 4–6 illustrates some solutions to enhance security. This chapter described hardware and software commonly used to enhance security. From an outside-in view of these measures, the firewall represents the first line of defense against potential intruders. To hide internal resources from prying eyes, proxy servers slow the work of hackers because they obscure the real network addresses of the internal resources. Smart card is a recent security measure that may gain importance in coming years. In addition to the physical access control, virus protection is the most common security protection implemented by most organizations.

With the rising importance of e-commerce, security will become an even more pressing concern. In this chapter, we introduced some of the issues and measures taken to secure a website or network. Within a business framework, management develops a set of policies and procedures aimed at securing the network from external and internal threats. Measures of authentication and encryption, essential to mastering information flow with data integrity, will be addressed in Chapter 5. While authentication, certificates, and encryption are highly complex matters, some simple steps were proposed in this chapter to protect the perimeter of the corporate network, as well as the internal usage of computing resources. After institution of policies and procedures, virus protection is often the first measure to be implemented in an organization. Virus scanning on individual hosts, scanning of incoming and outcoming e-mail, and newly installed software is a minimum step to enforce security. Protecting the perimeter of the network is often attempted with a combination of firewalls and proxy servers. They allow

FIGURE 4–6

Security elements

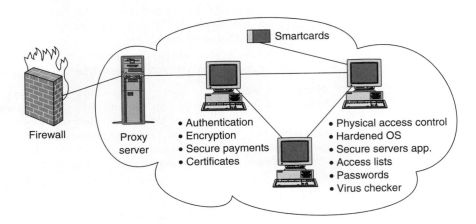

the organization to filter incoming and outgoing messages and to isolate the internal network. In order to recover in case of network meltdown, backup and recovery were mentioned as the second line of defense for company data.

A comprehensive security infrastructure will not be complete or manageable without the help of directory services. They will simplify the utilization of legitimate resources, while at the same time maintaining a stable degree of security. This newly embraced solution facilitates the integration of various networks and the access to multiple resources in a coordinated manner to the network manager portfolio of tools. With a global access list and unified log-in, information can be propagated with increased confidence.

Key Terms

Backup 122	LDAP 135
CCITT 135	Proxy server 128
Denial of service 134	Recovery 122
Directory service 135	Secrecy 111
Firewall 123	Single sign on 136
Integrity 111	Virus 119
Internet security 111	X.500 135

Review Questions

1. Differentiate between secrecy, integrity, and availability.
2. On the Web, access the site of one anti-virus vendor and list some of the most recent virus warnings. What do they have in common?
3. List the different implementation options in firewall architecture.
4. What is a proxy server? What functions are provided by a proxy server?
5. What is the role of directory service software? Find which solutions are the most popular in the marketplace. Why do you think it is so?
6. What type of person should conduct a security audit? Do you think that internal or external personnel are preferable?
7. Single sign-on is a solution aimed at simplifying the access to corporate resources by legitimate users. Is such a solution implemented at your workplace?
8. List five examples of virus-checking software.

Projects

1. Can a simple firewall be designed from standard computer equipment? What hardware components would you need for a proxy server?
2. What makes a firewall a good security investment? Accessing the Internet, find two or three firewall vendors. Do they provide hardware, software, or both?
3. Accessing the site for one of the firewall vendors, find out what solutions are offered.
4. Does the company you work for utilize a proxy server for Internet access? Is the proxy server intended to keep the hacker out of the network or control employees' access to the Internet?
5. Find out if your university or workplace has a backup policy in place. Is it followed and enforced?
6. Check a machine having access to the Internet. What kind of virus-checking software is protecting it? How old is the signature file? Download one or two virus-checking software packages and test a machine having access to the Internet. (You can find trial software at www.tucows.com.)
7. Hackers have readily available resources to create new viruses. How easy is it to find a virus writing kit? Search the Internet and find such a tool.
8. When files are normally erased from a hard drive they leave some residuals, which could expose their previous content. If you were in charge of network security, how could you alleviate such a risk? (Two avenues are to wipe out the file bit by bit or encrypt the content in the first place.)
9. Download one virus checker and read the documentation. How does it operate? What is the process of updating the virus signature file? How does the publisher charge for the product/service?
10. Inspect the virus checker installed on your computer. How old is the virus definition file? Do you think you are adequately protected? If not, what are the remedies?
11. Search the Internet for firewall providers. Find a few and a good review. What attributes would you look for in a firewall on your next security project?

References, Readings, and Hyperlinks

1. Baker, Richard H. *Network Security: How to Plan for It and Achieve It*. New York: McGraw-Hill, 1994.
2. Barrett, Daniel J. *Bandits on the Information Superhighway*. Sebastopol, CA: O'Reilly & Associates, 1996.

3. Carroll, John M. *Computer Security.* Woburn, MA: Butterworth-Heinemann, 1996.

4. Cheswick, William R., and Steven M. Bellovin. *Firewalls and Internet Security: Repelling the Wily Hacker.* Reading, MA: Addison-Wesley, 1994.

5. Ennals, Richard. *Executive Guide to Preventing Information Technology Disasters.* Heidelberg, Germany: Springer-Verlag, 1996.

6. Ghosh, Anup K. *E-commerce Security: Weak Links, Best Defenses.* New York: John Wiley & Sons, 1998.

7. Hruska, Jan. *Computer Virus and Anti-Virus Warfare.* Upper Saddle River, NJ: Prentice Hall, 1993.

8. Levin, Richard. *Computer Virus Handbook.* New York: Osborne McGraw-Hill, 1990.

9. McCarthy Linda. *Intranet Security: Stories from the Trenches.* Upper Saddle River, NJ: Prentice Hall, 1997.

10. Siyan, Karanjit, and Chris Hare. *Internet Firewall and Network Security.* Indianapolis: New Riders Publishing, 1995.

11. Turn, Rein. *Advances in Computer System Security.* Norwood, MA: Artech House, 1988.

12. UNIX Svr 4.2 Unix System Lab. *Audit Trail Administration.* Upper Saddle River, NJ: Prentice Hall, 1993.

13. http://www.BeyondSecurity.com/

14. http://www.securiteam.com/

15. http://www.epic.org/security/GAO_OMB_security.html
    (Details some security failures at U.S. defense sites.)

16. http://isrecon.ncsa.com/dox/FAQ/ISRFAQ.htm
    (Site with good resources, monitoring hacker activities and bulletin boards.)

17. http://www.cert.org
    (Site of an organization that supports research on network security violation and the appropriate warnings and remedies.)

18. http://www.raptor.com/lib/index.html
    (Site of the maker of one of the leading firewalls offering useful additional resources such as security-related articles in PDF format.)

19. http://ciac.llnl.gov/ciac/CIACVirusDatabase.html
    (While not maintained anymore, remains comprehensive resource for research on viruses.)

AUTHENTICATION, ENCRYPTION, DIGITAL PAYMENTS, AND DIGITAL MONEY

Chapter Outline

Learning Objectives

By the end of this chapter, you should be able to:

- Understand the importance of authentication.
- Understand the various encryption alternatives.
- Differentiate between symmetric and asymmetric encryption.
- Evaluate the strengths and weaknesses of the different solutions.
- Determine how and why encryption is important for e-commerce.

- Understand how security applies to e-mail, the Web, the intranet, and the extranet.
- Appreciate how virtual private networks are relevant to the future of e-commerce.
- Plan for strategies to fend off security threats.
- List and understand various e-commerce modes of payment.

Chapter Overview

Statements such as "We have a firewall and our network is secure" or "We scan all files for viruses and we're safe from hackers" are common. But this false security can be harmful to an organization. This chapter addresses security issues that will increase confidence in the system. These issues include identification and authentication—the first building blocks of security. They make the customer feel confident that the organization is serious about security. When sending messages within the network or through the Internet, message integrity and confidentiality need to be preserved through the use of strong encryption. The chapter also describes auditing, to track resource usage and to detect patterns of abusive use, and nonrepudiation, in which both parties agree a transaction is completed.

A Technical Vignette

Cracking encryption technologies is one way computer security professionals demonstrate the weaknesses of companies' protections. The small British specialty hardware firm, nCipher, which claims its encryption product is faster and more secure than most others on the market, staged a recent such attack.

One of nCipher's researchers created a program that can expose the secret keys, or digital codes, needed to process credit card transactions, thus creating the potential for fraud. The nCipher attack demonstrated that the barriers that separate companies' websites on the same server can be infiltrated and the secret keys obtained. Small companies and their customers are most at risk because they often share ISP Web servers with other firms to save money. The most popular operating systems that run Web servers, such as Microsoft Windows NT, Windows 2000, and Sun Microsystems' Solaris, were vulnerable to the attack.

After nCipher announced the creation of its attack program, it published the details of the program, making it accessible to hackers. At the same time the company also revealed its product to fend off such attacks. While some may consider such behavior unethical, it does help companies by revealing flaws in their security systems. Declining computer prices may also create a more secure environment as fewer merchants will have to share servers.

The wide acceptance of the Internet and its associated protocol, the transmission control protocol (TCP/IP), has made possible the transmission of information from one computer to another through a variety of intermediate computers and networks. This method exposes private messages to a number of third parties with the opportunity to interfere through eavesdropping, tampering, and impersonation. Fortunately, a set of well-established methods makes it feasible to take adequate precautions. Encryption and decryption, tamper detection, authentication, and nonrepudiation are some common preventive measures taken in comprehensive security architecture.

Source: Wayner Peter, "Attacks on Encryption Code Raise Questions about Computer Vulnerability," The *New York Times* on the Web, January 5, 2000.

Encryption

Encryption is the conversion of plain text or data into an unintelligible form by means of a reversible translation. In the electronic age, information that can benefit groups or individuals can also be used against such groups or individuals. For example, any online purchasing requires information about the customer; while this information facilitates the transaction, Internet thieves could use it to defraud the customer. Encryption is used to ensure customers' privacy, and it benefits both consumers and their business partners. Encryption is also used as a security measure to offset industrial espionage among highly competitive businesses. And those who want to exercise their personal freedom and enjoy their privacy may also wish to encrypt certain information.

The methods of data encryption and decryption are straightforward and easily mastered. Simple algorithms can keep information safe from indiscretion by making it difficult to decode. A message is encoded by the sender, using a special software making it unreadable to a third party, and decoded by the receiver, using the same software. The user is occasionally asked a password to access certain files. Encryption is often necessary if messages are to travel on public networks without being subject to third-party scrutiny.

In other uses of encryption, such as the deployment of information and the commercial distribution of software, applications may be provided through an encrypted authorization code. For example, such a scheme would allow companies to evaluate software before purchasing it. A similar situation would authorize a maximum number of users based on the licenses purchased by customers. Each of these features requires some type of encrypted data to ensure that the lockout works correctly and cannot be bypassed, thus protecting business interests and preserving the full-featured demonstration capability for customers.

Methods of Encrypting Data

Data streams can easily be encrypted through several software methods but not so readily decrypted when either the original or its encrypted data stream are unavailable. (When both source and encrypted data are available, code breaking becomes much simpler, though not necessarily easy.) The best encryption methods have little effect on system performance and may contain other built-in benefits such as data compression. The well-known PKZIP® utility offers both data compression and encryption. Similarly, database management systems packages often include some type of encryption scheme so that a standard file copy cannot be used to read sensitive information that might otherwise require a password to access. Databases also need high-performance methods to encode and decode the data.

The simplest of all encryption methods is the translation table. Each chunk of data (usually 1 byte) is used as an offset within a translation table, and the resulting translated value from within the table is then written into the output stream. The encryption and decryption programs each use a table that translates to and from the encrypted data. The 8086 central processing unit even has an instruction, 'XLAT,' that lends itself to this at the hardware level. While this method is simple and fast, the downside is that once the translation table is known, the code is broken. Further, such a method is straightforward for code breakers to decipher because such code preceded the advent of computers. A simple table of characters is devised to encrypt the message sent. On the receiving end, the algorithm is applied in reverse to obtain the plain text.

Following Figure 5–1, a simple message such as "the red fox eats the eggs" translates into "huodaoldewndobhmdhuodorrm." Decryption

Figure 5–1

Encryption translation table

	a	b	c	d	e	f	g	h	i	j	k	l	m	n	o	p	q	r	s	t	u	v	w	x	y	z
d	b	g	k	l	o	e	r	u	t		v	x	z	f	w	c	y	a	m	h	p	s	q	n	j	i

software could break the code in only a minute, but an inventive mechanism could rapidly make the code more difficult to crack. For example, after a number of characters in a block, the table could be rotated, such that the code would change and make the decryption much more lengthy. For general unintelligibility of encoded data, without adverse effects on performance, the translation table method lends itself well to encryption.

A modification to the translation table uses two or more tables based on the position of the bytes within the data stream, or on the data stream itself. Decoding becomes more complex because the process needs to be reversed. The use of more than one translation table, especially when implemented in a pseudo-random order, makes code breaking relatively difficult. An example of this method might use translation table A on all the even bytes and translation table B on all the odd bytes. Unless a potential code breaker knows that there are exactly two tables, even with both source and encrypted data available, the deciphering process is difficult.

Similar to a translation table, data repositioning lends itself to computer use, but it takes considerably more time to accomplish. A buffer of data is read from the input, and then the order of the bytes or other chunk size is rearranged and written out of order. The decryption program then reads this back in and puts them back in order. Such a method is best used in combination with one or more of the other encryption methods described here, making it even more difficult for code breakers. As an example, consider an anagram. An anagram is a transposition of the letters of a word or phrase to form a new word or phrase. The letters are all there, but the order has been changed, making it difficult to comprehend without knowing the logic of the changes. Some anagrams are easier than others to decipher, but a well-written one is challenging, especially if it is intentionally misleading.

Another favorite encryption method, however, involves something that only computers can do—word/byte rotation and XOR bit-masking. If the words or bytes within a data stream are rotated, using multiple and variable direction and duration of rotation in an easily reproducible pattern, a stream of data can be quickly encoded with a method that is nearly impossible to break. Further, if the code uses an XOR mask in combination with this (flipping the bits in certain positions from 1 to 0 or 0 to 1), code breaking becomes even more difficult. The best combination would use pseudo-random effects, the easiest of which would involve a simple sequence such as Fibbonaci numbers. In this method the sequence is easily generated by adding the previous two numbers in the sequence to get the next (1,1,2,3,5, . . .). Performing modular arithmetic on the result will make the code breaker's job even more difficult. The decryption program easily handles the added pseudo-random effect.

In some cases, the sender may want to detect whether the data have been tampered with and so encrypt some kind of check sum into the data stream itself. This is useful not only for authorization codes, but for programs as well. A virus that infects such a protected program would neglect the encryption algorithm and authorization/check sum signature. The program could then check itself each time it loads, and thus detect the presence of file corruption. Naturally, such a method would have to be kept secret, because virus programmers represent the worst of the code breakers (i.e., those who willfully use information to damage others). As such, the use of encryption is essential for any good anti-virus protection scheme.

A cyclic redundancy check typically uses the check sum method. It employs bit rotation and an XOR mask to generate a 16- or 32-bit value for a data stream, such that one missing bit or two interchanged bits are more or less guaranteed to cause a check sum error. This method, which has been used for file transfers for some time, such as with XMODEM-CRC, is somewhat well documented and standard. But a deviation from the standard CRC method might be useful for detecting a problem in an encrypted data stream or within a program file that checks itself for viruses.

In modern sophisticated cryptography, the power of keeping encrypted information secret is based not on the cryptographic algorithm, which is often widely known, but on a number called a key. The key must be used in conjunction with the algorithm to produce an encrypted result or to decrypt previously encrypted information. The goal is to make it virtually impossible to comprehend or decipher the message without the correct key. The first and most efficient method is called symmetric key encryption, but most common method is public key encryption.

Symmetric Key Encryption

In symmetric key encryption (see Figure 5–2) the sender and receiver of a message share a single, common key that is used to encrypt and decrypt the message. Implementation of symmetric key encryption can be highly efficient. Users do not experience any substantial delay as the result of the encryption and decryption. Also, authentication results because no other key can be used to decrypt the message. Security is preserved as

FIGURE 5–2

Symmetric key encryption

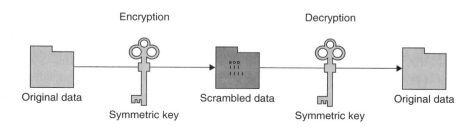

Encryption   Decryption

Original data   Symmetric key   Scrambled data   Symmetric key   Original data

long as the key is kept secret. If the key is divulged both confidentiality and authentication are compromised. A lost key can result in eavesdropping, tampering, and misrepresentation in both directions. Periodic distribution of new keys increases security, but this process has its own risk.

With all its risks, symmetric key is still the most efficient and transparent means of transmitting secure data. The security socket layer described later in this chapter makes the most of symmetric keys, using the less efficient but more secure asymmetric process to distribute the more efficient symmetric keys.

Asymmetric Key Encryption

The most common implementation of **public key encryption** is based on the patented RSA Data Security algorithm. The public key method, also called asymmetric key encryption, is composed of two different keys. The key pair is associated with entities that need to authenticate, encrypt, and sign data.

Public key cryptography involves two related keys referred to as the private key and the public key. The private key is used to encrypt the information. This encrypted information can then be decrypted only with the corresponding public key. Although the two keys are related, one cannot be derived from the other. The recipient verifies the digital signature using a reverse process and the public key. If the process confirms the validity of the digital signature, the document is deemed to be valid. Because only one party possesses the private key, the merchant can trust the document. If the key does not pass validation, then the merchant knows the document is either invalid from the sender's end or has been altered during transmission.

The public key is published and its owner keeps the private key secret. Anyone is able to send a message encrypted with the public key, but only the owner of the private key will be able to decrypt it (see Figure 5–3).

Because the two keys are different, decryption requires more computation than if symmetric keys are used. This method is not always appropriate when a large amount of data is transmitted. The schema in Figure 5–3 can be reversed where messages encrypted with the private

FIGURE 5–3

Public key encryption

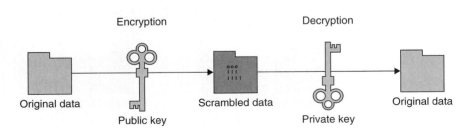

key can be decrypted only with the corresponding public key. This does not offer a good means to keep data secret as anyone has access to the public key. However, it is a useful method to assure authentication and is widely used in e-commerce for signing data with a digital signature.

A few concepts emerge from any scenario illustrating secure messaging or transaction. In a transaction, both participants want to be certain that the identity of the counterpart is valid. This is commonly achieved through authentication. Then only allowed resources should be used, and authorization takes care of this aspect. The next step is to insure that messages are delivered in the same condition as when they were sent, so a process of integrity control should be set up. Confidentiality of the parties should be secured, as unauthorized parties should not have access to the private message. Auditing should follow the trail of the transaction such that a security breach can be analyzed or prevented if events are detected outside the norm of regular operations. Finally, nonrepudiation denies the sender or recipient the opportunity to lie about the occurrence of an event. The following paragraphs address confidentiality, authentication, authorization, integrity, auditing, and nonrepudiation.

Confidentiality

Confidentiality, also called privacy, has come to the forefront of security issues as a result of highly publicized breaches of confidentiality and a number of lawsuits against prominent e-commerce firms. Espionage is no longer limited to the CIA but is part of everyday life. More concerned with money than ideology, unauthorized individuals can utilize stolen information to harm e-commerce participants. The confidentiality building block of security is developed to protect information from unauthorized eavesdropping as it flows through the network. Confidentiality has two aims:

- To use the digital signature or encrypted hash function to authenticate the identity of the sender.
- To protect the content of the message from eyes other than those of the intended recipient.

Cryptography is commonly used to implement confidentiality. Two distinct elements are involved in keeping messages confidential. In the first step, a clear message is encrypted and rendered incomprehensible as a cyphertext. The reverse aspect is the deciphering by the recipient through decryption (i.e., returning the cyphertext back to plain text).

Messages exchanged from the Web server to the Web browser often use secure socket layer (SSL) to ensure some confidentiality. SSL is a protocol developed by Netscape for transmitting private documents via the Internet. It uses a private key to encrypt data that are transferred over the

SSL connection. Both Netscape Navigator and Internet Explorer support SSL, and many websites use the protocol to obtain confidential user information, such as credit card numbers. By convention, Web pages that require an SSL connection start with **https:** instead of http:. The use of SSL is one way e-commerce businesses can build trust with customers and attract the repeat business essential to the long-term survival of any Web enterprise. Businesses should inform customers about the precautions being taken to protect information from third parties.

Reacting to U.S. and European government pressures to control unregulated e-businesses has led to a number of initiatives. A Federal Trade Commission (FTC) survey of 1,400 commercial websites found that 85 percent collected personal information, but only 14 percent provided any details about their information practices or their use of the information. More alarming is the fact that only 2 percent reported a formal privacy policy, and many of those could not enforce their published policies, leading to the current wave of lawsuits.

Where children are concerned, 54 percent had some disclosure notice, but only 23 percent informed children to obtain parental permission before divulging personal information about themselves or their families. The FTC concluded that incentives were necessary to trigger self-regulation. States have also initiated more comprehensive laws to protect financial and medical data. At the federal level, the Children's Online Privacy Protection Act of 1998 governs the disclosure of children's personal information. Depending on how the information will be used, different levels of authorization are required. If a site targets children, careful attention to this new legislation is required.

Self-regulation is an inherent part of insuring adequate privacy practices. The World Wide Web Consortium has developed standard technologies and procedures. The Platform for Privacy Preferences Project (P3P) and the **TRUSTe** program are publicly available at http://www.w3c.org and http://www.truste.org.

The Platform for Privacy Preferences Project (P3P) enables websites to express their privacy practices in a standard format that can be retrieved automatically and interpreted easily by user agents. P3P user agents allow users to be informed of site practices (in both machine- and human-readable formats) and to automate decision making based on these practices when appropriate. Thus, users do not need to read the privacy policies at every site they visit. The goal of P3P is to develop standards for allowing websites to disclose or exchange information practices in a machine-readable format. Browser, proxy, and agents for customers probe the P3P policies in automated fashion before information is exchanged. Only if the site meets the required level of privacy will the transfer of personal information occur.

TRUSTe awards its trustmark (label of privacy practice) only to websites that adhere to established privacy principles and agree to comply with ongoing TRUSTe oversight and dispute resolution procedures. While the organization does everything in its power to ensure the privacy of consumer personal information, it also relies on consumer vigilance. An online watchdog form is available reporting violations of posted privacy policies, specific privacy concerns pertaining to TRUSTe website licensees, and the misuse of the TRUSTe trustmark. Before filling out a watchdog report, TRUSTe urges users to complete the following three steps.

- Confirm that the website is a TRUSTe licensee.
- Make certain the complaint is a privacy matter relating specifically to the website.
- Contact the website licensee directly.

TRUSTe is concerned with privacy matters and not business practices, such as product quality, false advertising, pricing, merchandise delivery, and warranty. As such, TRUSTe is not intended to replace organizations such as the Better Business Bureau.

Firms should avoid privacy pitfalls. Some ideas may look like good ones but ultimately come back to hurt an organization. For example, Amazon.com collects information about who is buying what books, videos, and CDs. But some businesses fear their buying patterns could reveal their current interests and future strategies to their competitors, so Amazon.com now lets customers opt out of the program.

Authentication

Authentication is the process of identifying an individual or a message usually based on a user name and password or a file signature. In security systems, authentication is distinct from authorization, which is the process of giving individuals access to system objects based on their identity. Authentication ensures that the individual is who he or she claims to be. When filling out an application for an account or when requesting information when a user has lost his or her password, additional information is often requested. When accessing more information such as a bank's account, information such as mother's maiden name is often requested. As hackers become more familiar with additional identification practices, security policies need to be changed to more sophisticated methods. Customer service representatives often ask questions to verify client identity before initiating a transaction.

In private and public computer networks, identification and authentication—the most important building blocks of e-commerce security— often are limited to the use of log-in passwords. Knowledge of the password is assumed to guarantee that the user is authentic. Each user registers initially, using an assigned or chosen password. On subsequent

Figure 5–4

*Using a password to
authenticate the client
on a server*

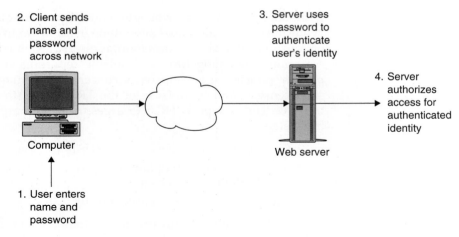

2. Client sends
name and
password
across network

3. Server uses
password to
authenticate
user's identity

4. Server
authorizes
access for
authenticated
identity

Computer

Web server

1. User enters
name and
password

use, the user must know the user ID and use the previously assigned password. Figure 5–4 depicts a schema using a password as the identification/authorization method.

The weakness in this system is that passwords can often be stolen, broken, erroneously transferred, or forgotten. Without being able to determine with certainty whether the individuals involved in the transaction are really who they claim to be, safe e-commerce is not possible. Even though identification and authorization are often used interchangeably, they have different purposes. Identification does not ensure that the user has a legitimate right to access the system. It only claims to have a certain identity. For example, John Doe could identify himself to a bank as being John Doe and he may, in fact, really be named John Doe, but this does not ensure that the person has an account with the bank.

Authentication goes one step further. It involves verifying the identity of the various parties in the transaction (client and organization). Three features are commonly used to identify and authenticate a user:

- Something the user knows, such as a user ID, name, and/or password.
- Something the user has, such as a badge, ID card, floppy disk, and/or smart card.
- Something that is part of the user, such as biometrics, fingerprint, retinal scan, or voice print.

Once the identification/authentication process has legitimized the user, the security system should proceed to the next step. Authorization is the process of verifying the rights assigned to the user and then channeling the user to the right resource. For example, a bank customer, once authenticated, can be presented with the choice of accessing his or her checking account, savings account, or mortgage account.

Digital Signature

A digital signature is a code attached to an electronically transmitted message to identify the sender. Digital signatures are means of remote authentication and an important factor in user confidentiality. Digital signatures facilitate the conversion of paper contracts to electronic contracts, saving companies both time and money. To be effective, digital signatures must be both memorable and convenient to use. A number of different encryption techniques are available to guarantee this level of security. Digital signatures are often used to both authenticate and verify the integrity of an electronic message. Figure 5–5 illustrates digital signature for a software buyer accepting a license agreement.

If buyer and seller wish to confirm their agreement with a digital signature, they will have to follow certain steps. These steps are transparent to the user and are performed automatically by software:

1. The sender composes the document.
2. The sender uses a hashing algorithm to create a "one-way hash." This one-way hash, sometimes referred to as "hash result" or "message digest," uniquely identifies the message, a kind of digital fingerprint. If the hash algorithm has been carefully selected, it is highly improbable that two documents would result in the same digest.

FIGURE 5–5

Digital signature and data integrity

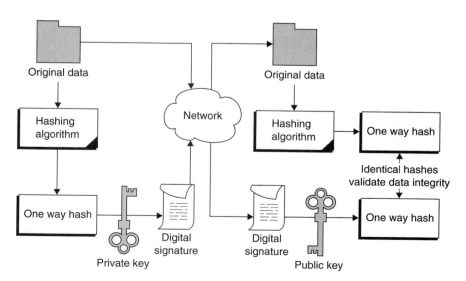

3. The sender uses his or her private key part of a public key system to encrypt the one-way hash to create the digital signature.
4. The sender then combines the original document with the digital signature to create a new signed document and send it to the receiver.

The signed document travels through the Internet and reaches the receiver address. The receiver takes the following steps to confirm the authenticity and integrity of the document. In other words, the receiver wants to make sure where the document is coming from and that it has not been altered.

1. The receiver separates the document from its signature.
2. The receiver decrypts the digital signature using the sender public key. If the digital signature is decoded, the authenticity of the document is established.
3. The receiver applies the hashing algorithm (usually part of Microsoft Outlook or Netscape Messenger) to the original electronic document to produce a new one-way-hash. If the newly created one-way-hash matches the decrypted one-way-hash then the message integrity is confirmed.

As the example illustrates, the advantage of a digital signature over a written signature is that each electronic document has a unique signature as compared to the signature for all written documents.

Digital Signature versus Electronic Signature.   Widespread confusion remains about signature technology. Many parties engaged in e-commerce misunderstand the differences between electronic signatures and digital signatures and their effect on the enforceability of electronic contracts. An electronic signature is any electronic mark, symbol, or process associated with a file, with the intent to sign the file. The definition is broad because it is intended to allow for any replacement of handwritten signatures. A digital signature, on the other hand, is more narrowly defined. This type of signature uses public key cryptography. A digital signature is an alphanumeric key attached to the document that identifies both the document and the author. Digital signature technology is part of many applications such as Microsoft Outlook and other e-mail systems.

Kerberos

Kerberos is an authentication system developed at the Massachusetts Institute of Technology for use on physically insecure networks, based on the key distribution model presented by Needham and Schroeder.[1] Kerberos is designed to enable two parties to exchange private information across an otherwise open network. It also provides for data stream integrity (detection of modification) and secrecy (preventing unauthorized reading) using cryptography systems such as DES. It works by assigning principals (user or services) a unique key, called a ticket. Each user who logs on to the network receives a ticket. The ticket is then embedded in messages to identify the sender of the message. Practically speaking, Kerberos is mostly used in application-level protocols (ISO model level 7), such as TELNET or FTP, to provide user-to-host security. It is also used, although less frequently, as the implicit authentication system of a data stream (such as SOCK_STREAM) or RPC mechanisms (ISO model level 6). It could rarely be used at a lower level for host-to-host security in protocols such as IP, UDP, or TCP (ISO model levels 3 and 4).

Two versions of Kerberos are currently in use, but they have limitations.[2] In particular, Kerberos is not effective against password guessing attacks; if a user chooses a poor password, then an attacker guessing that password can impersonate the user. Similarly, Kerberos requires a trusted path through which passwords are entered. If the user enters a password to a program that has already been modified by an attacker (a Trojan horse), or if the path between the user and the initial authentication program can be monitored, then an attacker may obtain sufficient information to impersonate the user. Kerberos can be combined with other techniques, such as onetime pass code and public key encryption, to address these limitations. In a later section in this chapter, we address digital certificates, used to allow third parties to confirm the signatures on documents.

Authorization

Authorization gives someone permission to do or have something. Once the security system has validated a legitimate user through identification and authentication, the next step is to allocate the resources and decide what actions the user will be allowed to perform. In multiuser computer systems, a system administrator defines for the system which users are allowed access and which privileges can be used. In the mainframe environment, this is achieved through a method called roles-based access control (RBAC). This method is effective in the centralized environment, but it is unlikely to succeed in the distributed Internet domain.

The access control system determines a valid user's access privileges and enforces them. Once an authorized transaction is initiated, the user will need to go through other steps to secure it. Authorization can be implemented at different levels within the system. Such access authorization can operate at the file directories level, restrict resources through access time, and allocate quotas for storage space. A computer operating system or application program may want to categorize what resources a user can be given during a session. Thus, a system administrator and the actual checking of established permission values are used to enforce authorization policies.

Authorized transactions should be completed successfully, and once set up, the transaction content should not be tampered with. For example, if a client agrees to pay an amount, say $500, to obtain some good through an auction, neither the seller nor the buyer should be allowed to modify the description, the quantity, or the price stated on the contract. This security process is called integrity.

Integrity

Integrity of the data during transmission and storage is crucial. Transaction participants want to be assured that unauthorized users will not alter the content of the transaction. At best, altered documents are an embarrassment to the company; at worst, the misstated financial statement could result in a lawsuit from the investors or even bankruptcy. In the traditional network environment, integrity is present in the form of a control redundancy check (CRC). This operation addresses the tampering or loss of information during a transfer. A file is submitted to an algorithm that generates a unique number for the message. On the receiving end, the file is processed again with the same algorithm, and the number generated is compared with the original.

In modern systems, hash functions are the principal approach used to ensure integrity. In the United States, the two most common hash functions are the Secure Hash Algorithm (SHA-1) and RSA's Message Digest (MD5).

SHA-1 was developed by the National Institute of Standards and Technology and published as a federal information processing standard. The algorithm takes a message as input with a maximum length of fewer than 2^{64} bits and produces a 160-bit message digest output. The message used as input can be long enough to accommodate most transactions. With the SHA-1 algorithm, every bit in the hash code is a function of every bit of the input message. As such, the complex repetition produces such a result that the message digest will very likely be unique. The designers of secure hash functions are reluctant to depart from a proven scheme. Original patterns such as DES were based on a Feistel cipher. Feistel ciphers are a special class of iterated block ciphers where the ciphertext is calculated from the plaintext by repeated application of the same transformation or round function. Sometimes they are called DES-like ciphers. Most subsequent schemes are based on the same method, with slight adjustments aimed at defeating newly designed cryptanalysis threats. While many cryptographers consider SHA-1 the stronger of the two methods, other methods have surfaced and gained wide acceptance.

MD5 is a message digest algorithm developed by Ron Rivest and supported by RSA security, one of the most trusted names in e-security. Netscape Navigator supports the cryptographic algorithm from RSA in its off-the-shelf version (Public Key Cryptography, MD2, MD5, RC2-CBC, and RC4). Likewise, Microsoft Internet Explorer contains licensed security software from RSA. Until the last few years, MD5 was the most widely used secure hash algorithm. It generates a 128-bit message digest, which is not long enough to resist brute force hacking.

Another noteworthy algorithm is RIPEMD-160, developed in Europe. Originally a 128-bit algorithm, it was subsequently extended to 160 bits. In its present form, it is very comparable in structure to SHA-1.

Public key hash functions supply fixed-length numerical message digests on messages of any length. The hash value provides an error detection capability. As with digital signatures, the value is unique to the document, and any bit modified will invalidate all the message content. The hash code generated, similar to the code generated with a public key, is a one-way function. The signature can be generated for the message, but one cannot infer the message from the originating key/function and the encrypted message.

Auditing

As no system will ever be completely secure, policies need to be devised where unauthorized usage will not occur. Any breaches should also be tracked. A discipline known as forensic security permits auditors to analyze the transaction trail and patterns of security breaches through system logs. This helps prevent future invasion. The audit trail should answer who did what, when, where, and how.

The intrusion detection and firewall noted in the previous chapter informs system administrators of a problem, but the sequence of events leading to the breach can be explained only through a deeper analysis of the transaction log. Examining the audit trail helps reconstruct the sequence of events leading to the breach. To be effective, the auditing process must incorporate all the above security elements.

Nonrepudiation

Nonrepudiation is a proof that a message has been sent or received. It provides stronger protection because the proof of delivery can be demonstrated to a third party. For example, if a recipient returns proof of delivery by signing a report, nonrepudiation of delivery is provided. Digital signatures provide nonrepudiation; the recipient can use a private key to acknowledge the delivery of the message, the way the receiver of a certified message signs to acknowledge delivery. Symmetric encryption cannot guarantee nonrepudiation. Since both the originator and recipient share the symmetric encryption key, either of both parties can generate the proof.

Nonrepudiation is important for the secure completion of online transactions. It is intended to collect, maintain, make available, and validate evidence concerning a claimed event or action in order to resolve disputes about the occurrence of the event or action. Nonrepudiation services are similar to their weaker counterparts (i.e., proof of submission, proof of delivery, and message origin authentication).

Unless time stamping is used, the nonrepudiation property cannot be obtained. A secure message handling system (MHS) will provide nonrepudiation of three factors—origin, submission, and delivery. Nonrepudiation of origin protects against any attempt by a message originator to deny writing a message. Nonrepudiation of submission protects against any attempt by a mail transport agent (MTA) to deny that a message was submitted for delivery, and nonrepudiation of delivery protects against any attempt by a message recipient to deny receiving a message. Nonrepudiation is essential for online auctions, where the identity of the bidder and the time of bidding is a crucial part of the transaction.

Digital Certificates

A digital certificate is a unique digital ID that can be used to verify the identity of a person, website, or JavaScript/Java Applet. It comes as an attachment to an electronic message, and it's most common use is to verify that a user sending a message is who he or she claims to be and to provide the receiver with the means to encode a reply. An individual or a business wanting to send an encrypted message applies for a digital certificate from a certificate authority (CA). The certificate authority verifies the identity of the requester and issues an encrypted digital certificate containing the applicant's public key and a variety of other items of identification information. The CA makes its own public key readily available through print publicity or on the Internet. The most widely used standard for digital certificates is X.509, a standard approved by the International Telecommunication Union (ITU).

The certificate always includes (1) a public key, (2) the name of the entity it identifies, (3) an expiration date, (4) the name of the CA that issued the certificate, (5) the digital signature of the CA, and (6) a serial number. These certificates use public key cryptography to sign and authenticate signatures and are protected by public and private key pairs linked by cryptographic algorithms. These keys have the ability to encrypt and decrypt information. Figure 5–6 depicts a typical certificate-based authentication.

In an e-commerce transaction, a customer places an order along with a certificate. The company validates the certificate with the known public key of the CA that delivered the certificate. When the company is certain of the customer's identity, it uses his or her key to verify the order.

FIGURE 5–6

Using a certificate to authenticate a client to a server

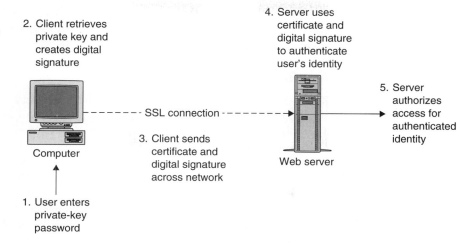

2. Client retrieves private key and creates digital signature

4. Server uses certificate and digital signature to authenticate user's identity

SSL connection

5. Server authorizes access for authenticated identity

Computer

3. Client sends certificate and digital signature across network

Web server

1. User enters private-key password

The certificate is only as good as the CA. Companies offering CA services include CyberTrust (a division of Baltimore Technologies), VeriSign, and Netscape. Typically, the CA has an arrangement with a financial institution, such as a credit card company, that provides it with information to confirm an individual's claimed identity. Digital certificates are part of the private key infrastructure (PKI) architecture (see Figure 5–7). The CA server issues, manages, and revokes certificates. In some cases,

FIGURE 5–7

PKI components

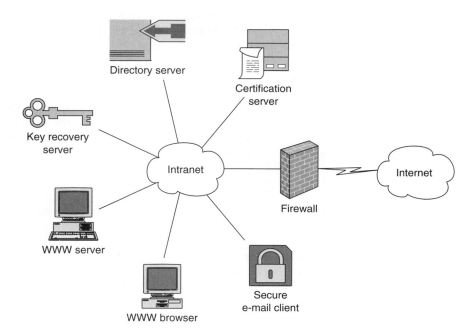

Directory server

Certification server

Key recovery server

Intranet

Firewall

Internet

WWW server

WWW browser

Secure e-mail client

CAs delegate their authority to issue a certificate, thereby creating a hierarchy. An ordered sequence of certificate from the last branch of the root is called a certificate chain.

Key Recovery Server

Key recovery servers enable the backup and recovery of encryption keys. This allows the secure recovery of encrypted e-mail and files and could also provide key escrow functions. In the United States, the Senate Commerce Committee on June 19, 1997, approved the McCain-Kerrey Secure Public Networks Act, which mandates access by federal and law enforcement agencies to session-based Internet traffic. This bill restricts the use of nonrecoverable strong domestic encryption technologies. This bill is inconsistent with the Commerce Department granting export license for non-key-recovery cryptographic software, and the issue will have to be resolved in the future. Problems of privacy and the potential for international industrial espionage have not been resolved to the satisfaction of the main trading partners of the United States.

Certificate Revocation List (CRL)

The administrator of a CA has to revoke a certificate to maintain the integrity of an organization's public key infrastructure (PKI) when the subject of the certificate leaves the organization or if the subject's private key has been compromised. If some other security-related event dictates that it is no longer desirable to have a certificate considered valid, then the certificate should be canceled. When a CA revokes a certificate, it is added to the CA certificate revocation list (CRL) and the list is propagated.

The browser may automatically import the latest CRL from an LDAP directory that receives regular updates from Netscape's Certificate Management System, and it may automatically check all certificates against the CRL to ensure they have not been revoked. If the browser does not do this automatically, or if there is reason to believe that the CRL is out of date (when the user's computer or the LDAP directory has been down, for example), it is necessary to check the master CRL or update the browser's version.

Online Certificate Status Protocol (OCSP)

The OCSP protocol [RFC2560] enables online validation of the reliability of a digital certificate. RFC2560 defines a mandatory-to-implement mechanism supporting the revocation status of the certificate and defines an optional extension mechanism to support a richer set of semantics (e.g., full path validation by the OCSP server).

In an effort to boost trust in e-business transactions, a process for validating digital certificates as quickly and accurately as validating credit cards is needed. Security companies such as RSA and ValiCert plan to achieve this goal through their OCSP Interoperability Initiative, a cooperative endeavor to advance this emerging Internet standard by establishing criteria and performing interoperability testing of third-party OCSP-enabled products to ensure they will work together. Some applications are more prone to security risks than others. Some back-office applications can be easily protected, while others are exposed due to their inherent nature and functions. E-mail is a primary contact point of any e-commerce setting, and its protection is the subject of the next section.

E-Mail and Internet Security

An essential component of e-commerce is a secure e-mail system. Customers should feel confident that their electronic communication with the business partners is tamperproof. The next sections discuss some of the most common alternatives employed to secure e-mail systems, including SSL, SET, PAP/CHAP, PCT, S/MIME, and PGP. The variety of the options discussed is a testament to the importance the industry attributes to this technology. While all the mechanisms mentioned provide the tools for securing e-mail systems, users should regularly visit advisory sites and the e-mail vendor for any flaws discovered that could compromise the system. Sites such as www.infosyssec.net/ consolidate the latest resources surrounding the security issues and can provide invaluable information to the networking professional.

Secure Sockets Layer (SSL)

As noted earlier, secure sockets layer (SSL) is a program layer protocol created by Netscape for managing the security of message transmissions in a network. This procedure is in wide use on the Internet. Messages are contained in a program layer between an application and the Internet's TCP/IP layers. Socket refers to the sockets method of passing data back and forth between a client and a server program in a network or between program layers in the same computer. Netscape's SSL uses the public and private key encryption system from RSA, which also includes the use of a digital certificate.

Many businesses use the industry standard security protocol of secure sockets layer to encode sensitive information, such as a credit card number, that passes between the customer and the business. SSL works by creating a temporary shared "key" (sort of a digital code book) that allows only the computers on either end of a transmission to scramble and unscramble information. To anything between the sender and the receiver, including all the servers that may relay the message, the SSL transmission is indecipherable gibberish. SSL makes online ordering as secure as using credit cards anywhere else. After millions of online transactions, no customer has ever reported misappropriation of a credit card number protected by the SSL technology.

When the client browser reaches a secure Web page, the server that is hosting the secure site sends a "hello request" to the browser. The browser then replies with a "client hello." The server responds back with a "server hello." Exchanging all these "hellos" allows the browser and the server's Web page to determine the encryption and compression standards that they both support. They also exchange a "session ID," a unique identifier for that specific interaction. Once they have greeted each other, the browser asks for the server's "digital certificate." It is an online commerce version of asking "Can I see some ID, please?"

Online companies obtain digital certificates from a certificate authority, such as RSA Security or VeriSign, which in late 1999 acquired Thawte Consulting, the second largest CA. A CA verifies an individual or a company's identification and then issues a unique certificate as proof of identity. After the browser and the secure server provider have shaken hands, so to speak, and after the browser has checked the digital certificate, the browser uses the information in the digital certificate to encrypt a message back to the secure server that only the server can understand.

Using that information, the browser and the server create a "master key," which is like a codebook that both sides can use to encode and decode transmissions. Only the browser and the server share that master key, and it's good only for that individual session. Using the unique, shared key, the browser and the secure server can exchange sensitive information, such as a credit card number, in a way third parties cannot understand or decipher.

When the customer quits a secure site, the master keys become useless because they are good for one session only. When the customer returns to the secure site, the computer and the secure server will again go through the entire process and then create another master key.

Customers can tell when they are on a secure site by looking at the drawing of a padlock or key somewhere along the bottom of the browser's window. If the key is unbroken or the lock is closed, and the image is golden or glowing, that means the user is protected by SSL. Most browsers can also be set to alert users when they enter and leave a secure site.

Two types of SSL certificates are commonly used. The first is a client SSL certificate used to identify clients to servers via SSL (client authentication). An example of such use could be a bank giving client SSL certificates to its customers to identify and authorize them to remotely access their accounts. Similarly, a business can provide an SSL certificate to its employee to secure access to its internal servers. The second type is a server SSL certificate used to identify servers to clients. The prime example could be Internet sites engaging in e-commerce that support encrypted SSL sessions, ensuring that personal information and credit card numbers cannot be easily intercepted.

SET

The Secure Electronic Transaction™ protocol (SET) enables the use of electronic payment methods, such as credit cards, for Internet commerce and provides assurances about the identification of the customers, merchants, and banks participating in the transactions. SET accomplishes this by providing encryption for secure Internet transmission of sensitive information and by using a public key certificate infrastructure to support established business trust relationships between customers, merchants, and banks.

SET promotes software interoperability and provides a secure environment for shopping on the Web. In real terms, SET lets customers purchase goods and services over the Internet with a high degree of confidence in the security of the transaction. Through varied alliances and partnerships, SET is fostered as the industry protocol for Internet payment.

The comprehensive, complex protocol is designed to accommodate a wide range of payment options and capabilities. As with any complex standard, adherence to the protocol alone does not ensure interoperability. Vendors may implement different options or interpret parts of the specification differently. To assure a high level of accuracy and uniformity in SET implementations, the credit card associations have established SET Secure Electronic Transaction LLC (SETCo www.setco.org) as an agency for the definition and compliance testing of SET. SETCo administers comprehensive compliance tests through its contracted agency, Tenth Mountain Systems (www.tenthmtn.com).

PAP/CHAP

Password authentication protocol (PAP) and challenge handshake authentication protocol (CHAP) are commonly used in conjunction with point-to-point protocol (PPP) to authenticate access before allowing data to flow on a PPP link. Both protocols work in a similar fashion—the router at one end of the link transmits a user name and password pair, and the router at the other end determines whether it will accept this as identifying a valid user. The router that is transmitting the user name/password is referred to as the peer, and the router that is receiving and checking the user name/password is referred to as the authenticator.

There are some significant differences in the details of the operation of the two protocols:

- With PAP, the password is sent as open text. With CHAP, the password is sent encrypted.
- With CHAP, the authenticator challenges the peer and expects to receive the user name and password in response. A challenge occurs during the initial link negotiation process and then again

at 10-minutes intervals throughout the time the link is open. With PAP, the peer offers its user name and password once at link negotiation time but never again.

PCT

The private communications technology (PCT) is a Microsoft security initiative. The protocol offers the following elements of transmission security for client/server relationships over the Internet:

- Provides symmetric session-encryption keys between servers and clients.
- Accommodates authentication of server to client via certificate of authority (CA) trusted public keys. Optionally, it also authenticates clients to server.
- Verifies message integrity with hash function message digests, similar to the SET protocol.

PCT assumes the existence of a network transport layer, most commonly TCP/IP, but not a particular application protocol. Thus, PCT can be implemented to coexist equally with both HTTP and FTP. The PCT protocol is similar in record format to Netscape's SSL scheme of securing transmission between a Web server and a Web client. In addition, however, PCT offers other advantages. First, PCT permits stronger authentication because it separates the authentication and encryption functions. In SSL, these two functions are bound, making SSL subject to the current 40-bit encryption key limit that the U.S. government places on exports. (This limitation may soon be void.) The public/private key pairs used to authenticate messages are specified to be different from the encryption keys. There is no built-in requirement to encrypt a message at all, although authentication can still occur. Second, PCT has a more streamlined handshake phase than SSL, resulting in faster server authentication.

S/MIME

The secure multipurpose Internet mail extensions (S/MIME) is a secure method of sending e-mail that uses the RSA encryption system. It provides a consistent way to send and receive secure MIME data. Based on the popular MIME standard, S/MIME provides the following cryptographic security services for electronic messaging applications: authentication, message integrity and nonrepudiation of origin (using digital signatures), and privacy and data security (using encryption). S/MIME is included in the latest versions of the Web browsers from Microsoft and Netscape and is endorsed by most other messaging vendors. RSA has proposed S/MIME as a standard to the Internet Engineering Task Force (IETF). An alternative to S/MIME is using PGP, which has also been proposed as a standard and is described in the next section.

MIME, described in the IETF standard called RFC 1521, specifies how an electronic message will be organized. S/MIME details how encryption information and a digital certificate can be included as part of the message body. S/MIME follows the syntax provided in the Public Key Cryptography Standard (PKCS) format 7.

Pretty Good Privacy (PGP)

PGP is the world's de facto standard for e-mail encryption and authentication with over 6 million users. PGP 6.5.1 MIT freeware supports RSA, PGP e-mail, and secure client-to-client connections using PGP certificates. It is available for noncommercial use only.

The commercial PGP virtual private network (VPN) client is available from Network Associates and is fully IPSec compliant with support for X.509 certificates from industry leaders such as VeriSign, Entrust, and Net Tools and from VPN gateway support, to create encrypted network connections to a company for secure remote access. The commercial client also includes PGPdisk, advanced utility software for fast disk, file, and directory encryption and authentication.

E-mail sent over the Internet is more like paper mail on a postcard than mail in a sealed envelope. It can easily be read or even altered by anyone with privileged access to any of the computers along the route followed by the mail. Hackers can read and forge e-mail. Government agencies may eavesdrop with a court order on private communications, and corporate competitors may attempt to derive information from employee e-mail.

In August 1999, hackers discovered a way to breach the security of Hotmail e-mail accounts, and the details were made public on the Internet, thus putting the privacy of 50 million subscribers at risk. The entire Hotmail system was closed for a short time, while steps were taken to fix the problem. It is difficult to be confident that e-mail is secure.

Virtual Private Network

A virtual private network is a network available when the user needs it. The concept behind on-demand networking is that the node can join the network for any desired function at any time, for any length of time. The common approach is to tunnel IP within IP, with some layer in between to provide the on-demand management. Two technologies are emerging for this, L2TP (layer two tunneling protocol) and IPSec (IP security protocol). The next sections cover the three major protocols for virtual private networks.

The IPSec protocol is defined by a large number of standards and recommendations that are codified by the Internet Engineering Task Force (IETF). There are many flavors of IETF standards, recommendations, statements of common practice, and so on. Some of the protocols used in IPSec are full IETF standards; the others are often stable enough to be treated as standards by people implementing IPSec.

IP Security Protocol (IPSec)

IPSec provides network-level security for IP. Its management protocol, ISAKMP/Oakley, is also a security protocol and protects against man-in-the-middle attacks during the connection setup. IPSec in hosts as OS components or BITS ("bump in the stacks") implementations can work with gateway or router implementations such as BITW ("bump in the wire") to create secured, on-demand network connections. The distinction between L2TP and IPSec is an important one. L2TP supports on-demand connections that can be secured. IPSec provides security that supports on-demand connections.

Layer Two Tunneling Protocol (L2TP)

Layer two tunneling protocol combines a number of existing technologies to deploy manageable on-demand networks. L2TP is an emerging IETF standard that combines the best features of two existing tunneling protocols: Cisco's layer two forwarding (L2F) and Microsoft's point-to-point tunneling protocol (PPTP). L2TP is an extension to the point-to-point protocol (PPP). Using L2TP, users and telecommuters can connect to their corporate intranets or extranets. VPNs are cost-effective because users can connect to the Internet locally and tunnel back to connect to corporate resources. This not only reduces overhead costs associated with traditional remote access methods, but it also improves flexibility and scalability.

L2TP does not claim to offer enhanced security. Two avenues for enhancing security are using IPSec in its transport mode or using a much weaker PPP security. L2TP, as its name implies, tunnels a link-layer protocol over IP. This allows for support of multiple protocols over an IP network, such as IPX or AppleTalk. The connection management protocol within L2TP lets the network administrator control the valid L2TP links. L2TP is targeted for remote clients, but some servers, routers, and gateways will support it for network-to-network links. L2TP may not be common in firewall products, as its security is not recognized as fully secure.

FIGURE 5–8

Example of architecture using L2TP

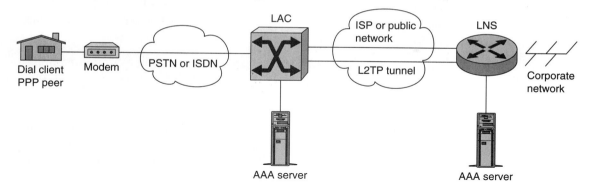

Figure 5–8 illustrates how L2TP is used to connect a remote user to the corporate network. The L2TP access concentrator (LAC) is a device that the client directly connects to and whereby PPP frames are tunneled to the L2TP network server (LNS). The LAC needs only to implement the media over which L2TP is to operate and pass traffic to one or more LNSs. It may tunnel any protocol carried within PPP. The LAC is the initiator of incoming calls and the receiver of outgoing calls. L2TP is analogous to the layer two forwarding (L2F) network access server (NAS).

As it becomes more popular, L2TP promises a variety of benefits:

- Vendor interoperability.
- Ability to be used as part of the wholesale access solution, which allows ISPs to offer VPNs.
- Ability to be operated as a client-initiated VPN solution, where enterprise customers using a PC can use the client-initiated L2TP from a third party.
- Currently available value-added features from Cisco's L2F and others.
- Load sharing and backup support, which will be available in future releases of L2TP.
- Support of Multihop, which enables Multichassis Multilink PPP in multiple home gateways, allowing the stacking of home gateways so that they appear as a single entity.

Transport Layer Security (TLS)

Transport layer security is used for encapsulation of various higher-level protocols. One such encapsulated protocol, the TLS handshake protocol, allows the server and client to authenticate each other and to negotiate an encryption algorithm and cryptographic keys before the application protocol transmits or receives its first byte of data. The TLS handshake protocol provides connection security that has three basic properties:

- The peer's identity can be authenticated using asymmetric, or public key, cryptography (e.g., RSA or DSS). This authentication can be made optional, but it is generally required for at least one of the peers.

- The negotiation of a shared secret is secure. The negotiated secret is unavailable to hackers, and for any authenticated connection the secret cannot be obtained, even by an attacker who can place himself in the middle of the connection.

- The negotiation is reliable. No attacker can modify the negotiation communication without being detected by the parties to the communication.

Encryption Export Policy and Key Recovery

Companies operating on a global basis are subject to rules and regulations affecting their use of encryption technologies. Export controls on commercial encryption products are administered by the Bureau of Export Administration in the U.S. Department of Commerce. Regulations governing exports of encryption are found in the Export Administration Regulations (EAR), 15 C.F.R. Parts 730-774.

New export policies approved in early 2000 relaxed the restriction on utilization of strong encryption in foreign countries. This policy should help business and promote e-commerce by adjusting U.S. regulations to marketplace realities faced overseas. The regulation further streamlines requirements for U.S. companies by permitting exports of any encryption item to their foreign subsidiaries without a prior review. Foreign employees of U.S. companies working in the United States no longer need an export license to work on encryption.

Telecommunications and Internet service providers can obtain and use any encryption product under this license exception to provide encryption services, including public key infrastructure services for the general public and subsidiaries of companies operating e-commerce operations. As previously mentioned, the new McCain-Kerrey act contradicts the newly adopted export regulations, and the two will have to be reconciled to provide a seamless global e-commerce framework.

Advances in Hardware and Threats to Security

Advances in security and encryption technology are bringing certain benefits to e-commerce in the form of increased trust and lower commercial risks. However, counterbalancing opportunities exist for hackers to use the hardware innovation and shared processing to exploit remaining weaknesses. The previous chapter described how distributed denial of service used multiple software agents to cause business disruptions. The potential of modern hardware is still mostly untapped by hackers, but this environment could change rapidly.

Parallel Processing

A core concept of the computer revolution, Moore's Law, states that the power of a microprocessor doubles approximately every 18 months. Thus, in 1984, a desktop computer could execute 2 million instructions per second, but by 1994, the same machine was capable of 256 million instructions per second. Such advancement in computer power threatens security at an accelerating pace. The remedy has been to successively increase the length guarantees of encryption keys and try to find more convoluted algorithms. In the long term the intelligence community acknowledged the high risks of failure.

Moore's Law makes the focus on encryption key length almost irrelevant. The strong encryption is only "strong" compared to a single processor of available computing power to crack the string of numbers that comprise the key. As computing power doubles every 18 months, no encryption scheme will remain strong for long. Also, advances in parallel processing and clustering architectures have rendered the evaluation based on a single processor obsolete.

Groups such as the Progress and Freedom Foundation have warned of the threats posed by weak encryption. Partitioning the range of possible keys among a number of processors with idle processing power will extend the breaking power to unbelievable levels. To counter such threats, software encryption is almost defenseless or information transfer would be so slow (taxed by highly complex encryption measures) as to become irrelevant. One avenue to a temporary solution is to use special chips to encrypt all outgoing data.

From Real-World to Digital Payment Systems

Payments for transactions have evolved through time, changing first from barter to real money then to representation of value. E-commerce can use a number of instruments to settle a transaction from cash, to purchase orders, to checks, or transferring balances to a bank account. Even in the United States, about 40 percent of the population operates without credit cards. As a result, a number of alternative payment methods have been devised.

Cash

The value of cash is symbolic and will become totally virtual with on-line transactions. Paper money has no value in itself but represents the promise to be able to use it in future transactions. The government of the country issuing the bills guarantees paper money. Cash has some well-recognized properties—it is generally accepted, it carries no buyer or seller transaction cost, and it is anonymous and convenient. Apart from the potential for counterfeit bills, the risks incurred in cash trans-actions are nonexistent on the seller side and limited to the difficulty of proving that the transaction has taken place on the buyer side.

Checks

Check payments have a higher risk than cash. The institution issuing the check will honor the payment only as long as the check issuer has the amount in an account. Warranty of the payment also depends on the sol-vency of the bank. Banks and other third parties issuing checks have more questionable stability than cash. Checks are familiar instruments for real-world payments. Both individuals and businesses use checks to complete transactions. A check is written by the consumer and authenticated by a signature. It is then presented to the merchant, who endorses it before presenting it to the bank for payment. If both parties have the same bank, then the bank operates as a simple transfer agent; if the banks aren't the same, the check is sent to a clearinghouse or the Federal Reserve Bank for settlement. If the check is certified, then the seller has total assurance that he or she will be paid. If the check is a personal one, there is always the possibility that the buyer does not have the funds to cover the purchase. Checks (e-checks) are becoming relevant to e-commerce through software that makes it possible to accept personal and business checks by tele-phone, fax, or e-mail. The customer's manual signature on the check is not necessary, and the check can be deposited on the same day.

Money Orders

Money orders are similar to certified checks, as a known third party such as the U.S. Postal Service, American Express, Western Union, or a bank guarantees their value. The transaction cost is small and the advantage is that it can be sent to the named receiver. The payment still carries some degree of anonymity. If the issuer preserves the privacy of both the seller and the buyer, the transaction is well protected.

Credit Card Payments

A credit card system is based on some trust and provides the customer with a means of purchasing goods and services while deferring payment. The merchant is assured of payment, and the card issuer bears the responsibility for billing the customer and collecting the money. In a traditional transaction, the customer presents the credit card, and the merchant validates the signature and submits the transaction for authorization (an operation routinely done online) and obtains an approval code. If the merchant accepts credit cards through the mail, phone, or the Internet, the card issuer accepts the risk of nonpayment, but the merchant stands the risk of fraudulent card usage (e.g., when the buyer is not whom he or she claims to be). The merchant bears the risk and cost of accepting credit cards in order to expand the business. Under U.S. law, cardholder liability is limited to $50 if a third party fraudulently uses the card.

Electronic Money

Payment security is a key factor in the success of Internet commerce. Electronic transactions need to be safe for all parties involved, and transaction cost is often an issue in business-to-consumer operations. Cash, money orders, and checks are not convenient means of conducting business on the Internet. Credit card processors and banks are reticent to provide free support for transactions with minimal amounts. As a response to these hurdles, a few payment services offer alternatives to both consumers and merchants. Merchants want to make sure their investment in payment solutions will work in the long term. Market acceptance is now centering around a few options.

CyberCash

The Internet electronic payment industry is consolidating through mergers. Bill Melton, the co-founder of CyberCash, has acquired and taken over the Internet payments customer base of the pioneer Internet-payment company, ICVerify, an early participant in the industry. Melton was one of the pioneers and creators of VeriFone, now a unit of Hewlett-Packard, the world's dominant supplier of electronic payment systems to retailers. CyberCash's payment method involves easy-to-carry electronic "wallets," substituting for cash and credit cards, and uses secure transactions, digital signatures, and identification. After a bad experience with its early electronic wallets, CyberCash launched InstaBuy, a one-click product aimed at boosting buying ease. For InstaBuy, the buyer does not have to provide personal details. Banks, which hold the customers' trust, are vouching for the safety of the instrument and issue the card to their consumers.

The CyberCash solution operates similarly to SSL or SET by encrypting the credit card details. CyberCash transactions flow through seven steps:

1. Information about the purchase price of the selected item is sent from the merchant to the buyer.
2. The browser of the buyer sends encrypted order and credit card information to the merchant.
3. The merchant forwards the encrypted payment information to the CyberCash server along with its own signature.
4. The transaction amount is forwarded to the merchant's bank.
5. The bank gets payment approval from the issuer bank.
6. The bank payment server confirms or denies the transaction.
7. The transaction is completed or aborted.

Allowing secure transactions with the added benefit of confidentiality (the merchant has no access to credit card information, and the bank has no information about the item bought) is one of the advantages of the CyberCash approach. Stored value cards, discussed later, provide some of the same benefits.

VeriFone

Now a unit of Hewlett-Packard, VeriFone is pursuing both the electronic payment market as well as the conversion of paper checks to electronic checks. Based on a study conducted by the U.S. Federal Reserve, electronic processing can reduce the cost of check handling by up to 50 percent, saving financial institutions and merchants billions of dollars annually. The point-of-sale check conversion service from Vital Processing Services® provides value to merchants by increasing cash flow with the reduction of bad check losses, improvement of check collection efficiency, simplification of funds management, and quicker checkout time.

Vital has certified a solution that enables VeriFone's suite of Omni terminals to accept credit and debit card payments as well as to process point-of-sale (POS) check conversion. Vital has also entered into a reseller agreement with BankServ to provide connectivity to the BankServ host system for settlement of checks. Leveraging VeriFone's Omni terminals, paper checks are converted into an authorized electronic check transaction, providing the merchant with the electronic movement of funds and eliminating the need to submit the paper check to the bank for payment. VeriFone's terminals also support credit and debit card payment capabilities using additional software. VeriFone has a similar agreement with Concord E.F.S and National Data Corporation.

The VeriFone Integrated Payment Solution (IPS) addresses these needs through a modular framework built for rapid change and expanding capabilities. It is cost-effective, highly flexible, and future-proof. The IPS framework includes the following:

- A collection of core technologies that streamlines the development and delivery of payment and payment-related applications.
- Modular application components from VeriFone Internet-based technology that forms a bridge between traditional storefronts and the Internet.
- High scalability, security, and reliability to ensure high-quality performance.

Stored-Value Smart Cards

Smart cards look similar to credit cards but have the added feature of incorporating an embedded microchip. The cards have metallic contacts that represent their interface to the world and memory to store information and value. Smart cards have been used extensively in Europe for the past few years, mostly as a **stored-value** telephone card. European telecommunications companies have fully endorsed smart cards; public phones in Europe no longer accept coins. Many cities have similarly adopted these cards as a medium to store parking meter units. As an authentication mechanism, smart cards are highly useful because they can store encrypted information about the carrier. Smart cards are widely used in Canada for health care. In the banking industry, their adoption has been slower because most U.S. banks have not embraced the technology.

The stored-value smart cards have a number of attractive features.

- They are highly portable, allowing the owner to carry around readily available currency.
- They are secure and mostly tamperproof.
- They offer a foolproof authentication mechanism if the system accessed is equipped with a card reader.
- They cannot be as easily forged as regular credit cards.
- They can be a reliable mode of payment for small transactions and are widely available through Visa Cash Mondex.
- They do not involve individual transaction paper trails and have minuscule transaction costs.

Although they have been plagued by the lack of a standard interface, smart cards have compelling advantages that should increase their adoption in the years to come. They can be used in e-commerce on the client to support standard protocols such as SSL and SET and can be used for encryption, storing the keys and certificates used by the protocols.

Digital Cash

Transactions can be performed with electronic cash using either smart cards or cash cards. One of the hurdles of credit card transactions is the high transaction cost when used for the purchase of small items; these technologies overcome that barrier.

Visa Cash.   Visa Cash uses embedded logic such that the card can be used until the stored money is depleted. In some cases, the card can be reloaded and reused. Visa Cash technology is not appropriate for use on open networks because it assumes a secure channel to the card reader.

Mondex.   The Mondex cash card system was launched in Great Britain in 1995 using an integrated circuit card (ICC), a normal plastic card with a small microcomputer chip embedded in it. This microcomputer is programmed to function as an electronic purse. The electronic purse can be loaded with some value that is stored until it is used as payment for goods and services or transferred to another Mondex card by inserting the card into a card reader. The electronic purse can also be locked using a personal code so that only the card's owner can access its value. Mondex chips are designed to withstand normal extremes of cold and heat, damp, X-rays, and electrical interference.

The card has not been widely deployed in the United States, where a pilot venture between AT&T, HP, and Mondex has met with a lukewarm welcome.

Digicash.   Digicash offers online person-to-person payments. ECash Technologies is the first company to offer general consumer-to-consumer payment solutions to banks. With eCash P2P, financial institutions can offer person-to-person payments to their customers. Already deployed in Germany through a partnership with Deutsche Bank 24 AG, the eCash person-to-person solution is an easy-to-implement payment product that can be installed directly at financial institutions or accessed seamlessly through a hosted service. The eCash system has been in use for over five years in global pilot programs. Having achieved recognition for bulletproof security, consumer privacy, and simplicity of use, eCash is ready to offer its system in the United States.

Micropayment

Micropayment is a term used for amounts as low as one cent and allows vendors to sell content, information, and services over the Internet at very low unit prices. Several companies offer micropayment solutions.

IBM Micro Payments targets a wide range of domains, including banks and financial institutions; telephone companies; Internet service providers; content providers offering games, entertainment, reference information, archives, reviews, and consumer information; service providers offering fax, e-mail, and phone services over the Internet; premium search engines; and specialized databases. The IBM solution claims a number of advantages:

- Universal acceptance of payments.
- Scalable, decentralized design.
- Transaction amounts as low as one cent.
- Simple "click-and-pay" user interface.
- Negligible delay for transactions.
- No special hardware required.
- Security against forgery and overspending.
- Completely exportable.
- Support for multiple currencies and multilingual support.
- Application Programming Interface (API) for integration of legacy systems.
- Automated compiler tool for HTML authoring.
- Existing relationships enhanced.

Compaq's alternative, the MilliCent™ microcommerce network, provides new "pay-per-click" and "earn-per-click" functionality for Internet users. It is designed for buying and selling digital products costing as little as 1/10th of a cent. Websites can use MilliCent to build parallel revenue streams through the simultaneous use of pay-per-click purchases, subscriptions, and advertising. It can also be used to make direct monetary payments to users.

CyberCash's InstaBuy offers merchants and potential customers easy sign-up for the service. Merchants who offer InstaBuy display the InstaBuy logo. During checkout, the customer simply clicks the logo to sign up, completes the online form, and then makes the purchase using InstaBuy. The form asks for the user's shipping address, billing address, credit card number, and password. Currently, InstaBuy has not been widely deployed and the volume of transactions does not cover its costs. However, the advancement of technology and a partnership with the utility companies may allow customers to charge their small purchases to their utility bills.

Payment Services

Payment services can turn a website into an e-commerce store quickly and easily. With a good payment service, a business can process most major forms of online payment. Payflow Link from VeriSign is an HTTP-based solution designed for businesses that want a fast and easy way to conduct secure transactions over the Internet. Payflow Link enables merchants to connect their customers to a secure order form that automates order acceptance, authorization, processing, and the management of transactions. The process is as simple as entering an HTML hyperlink into the existing website. Payflow Link can also be used in combination with shopping carts and other e-commerce solutions.

Payflow Link

- Accepts credit cards, debit cards, and Internet checks.
- Makes transactions occur over a secure SSL connection.
- Authorize payment in less than three seconds.
- Installs easily with a piece of HTML code.
- Supplies back-end reporting tools to help manage profits.
- Modifies the look and feel of the hosted forms to suit the website.

Summary

Network security is one of the remaining frontiers in the computing arena. Networks and systems have to be secure to provide a safe infrastructure for e-commerce and personal and business use. This chapter addressed issues relevant to the encryption of messages sent through the network. In its various forms the goals of encryption (safe, authentic, efficient transmission of messages) can be achieved through a combination of techniques including symmetric and public key encryption. Methods of payments useful for e-commerce were surveyed, including the traditional payment systems and the more specific electronic payment mechanisms. Among the network applications most subject to hackers' attack, e-mail deserves the most attention and the industry has responded with a set of technologies enabling safe communication through this medium. We also introduced techniques that allow businesses to use the public network infrastructure as a surrogate for a private network through the use of virtual private networking. Finally, users should be aware that security is a very fluid field and that hackers will always be ingenious and have access to tools to compromise encryption systems either by brute force or by mascarading as an authorized user.

Key Terms

Asymmetric key 148	CRL 160
Auditing 157	Digital certificate 158
Authentication 151	Digital signature 153
Authorization 155	Encryption 144
Confidentiality 149	Integrity 156

Review Questions

1. What are the leading means of encrypting data?
2. What is the distinction between symmetric and asymmetric key encryption?
3. What are digital signatures and how can they be applied in e-commerce?
4. What are the leading payment systems used in business-to-consumer and business-to-business e-commerce?
5. How do you know when the browser is working in encrypted secure mode versus insecure browsing mode?
6. What are the alternative technology solutions available for e-mail security?
7. What is PGP? What security issues does it address?
8. How does PGP integrate with current e-mail programs?

Projects

1. Visit an e-commerce website and survey the mode of payment allowed. Would you trust the site with your business?
2. Global e-commerce presents challenges exempt from domestic e-commerce. What security concerns add to the complexity of international e-business?
3. What measures should e-commerce providers take to create trust among their potential customers? What measures can be verified by the customer?

4. Visit 10 e-commerce websites. How many mention security on their home page? Is privacy mentioned? How many of them belong to the TRUSTe association?

5. Visit the VeriSign website (www.verisign.com). What solutions does it offer for e-commerce?

6. Visit your e-mail or WWW browser provider site and search for security. What technologies are supported by your particular product?

7. Visit the TRUSTe website (www.truste.org). Describe what services and solutions are offered.

8. Get the latest PGP freeware from web.mit.edu/network/pgp/pgp.html. Install it on two machines and encrypt a message on one machine and decrypt it on the other.

References, Readings, and Hyperlinks

1. Friedman, W. F. *Advanced Military Cryptography*. Laguna Hills, CA: Aegan Park Press, 1996.

2. Van der Lubbe, J. C. A. *Basic Methods of Cryptography*. Cambridge: Cambridge University Press, 1998.

3. Johnson, B., and L. Daste. *Break the Code: Cryptography for Beginners*. Mineola, NY: Dover Publications, 1997.

4. Rhee, M. Y. *Cryptography and Secure Communications*. New York: McGraw-Hill, 1994.

5. Menezes, Alfred J., Paul C. Van Oorschot, and Scott A. Vanstone. *Handbook of Applied Cryptography*. Boca Raton, FL: CRC Press, 1996.

6. Zimmermann, Philip R. *The Official PGP User's Guide*. Cambridge, MA: MIT Press, 1995.

7. http://www.perkinscoie.com/resource/ecomm/digisig/digsig.htm
The digital signature resource center offers information about electronic authentication laws at the model (United Nations Commission on International Trade law), international, federal, and state levels. The site lists additional pages on policy development, related issues, and background information relevant to digital signature.

8. http://www.abanet.org/scitech/ec/isc/dsg-tutorial.html
The American Bar Association offers tutorial and guidelines for digital signatures.

9. http://www.merchantrust.com/
The MerchanTrust™ product line delivers powerful, yet simple-to-use transaction processing that integrates into existing websites and popular "shopping cart" software. It provides real-time credit card transactions and personal check acceptance. Customers can use recurring debiting and membership password services to create subscription services on websites.

10. http://mkn.co.uk/bank
The BankNet service is an online banking service. It is a joint venture between MarketNet and Secure Trust Bank plc. The BankNet account offers all

of the facilities of a Secure Trust current account (no transaction charges even if overdrawn, interest on credit balances, check book, guarantee card, cash card). In addition, however, these accounts offer:

- An online opening form where you print the form on your own computer (live).
- The ability to look at your account through the World Wide Web (live).
- The ability to write electronic checks (live). These are digitally signed checks using public key/private key cryptographic techniques. It is linked to HTML and available for Windows 3.1, Windows 95, and 98.
- The ability to arrange a number of other processes online.

11. http://www.checkfree.com/
    Customers who enroll for the service provided by the U.S. Postal Service will be able to view and pay electronic bills live from leading companies including AT&T, MCI Worldcom, Sprint, GTE, BellSouth, Qwest, Countrywide Home Loans Inc., Homeside Lending, Amoco Oil, Florida Power & Light Company, and regional telecommunications, utility, cable, and wireless providers.

12. http://www.lclickcharge.com/html/merchant.html
    Pay-per-use creates a low-risk way for customers to buy and can increase sales of subscriptions and other premium content.

13. http://www.commerce.net/resources/

14. http://www.cybercard.com/
    This credit card is designed for Internet commerce with special features addressing secure transactions, age verification, and Internet privacy.

15. http://www.cybercash.com/
    CyberCash provides the broad connectivity with connections to over 95 percent of acquiring banks through the following processors: First Data Corporation, Paymentech, NDCeCommerce, Vital, Checkfree, Wells, NOVA, NPC, and Sligos (European).

16. http://www.cybersource.com/
    CyberSource Commerce Component services are accessed in real-time via the CyberSource Commerce Component installed on a secure NT or UNIX server. This component is available as a ready-made plug-in or set of development libraries in C, Perl, or Java. All libraries and plug-ins use the open simple commerce messaging protocol (SCMP) to facilitate secure messaging between the merchant server and CyberSource. Production-ready software and documentation are available for download at no charge.

17. http://novaplaza.com/debitnet/
    DebitNet changes the customer's account number with each transaction. Whether selling items at $10 or $.10, the DebitNet's Secure Internet Payment System works the same, making consumers comfortable purchasing over the Internet.

18. http://www.ietf.org/html.charters/pkix-charter.html
    IETF and the PKIX working group within IETF are active in the area of digital signatures and digital certificates and have developed standards and draft documents in this area.

19. http://www.iso.ch/jtc1/sc27/
    The ISO has produced guidelines on the use and management of TTP services (ISO/IEC PDTR 14516). In addition, it has a number of relevant security standardization initiatives.

20. http://www.w3.org/DSig/
The World Wide Web Consortium, in the context of developing standards for XML, has looked at issues relating to electronic signatures and XML. It has formed a working group with IETF in this respect.

21. http://www.rsa.com/rsalabs/pubs/PKSC/
RSA Laboratories public key standards (PKSC) were developed in conjunction with a number of IT companies. The standards cover RSA encryption certificate request syntax.

22. http://www.mondex.com/

23. http://www.millicent.org/home.html
MilliCent is a micropayment system optimized for buying and selling digital products over the Internet. The site offers articles, newsletters, real-time data feeds, streaming audio, MP3 music, electronic postage, video streams, maps, financial data, multimedia objects, interactive games, software, and hyperlinks to other sites.

24. http://www.ini.cmu.edu/netbill/
The NetBill electronic commerce project at Carnegie Mellon's Information Networking Institute is researching design issues of highly survivable and secure distributed transaction processing systems, as well as accounting and access control for digital libraries. NetBill is addressing these issues by developing the protocols and software to support network-based payment for goods and services over the Internet. These protocols and software have been implemented in a test system, currently in its Alpha trial, on the Carnegie Mellon campus. This system enables consumers and merchants to communicate directly with each other, using NetBill to confirm and ensure security for all transactions.

25. http://www.ietf.org/internet-drafts/draft-ietf-pkix-ocspx-00.txt
This document defines Internet-standard extensions to OCSP that enable a client to delegate processing of certificate acceptance functions to a trusted server. The client may control the degree to which delegation takes place. In addition limited support is provided for delegating authorization decisions.

26. http://www.alhamy.net/faqs/crypto/
Cryptography frequently asked questions.

Endnotes

1. R. M. Needham and M. D. Schroeder, "Using Encryption for Authentication in Large Networks of Computers," *Communications of the ACM* 21, no. 12 (December 1978), pp. 993–99.

2. S. M. Bellovin and M. Merritt, "Limitations of the Kerberos Authentication System," *Computer Communication Review* 20, no. 5 (October 1990), pp. 119–32.

SERVERS FOR
E-BUSINESS

6

SERVER PLATFORMS IN E-COMMERCE

Chapter Outline

Learning Objectives

By the end of this chapter, you should be able to:

- Define the main components of an e-commerce platform.
- Identify appropriate platforms for various situations.
- Differentiate between the critical and nonessential features of e-commerce architecture.

- List the components necessary for the front-end and back-end of e-commerce transaction systems.
- Describe the steps involved in establishing an e-commerce website.

Chapter Overview

In a traditional computing environment, a platform is the underlying hardware and software for a system. For example, the platform might be an Intel Pentium III processor running Microsoft Windows NT version 4.0 or it could be a Sun UNIX machine running Solaris version 8.0 on an Ethernet network. A platform defines a standard around which a system can be developed. Once the computing platform has been selected, software developers can adopt appropriate application software and managers can purchase appropriate hardware.

Until the mid-1980s, computing platforms were centralized. Corporations operated their systems on expensive, powerful mainframe computers running all the software and providing results through display terminals or printed reports. The current computing architecture is mainly based on distributed processing with clients and servers. Sometimes called a two-tier architecture, the client/server platform is a network architecture in which each computer or processor on the network is either a client or a server. Servers are powerful computers dedicated to managing disk drives (file servers), printers (print servers), network traffic (network servers), or applications. Clients are personal computers, workstations, or other devices on which users run applications. Clients rely on servers for most resources, such as files, devices, and even processing power. In a two-tier client/server setting, the client is mostly responsible for the presentation of data either in text mode or in modern systems with a graphical user interface. The latest client/server systems have evolved toward a multitier architecture in which additional layers of computing power have been inserted between the client and the server in a networked environment. The intermediary layers are computers that may assume some processing burden from either the client or the back-end server.

This chapter discusses the specifications for client/server architectures. The software and hardware for the client and the server are discussed. Middle-tier servers, the most advanced e-commerce solutions, are also explained. The network elements of the architecture were considered in Chapters 2 and 3.

Figure 6–1 depicts an overview of e-commerce architecture. The first step of an e-commerce initiative involves placing the company information and a catalog on the Web using a Web server. The second phase deals with such factors as receiving orders, managing inventory, and collecting invoices. The third phase involves redesigning business processes and technology to create a seamless flow for the e-commerce supply chain. The third step is technologically more complex because it involves the interface of multiple additional components. This chapter does not go into the details of the architecture necessary in the third phase, but businesses involved in e-commerce will all have to

Figure 6-1

Standard e-commerce architecture

Basic e-commerce architecture

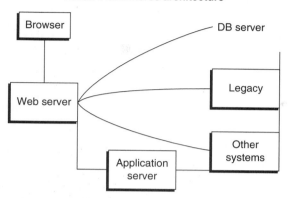

eventually face the integration issue (through enterprise resource planning, supply chain management, and customer relationship management). Chapter 11 addresses data warehousing and data mining aimed at collecting the customers' data and transforming them into valuable business intelligence for customer relationship management. Chapter 11 tackles the infrastructure business backbone provided by enterprise resource planning.

This chapter considers the components of a typical e-commerce platform, including Web servers, Web browsers, application servers, and packaged software.

A Business Vignette

The general public is becoming more aware of the possibilities offered by the Web, and e-commerce transactions are increasing rapidly. Recent reports have outlined the rapid global increase in the number of Internet users. In the United States, it has become common to list Web addresses on TV, newspaper, and magazine advertisements. In Europe, one out of four people use online services, and similar trends are under way in the Far East. The Internet is a global trend affecting both business-to-consumer and business-to-business relationships. The following is just one example of a rapidly growing business taking advantage of the Web.

In Sweden, Fish-co is a long-standing supplier of luxury seafood to the royal court as well as to top restaurants. When the company decided to expand into the consumer market in 1997, it chose the Internet as a channel rather than opening expensive brick-and-mortar retail stores. The main barrier the firm encountered was logistical—how to deliver perishable food over long distances within guaranteed time frames. To solve this problem, Fish-co worked with a Swedish company, Packaging-co, which developed a special packaging material to keep seafood cold, and the Swedish post office. The post office was interested in piloting a home delivery service for perishable food in order to develop such a capability in the future. Fish-co began selling luxury seafood through its Swedish-language website in April 1998 (www.cedlerts.se) and now receives 40 orders a week, with an average order value of about $120. The company is also finding that its traditional customer base, restaurants, is beginning to order electronically also. Fish-co buys seafood from fishermen and agents around the world, but these suppliers are resisting electronic purchasing.

Fish-co spent $140,000 establishing its new business and was fortunate to work with organizations, such as Packaging-co and the Swedish post office, that had a vested interest in developing the services it required. The company's risky investment in e-commerce is paying off: Profit margins are considerably higher on its consumer business than the restaurant business, and it intends to exploit the powerful marketing opportunities made possible through the combination of the Internet and its membership cards (issued to loyal repeat customers). Logistics remains the stumbling block to expansion to other geographic markets. The firm has now fulfilled orders to Denmark and intends to offer its services in Germany and France once it has translated its website into the appropriate languages.

Fish-co's effort involved a number of e-commerce applications: messaging and information access (e.g., e-mail, and website browsing), marketing (e.g., website for advertising and promotion), sales (e.g., receiving orders from customers), postsales supply to customers (e.g., electronic delivery or confirming nonelectronic delivery), customer support (e.g., answering commercial or technical queries), customer monitoring and relationship development (e.g., needs and satisfaction research, and consultation).

Overview of Computing Platforms

The next three sections outline the successive platforms that have dominated the computing industry for the past 30 years. The first wave of computing was comprised of centralized operations based on mainframes. The first shift from this option followed the introduction of the minicomputer, but it still followed the same primary architecture. The second significant wave occurred with the introduction of the personal computer in the early 1980s and the following introduction of the client/server architecture. The most recent transformation is toward a heterogeneous Internet platform. While the host-based platforms and client/server architecture remain important, new businesses focus on the ubiquitous Web platform.

FIGURE 6-2

The host architecture

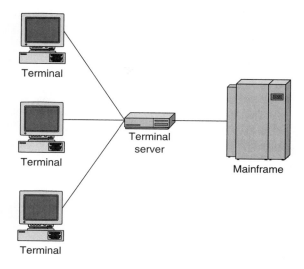

Host-Based Platform

In this centralized computer architecture, a single computer executes the business rules and the shared applications. Attached terminals provide the user interface, or the requested jobs are executed in batch and the results are provided to the user via printed reports. A high-performance database engine executes on the same computer and provides shared data to all other applications. No processing is done on the dumb terminals. Often, to spare the computing capacity of the mainframe, a terminal server or front-end processor (FEP) is inserted to take care of the connection and authorization services (see Figure 6–2).

Functionally, the terminal is charged with the display and the host carries the remaining three functions of interface logic, business application, and database. The flow of processing consists of the terminal sending a request to the host and the host providing a report after complete processing.

Client/Server Platform

In a client/server (C/S) architecture, there are clients and a server. In this arrangement, the client carries a substantial part of the processing. The software functions are divided into applications, database, interface logic, and interfaces. In a traditional C/S system, the server executes only the database function, while the client carries the other three. This is in sharp contrast with host-based systems, where the client provides only a character-based display and the server executes the other three functions.

FIGURE 6–3

Contrast host and
client/server systems

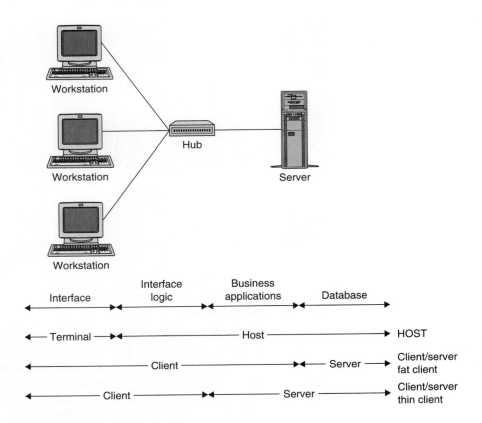

In a fat-client system, the client carries the heavier load, including the interface logic and the business logic, and performs a relatively heavy portion of processing. In contrast, a thin-client architecture allocates only the interface and the display logic to the client, leaving the application logic, processing, and database processing to the server. Figure 6–3 compares the allocation of functions for host system, client/server with a fat-client system, and client/server with a thin client. In an extension of the thin-client system, the server's responsibilities are separated into two or more tiers. The first-level server executes the application and the second-level server executes the database. This is known as a multitier or n-tier client/server system.

One application of client/server platforms is the transactional C/S system, which can be differentiated from a host-based system in a number of ways. First, the client in a two-tier C/S system runs on a much more powerful machine than a terminal, usually a personal computer or computer workstation. Second, the client processes a significant part of the total transaction load, more in the case of the fat client and less in the case of the thin client. Third, the interface in C/S systems is achieved through a graphical interface. In most cases, the interface allows for the use of a mouse, menus, windows, and graphical controls such as command buttons and text boxes. Finally, in the case of the C/S architecture, depending on the application, the network capacity required may be high or low.

Most C/S systems were initially implemented on local area networks. Client/server platforms are often located on LANs implemented under the control of a single organization at its own location or on a wide area network controlled by many entities. C/S platforms on LANs operate at high speed and high bandwidth. Technologies used on the local area networks include communication protocols such as SPX/IPX, the network protocol from Novell, and the standard transmission control protocol/ Internet protocol (TCP/IP) used by Microsoft and the UNIX computing platforms. SPX, the sequenced packet exchange which is a transport-layer protocol, was explained in Chapter 2. SPX is used primarily by client/server applications on the local network and is rarely used in e-commerce.

TCP/IP is the suite of communications protocols used to connect hosts on the Internet. A TCP/IP stack uses several distinct protocols, the two main ones being TCP and IP. TCP/IP is built into UNIX operating systems, including Sun Solaris and Linux, and is used widely by the Internet, making it the de facto standard for transmitting data over networks. Faced with the radical growth of the TCP/IP protocols, even network operating systems that have their own protocols, such as Netware, are now supporting TCP/IP.

World Wide Web Platform

Larger C/S systems are implemented on wide area networks running over private or leased lines. While the technologies used in C/S are still proprietary, the underlying enabling standards are usually universally accepted. On the Microsoft platform, standardized components (COM) encapsulate the functionality of the applications, and Structured Query Language (SQL) is universally recognized for relational databases.

The World Wide Web (WWW) is a subset of the wide area network. The Web includes numerous Internet servers that support specially formatted documents. These documents are formatted in a language called Hypertext Markup Language (HTML) that supports links to other documents, as well as graphics, audio, and video files. This means users can jump from one document to another simply by clicking on linked hot spots. The WWW is a vast distributed system comprised of millions of servers where information is stored across many computers and shared through a network supporting the TCP/IP suite of protocols. Web pages are sent over the Internet from the Web servers to the browsers. Pages can be a plain text file, an audio file, an image, or a video clip. These documents can be related through hyperlinks for moving from one topic to another. As users choose different links and move from one document to the next, they may be jumping from one server on the Web to another without knowing it, while the WWW handles all the connections. Hypermedia is the basis of the WWW.

The WWW is also a client/server system. The server is a repository of information and the clients are computers that request the information. Because the information is distributed over many Web servers, the WWW is described as an n-tier distributed client/server platform. These servers manage a collection of Web pages.

In the case of the WWW, the browsers on personal computers act as clients and are served by the Web servers. In the future, website developers will optimize content for a more diverse set of browsing devices including personal digital assistants (e.g., Palm Pilot) and cellular phones. Often, the Web server must process a client's request before it can send the information.

Web servers are often dedicated machines that act as repositories for Web pages. A server consists of:

- Hardware, which could be a personal computer, a workstation, or a mainframe computer.
- An operating system such as Windows NT, UNIX, or some mainframe operating system such as MVS and VMS that runs on the hardware.
- The Web server software, which runs on top of the operating system. Some popular Web server products are Microsoft's Internet Information Server, iPlanet Enterprise Server, and Apache Web server.

To display the Web pages, a user needs to have a WWW client program called a **browser.** Common browser programs are Netscape Navigator, Microsoft Internet Explorer, Sun Hotspot, and Opera Browser. The browsers run over a variety of platforms such as Windows, UNIX, and Mac OS. In the WWW, any server running on any platform can interact with any browser running on any client machine connected through the Internet. This makes the content of the WWW system universally available all over the Internet. Figure 6–4 illustrates a website with a number of Web clients linked to the Internet. These clients can be linked either through a dial-up line using a modem or digitally directly to the Internet through leased line, digital subscriber line (DSL), or cable modem (using the cable TV network to digitally access the Internet). Access to the Internet can be provided either by the telephone companies or **Internet service providers** such as America Online, CompuServe, and Prodigy.

FIGURE 6–4

Website transmission

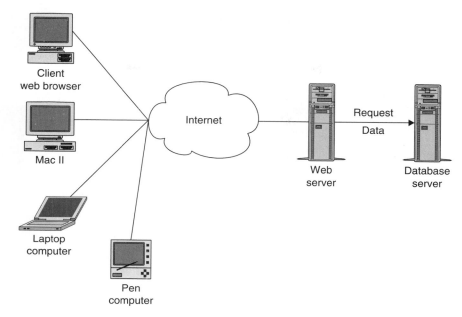

Internet service providers such as AOL traditionally offer dial-up access to a communication server. Once connected, the client submits requests for Web pages and the domain name server translates the address into a physical location and finds the path to the page location. A gateway at the ISP passes the request to the next node of the Internet (symbolized by a cloud, a vast assembly of routing devices linked by communication lines).

Implementation of an e-commerce solution can evolve in numerous fashions from an initial pilot site to a completely integrated solution. The last part of the chapter discusses the steps involved in building, buying, or renting e-commerce process chains.

In the simplest form, a website consists of the following components: (1) an informational website hosted on a Web server on the company side, (2) the Web browser on the visitor's side, (3) access to e-mail for both the business and the client, and (4) the core editing/development tools associated with the platform (see Figure 6–5).

More sophisticated e-commerce sites supplement the core components with software that enables secure transactions (see Figure 6–6). These include the commerce, applications, and database servers. Links to the back-end processing, to external credit checking and payment processing suppliers, and to the delivery mechanism complement the architecture portfolio. The most complex e-commerce sites incorporate integration with enterprise resource planning and the customer relationship

FIGURE 6–5

*A simple
informational website*

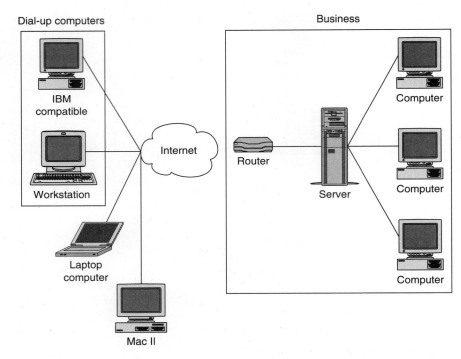

FIGURE 6–6

*A secure transactional
commerce site*

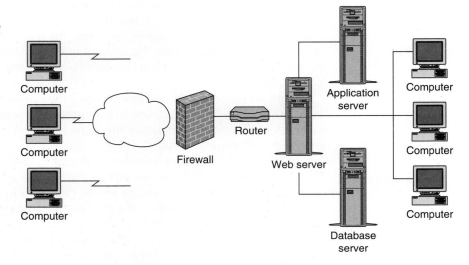

apparatus (see Figure 6–7). The long-term success of an e-commerce initiative may rely on the ties between enterprise resource planning (ERP)
and customer relationship management (CRM). These two functions can
use the details collected from customers to derive useful information for
customizing services and to control revenues.

FIGURE 6–7

*An integrated
e-commerce site*

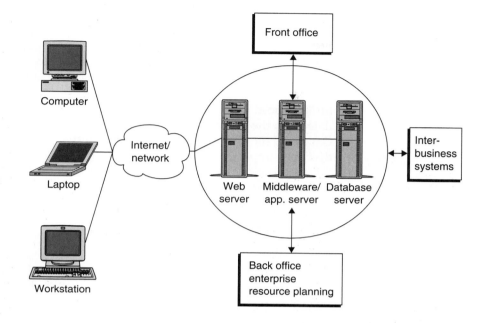

E-Commerce Components

The following components are often associated with a website:

- The clients with associated hardware and software capabilities (i.e., communication software and browser).
- The Internet.
- The routing devices at the boundary of the enterprise.
- Extra devices (covered in Chapters 4 and 5) that defend the perimeter against potential hackers.
- The Web server (in most cases) or/and a commerce server (in advanced systems).
- The application servers (in advanced systems), which are intended to integrate the e-commerce function with other functions.
- The back-end transactional software, such as transaction processing (TP) monitors, which will schedule the transactions; the database management system, which will support the storage, manipulation, and retrieval of operational data; and the data warehouse, which will support managerial decision support.

A transaction processing monitor is a program that monitors a transaction as it passes from one stage in a process to another. The TP monitor's purpose is to ensure that the transaction processes completely or, if an error occurs, to take appropriate action of rolling back the partial changes. TP monitors are important in three-tier architectures that employ load balancing because a transaction may be forwarded to any of several servers. The TP software is aimed at coordinating the enterprise resource planning (ERP), the supply chain, and/or relationships with suppliers' SCM (in advanced integrated systems). Both classes of software should pull data from the operational data store as well as from the data warehouse. Gateways should be able to aggregate external data with internal data for decision support systems.

We now consider the various components of a typical e-commerce system starting from the client and tracing the flow toward the back-end system.

Web Browsers: Internet Explorer and Netscape Communicator

The material distributed on the Internet is displayed with a heterogeneous set of browsers. Acknowledging and understanding this diversity can help avoid costly mistakes and incompatibility of the content with the leading Web clients.

The original Web browsers (e.g., Lynx) were simple tools able to display limited text. The next generation added the ability to display images without consuming large computing resources. In their latest iterations, Internet browsers encompass a range of functionality but at the cost of highly extended resource requirements conflicting with emerging trends such as wireless access through low bandwidth devices (e.g., cellular phones, Palm Pilot).

The desktop market is currently dominated by two browsers and supplemented by a number of marginal products. Internet Explorer's extended features and its closer integration with the desktop operating system have accelerated the dominance of Microsoft. From a clearly dominant position only three years ago, Netscape has been turned upside down, with Microsoft now claiming three-fourths of the market. Both Microsoft Internet Explorer and Netscape Communicator are free products and have an extensive list of capabilities.

Microsoft IE 5.5 offers a full assortment of features:

- Browser for display of Web pages.
- NetMeeting for collaboration.
- FrontPage Express for building Web pages.
- Outlook Express for fully functional e-mail.

Both Microsoft Internet Explorer and Netscape Communicator support additional Internet capabilities, such as file transfer protocol (FTP), Gopher, and NNTP newsreader and have support for execution within the browser of programs written with a scripting language. JavaScript capabilities exist in both cases. IE 5.5 has strong support for VBscript. (Scripting languages are considered in Chapter 7.) ActiveX is the preferred form of component inclusion within Microsoft IE.

Netscape Communicator has followed the same route as Microsoft IE, adding features at each generation, but it has been slower to deliver on its latest version. Netscape lacked a new product release from 1998 to 2000, and Microsoft slowly gained a majority of the browser market. While still offering Netscape Navigator without all the accessories, Netscape emphasizes the Netscape Communicator product. Netscape Communicator offers:

- Netscape Navigator (the browser itself).
- Netscape Messenger (fully configurable e-mail client).
- Netscape Composer (HTML editor).
- Netscape Conference (for telephony interface).
- Collabra discussion (for news groups).
- Netcaster (for push technology).
- Ability to snap-in an extensive set of add-ins.

Netscape recently released the new version of its browser (version 6) based on an open-source code base (Mozilla). The browser has gained better support for the latest standards, including the extensible markup language (XML), but has lost in stability.

Java is also somewhat supported by both browsers, but none currently supports Java 2. The browsers come with their own Java virtual machine (JVM). Java™ plug-in from Sun enables business customers to execute applets or beans in more uniform fashion. Mozilla.org, an open-source spinoff from Netscape, conducts a parallel effort with the MacOS Runtime for Java (MRJ). This plug-in enables current Netscape browsers (version 4.X and later) on Mac OS to use MRJ to run applets. Java applets can be written and executed within both browsers.

Other Browsers.   When almost every software upgrade requires a significant investment in new hardware as resource requirements continuously rise, Opera Software offers a refreshingly different approach, with a browser optimized for space and speed. In a small package, Opera 5.0 is a powerful alternative to the two market share leaders. Among Opera's notable features are strict adherence to HTML standards, sophisticated and speedy Web browsing with news and e-mail, and secure 128-bit SSL encryption. This selection is ideal for older machines and mobile computing with less available memory or disk space. The software also runs as a native 16-bit application under Windows 3.1 and 3.11. Ports to other platforms, such as BeOS, Linux, and Mac, will soon be available. The latest version is available free for download and is sponsored by advertising banners.

Sun, the developer of Java, has produced a Java Web browser called HotJava that has gained limited acceptance in the market. The browser has small requirements and is designed to work on a variety of devices.

As a commerce site, a business cannot afford to limit its market by supporting only one type of browser. Careful testing of the site with a range of clients will limit unexpected and poor experiences. Many of the advanced designs use nonstandard functionality existing in only one of the browsers and thus keep potential customers away from the site. Even using common techniques, such as style sheets (a type of formatting templates discussed in Chapter 7), to enhance the appearance of Web pages could lead to irregular display on the client monitor.

An open-source project, www.mozilla.org, is developing another alternative to commercial Web browsers. Mozilla is a modular Web browser, designed for standards compliance, performance, and portability. The browser is targeted to be across-platform software. It has not been released in an official version but is downloadable as is. The current porting efforts include MacOS, UNIX, IBM OS/2, BeOS, Sparc Solaris, SGI-Irix, and Linux. The browser is expected to run under other devices (e.g., Palm Pilot) in a pure Java version. Additional projects such as DocZilla are intended to enhance the browser with better support for XML and SGML.

Browsers will have to be developed to support emerging technology with different needs. Microbrowsers are at various stages of development to adapt display to mobile devices with limited screen space and bandwidth (i.e., cellular). E-commerce organizations will have to adopt some of these new technologies to take advantage of emerging trends.

Web Servers

In a typical e-commerce project, selecting a Web server is a critical step. A **Web server** is a computer and associated software that is attached full-time to the Internet. The main software component of the Web server is the HTTP (hypertext transfer protocol) server. While it is referred to differently under various platforms, this component is present in all products to respond to HTTP requests. Under UNIX, it is called a daemon and is named HTTPD, a process running continuously. Under Microsoft Windows NT/2000, a similar service, named https, provides the same functionality. The software works by constantly monitoring network traffic and tending to requests for pages.

The legacy software, the back office, the network, the administrator preferences, and the development skills of the staff often dictate the decision. Web development tools and Internet trends are also part of this decision making.

A Web server is usually evaluated for overall performance and compatibility and interoperability with other components (internal and external). The first selection criterion for a Web server is performance. Users have a short attention span and will surf away from a site if performance is unacceptable, never to return. Development is a close second among the influential factors, since the developer needs a platform where the initial content can be developed effortlessly and successive changes will not be overly difficult once the e-commerce process is ongoing. A heterogeneous development/deployment platform is not unusual, but developers should be aware of the inherent risks.

A secure server needs management features to create classes of users, easily model the site, and assign different access rights to different users. To have the ability to scale up, multiple types of CPU, hardware, and operating systems should be supported. The various servers will likely run on different machines, for example, the Web server might run on an Intel platform under Microsoft NT or Linux and the database server could execute on a Sun SPARC server. A multiplatform solution provides some insurance that the architecture will not be overgrown too quickly and that the site is not locked in to a particular supplier or commerce service provider (CSP). Clustering capabilities and automatic fail-over could also be critical Web server adoption factors. Stability and reliability remain difficult issues. The server's stability has a tangible effect on availability and staffing levels. In a multiserver environment, restarting the servers numerous times during operations could shatter the company's image.

Functionality Checklist. The Web server is at the heart of most e-commerce platforms. It should support most of the following attributes:

- High-performance HTTP engine. This component is present in all products. Four common measurements of Web server performance are connections per second or requests per second; bytes per second; round trip or response time; and errors. In addition, a brief checklist addressing the performance issue of the HTTP engine should include functional compliance with HTTP version 1.1 or later, including persistent connections. Scalability of the architecture, potential to host multiple websites on the same machine (this also has security implications), integration of clustering for fault-tolerance, load balancing, and reliability and performance are also dimensions affecting real-world performance.

- Security. With the availability of a stronger encryption technology on a worldwide basis, this item will become a prominent factor on any Web server functionality list. As was discussed in Chapters 4 and 5, strong security can slow performance as all communication is filtered and encrypted. Hardware encryption will alleviate some performance bottleneck otherwise noticeable on low-end server hardware platforms.

- Interface to back end. The Web server is expected to offer integration with the back-end applications. Among these integration capabilities are support for common gateway interface (CGI), cross-platform interoperability for Internet server application program interface (ISAPI) and Netscape server application program interface (NSAPI) extensions and filters, Java servlets, Java server pages, open database connectivity through Java database connectivity (JDBC) and open database connectivity (ODBC), as well as remote method invocation (RMI) and common request broker architecture (CORBA) ORB support. ISAPI is a set of Windows program calls developed by Microsoft that permit the writing of a Web server application. NSAPI is the counterpart set of calls designed by Netscape to integrate applications with its servers. Both approaches are tightly matched with the Web servers and will run faster than a CGI application.

- Publishing capability. Most users also expect authoring and publishing tools for seamless development. While ad hoc methods can connect Web-authoring tools to any Web server, the popular Microsoft FrontPage extension facilitates remotely updating a site. Similarly, remote Netscape Composer file transfer protocol (FTP) capabilities, an integrated search engine, and automatic indexing server are useful benefits.

- Management and administration. On-site hosting ensures ready physical access to the Web server hardware, but remote hosting makes remote configuration capability a mandatory feature. The Web server should ideally be fully configurable through a secure Web browser. A graphical configuration interface will also facilitate rapid changes. However, editing of configuration files in a textual mode should still be available if the Web server is initially not running or if the configuration files are corrupted. When the e-commerce software is layered on the Web server software, integration of the two products should allow browser-based management of the Web store as well.

Comparing Web Servers.   With e-commerce websites, availability is a high priority. The Web server must have the underlying operating system capability to sustain lengthy operations without interruption. The ability of the Web server to add functionality and to control the website's content is the second priority. Various Web servers can be acquired for a variety of platforms. Table 6–1 lists the most popular Web servers and the platforms with which they are compatible. A more comprehensive

TABLE 6–1   Sample Web Servers

Server/Version	Operating Systems Supported
Apache 1.3.x (Version 2 Beta)	NetBSD, Digital UNIX, BSDI, AIX, OS/2, SCO, HPUX, Windows NT, Linux, Windows 95/98, FreeBSD, IRIX, Solaris
Commerce Server/400	AS/400
Microsoft Internet Information Server 5.0	Windows server 2000, Windows 2000 Professional
Java Web Server 1.1	OS/2, HPUX, Windows NT, Linux, Windows 95/98, IRIX, Solaris
Lotus Domino Go Webserver	Digital UNIX, AIX, OS/2, HPUX, Windows NT, Windows 95/98, IRIX, Solaris
iPlanet Enterprise Server	Digital UNIX, AIX, HPUX, Windows NT, IRIX
Oracle Web Application Server	HPUX, Windows NT, Windows 95/98, Solaris
Website Professional	Windows NT, Windows 95/98
Zeus Web Application Server	Digital UNIX, AIX, HPUX, Windows NT, Linux, IRIX, Solaris

alphabetical list of available Web servers and associated OS platforms is available at http://webcompare.internet.com.

Web servers are often used in conjunction with development tools to add content and functionality to the site. Affinity of the development tools and the Web server will improve productivity of both the development and the operating teams.

Other factors to be considered in selecting a Web server are:

- Product feature set, current availability, and likely product evolution path.
- Security.
- Built-in database connectivity and the availability of application development tools.
- Manufacturer's reputation, quality of technical support, and prior experience with this manufacturer.
- Purchase price, licensing, and maintenance cost.

Netcraft reports on almost 10 million sites, analyzes the leading Web servers, and lists what hardware/OS developers run on their websites.

The site also offers the capability of checking a site's security and the encryption services supported by its servers. Three Web servers account for almost 90 percent of the 10 million sites surveyed. At the beginning of 2001, the three Web servers at the top of the list are Apache (60 percent), Microsoft Internet Information Server (19 percent), and Netscape Communications Enterprise server, now renamed iPlanet Enterprise Server (6 percent).

The Apache Web Server. The Apache server, available free at www.apache.org, (see Figure 6–8) reliably and quietly serves more than 60 percent of the currently posted websites. The fact that it is free is only a partial explanation for its popularity. It is available on many platforms in both binary and source code format and has earned the reputation of being the most reliable Web server available.

Unfortunately, the production version of the Apache server's management is not easy to figure out. Its textual user interface is not user-friendly and remains an impediment to even greater success. In view of this weakness, an effort is under way to provide a graphical user interface to the configuration process. COnfiguration MANager for apaCHE (Comanche), as part of the Apache graphical user interface

FIGURE 6–8

Apache.org home page

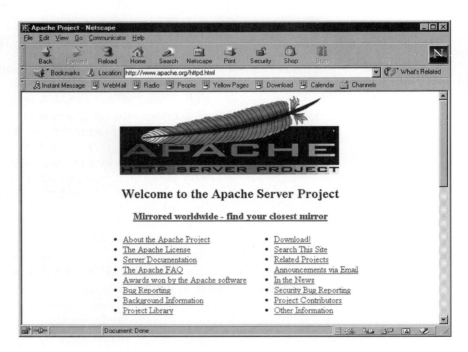

project, will provide a quality cross-platform graphical tool for configuration and management of the Apache Web server and related software. Comanche will run on most flavors of UNIX and Windows and even on Apple's Macintosh. In the meantime, the Apache server versions 1.3 and above use a new batch configuration method called Apache autoconf-style interface (APACI). This script streamlines the installation and configuration procedures. As noted, the product's availability in binary form for a number of operating systems and hardware and its source code availability ensure that the product will be supported by multiple sources.

As an open-source Web server, the Apache server benefits from many contributions from Web developers. They are available in the form of modules and are supported in many commercial distributions. While no software is bug-free, bug fixes are rapid in this open-source environment, and the product development cycle is timely. The server gets a growing number of features from numerous initiatives such as Jakarta, Tomcat, XML-Apache, Java-Apache, mod-perl, Apache::ASP, and mod-php. Large software house such as IBM have put their weight behind the effort. Jointly, these projects will support Java with Jserv, servlets, and Java server pages. With the upcoming version 2.0, in combination with the scripting ability (mod Perl, mod Php, and XML), Apache will reach a level of functionality that others will have difficulty matching.

On a lower-end server (e.g., an Intel Pentium PC with 64 MB to 128 MB of memory), the Apache–Linux combination performs better than Windows NT running IIS. This should be considered if performance problems occur with an underpowered setting. With a less powerful hardware server, *PC Magazine* found that the performance flattened out at an 8-client run for IIS, while with lower resource requirements, Linux flattened out at the 12-client level. Firms concerned with response time should watch for bottlenecks associated with the platform.

Microsoft Internet Information Server.   The second most popular Web server is the Microsoft Internet Information Server. Version 5 of IIS was released with Windows 2000. It now offers similar functionality in both the Windows 2000 server and Windows 2000 Professional products. Version 4.0 is still widely used. Microsoft released IIS with its NT server as a free component tuned for performance on the Intel platform. IIS 5.0 is installed by default with the Windows 2000 server but not with Windows 2000 Professional. A simplified version of IIS 4.0 was bundled for personal use as the Personal Web Server (PWS) running on Windows 95 or 98. While suitable for simple and rapid prototyping under Windows 95 and 98, it is not advisable to use PWS for a production e-commerce initiative.

FIGURE 6–9

*A Microsoft
information site*

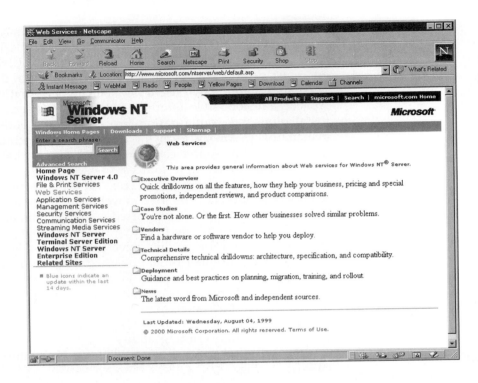

As the antipode of the Apache product, Microsoft IIS is intended to run on a single platform (e.g., Intel compatible processors and the Windows NT OS). IIS already dominates the NT market segment as an intranet server, winning numerous awards including Editors' Choice from *PC Magazine.* Additional information can be obtained from the Microsoft support website (www.microsoft.com/ntserver/web/default.asp) as shown in Figure 6–9.

The IIS popularity has spurred software developers to create an array of add-ons. Microsoft and its partners offer solutions for a full range of functions for the Web platform. Database access tools, e-mail, security, and managing and monitoring tools are relatively easy to find. While Microsoft optimizes the product for its own offerings, sites do use alternative technologies, such as script language and interpreter Practical Extraction and Reporting Language (PERL) or Personal Home Page Tools (PHP) instead of Active Server Pages (ASP) or Java Server Pages (JSP) and Java instead of Visual Basic, for their integration aspirations.

IIS is managed from the Microsoft Management Console (see Figure 6–10). This new mode of operation and its ease of use are the IIS's primary advantages. The IIS solution has scored well on benchmark tests

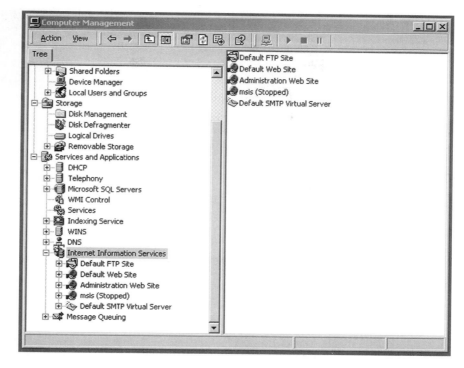

such as WebBench. IIS on Windows NT 4.0 ISAPI outperformed the competition, with more than 2,000 requests per second for simple dynamic comparisons and only slightly fewer for e-commerce dynamic comparisons. These measures, performed on a single server, bode well for the future of this solution, given that some of the alternatives, including Stronghold on Solaris and Sun Web Server (SWS) on Solaris, had fewer than 500 requests per second.

IPlanet Enterprise Server.   While it has lost some ground against both the free Apache products and the bundled Microsoft IIS, Netscape Communications' iPlanet Enterprise Server, under the corporate umbrella of America Online (AOL), excels in certain areas.

The Netscape Enterprise administrative console is intuitive to use, manage, and configure. The iPlanet servers support a range of platforms from Sun Solaris on Sparc and Windows NT. This solution has the advantage of working with most enterprise hardware. While the merger of AOL and Time Warner has raised some speculation for future development of this Web server, the current offering is a definitive alternative when running a Web server on a non-Intel platform. This stable server seldom requires rebooting and does not have system failures apart from

FIGURE 6–11

The Netscape server configuration screen

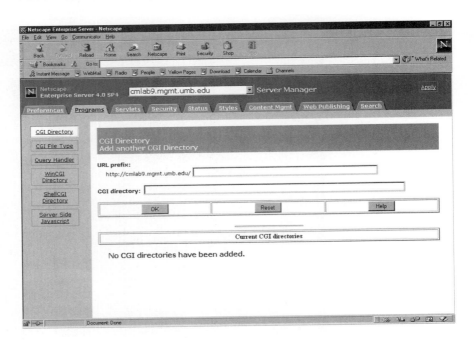

potential hardware problems. The Enterprise server is on a par with Microsoft IIS on Intel hardware and surpasses the Apache server under dynamic testing. The server can be configured through editing of the configuration text file. The newly reengineered Web user interface (WUI) has made it even easier to configure than Microsoft IIS. The WUI can be used to set up the server (see Figure 6–11), either from a Microsoft Internet Explorer or Netscape Navigator browser. Plus, an inexperienced user will welcome the well-designed context-sensitive online help.

Netscape has a strong alliance with Sun and emphasizes Java. The Web server ships with a number of Java libraries from Netscape. Users can download the latest development kit from Sun as an alternative to the Java libraries provided, but they should test previously developed servlets before installing a full upgrade to ensure compatibility of the upgrade with their applications. The iPlanet Enterprise runs on Windows NT, Solaris 2.6, 7 (binary compatibility), IBM AIX 4.2, 4.3 (binary compatibility), Digital UNIX 4.0d, SGI IRIX 6.5, HP-UX 11.0, and Microsoft Windows NT 4.0 (SP4+). Support for Linux, which runs many websites, was added with the introduction of version 4.1.

IBM/Lotus Domino. The IBM/Lotus Domino server was a popular solution for intranets and extranets of some large companies, but it is rapidly being supplanted by the IBM HTTP Server powered by Apache.

The IBM/Lotus Domino server, while not a Web server per se, offers an integrated messaging and Web application software platform for growing companies seeking improved customer responsiveness and streamlined business processes. For those growing organizations that want to deliver secure, interactive Web applications along with a solid infrastructure for messaging and collaboration in an IBM/Lotus environment, Domino servers are a good choice. Domino helps leverage existing investments in people, skills, tools, and back-end systems if the firm's legacy system used Lotus Notes. It works well with multiple software products for messaging, security, systems management, and data distribution and replication. It offers support for some platforms (e.g., AS/400 and IBM S/390) that have otherwise limited alternative Web servers. The Domino server is available for the other most popular operating systems, including Windows NT, Solaris, HPUX, IBM AIX, Linux, and OS/2.

Monitoring Web Server Performance. With corporate websites getting millions of hits per day, the performance of Web servers is a critical issue. For example, the 1999 Christmas season was marked by a number of highly publicized Web server outages. The 2000 buying season also experienced disruptions, crippling both Amazon.com and eBay.com. Most Web performance analysis has concentrated on two issues: overall network traffic and the performance of Web server software and platforms. Web servers that do not respond quickly under heavy loads can slow network connections. In an effort to improve Web server performance, benchmarks have been developed that include three main components: the load generator (clients); the workload(s); the measurements and metrics. The Internet Engineering Task Force (IETF) also is working on standards, and additional information can be found at http://io.advanced.org/IPPM/. Mindcraft is also a source for a number of well-known tools and reports on Web performance testing.

Performance Planning and Monitoring Tools. Performance planning and monitoring are essential to estimate the capacity requirements of a website. Web server performance can be studied in multiple ways: analysis of logs of active servers; instrumentation of network, server operating systems, and Web software; and laboratory testing (benchmark). A variety of companies offer monitoring tools.

- Mindcraft's WebStone was among the first software offered in the benchmarking arena. This free tool simulates a load on a Web server by channeling the activity of multiple Web clients, which can be thought of as users, Web browsers, or other software that retrieves files from a Web server. This simulation is carried out using multiple Web clients running on one or more computers.

It is possible to run in excess of 100 simulated Web clients on a single computer.

- WebBench 3.0 offers e-commerce test suites for each platform it supports. The product is distributed by Ziff Davis. The WebBench benchmarks are published for various Web server softwares running on the same hardware or by running a given Web server package on various hardware platforms. WebBench's standard test suite produces two overall scores for the server: requests per second and throughput as measured in bytes per second. It provides both static standard test and dynamic standard test suites, which execute applications that actually run on the server. In addition, users can easily create their own tests. PC clients must be running either Windows 95/98 or Windows NT, and the controller must be running Windows NT. Ziff Davis has other utilities such as ServerBench, to test the application server, and BrowserComp, to evaluate the features of various Web browsers.

- SPECweb96, which is available from Standard Performance Evaluation Corporation (SPEC), is a standardized benchmark for measuring basic Web server performance. It features full disclosures of the tested platforms on Standard's website. As the successor to SPECweb96, SPECweb99 continues the SPEC tradition of giving Web users an objective and representative benchmark for measuring a system's ability to act as a Web server.

- Web Capacity Analysis Tool (WCAT) and InetLoad from Microsoft are used to test Web, proxy, e-commerce, directory, e-mail, news, and cache servers. They run simulated workloads on client/server configurations. WCAT can test how Internet Information Services and network configurations respond to a variety of client requests for content, data, and HTML pages. The results of these tests can be used to determine the optimal server and network configuration. WCAT is specially designed to evaluate how Internet servers running Windows 2000, Windows NT, and Internet Information Services respond to various client workload simulations.

- Technovations offers two products relevant to e-commerce: WebSizr and WebCorder. WebSizr is a performance analysis application designed to size, benchmark, and debug applications using HTTP servers and applications. It can simulate workloads from hundreds of Web browsers. WebSizr can be used to characterize Internet/intranet and electronic commerce applications under load, in addition to sizing HTTP servers. It measures the various flavors of GET and POST requests. WebSizr also supports advanced paradigms, such as authentication, cookies, and redirects, to help the application developer engineer a high-performance application by providing the ability to scope into problems under user load. WebSizr also helps a system architect optimize and tailor an application to specific content and computing infrastructure.

• WebCorder is designed to capture and record HTTP transactions. In addition to the base HTTP requests, captured details include think times, client caching characteristics, browser signatures, and authentication. This gives developers rapid insight into any browser's conversation with the server. WebCorder records all these requests in a format compatible with WebSizr, which can replay these requests for load testing and performance analysis. WebCorder reduces the investment in developing scripts for WebSizr.

Another notable method used to measure both the performance and marketing aspects of a website is log analysis. When a visitor views the site, the date and time and the page visited are entered into the Web log file. Inspection of this file using an analysis tool can provide information about the navigation patterns and potential problems with the site, including potential breach of security. Examples can be found at www.infoport.com/loganal.htm.

• Net.Genesis offers two products for site analysis: Net.Analysis and CartSmarts. Net.Analysis provides the site analysis and insight required to increase sales, advertising revenue, and brand awareness and to improve customer service. It enables businesses to align customer data with business goals and benchmark and monitor these results over time, thus achieving a more competitive edge in the marketplace. CartSmarts creates more than 40 automated reports, such as purchase path conversion, shopping cart activity, purchase frequency and recency, and acquisition source, that help e-commerce companies better understand online visitor behavior patterns within the context of the online shopping cart environment.

• Aria by Andromedia, acquired by Macromedia, introduces a range of capabilities supporting both marketing and performance analysis. While the focus is on business intelligence (customer data analysis), many of the reports offer insight into a site performance. Among the reports generated are visitors, site objectives, traffic, navigation, and content reports.

• WebTrends offers a log analyzer as well as a comprehensive suite of products, including eBusiness Intelligence Solutions, eBusiness Systems Management, and eBusiness Security Management. The WebTrends Log Analyzer provides comprehensive analysis and reporting of Web server traffic. It can be installed on a Web server system or on any system that has a mapped drive, FTP, or HTTP access to the log files. The tool reports on Microsoft IIS and Site Server, Netscape, Apache, CERN, NCSA, WebSite Pro, Lotus Domino, Oracle, Open Market, IBM, and Novell. The reports review visitor behavior, advertising views, referring sites, visitor paths, and demographics. The WebTrends Log Analyzer generates customizable reports in HTML, Microsoft Word, Excel, ASCII text, and comma delimited format.

The number of software vendors offering log analysis with performance monitoring and business intelligence capabilities is increasing. Because only a small number of e-commerce site visitors make a purchase, it is difficult to evaluate the volume of connections from actual sales. A log analysis provides information about aborted transactions, statistics about the most and least visited pages, as well as other useful data. For example, WebTrends Commerce Trends Analysis keeps track of total visits, engagement rate (the percentage of visitors who become shoppers), conversion rate (the percentage of visitors who become buyers), total buyers, total shoppers, and total visits. The statistics help distinguish between the Internet surfers, visitors who have purchasing intentions, and visitors who will complete an order.

Application Servers and Database Servers

Advanced commerce website solutions include additional layers elicited either by the middleware/application server or the database server. This layer is illustrated by a database management system and a number of add-ons linking the system to the functionality of external partners. A **database management system** often acts as a buffer between the front-end processing linked to the Internet and the back-end functionality focused on administration, accounting, and logistics. Application servers play a role in the integration between the internal and external infrastructures of e-commerce.

Application Servers.   A recent addition to e-commerce architecture is the **application server.** There is no clear consensus as to what an application server is, but the software category is an extension of a middleware solution. The new goal for e-commerce is to achieve seamless integration of a supply chain, and application servers are part of the proposed blend of solutions. An application server is designed to make it easier for developers to isolate the business logic in their projects as well as to develop multitier applications with flexible connections. The trend is for application servers to be offered as components of more encompassing solutions integrated with Web development tools.

The functionality offered by the application servers is quite diverse. Before purchasing an application server, which can be expensive, answering a series of questions can delineate its fit to the existing or prospective e-commerce environment:

- What platforms are supported by the software? Most of the offerings will be for NT or UNIX, and alternative platforms such as Novell, IBM AS-400 or MVS, and Compaq VMS are rarely supported.
- Who makes the application server? In the current environment, mergers and acquisitions have a high impact on the survival rates of product lines.
- What programming language interface does the application server support? It should support a native interface to a number of programming languages such as C++, Java, and Visual Basic. Encapsulated interpreted code could be feasible, but at the cost of performance degradation.
- What portion of the existing applications portfolio will have to be rewritten to accommodate the new environment?
- What interfaces to the existing database management system are feasible? With the predominance of database-driven commerce websites, performance is more and more dependent on the connectivity between the application server, the Web server, and the database. Solutions to this connectivity include open database connectivity, Java database connectivity, and native drivers. The pooling of connections can help reduce the number of channels to the site and simplify resource allocation.
- What will be the direct and indirect costs of purchasing the software? Some software licenses are sold for a onetime payment; some involve license renewal every year or the payment of periodic maintenance and support fees. Some contracts include support and some imply a cost for support based on incident (e.g., through a telephone help desk).

A large number of application servers exist for many platforms. Application server suppliers include some of the Web server specialists and other heavyweights of the computer industry (e.g., IBM, Oracle, and Sun Microsystems).

- IPlanet application servers (www.iplanet.com/products/ infrastructure/app_servers/) list the products of the Sun–Netscape alliance, combining the existing technologies of the Netscape application server (with components acquired from the previous purchase of Kiva) and Sun's NetDynamics application server. This duality has led Sun to cease investing in the

FIGURE 6–12

*Oracle application
server*

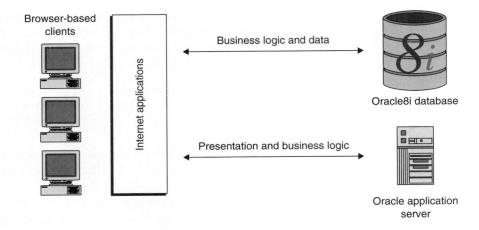

NetDynamics application server line. Associated with the Sun
tools division, reinforced by the acquisition of Forte and
NetBeans, the new emphasis is on Java-based tools.

- Oracle application server (www.oracle.com/appserver),
previously named the Oracle Web application server, is well
integrated with the Oracle DBMS and other Oracle development
tools, including JDeveloper, a Java-integrated environment
obtained under license from Borland (see Figure 6–12). Oracle
WebDB is an associated product that allows the development of a
website with the help of a set of wizards. In the latest version of
Oracle tools, there is also a clear trend to support the forthcoming
XML interoperation solutions.

- IBM WebSphere application server's (www-4.ibm.com/software/
webservers/) Commerce Suite 4.1 offers new, advanced
functionality necessary for the next generation of e-commerce
businesses. Businesses can attempt to increase revenues through
business intelligence, targeted customer loyalty, and relationship
marketing programs, including personalization, merchandising,
business analysis and reporting, order management, auctions, and
integration with existing systems and processes. This IBM offering
seamlessly integrates with other tools in the IBM development suite,
such as Visual Age for Java. A comprehensive support on the IBM
hardware platform is similarly expected up to the mainframe level
with e-commerce products for Z/OS and OS/390 operating systems.
IBM is working with a set of partners, such as i2 for the supply
chain and Ariba, to offer a complete solution to Web commerce.

- Sybase Enterprise application server (www.sybase.com/products/
easerver) provides a highly scalable, robust deployment

foundation for Web and distributed applications. As anticipated, the Sybase offering provides clear integration with Sybase DBMS products. Similarly, Sybase has enabled its development tools, Powerbuilder and PowerJ, with strong support for Web development. The Enterprise application server incorporates the capabilities of a component transaction server with a dynamic Web page server and support for Java 2.

- The BEA WebLogic application server (www.beasys.com) is part of the BEA WebLogic software suite, which delivers an e-commerce transaction platform for Web-based solutions and applications built using the latest distributed object technologies, including Enterprise Java and CORBA. BEA systems and Warburg, Pincus Ventures have established a new company (Web Gain) to develop a line of e-commerce tools targeted at simplifying e-commerce. They acquired the assets of Symantec's Visual Café and its pioneering Java product line to provide seamless development solutions.

- Borland application server (www.borland.com/appserver) simplifies and accelerates the development, integration, deployment, and management of thin clients and distributed enterprise software systems (see Figure 6–13). The environment is the output of strong experience with the ORB architecture from

FIGURE 6–13

Inprise application server

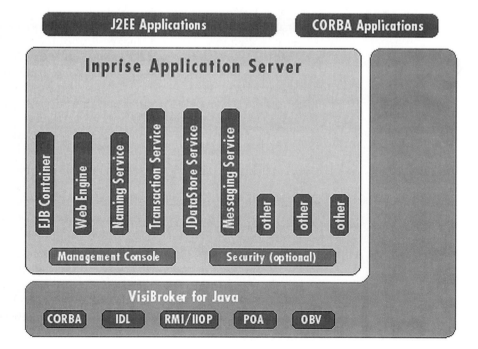

FIGURE 6–14

Allaire Spectra

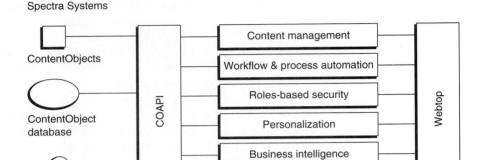

Source: Allaire 2001

Visigenics (a standard in CORBA solution), MIDAS, and the Borland programming tool set. Borland offers Delphi, C++Builder, as well as its Java tool, JBuilder, which is similar to the Oracle Jdeveloper product.

• Allaire ColdFusion (www.allaire.com/Products/ColdFusion) provides a fast way to build and deploy scalable solutions integrating browser, server, and database technologies. Allaire also offers Homesite, an HTML development tool. While its server uses proprietary tags, the integrated solution, combined with strong customer support, makes it popular with a number of small and medium-sized companies. In early 2001, Macromedia expressed its intention to acquire Allaire. If the merger materializes, the merged company should offer a strong offering from page construction software, graphics design, and content management to enterprise application servers. In addition to Coldfusion, Allaire provides Spectra (see Figure 6–14), which includes six core services useful to e-commerce.

• Apple's WebObjects (www.apple.com/webobjects) comes enhanced with new tools for building Java-based network applications (see Figure 6–15). The new development environment inherits the strong object-oriented foundation derived from the Next development tools and is a preferred tool for the Apple server platform.

The integration of the application server with the database server is an important factor in the overall performance of an e-commerce system.

Database Management System (DBMS).   Most DBMS vendors provide solutions or partnerships for e-commerce. While the priority of the

FIGURE 6–15

Apple WebObjects

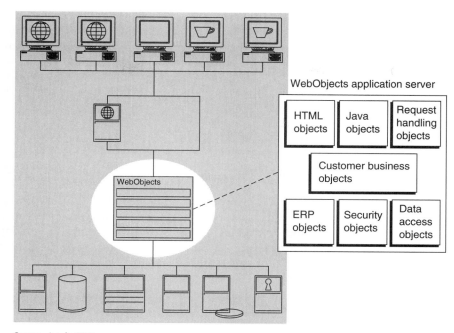

WebObjects application server

| HTML objects | Java objects | Request handling objects |

Customer business objects

| ERP objects | Security objects | Data access objects |

WebObjects

Source: Apple 1998

vendors a few years ago was to integrate with the leading ERP products, being an e-commerce component has become a new main objective. All the major software firms, including IBM, Oracle, Sybase, Informix, and Microsoft, have such initiatives. Smaller vendors, such as Progress Software, also have solid niches. All these providers, on their respective platforms, can sustain a Web initiative.

One key to success for transactional e-commerce is the smooth integration of the database with the storefront facing the customer and the ERP, the accounting systems, and the **customer relationship management** on the back end. Database vendors are also concerned with supporting online analytical processing and data mining as new essential components of a solid customer relationship management. For performance reasons, it is prudent to separate the operational database from the analytical processing of the data in a data warehouse. While the latter can tolerate asynchronous responses, the transaction system should be as close to real time as possible.

More Back-End Integration

The e-commerce components on the storefront are very important. Application servers and databases address the need for business logic in a layer inserted between the Web server and the back office. While they provide data access, validation, and manipulation, they do not provide all the functionality for end-to-end information flow. A comprehensive e-commerce strategy should also consider other components of a business system such as the accounting systems, ERP systems, inventory, billing, customer profiling, and customer relationship management.

Enterprise Resource Planning.   While **enterprise resource planning (ERP)** is considered in Chapter 11, here we discuss its importance for a successful integrated e-commerce project. In the 1980s, a business-to-business commerce solution called electronic data interchange (EDI) slowly made inroads in replacing telephone, fax, and proprietary systems. Key functions, such as order management, transportation, logistics, inventory management, warehousing, and tax management, were being integrated into a supply chain. After inventing, perfecting, and selling ERP, the major vendors are shifting gears from making the applications that streamline business practices inside a company to focusing outward to the rest of the world.

Outward-looking (the Internet) post-ERP models being developed include electronic commerce, planning and managing the supply chain, and tracking and serving customers. Most systems still lack integration, and mainstream ERP vendors have been slow to develop offerings for these areas. Inheriting monolithic systems, they face stiff competition from more nimble niche vendors. Nevertheless, ERP vendors have the advantage of a huge installed base of customers, a virtual stranglehold on back-office functions such as order fulfillment, and a good understanding of a variety of industries. Some ERP vendors are focusing on being the back-office engine that powers electronic commerce, rather than attempting to be in all the software niches that are necessary for a good commerce website. As the niche vendors make their software easier to hook into the supply pipeline, and as middleware vendors make it easier for information systems departments to join applications from different vendors, heterogeneous systems will become easier to integrate.

Electronic commerce represents a post-ERP architecture with the necessity of tightly managing the supply chain and tracking and serving customers on a faster cycle. Suddenly, businesses need to be concerned with the way the software looks, the way it requests information when reconfigured, and how the technology fits with staff skills.

In the information age economy, size is no warranty of stability. To respond to the e-commerce challenge, SAP, the leading ERP vendor, formed a new company in association with Intel, investing billions of dollars. The Pandesic architecture was a multitier, client/server architecture

FIGURE 6–16

Pandesic e-commerce platform

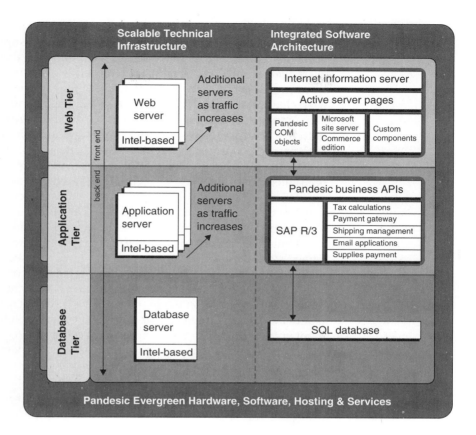

that clearly separated data, applications, and user interfaces using industry-standard data storage, transaction processing, and Web server software (see Figure 6–16). When demand for the solution failed to materialize, the partnership dissolved, leaving existing customers without any support.

Organizations need to keep their Web solutions options open, even if limited compatibility exists between the system components. Two technologies facilitating interoperability have been increasingly adopted, Java and XML. The extensible markup language (XML) covered in Chapter 7 represents the logical evolution from HTML to a more extensible Internet development language. Forthcoming support for Java and XML should accelerate the connectivity between tools. Seamless integration is often a key factor in the ultimate success of an e-commerce operation. Unable to accomplish a tight integration with its back-end ERP, a firm found that it was five times less efficient to take orders from the website and re-enter them into the ERP system than it was to merely take the orders over the phone.

SAP and many of its competitors, such as PeopleSoft and J.D. Edwards, are working to develop a new lineup of applications that are built from more Internet-friendly technologies than R/3, the SAP client/server product. Collectively called New Dimensions initiatives, these products, intended for supply chain management, business-to-business electronic commerce, business intelligence, and customer relationship management, are supposed to have friendlier user screens, work well with the Web, and be easier to use and maintain. But most of these promised products are not yet available, and those that are, do not have as much functionality as does software from a number of smaller, more nimble competitors, such i2 Technologies, which leads the supply chain market, and Siebel Systems, which dominates the customer relationship market. Given the rising importance of customer intelligence and personalization, this topic is explained in more detail in Chapter 11.

While it is important to integrate an e-commerce initiative with the legacy systems, most businesses do not have the necessary expertise. In an outsourced alternative, few **commerce service providers (CSP)** currently support the integration of the hosted site to the back-end processing of the firm based on the market leaders' ERP, such as SAP, PeopleSoft, Baan, and Oracle Financials, or emerging customer relationship management software such as Siebel and Vantive.

CSPs seldom support proprietary back-end systems, unless there are market pressures to do so. The quality of service and higher competitive pressures have encouraged CSPs to extend their flexibility. Integrating newly developed Web distribution channels with the existing architecture and culture of the firms will remain a major issue over the next few years. Most Web initiatives will live with their preexisting environment and will have to assemble their systems from heterogeneous parts.

Supporting Technologies

Web transactional systems use a number of associated technologies that support the integration of the heterogeneous components. Following are some definitions of terms associated with the Internet that are used repeatedly in the remainder of the book.

HTTP.   Hypertext transfer protocol (HTTP) is the underlying set of rules used by the World Wide Web. HTTP defines how messages are formatted and transmitted and what actions the Web servers and browsers should take in response to various commands. For example, entering a URL in a browser sends an HTTP directive to the Web server ordering it to fetch and transmit the requested Web page.

CGI.   Common gateway interface (CGI) is a specification for transferring information between a World Wide Web server and a CGI program.

A CGI program is any program, written in any programming language including C, PERL, Java, and Visual Basic, designed to accept and return data that conforms to the CGI specification. CGI programs are the most common way for Web servers to interact dynamically with users. Many HTML pages that contain forms, for example, use a CGI program to process the form's data when it is submitted.

PERL.   Practical Extraction and Report Language (PERL) is a programming language aimed at processing text. Because of its strong text processing abilities, PERL has become one of the most popular languages for writing CGI scripts. It is an interpretive language, thus making it easy to build and test simple programs. This multiplatform language has been widely adopted in the Web developer community.

Application Service Provider (ASP).   **Application service provider** is a new hosting service for applications where the user does not have to purchase the application but is remotely using the service executing on the provider premises. It is increasingly used for expensive or rapidly changing applications such as ERP. Using the same acronym as active server pages, it has created some confusion in the terminology.

Active Server Page.   **Active server page** (ASP) is a specification for a dynamically created Web page that utilizes ActiveX scripting, usually VBScript or JScript code. When a browser requests an ASP, the Web server generates a page with HTML code and then sends it back to the browser. ASPs are similar to CGI scripts, but they enable Visual Basic programmers to work with familiar tools. As CGI scripts, they suffer some performance degradation when multiple concurrent requests hit the Web server.

ActiveX.   ActiveX is an increasingly common way to provide dynamic feedback for Web users. It includes scripts or programs that run on the user's machine rather than on the Web server. These programs can be Java applets, Java scripts, or ActiveX controls. These technologies are known collectively as client-side solutions, while the use of CGI is a server-side solution because the processing occurs on the Web server.

An ActiveX control can be automatically downloaded and executed by a Web browser. ActiveX is not a programming language but rather a set of rules for how applications should share information. Programmers can develop ActiveX controls in a variety of languages, including C, C++, Visual Basic, Delphi, and Java.

Java Applets.   Java applets are programs executed from within another application. Unlike an application, applets cannot be executed directly from the operating system; they need a host application such as a Web browser to run. With the growing popularity of object linking and embedding, applets are becoming more prevalent for add-in and flexible component executing on demand.

Java Servlets.   Servlets are similar to applets except they run on a server. In general, the Java servlet runs within a Web server environment. Servlets are becoming a popular alternative to CGI programs. The major difference with CGI is that a Java servlet is persistent; that is, once it is started, it stays in memory and can fulfill multiple requests. In contrast, a CGI program disappears once it has fulfilled a request and must be reset at each invocation.

A number of servlets are available that enable the server side to answer **Java Server pages** (JSP) commands.

- Apache JServ distribution contains a module closely tied with the Apache Web server.
- Allaire, a pioneer of Web development tools, offers Jrun, which is one of the most widely adopted engines for developing and deploying emerging server-side Java applications that use Java servlets and Java Server pages. The first commercially available product to fully support the JSP 1.0 specification, JRun enables developers to add the functionality of server-side Java to their existing Web servers, including Microsoft's IIS, Netscape's iPlanet Enterprise server, and Apache.
- ServletExec 2.0 is a Java-based Web application server that implements the Java servlet API and Java Server pages standards. A developer can use ServletExec to quickly build reliable, portable, high-performance Web applications that can be deployed on any major Web server and operating system, including Microsoft IIS, Netscape FastTrack and Enterprise servers, Apache server, and Mac OS Web servers.
- ServletFactory is a free servlet development and deployment toolkit that enables users to deploy servlets on an ISP's Web server that supports only CGI.
- WebSphere application server is IBM's Java servlet-based Web application server that helps users deploy and manage Web applications, ranging from simple websites to powerful e-business solutions. The updated version of WebSphere provides users with an optimum foundation for Java-based enterprise applications.

Java Server Pages (JSP).   JSP is similar in principle to active server pages. As with ASP, JSP operates with a pair of technologies. The client page has embedded call, and the server side provides the functionality and transfers the resulting data back to the client. The difference between the two technologies is that the code embedded between the $<$% and %$>$ tags in JSP is exclusively Java, whereas ASP uses Microsoft Visual Basic. According to Sun Microsystems, JSP works with 85 percent of the Web server market, including Apache Web server, Netscape servers, and Microsoft IIS 4.0 with a required plug-in. A plug-in is a helper application that locks to the Web browser and extends its functionality.

The JSP technology is an extension of the servlet technology created to support authoring of HTML and XML pages. It makes it easier to combine fixed or static template data with dynamic content. Even if users are not comfortable writing servlets, there are several reasons such as portability, modularity, security, and scalability to consider JSP technology as a complement to existing work.

COM and COM+.   Microsoft **Component Object Model (COM)** is a model for binary code that enables programmers to develop objects that can be accessed by any COM-compliant application. Both object linking and embedding (OLE) and ActiveX are based on COM. COM is a framework for developing and supporting program component objects. It provides similar capabilities to those defined in Common Object Request Broker Architecture (CORBA), a framework for the interoperation of distributed objects in a network that is supported by other major companies in the computer industry. Whereas Microsoft's OLE provides services for the compound document that users see on their display, COM provides the underlying services of interface negotiation, life cycle management (determining when an object can be removed from a system), licensing, and event services (putting one object into service as a result of an event that has happened to another object).

DCOM.   The **Distributed Component Object Model (DCOM)** is a set of Microsoft concepts and program interfaces in which client program objects can request services from server program objects on other computers in a network. DCOM is an extension of COM and provides interfaces that allow clients and servers to communicate within the same computer that is running Windows 95 or a later version.

CORBA.   The **Common Object Request Broker Architecture (CORBA)** enables pieces of programs, called objects, to communicate with one another, irrespective of the programming language they were written in or the operating system they run on. CORBA is a nonproprietary alternative to Microsoft COM developed by an industry consortium known as the Object Management Group. The essential concept in CORBA is the object request broker (ORB). The ORB support in a network of clients and servers on different computers means that a client program, which may itself be an object, can request services from a server program or object without having to understand where the server is in a distributed network or what the interface to the server program looks like. To make requests or return replies between the ORBs, programs use the inter-ORB protocol (IOP). On the Internet, the Internet inter-ORB protocol (IIOP) maps requests and replies to the TCP layer in each computer.

JavaBeans.   JavaBeans is a specification developed by Sun Microsystems that defines how Java objects should interact. An object that conforms to this specification is called a JavaBean and is similar to an ActiveX control in the Microsoft environment. It can be used by any application that understands the JavaBeans format. The principal difference between ActiveX controls and JavaBeans is that ActiveX controls can be developed in any programming language but executed only on a Windows platform, while JavaBeans can be developed only in Java but can run on any platform.

Developing an E-Commerce Platform

Once the technology involved in creating an e-commerce website is understood, the project can start. The issue of building, buying, or renting e-commerce solutions should be addressed in initial site construction and in site upgrade, as well as part of site management. A decision to outsource has both technical and political facets, which need to be addressed early in the decision-making process. Various levels of size and complexity lead to a variety of alternatives. Figure 6–17 gives an overview of the alternative deployment practices.

FIGURE 6–17

Deployment practices

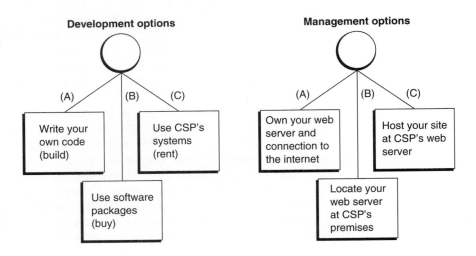

Part 1: Alternative Scenarios

At the most simple level is an informative site without transaction capability. This cannot really be considered an e-commerce solution, but it offers a new channel for providing information. An Internet service provider can host the website or it can be hosted by the organization itself at a higher cost but with more control. The Web pages can be developed either by an organization employee or a contractor using end-user tools such as Microsoft Front-Page, Adobe Golive, Macromedia Dreamweaver, or any other HTML editor. The most popular development platforms are Microsoft Windows and Apple Macintosh. Most ISP accounts provide an e-mail account that can be used to communicate with potential customers in asynchronous mode. In addition, support files (e.g., maintenance manuals, notice for upgrade, presentations, investors and partners relation news) can be stored or downloaded by visitors. If a site is to be only informational, design issues will not be overwhelming. Chapter 10 addresses issues such as what graphic format should be used to optimize bandwidth and look. At this level, the interactive features are limited and the maintenance is more static than for the other alternatives.

For small businesses that need transactions support, the scope of services is somewhat higher. For a hosted site, the basic hosting service offers disk space and the capability to conduct transactions. Additional services are charged according to the number of transactions. The service provider channels notification of the completed transactions back to the seller who takes care of the back-office functions such as shipping the product to the buyer from the warehouse. Merchant services in the form of a gateway to payment intermediaries add fraud prevention and detection to the site capabilities.

Hosted solutions have multiplied in the past two years as many small businesses and individuals enter the field and develop their own storefronts. In general, outsourced Web store hosting is suitable for small operations with a limited number of items listed in their catalog and marginal trading. The Web store developers have access to the most affordable e-commerce solutions, usually charging a low monthly fee ranging from $10 to $50. Large service providers also have entered this field in an aggressive manner along with the telephone companies. Most low-volume transactional sites either opt for a hosted solution with an ISP or a low-end package as follows:

- OLM with Miva Order has a Web-based order system and back-end processing that offer cross-platform (UNIX or Microsoft NT) support and integration with an existing site. It claims to currently be hosting in excess of 65,000 domains worldwide and offers a solution at $49.95 per month for a site of 8 gb transfer per month.

- The well-known e-retailer Amazon.com recently entered the fray of store hosting with its Zshop and a slightly different pricing model involving a listing fee and a completion fee based on the price of items sold. This may allow Amazon.com to leverage its investment in surplus capacity.
- E-BizBuilder advertises easy access to its online control panel. There a seller starts a Web store, enters the page content including graphics and log, adds shipping and taxes options, and then publishes the site.
- Yahoo!, the forerunner of Web portals, has its Yahoo!store, which offers unlimited bandwidth and 25 megabytes of disk space for a monthly fee of $29.95.

Most of the hosting solutions follow a sequence of steps in the Web building process and utilize Web-based wizards to enter or modify the catalog.

Before selecting an ISP, an organization needs to establish criteria to filter the crowd trying to assert themselves as e-commerce hosting services.

Selecting a Commerce Service Provider.   A set of criteria can be established to select the appropriate CSP for e-commerce websites. These criteria fall into four categories (see Figure 6–18):

1. Factors that facilitate the building of the site.
2. Factors that enhance the image of the vendor.
3. Factors that facilitate transactions.
4. Factors that expedite shipping and payment.

Factors Facilitating the Building of the Site.

- Portability of the site. This is a particularly complicated aspect because some site-building wizards can store a site in a proprietary, not downloadable format.
- Bandwidth of the host site. The published use of T-1, T-3, and OC lines will give only an indication of the available speed of the site. Another important statistic is the bandwidth ratio to hosted site (e.g., one T-1 line for 50 sites).
- Maximum number of items in the catalog. Restrictions can be either technical or monetary.

FIGURE 6–18

E-commerce deployment

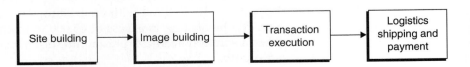

- Type of servers used. Operating systems and serv
  indicate the installed stability and security. In shared
  the operating system is a significant performance determ
- Support and backup systems offered. Support should be
  accessible on a round-the-clock basis. It would be a catastrophe t
  lose the site as a result of a crash and not be able to recover.

Factors That Enhance the Image of the Vendor.

- Flexibility of the site-building process. Most vendors want a
  branded storefront to build their own identity, rather than having
  a site under a hosting umbrella (e.g., www.interflora.com versus
  www.yahoo.flower99.com).
- Look and feel of the site. Look and feel should be fully configurable
  with the vendor templates, background, images, and looks.
- Promotional capabilities. It is important to find out what
  promotional capabilities the hosting agency offers, such as cross-
  selling if the agency acts as a mall.

Factors That Expedite Transactions.

- Order notification. The mechanism used for merchant notification
  could be e-mail, paging, or fax, depending on the merchandise.
- Administration security. It is important to find out if the orders
  are secure and what solutions are being deployed (e.g., firewall,
  encryption).
- E-mail capabilities. A number of accounts are provided. Standard,
  forwarding, and broadcast capabilities should be such that they
  will support transactions.

Factors That Facilitate Shipping and Payment.

- Automatic tax calculation. The tax solution should be flexible in
  terms of buyers' location and user location. Some states claim tax
  if the host is located on its premises (e.g., the vendor is in
  Massachusetts, the host is in California, and the buyer is in New
  York). The tax laws for e-commerce are being scrutinized.
- Payment options. Common options include simple credit card
  validation, CyberCash, CyberSource, CardService, and
  PaymentNet.
- Calculation of base and weighted shipping charges. The site
  should be able to allocate the shipping charge and assign a
  tracking number.
- International trade. The site should be able to address multiple
  currency formats.

...st outlines the complexity of the factors to be considered be-... decision is reached. Pricing structure of the service is another ...factor in selecting a provider. Price may depend on the num-...ms listed, the bandwidth available or used, the storage space, or ...ber of e-mail accounts provided. Some less technical issues such ...cial stability, security, and experience of the firm should also be ...ered before selecting an ISP.

...ne lower-end packaged approach is often used in conjunction with ...eb hosting service. An example of simple packaged software is ...uilder (see Figure 6–19). First, the site is developed offline and then ...loaded to the hosting networked computer. With many of these pack-...ges, configuration of the e-commerce site consists of taking steps through a wizard.

Most low-end packages provide an electronic **shopping cart**—software components or script (e.g., written in JavaScript) that allow the user to add/remove items to/from an order, total the order, and proceed to the checkout process where customer information such as shipping address and payment is entered—and facilitate the establishment of a merchant account with a bank or credit-processing organization. Cyberstore software such as Carello, Freemerchant, Web Business Builder, and iHTML Merchant Pro are available for free or for just a few hundred dollars and provide an inexpensive solution for getting started.

FIGURE 6–19

EcBuilder Pro software

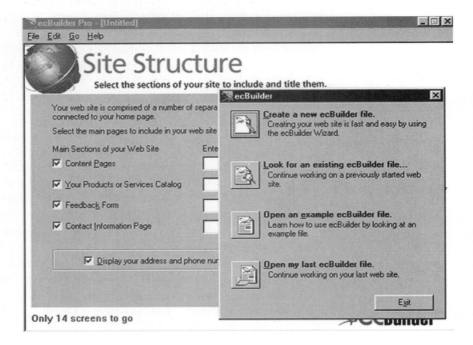

If organizations decide to assemble the site from components instead of a package, a simple electronic shopping cart can be extended with custom programming. The shopping cart should let users:

- Place an order for a product on the same page on which it is pictured and described. With a simple form that doesn't have that ability, customers have to write down the product name and catalog number so that when they get to the order form they can remember what they wanted.
- Order multiple times the same item with some variations, as well as different items. If customers leave a simple order form to find another product, it is possible to lose the information on the order form.
- Total all the items along with tax and shipping charges. Simple forms do not do any calculations or do so with extreme difficulty.

Examples of shopping carts include WebGenie, eCongo free commerce, EasyCart, FreeMerchant, Merchant Manager, and MerchandiZer. The carts are frequently offered in conjunction with hosting services. In addition, a number of carts implemented as JavaScript have been released as freeware (e.g., Xcart).

The Freemerchant site shown in Figure 6–20 is used by a number of small businesses or e-commerce cottage industries such as candy, yarn,

FIGURE 6–20

Freemerchant.com

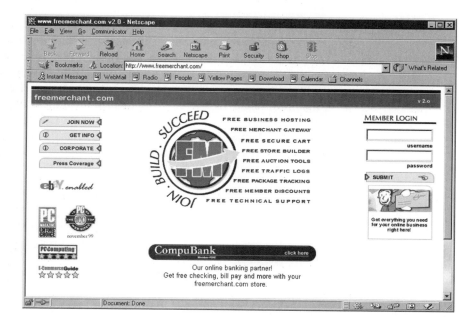

floral, gift, and handbag shops. Sites such as these benefit entry-level e-commerce solutions.

Building a Complex Site.   Medium-sized companies and organizations whose main distribution channel is the Web need to exercise caution in the transaction system. In this environment, the same logic applies in developing an e-commerce platform.

- Determine if the firm wants to develop its own website or buy one of the high-end, fully functional packages.
- Determine if the firm will host its own website or outsource to a CSP.
- Determine if the firm will manage its content or outsource.

Building a complex site also involves registering the site with its own domain name. Domain names can be acquired from a number of sources such as VeriSign, Register.com, and America Online. The maintenance of the domain right is secured by paying periodic fees.

For a medium to large organization, the lower-end packages will typically not be adequate to sustain the transaction level of an active e-commerce initiative. The average budget for a large e-commerce initiative exceeds $1 million. When deciding on a packaged versus a component-based design, the trade-offs are mostly a timing of the expense. For example, the Art Technology Group offers a commerce server with strong Java-based components architecture. While the initial costs can be as high as 30 to 40 percent of the budgeted investment, they can be recouped through lower development expense and flexibility when maintaining the site.

The packaged approach offers faster time to market. Both Microsoft and IBM are aiming at this segment with, respectively, Site Server Commerce Edition and the Websphere suite, which IBM offers through its line from the NT, UNIX, AS400, onto the large S/390 mainframe. Ease of maintenance within a vertical domain is promised by the offerings from BroadVision's One-to-One Commerce, InterWorld's Commerce Exchange, Netscape's SellerXpert or MerchantXpert, and Open Market's Transact. BroadVision, one of the larger e-commerce software specialists, has a number of prominent customers in a variety of sectors, such as financial services, retail, distribution, technology/manufacturing, telecommunications, and travel. Building on its strength and support by a number of consultancies, it is supporting such clients as American Airlines, Credit Suisse, Home Depot, Nortel, Sears, Xerox, and Wal-Mart. Most of these sites sustain a high load of transactions in real time (see Figure 6–21).

The greater up-front cost of these highly integrated solutions is balanced by less development and integration effort. The trade-off resides in the closer dependency on the provider and an ability to evolve with the

FIGURE 6–21

*Heavy traffic
transactional site*

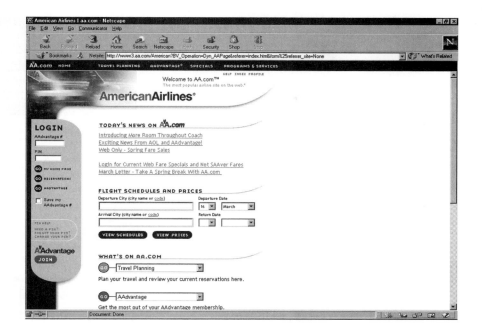

market. Most participants in the medium to large nonintegrated category use some external consultants to establish their sites.

Creating a Customized Site.   The most cutting-edge organizations, with large volumes of transactions, are likely to customize their sites to accommodate the volume of transactions and offer features such as personalization and integration with their back-office applications (for more on these issues, see Chapter 11).

While most of the software packages listed above aim at integration, none of them can cover an end-to-end service. Most of the sites from the largest e-commerce pioneers add some customized features. To provide information to the customer on an individual basis and targeted data to the marketing department, personalization and data mining are often implemented together. Netperceptions, one of the products offered in this segment, integrates with a number of e-commerce suites such as Allaire Cold Fusion, ATG Dynamo, BroadVision, IBM Net.Commerce, Intershop, Interworld, Microsoft Site Server, Open Market, Oracle I-Sales, and Vignette Story Server.

These customized sites often are used by organizations that are on their second iteration e-commerce solution. A typical example in this segment is Amazon.com, which has evolved to include a user-friendly customized interface and a personalization component tracking the history of the client (see Figure 6–22).

FIGURE 6–22

Amazon.com

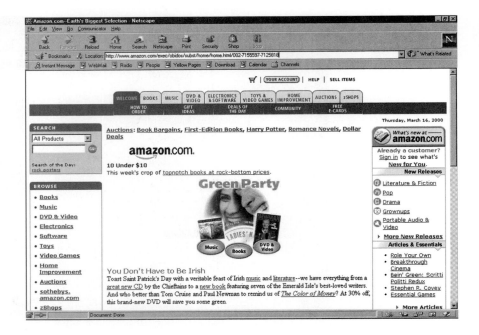

Part 2: Remaining Issues

Many questions have to be answered when developing an e-commerce integrated solution, including:

- Given constraints of time, budget, and business policies, should the firm adopt an off-the-shelf package, a customized solution assembled from heterogeneous components, or rent a turnkey solution from a Web hosting company?
- How can the firm create an end-to-end flow in the ordering process? This concern appears in competitive environments and is becoming more apparent as the industry attempts to become more efficient.
- Should the firm host its own site or host it at a CSP?

Deciding to build an e-commerce site is becoming a strategic decision. All organizations are likely to become more dependent on e-commerce for some aspect of their operations. In contrast to the pioneers of electronic commerce, many alternatives are now available. Many packages exist in the market and determining which one to use, if any, is complex.

As the volume of transactions increases, a potential traffic bottleneck becomes more likely. Full capacity or marginal capacity can be acquired from colocation providers.

Colocation and Managed Sites.   **Colocation** is hosting the server at some Internet backbone location, either at an ISP or one of the telephone companies. Colocation preserves the ownership of the equipment and content, and the firm's employees do the administration remotely. Managed sites have features similar to colocation, but the administration of the site is relegated to the CSP as an outsourcer. Colocation is a variation on the store hosting option that is primarily used by large e-commerce sites. This solution affords more options for control and customization from the site developer. The firms can have their own software and hardware but leverage the bandwidth capacity of the ISP. In addition to ready access to a larger bandwidth than the organization would otherwise afford, lower maintenance is also an advantage. This complex and expensive solution still relies heavily on the hosting organization for support. The more extreme solution is to outsource the management of the site to the CSP. In this environment, the CSP operates the site, including its security, its backup, and in some cases the maintenance of the commerce software. Familiar examples of bandwidth, content delivery, and colocation providers are Exodus (see Figure 6–23), IBM, GTE, and Akamai.

The Purchasing Decision.   Purchasing an e-commerce system can range along a continuum from a platform and toolkit approach to an integrated

Figure 6–23

Exodus.com

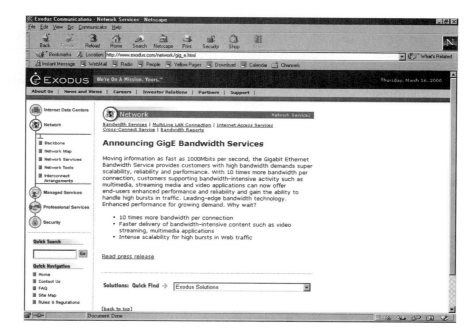

software package approach. One of the main differences between the two approaches is the dissimilar blend of expenses along the life cycle. With a platform and toolkit, the initial investment is relatively modest, but customization efforts and maintenance are more costly and complicated. With a packaged solution, the initial cash outlay is large, with the expectation of less operational costs. The current average cost of an integrated commercial storefront is about $1 million, with an estimated 70 percent going to customization and installation fees. In the case of the platform and toolkit option, the initial spending may account for only 5 percent of the total budget.

As solutions abound in the integrated suite category, it is useful to present a comprehensive set of evaluation criteria for an enterprise commerce server. The following is a partial list of items important in the decision:

- Functionality, as measured by the ability of the product to address all aspects of the selling side of e-commerce. In addition, if integration with the supply chain (internal and external) is the main objective, additional requirements should be included. Functionality can be organized along the lines of:
  - User interface tools/components (front office).
  - Performance monitoring tools/components (background process).
  - Authentication and security tools/components (front office).
  - E-business service/transaction tools/components (main functionality).
  - Supply chain management package (interface).
  - Commerce payment services tools/components (partner/third party).
  - E-relationship management services tools/components (marketing).
  - Decision-support services tools/components (back-office data analysis).
  - Application integration tools/components (gateway to CRM, ERP, and external systems).
  - Enterprise e-business application services (glue between the Web server and the rest of the transactional functionality).
- Cost criteria, based on acquisition expenses, license fees, application development, integration and customization, additional hardware, and networking devices. While cost is likely to be very diverse from one solution to another, it is important to have an encompassing checklist. Due to the competitive/strategic nature of most e-commerce initiatives, management is unlikely to deny spending large amounts associated with e-commerce but will be very concerned about erroneous estimates.

- Time to market. Often, due to the seasonal and competitive nature of the field, a delay of just a few weeks could amount to large opportunity losses. It is important to obtain estimates of schedules, client references, and templates to hasten the implementation.

- Ease of use for developers, administrators, content managers, and customers. While the use of consultants and external contractors is a general practice during the initial e-commerce project, the ongoing operation should be smooth and practical. Internal content developers should have an easy method to evolve the site within flexible architecture.

- Performance from an internal and customer perspective. Many aspects of performance bind the e-commerce solution. A scalable system should have a resilient core and paths to adapt the site to an increased load. To predict performance, stress and load pilots and simulation should be conducted using some of the performance measuring tools previously mentioned. Under real load, benchmark tools can be used to duplicate burst in connections (for example, using Microsoft inetload, Ziff-Davis WebBench, or Mindcraft WebStone). This provides an evaluation of responses to stress and helps uncover the limits of some alternatives. For example, components linked by smart CGI programs could perform well under light usage but collapse past a breaking point when subject to heavy usage. If the site has to be re-architected, it is better to know it in advance. Simulation and benchmarking are also useful in determining the effects of variations due to the graphics (or scripts or applets) intensity of the pages. Building the infrastructure to accelerate a site may require the purchase of better servers, page caching, network bandwidth, hardware encryption, and load balancing between replicated sites.

- Extensibility, the ability to integrate with third-party add-ons. Both platform and toolkits and packaged solutions offer this attribute. The important criterion is to have flexibility to extend the solution or have embedded mechanisms to bolt in third-party modules. Different vendors opt for either a bolt-on approach or a partnership allowing inclusion with the package. Microsoft Site Server Commerce Edition adopts a processing pipeline with steps where partners such as VeriFone, CyberCash, Trintech, ICVerify, and PaylinX can add their functionality to the base platform. InterShop has a Visual Pipeline Manager and Pipeline Orchestrator within "enfinity," which offers predefined standard and customizable configurations. InterWorld calls its solutions business adapters, which facilitate integration with ERP, supply chain management, customer asset management, sales tax calculation, shipping and fulfillment calculation, payment processing, digital product clearinghouse, and ZIP code. Other providers have parallel answers based on the same set of prime providers.

- Flexibility and nimbleness. Business processes change and alliances shift rapidly, inducing changes in configuration and expected functionality. The future will involve more customization for one-to-one sale, distribution of the delivery process while retaining control of the end-to-end supply chain, and globalization of e-commerce.

The vendors themselves should be evaluated with regard to long-term viability and quality of service. The performance of business partners, from hardware providers to the CSP service level, will be reflected in the opinion customers have of the organization. A customer-oriented system will lead development of the website as customer taste evolves. The software and, in a large measure, the skills available to the organization will influence the platform that can be adopted.

In addition to the marketing and selling function, e-commerce is also charged with the fiduciary/agency role of managing the information assets collected from customers. This additional role has its potential and threats. The potential is the competitive advantage of mining customer data to better serve these stakeholders, thus increasing profits. The reverse side is the potential threat to privacy and its concurrent legal entanglement.

While the business-to-consumer market has been in the limelight, business-to-business volume will count for a much larger share of the traded value and increase e-commerce predictability. Business-to-business commerce is based on the tradition of the EDI legacy and benefits from understood procedures and protocol. Establishing an e-commerce site for this market is aided by the ability to better forecast transaction volume and timing. The somewhat simplified workflow of a business-to-business transaction is as follows:

- The buyer browses the supplier website.
- A custom catalog is presented to the buyer.
- The buyer orders items.
- The order and payment method are confirmed.
- The order is accepted and forwarded to back-office applications for processing.

The key requirements for the business-to-business site are a high level of security and trust. The payment mode is dominated by corporate procurement, and store prices are adjusted for each vendor–buyer pair. A purchase order should be an option in the system.

In the business-to-consumer market, a planning and purchasing pipeline is a useful framework for building the website. This top-down model allows for decomposition and outsourcing of segments along the workflow process. The common elements of a planning pipeline include:

- Collection of product information.
- Merchant information.
- Shopper information.
- Order initialization.
- Order check.
- Item pricing.
- Item price adjustment.
- Order total.
- Shipping arrangement.
- Handling arrangement.
- Taxation.
- Inventory management.

The purchase pipeline involves:

- Checking the order.
- Checking the payment.
- Accepting the contract.

Website design decisions are influenced by customers becoming more educated about the market and competition constantly adding value and features to their solutions. The customers are expecting value and timely (24 hours a day, seven days a week) availability for execution of their orders, and they are increasingly using intelligent buying agents to probe the Internet in search of a bargain. They also wish to order anytime, from anywhere, and track the shipment of their goods in near real time.

Platform decisions may be influenced by the capability of the organization's employees and the budget, but other factors should be considered when refining the e-commerce architecture. A firm may list the desired Web server, commerce software, and design concept and then decide to build and host the site itself or look for a CSP that supports the chosen options. The alternative is to look at various CSPs and their supported platforms and then adapt the firm's vision to that offering.

Summary

During the next two years, the e-commerce landscape will change radically. The pendulum is swinging between the alternatives for companies of running their own e-commerce infrastructure or using storefront services. All solutions will float toward similar end results. At the beginning of the chapter, we described the array of components of e-commerce architecture: the Web browsers, the Web server, the application server, the database server, and the ERP and accounting subsystems.

Many organizations are beginning to realize that scaling up remains a major issue. Informational and transaction sites have content that can be delivered more efficiently by third parties with the proper infrastructure. Large firms should consider service providers for content distribution as a complement to their own bandwidth capacity. While better e-commerce packages appear on the market, the level of specificity of the website will mandate either a packaged solution or a custom design.

In e-commerce, many firms are going back and forth attempting to identify a better alternative to their current situations. For example, Britannica.com Inc. is considering scrapping its Open Market Inc. catalog software because it is not flexible enough. VitaminShoppe.com hinted that it would likely replace its Microsoft Site Server, which has provided it with a quick and relatively inexpensive entry to e-commerce, with a customized database-driven site. On the other hand, a number of firms flock every day to managed CSPs after they realize that they have neither the time nor the skills to develop and host their own solutions. Others are joining Web marketplaces, where they benefit from a standard Web presence without incurring high costs, but they may miss out on the competitive advantages of a unique Web presence. A mixed approach to e-commerce supplements packaged solutions with components, such as customization, personalized marketing, and customer profiling. Table 6–2 shows available e-commerce approaches.

Many small companies tend to adopt low-end packaged solutions or are lately moving to storefront services. The low-end packages are a way for firms to engage in e-commerce with an initially low investment or to supplement traditional distribution channels. Web hosting solutions are appearing at both the low end and high end of the spectrum. At the low-end websites, hosting solutions are appropriate for low transaction volume and a small number of listed products. Many companies in the small to medium-size range of less than $1 billion are opting for either packaged software or hosted storefront service. Large companies mostly elect sophisticated integrative packages, including links to front and back offices, or built-to-order solutions. At the high end, expensive integrated packages are adequate with customization for the high volume and numerous listings. Waiting for a perfect alternative is not feasible. In the meantime, having a flexible platform is a necessity. An agile platform will ensure survival of the firm in the event of growth, downsizing, and merger.

TABLE 6 – 2   E-Commerce Solutions

Company Size	Level of Customization	Suggested Hosting	Package	Transaction Volume	Nature of Site
Small	Low	ISP	Custom	None	Information site
Small	Medium	ISP	Entry	Low	Entry-level, transactional
Small	High	ISP	Entry+	Low	High impact, low budget
Medium	Low	CSP	Package	Low	Low impact, supplemental channel
Medium	Medium	Host	Package+	Medium	Important, medium budget
Medium	High	Host/CSP	Custom	High	High impact, high budget
Large	Low	CSP	Integrated Package	Medium	Low impact, supplemental channel
Large	Medium	Host	Integrated Package+	High	Strategic, integration
Large	High	Host/CSP	Components Custom	High	Strategic, competitive+

Key Terms

Application server   208
Active server page   217
Application service provider   217
Benchmark   205
Browser   194
Colocation   229
Commerce service providers (CSP)   216
Common object request broker architecture (CORBA)   219
Component object model (COM)   219
Customer relationship management   192

Database management system   212
Distributed component object model (DCOM)   219
Enterprise resource planning (ERP)   214
Hardware   186
Hosting   221
Internet service providers   221
JavaServer pages   218
Shopping cart   224
Web performance   205
Web server   196

Review Questions

1. List the most common Web browsers.
2. Access the Web and use a search engine to find the latest version of the most popular Web browser. What are its new characteristics? How much does it cost, if anything?
3. What are the hardware requirements of the most popular browser? How much storage space does it require? What type and version of operating system does it require?
4. When were the current versions of the most popular Web browser released?
5. List some application servers. Access the Web and find the latest version of the application servers mentioned in the text. When were they released? Can you make any conclusion about the release cycle of Internet software in comparison to other business software (e.g., spreadsheet, word processor, accounting packages)?
6. List some commercial database management systems. What are the current characteristics of these products?
7. Go to the websites of IBM, Oracle, Informix, and Sybase. Is there any mention of e-commerce associated with their database products? What suite or partnership do they list with related e-commerce offerings?
8. List the main Web servers. What types of companies are offering the leading servers? Distinguish between the open source and proprietary products. Who is providing support for the products? How much do they cost? Do you think the Web server purchase price is a significant factor in the budget considerations for a large e-commerce initiative?
9. List some software solutions available for small, medium, and large e-commerce sites.
10. Access the Web and find the current rate for website hosting. What are the criteria used by the ISP for pricing?
11. Why is the perception that integration will become a critical factor gaining in importance? What is the role of ERP within the enterprise software architecture? What is customer resource management and why is it important to e-commerce?

References, Readings, and Hyperlinks

1. Cataudella, Joe, Dave Greely, and Ben Sawyer. *Creating Stores on the Web*. Berkely, CA: Peachpit Press, 1998.
2. Minoli, Daniel, and Emma Minoli. *Web Commerce Technology Handbook*. New York: McGraw-Hill Series on Computer Communication, 1997.

3. Mougayar, Walid. *Opening Digital Markets: Battle Plans and Business Strategies for Internet Commerce.* New York: McGraw-Hill, 1997.

4. Nemzow, Martin. *Building CyberStores: Installation, Transaction Processing, and Management.* New York: McGraw-Hill, 1997.

5. Treese, G. Winfield, and Lawrence C. Stewart. *Designing Systems for Internet Commerce.* Addison-Wesley, 1998.

6. www.ecommerceadvisor.com/articles/index.html publishes articles from website basics to reports on specific topics of e-commerce.

7. www.ecommerce.internet.com distributes news about e-commerce. It also hosts a number of guides related to e-commerce servers, auction builders, portal, payment solutions, and storefront builders.

8. www.WebDevelopersJournal.com publishes a number of related articles covering e-commerce. Topics range from building a simple e-commerce site, to e-commerce tutorial, to comparison of shopping cart software.

9. www.webreview.com illustrates many useful topics related to e-commerce including articles on storefronts and discussion about the issue of building or buying.

10. www.zdnet.com/ecommerce/filters/resources/0,10385,2181778,00.html site offers information and tips about e-commerce.

Appendix 6.A
Hardware

The hardware in the front and the back office should operate transparently to support user-friendly e-commerce software. Visiting the commerce website should be a rewarding experience. The decision to purchase particular hardware is highly dependent on the chosen software. Thus, hardware acquisition should be postponed until the firm has decided where to host the website.

Since an Internet business is intended to operate around the clock, downtime has to be avoided so a system resilient to failure is essential. Fault tolerance can be achieved by having multiple systems running in parallel with some fail-over mechanisms or by having alternative sites as hot backups. In addition, the production system should be protected by redundancy storage capacity. While a traditional business could schedule offline time for backup, an e-commerce business can achieve a safe status only with incremental backup associated with some Redundant Array of Inexpensive Disks (RAID) system, which is an array of inexpensive drives offering redundant storage of data. When designing the website architecture, adding a RAID system, in which disks can be swapped without shutting down the system, contributes to achieving resiliency. As such, when deciding on the hardware for the Web server, the application server, the commerce server, and the variety of back-end servers, this capability should be considered.

A server should demonstrate reliability, high availability, serviceability, manageability, scalability, and expandability. If the system cannot be shut down to install hardware and software upgrades, a mechanism should be in place to allow online substitution of modules. This capability has been in place since the 1980s on mainframe and UNIX computers, but it is only starting to emerge on Intel-based machines. Hot-plug and hot-add peripheral component interconnect (PCI) capabilities on the Intel platform should be assisted by management features leading to early detection of failure.

A partial checklist for evaluating hardware servers should include attributes measuring performance, availability, manageability, and service:

- Processor support in terms of type, number, and microprocessor speed.
- Front-side bus mode and speed.
- Cache levels and size.
- Memory supported minimum, standard, maximum, and type; error conecting code (ECC) with reporting.
- Disk storage, number of free bays, type, and access speed.
- Hot swap drives: number and maximum capacity.
- SCSI controllers: number, type, and fault tolerance features.
- Other internal storage and other external storage support.
- Support for PCI-X or Net Generation I/O (NGIO) and support for Fibre-Channel or Intelligent I/O; total IO slots.
- Clustering support.
- Automatic server restart.
- Redundant network interface card IC: how many?
- Integrated disk array controller; RAID level supported: standard or option; cluster management software.
- Vendor support: where, when, service level agreement, and costs.
- Web hardware monitoring.
- Ability to exchange components while the system is in operation: hot-plug hardware; hot-swap fans; hot-swap power supply; availability in rack form for space management.

PART

4

SOFTWARE SOLUTIONS FOR E-BUSINESS

CHAPTER

7

LANGUAGES FOR THE WEB: HTML, XML, AND BEYOND

Chapter Outline

Learning Objectives

By the end of this chapter, you should be able to:

- Differentiate between HTML and XML and appreciate the role of XML in e-business.
- Create an XML document that uses a simple cascade style sheet and displays its content in an Internet Explorer browser.
- Learn how to use an external document type definition (DTD) file to specify the document structure required for an XML document.
- Write an extensible style sheet (XSL) to specify the formatting requirements of a document and appreciate how its programming features are used.

- Distinguish between the static and dynamic modes of a Web page.
- Define the current state of the practice in Web page composition.
- Practice with the most common events of DHTML.
- Describe how the choice of image format affects performance in the context of limited bandwidth.
- Have a brief overview of programming options.
- Understand the important trends coming in the near future.
- Comprehend the standardization effort of various associations.

Chapter Overview

The chapter introduces the programming languages and building blocks of the World Wide Web. Different languages enable the publication of interactive e-commerce websites. The chapter covers three aspects of content delivery. The first covers the group of languages (including HTML, DHTML, and style sheets) aimed at formatting the content and focusing on the aesthetics of the page. The second facet (XML) addresses the structural and semantics aspect of the content. The third provides a capsule description of the scripting languages, which execute the procedural aspect of content interaction. From the old tools such as HTML to the newer approaches exemplified by XML, a range of techniques and languages help the developer compose Web pages for e-commerce. Most documents stored on Web servers are displayed through some version of HTML. After introducing the basic types of HTML, the chapter considers some of the more recent introductions to Web page technology, such as dynamic HTML, style sheets, and various aspects of XML. The rising number of applications built on XML illustrates the dynamism of the technology. From RosettaNet and XML style sheets to Biztalk, the tide of XML applications relating to e-commerce is growing dramatically.

Scripting languages are powerful tools that enable the processing of data and the interface of Web pages to external applications. From traditional CGI to the most recent use of active server pages or Java server pages, the options available to connect a website to the back-office processing have proliferated. This chapter discusses standard solutions such as JavaScript and VBScript as well as some of the less common alternatives such as Coldfusion and PHP. Finally Java, the programming language most related to network and the Internet, is briefly described.

A Business Vignette

Harbinger Net Services, now a part of Peregrine Systems, a worldwide supplier of electronic commerce software, services, and solutions, revealed that its customers are adopting eXtensible Markup Language (XML) and Internet e-commerce technologies at a record pace. More than 40 percent of the company's desktop customers moved to XML-enabled technologies in 1999. XML is an emerging data standard that greatly facilitates the exchange of e-commerce transactions over the Internet and promises to further accelerate the widespread adoption of business-to-business e-commerce.

Harbinger registered its 5,000th XML customer in December 1999, when ABSCOA Industries, a distributor of critical parts to the aerospace industry, signed on for service on the company's business-to-business e-commerce portal. In doing so, ABSCOA benefits from the new technologies, including the capability of performing real-time transactions and having access to a host of free and low-cost services such as around-the-clock online customer care, instant downloadable software for new releases, enhancements and upgrades, and free access to Harbinger's online e-commerce resource center.

Harbinger expects the rate of conversion to XML and Internet technologies to continue to rise at a steady pace, and industry analysts tend to concur. The latest estimates in a study from Reuters project business-to-business e-commerce to rise an estimated 33 percent by 2003, to $2.8 trillion, equaling one-quarter of all corporate purchasing, according to the Boston Consulting Group.

Source: "Higher Growth Rates Predicted for B2B E-commerce" Boston Consulting Group, December 1999.

Introduction

The Web has a short history, but from the beginning, it has been a fertile ground for experiments and innovation. The mode of expressing content for display or processing through the Internet has followed cycles associated with a changing focus. The original intent was to get something on the Internet with simplified tools. To that end, the pioneers adopted the Standard Generalized Markup Language (SGML), maintaining the idea of the markup language and the hypertext paradigm of navigation and eschewing all complex features. The result was the HyperText Markup Language (HTML). The original initiators were physicists who did not want to get overwhelmed by marginal issues not part of their main interest, the distribution of preliminary physics research. As a presentation and navigation language, HTML had apparent weaknesses, and as it evolved, complexity found its way back into the language.

Capabilities were added to position the content within the pages, but these features were relatively fragile. The next idea to emerge was to make the language more flexible. Dynamic HTML (**DHTML**) was developed outside a standardization process and as a result, it has not been widely adopted due to the divergent support from the leading browsers. This difference between browsers still exists and if DHTML is utilized, careful testing is essential.

A new development used to develop coherent content is the segregation of the content from formatting. Standardization and policies enforcement can be achieved by the creation and use of a style sheet. Two successive recommendations were adopted by the W3C: (1) cascading style sheet (CSS1), which is becoming widely adopted by the major browsers, and (2) CSS2, which adds more capabilities and complexity to the use of style sheets and is not yet widely supported. A modularized standard effort is now under way as cascading style sheet 3 (CSS3). The goal is to streamline the standardization process and be able to build specific tests for various modules of the recommendation. This will help implementers in deciding which portions of the CSS to adopt and support.

The latest development of the Internet community is the eXtensible Markup Language (XML). XML has attracted a wide range of support from Microsoft to IBM. It could be the most relevant upcoming standard to enable the next generation of websites. From an e-commerce perspective it is very important because XML will provide a means of defining structures bridging front-end to back-end subsystems.

Another meaningful document format on the Web is Adobe PDF (portable document format). The proprietary format allows organizations to distribute complex documents preserving their original style. Viewers and add-ins exist for most platforms. Available for free, these viewers have extended the reach of an otherwise marginal tool. The PDF is not intended as a Web page design method, but as a powerful downloadable method.

The Origins of Web Languages: SGML

The **Standard Generalized Markup Language (SGML)** grew out of development work on generic coding and markup languages in the early 1970s. SGML is a formal standard, forged and agreed on by an international community working under the auspices of the International Organization for Standardization (ISO). The full name is ISO 8879 Information Processing Text and Office Systems—Standard Generalized Markup Language (SGML). The first edition was published in 1986, and its first amendment in 1988.

SGML prescribes a standard format for embedding descriptive markup within a document. More importantly, and crucial to its real value and power, SGML also specifies a standard method for describing the structure of a document. It has an open-ended definition, reflecting the diversity of information needs in industry. SGML does not directly define any types of content data and thus does not restrict the type of data contained in a document. It is sufficiently flexible to be able to describe any logically structured set of information, whether it is a form, a memorandum, a letter, a report, a book, an encyclopedia, a dictionary, or even a spreadsheet or database. SGML's sophistication has preempted wider adoption on the Web. It is aimed primarily at professional content developers and has its own constituency that is attempting to standardize information exchange among members.

SGML itself is not a markup scheme. It does not define markup tags nor does it provide a template for a particular type of document. Rather, it denotes a means for describing any markup scheme. By using SGML, many markup schemes can be developed, one for each document type or class. This is both a strength and a weakness in SGML.

SGML is still mostly viewed as a format for use in publishing printed documents and multimedia CD-ROMs. Publishing was the original purpose of the standard, but it was soon apparent that it had far greater potential outside the publishing industry. SGML is regarded as a possible means to save information for the long term in a stable format at the cost of higher complexity. The Association of American Publishers (AAP) has developed the electronic manuscript preparation and markup, a general-purpose document type definition (DTD) for publishers, authors, and editors. The Air Transport Association (ATA) has several DTDs under the ATA-100 specification. Similarly, the American Trucking Associations has initiated a task force to establish the standard for electronic service information. The U.S. Department of Defense created the computer-aided acquisition and logistic support (CALS), recently renamed the continuous acquisition and life-cycle support, which is intended to reduce the cost of supporting and maintaining military equipment.

While SGML is still important as a structuring language, it has not made any significant inroads into mainstream e-commerce. In fact, it has recently lost its glamour to more upcoming technologies such as XML.

HTML

The **Hypertext Markup Language (HTML)** evolved from the rejection of SGML's complexity. From its inception, HTML was adopted and supported by the major Web browsers. The primary form of representing Web pages remains HTML.

Browser Support

Both Microsoft Internet Explorer and Netscape Communicator have gone through a number of iterations following the progress of the underlying description language. The browsers' support for the various elements of HTML's successive releases is uneven. A related problem is that browsers have been developed with some resilience to coding errors. As browsers attempt to comply with new recommendations, they may lose support for deprecated syntax. Sound advice is to test all pages with a variety of browsers and browser versions.

Empower the Users

HTML has been widely adopted and has gone through a few iterations. The rapid diffusion of the technology can be partly explained by the pre-existing void for accessible technology and partly by the ease of use for the novice Web developer. HTML brought power to the users within a simple framework where the content can be formatted with the addition of a few tags. In its latest inception, version 4.01, HTML is used for static pages, forming the scaffolding of most websites.

HTML is also increasingly created by dynamic code generators or from templates. For the nonprogrammer and the casual user, modern word processors offer the option of exporting any document in HTML format. The latest edition of Microsoft Office goes as far as accepting HTML as native format for a document. While the results are not always predictable, the document can easily be modified and edited with one of the more specialized Web development tools.

As HTML became the lingua franca of the Web, other applications have added the capability of exporting to this format. Examples of such applications include the Excel spreadsheet, Access database, and PowerPoint graphics software of the Microsoft Office suite. Other office suites such as Corel Office can also save to HTML. This provides a productive shortcut to publish a static document to a Web page with only the overhead of a few redundant tags.

A Fixed Set of Tags, Easy to Master, Difficult to Extend

The HTML offers a limited number of fixed tags, which allow the user to design a Web page, a document displayed through a browser. The principal elements of a Web page include a title, the body of the page, and the background of the page similar to wallpaper under windows. The normal text of the page can be presented in paragraphs, lists, tables, or forms and be emphasized with a number of attributes such as bolding, italicizing, or underlining.

To add vigor to the content, visual effects are often added with images and backgrounds. Java applets and ActiveX add functionality and hypertext links allow the user to navigate to other pages. A number of tools can be used to develop HTML documents, ranging from the primitive MS Notepad to the most sophisticated HTML specialized editors offering WYSIWYG. Table 7–1 provides the mainstream tags offered by all HTML versions.

Interpreting known tags, the browser separates content from markup and uses the latter to format the displayed information. Current browsers are quite permissive of small programming errors. In the future, Web pages will be tested more stringently as newer versions of HTML and XML enforce the syntax. Limitations of HTML become apparent when the developer is cornered without a tag to specify some new structure or format.

Insertion of Pictures on a Web Page

The ability to add images to Web pages was an important factor in the success of the WWW. The Internet existed for a long time before suddenly becoming popular when browsers with the ability to display pictures appeared. Two classes of images are used on Web pages. Inline images are

TABLE 7–1 **Most Common HTML Tags**

HTML Tags	Function
<HTML> </HTML>	Marks the beginning of the document and the end
<HEAD> </HEAD>	Specifies the beginning and end of the header information
<TITLE> </TITLE>	Indicates the title of the document; not displayed on Web page
<BODY> </BODY>	Indicates the main part of the Web page
<Hn> </Hn>	Specifies the size of heading from 1 (largest) to 6 (smallest)
<P> </P>	Delimits a paragraph with a blank line
<UL> </UL>	Delimits the beginning and end of an unordered list
<LI> </LI>	Marks the item as part of a list
<HR>	Inserts a horizontal rule
 	Indicates a cut in the text flow going to next line
<B> </B>	Indicates that the text within is emphasized
<I> </I>	Indicates that the text within is italicized
<U> </U>	Indicates that the text within is underlined
<TABLE> </TABLE>	Inserts a table in the document
<FORM> </FORM>	Inserts a form in the document

displayed on the page directly without any action from the visitor. External images are stored independently and displayed when the visitor clicks on a link.

As described in Chapter 10, three types of raster graphics are used on Web pages: GIF, JPEG, and the newer PNG. They use the standard extensions (.gif, .jpg, and .png) and are readily displayed in modern browsers without the need for plug-ins. The simple syntax for inserting an inline image is the statement in the body of the page:

```
<html>
<head>
<title> Picture of a dog </title>
</head>
<body>
<IMG SRC="dog.jpg" border=0>
</body>
</html>
```

FIGURE 7–1

*Image inserted on a
Web page*

This will display the image within the Web page as shown in Figure 7–1.

A number of attributes can change the final appearance of the picture within the Web page. Attributes are assigned values as Border = 1 within the statement.

- ALIGN can take values bottom, top, left, middle, and right.
- ALT will give an alternative displayed text if the image cannot be found.
- BORDER defines a border width.
- HEIGHT determines the height of the image and allows resizing for performance.
- HSPACE defines the horizontal space between the image and the surrounding text.
- SRC gives the URL of the image (may be on the same server or a separate server).
- VSPACE defines the vertical space between the image and the surrounding text.
- WIDTH defines the width of the image and allows resizing for performance.

Care must be exercised when resizing the image that proportion is maintained to avoid distortion.

The effect from a plain page background can be obtained with a statement such as:

<body bgcolor="#99CCFF" >

The three pairs of numbers express the value of the colors red, green, and blue in hexadecimal.

If a picture is used as background, the statement is only slightly different:

<body background="lightgreen.jpg">

Adding images is only one of the numerous tools that enable the designer to enhance pages. One can use a Java applet to add functionality. Figure 7–2 shows an applet packaged with IBM HotMedia to add animation to a page.

The code to insert an Applet is straightforward. It points to the compiled Java class (hm30.class) file in the same directory with a description of the size of the displayed region on the page.

FIGURE 7–2

Animation Java applet

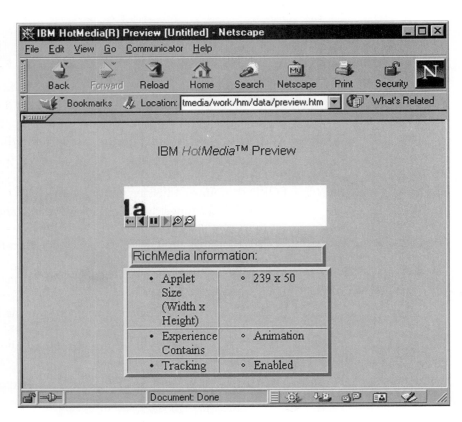

```
<APPLET
CODEBASE="..”
CODE="hm30.class"
NAME="HotMedia"
WIDTH="239"
HEIGHT="50">
<PARAM NAME="mvrfile" value="data/preview.mvr">
</APPLET>
```

Links to Other Pages

The hypertext feature of the Web is among its most attractive attributes. Links are used within a website to suggest paths to visit. Links can direct users to external resources or related pages on the same site. In e-commerce sites, links are often used to balance the load among various servers or to help delegate long operations to content service providers. Examples abound. For example, Conxion is a managed hosting service carrying a 99.999 percent uptime guarantee. Similarly, Akamai Technologies and Exodus Communications can host large graphics files and allow users to concentrate on the business side of their operations.

The syntax for a link within the body of a Web page is:

<A HREF="second.htm">second page </A>

The pair <A> and </A> is used to create the link or anchors for the link. The HREF attribute indicates the URL of the target page. If the HREF is followed by a Mailto:user@address statement, the link can be used to call an e-mail client and send messages to this address. Links can be built among pages as well as within the page between various sections.

Publication of Pages on the Web

Publishing pages on the Web is a simple process. If developed on the Web server, the file representing the Web page can be moved to the directory containing the documents to be published. The page can then be called by other documents or accessed directly with the proper access rights. A Web server should be running on the computer where the document is posted if access from the Internet is desired. For remote insertion of pages on a Web server, many of the latest Web page editors allow file transfer protocol (FTP) to upload pages to the server. Often this is done transparently through a publishing feature.

While HTML programming is not overly difficult, many users do not want to get too involved with coding. To this end and to enhance productivity, a number of readily available tools have been developed.

HTML Editors. Many HTML editors exist, ranging from simple free software to the most sophisticated environment. Some users even employ Windows Notepad to compose a home page. Most editors offer changing features with support for some of the latest technology. Since none of them has the full spectrum of attributes, a business should base its selection on chosen relevant factors (e.g., use of standard, style sheets, dynamic HTML, and support for the scripting language of choice). Developing competitive Web pages requires more coding than possible with version 1 or 2 of HTML. The tools should be chosen accordingly. Fortunately, along with higher-tech Web pages come higher-tech HTML editing programs, many offering visual programming and a WYSIWYG preview option facilitating rapid prototyping.

HTML editors' useful features include:

- Collaboration and site management.
    Check in/check out of Web pages from the site.
    Integration with version control tool.
    Ability to navigate and control the site from the editor.
- Database features.
    Tools for database integration from form to any database through ODBC or JDBC.
    Ability to send form data to e-mail address.
    Ability to save form data to file.
- Deployment features.
    Support for multilingual editing.
    Easy FTP to Web server.
- Design features.
    JavaScript and VBScript support.
    Easy integration of CSS1 and CSS2.
    Support for DHTML with cross-browser tuning.
    Visual wizard for forms, tables, and frames definition.
    Support for image composition and mapping.
    Pixel-precise positioning.
    Drag and drop support.
    Preview in browser for pages and images.
    HTML syntax checking.
    Spell checker, local and across the Web.
    Site navigation overview.
- HTML editing features.
    Customizable template for Web page development.
    HTML validation tool and HTML XML compliance tool.
    Search and replace over multiple files.
    Support for Java applets, ActiveX, and CGI.
    Syntax coloring for latest HTML standard.
    Prebuilt DHTML scripts or wizard.

Ability to import and view/play multimedia files such as GIF,
JPEG, BMP, WAV, or Midi.

Some Web server providers as well as many independent small software
boutiques sell HTML editors. These include the following:

- Microsoft FrontPage supports a comprehensive list of features that
are highly extended in its latest version. MS FrontPage extension's
seamless integration with Microsoft IIS makes this product a strong
competitor. Many CSPs hosting e-commerce sites on Windows NT
will support easy uploading of pages through FrontPage.

- Allaire HomeSite has a strong reputation as an industry leader. Its
intuitive WYSIWYN (what you see is what you need) interface
presents all the necessary site-building tools, leading to increased
user productivity.

- A freeware called 1rst Page 2000 from evrSoft has a strong feature
set and is also worth considering.

- SoftQuad has products addressing most editing needs, from
HTML, to SGML and XML. SoftQuad Software is the producer of
award-winning standards-based structured document tools
XMetaL 2.0 and HoTMetaL PRO 6.0.

- HotDog Professional from Sausage Software is one of the best
HTML editors available. The interface is attractive, very powerful,
customizable, and easy to use with simplified menu commands.
HotDog Professional can easily be integrated with programs such
as Linkbot to verify the integrity of the website and Interactor to
provide the website with some of the best accessories available.

- Adobe has both a simple tool with PageMill and one of the most
complete products in GoLive, both operating on the Apple
Macintosh as well as under MS Windows. GoLive is aimed at
visually building e-commerce and dynamically generated
websites with Dynamic Link. Adobe GoLive Dynamic Link for
active server pages (ASP) creates complex, dynamically driven
websites without hand coding, regardless of the back-end
environment on a Microsoft Web server. It offers an attractive
solution for e-commerce storefronts, online catalogs, and
personalized content, as well as any database-driven information.

- Macromedia is another software provider that has strengthened
its Web development product line. Its Drumbeat 2000 software
introduced versions with active server pages or Java server pages
(JSP) as well as an eCommerce edition that has all the features
and capabilities of Drumbeat 2000, plus additional features for
building secure, fully customizable online stores. The other
products, Dreamweaver and Fireworks, are all that is required to
build fine sites. Web graphics can be created in Fireworks and

then integrated seamlessly into Web pages built with Dreamweaver. In Dreamweaver, round-trip HTML offers total control over code. In Fireworks, professional vector and bit map editing tools allow users to produce comprehensive graphics and modify files from any graphics source and edit anything, anytime. In the latest version, Macromedia folded the capabilities of Drumbeat within Dreamweaver with the release of Dreamweaver Ultradev.

- Barebones Software has a long-standing group of loyal followers in the Apple community.

Similarly to shareware, most commercial products are available for download in trial version for 14 to 60 days. Most of the HTML editors are available on the Microsoft Windows platform and a few on Mac or UNIX. By downloading from a shareware site, such as www.tucows.com, developers can evaluate several tools in both classes of editors. Using a WYSIWYG with graphical layout or a specialized editor with visible tags is a matter of choice. The developer can practice with freeware or shareware before making a final choice. The same site offers a number of utility tools such as Image editors, which are useful in other aspects of e-commerce site development.

Advanced HTML and DHTML

Developers using only HTML still face limitations and static aspects of the language. The dynamic behavior of a Web page may be created using a number of technologies such as JavaScript, VBScript, the Document Object Model (DOM), layers, and cascading style sheets (CSS). One attribute common to many of these technologies is that the display of the Web page can be changed after the page loads. Although **dynamic HTML (DHTML)** works only with the latest generation of browsers (Microsoft IE 4.0+ and Netscape Navigator 4.0+), the wide adoption of these browsers makes it reasonable to consider the advantages of DHTML.

DHTML can be implemented with diverse tools, but two aspects of DHTML dominate. CSS is used to adopt a uniform look and feel. Laying out pages in a consistent manner is important to improving the usability of an e-commerce website. The second attribute is adding animation to the pages. While making images fly through pages may seem foolish, adding event-driven animation in response to user input has certain advantages.

The first step in controlling page layout is learning to use the <div> and <span> tags. Due to disparity between browsers, the safe method is to use <div> as a generic container. We will create a box and position it on the page. The container can then be filled with whatever content we see fit (i.e., image, text).

```
<!DOCTYPE HTML PUBLIC "-//W3C//DTD HTML 4.0
   Transitional//EN">
<HTML>
<STYLE type="text/css">
<!--
#pic1 {
POSITION: absolute;
Z-INDEX: 1;
LEFT: 30px;
TOP: 30px;
Visibility: visible}
-->
</STYLE>
<BODY>
<div id=pic1>
<img src="http://mis.mgmt.umb.edu/euni.gif" width=100
   height=50 alt=" " border="0">
</div>
</BODY>
</HTML>
```

Any text or element can be inserted between the boundaries of the div. Note the use of the absolute parameter. The two alternatives, absolute or relative, will affect the positioning on the page. Absolute means that the positioning is fixed relative to the corner of the Web page. As a result, objects can be superimposed and take no space within the flow of the HTML. With a relative parameter, the boxed element is positioned within the flow of the page relative to preceding elements displayed. As an exercise, try variations of these two options.

Dynamic HTML offers advantages over the use of tables for positioning elements one on top of the other. Overlapping text and image is impossible with tables, and the Web designer often needs to resort to using large bit maps. A drawback of large images is the increased downloading time with slow connections and a lack of flexibility with various screen sizes.

Elements That DHTML Can Control

DHTML can control a number of components on a Web page. This allows the developer to specify changes to the page after it has been loaded. Part of DHTML's power is its ability to hide and expose portions of pages. This means whole sections of pages can be hidden until a user performs some action that will expose them. The display attributes of style sheets enable a user's enhanced interaction with the website. In practice, style sheets and HTML concepts are inherently associated. DHTML can control text, background, form field, images, frames, tables, and paragraphs.

DHTML Examples

With all the sites and hundreds of channels available from well-funded content providers such as CNN and ABC and their respective partners, businesses need all the help they can get to make their websites stand out. Aside from animated gifs and applets, most sites are relatively static. DHTML has the potential to bring HTML pages to life and make them more interactive. For example, text and graphics can be moved around the screen after the page is loaded; text color can be changed on mouseover or at the click of a button; scroll bars can be used to let users explore additional information without leaving the page; and ticker objects can be created to scroll text.

The following code illustrates some of the remaining compatibility problems with DHTML. With divergent implementations, dynamic channel providers have fragmented the market, forcing providers to choose among a set of incompatible solutions.

An example with JavaScript:

```
<!DOCTYPE HTML PUBLIC "-//W3C//DTD HTML 4.0
   Transitional//EN">
<HTML>
<HEAD>
<SCRIPT LANGUAGE="JavaScript">
<!-- Begin
function popUp(URL) {
day = new Date( );
id = day.getTime( );
eval("page" + id + " = window.open(URL, ' " + id +
" ', 'toolbars=1, scrollbars=1, location=1, statusbars=1" +
", menubars=1, resizable=1, width=200, height=150') ; ");
}
// End -->
</script>
<BODY>
<form>
<input type=button value="Open the Popup Window"
   onClick="javascript:popUp('http://www.umb.edu')">
</form>
</BODY>
</HTML>
```

The code will call a pop-up window when a button is pressed. While the code is simple, it illustrates the difference in implementation between the MS IE and Netscape. IE will pop up the window with the correct dimensions, but Netscape will display it maximized without taking the height and width into consideration.

An example with VBScript:

```
<!DOCTYPE html PUBLIC "-//W3C//DTD HTML 4.0
  Transitional//EN">
<HTML>
  <HEAD>
<SCRIPT language="VBScript">
    ' This line executes when the script tag is parsed.
    Call PrintWelcome
    Sub PrintWelcome
        Dim h
        h = Hour(Now)
        If h < 12 then
           Document.Write "Good morning! "
        ElseIf h < 17 then
           Document.Write "Good afternoon! "
        Else
           Document.Write "Good evening! "
        End If
        Document.Write "Welcome to the world of VBScript. "
        Document.Write "Simple time machine              "
        Document.Write Time() & " on the " & Date() & "."
    End Sub
</SCRIPT>
    <TITLE>Example of VBScript
    </TITLE>
  </HEAD>
  <BODY>
    <BR>
    hello
  </BODY>
</HTML>
```

This example greets the visitor with the time and date and a "Good morning," "Good afternoon," or "Good evening." The use of VBScript restricts the target audience to users of IE Explorer, as most other browsers will not display any message.

Using DHTML Events to Manipulate Loaded Web Pages

As more applications are developed that are targeted at HTML 4 browsers, the back-end processors will handle most of the functionality. However, a prudent use of DHTML event handlers can alleviate problems and send cleaner data to be further processed. Events on the client can also address irregularities that occur while manipulating the pages. The following code segments illustrate a wide range of commands and briefly explains them.

```
<!DOCTYPE HTML PUBLIC "-//W3C//DTD HTML 4.0
   Transitional//EN">
<html>
<head>
    <title>DHTML events</title>
</head>
<body BGCOLOR="lightgrey"
onBlur="document.bgColor='lightgrey' "
onFocus="document.bgColor='antiquewhite' ">
The following illustrates some DHTML events
<br>
```

The two tags onBlur and onFocus have opposite meanings. In onFocus, the element under consideration, in this case the document, will take the color assigned as antiquewhite. When the document loses focus, either because the user has clicked outside the document or has tabbed to another window, the document will take back the color lightgrey. These events may apply to Body, Select, Textarea, or Input elements of the page.

```
<SCRIPT>
var dataOK=false
function checkData (){
if (document.myForm.threeChar.value.length == 3) {
  document.myForm.submit()}
  else {
    alert("Enter exactly three characters. " +
    document.myForm.threeChar.value +
      " is not valid.")
    return false}
}
</SCRIPT>/
```

The function checkData will validate entries and assure that the entry has three characters.

```
<script>
imageA = new Image(150,150)
imageA.onload=displayAlert
function displayAlert(theImage) {
   if (theImage==null) {
      alert('An image loaded')
   }
   else alert(theImage.name + 'has been loaded.')
}
</script>
```

Onload will indicate that the image has been loaded. The command Onload may be used to move elements around within the page or load additional elements such as images.

```
<script language="JavaScript">
function submitting() {
// return ...
return window.confirm("are you sure you want to send this form?")
}
</script>
<br>
<IMG src="euni.gif"
onAbort="alert('You didn\'t get to see the image!')">
<br>
```

OnAbort indicates that the transmission of the image has been stopped. This could add a level of flexibility over the standard "alt=" command of HTML. A specific action can be taken, instead of displaying the fact that the image is not loaded.

```
<INPUT TYPE="text" VALUE=" " NAME="userName"
onChange="checkValue(this.value)">
<br>
```

OnChange indicates that the value of the element has changed. When the element loses its focus, a specific action can be taken. In this case, the function checkValue will be called to validate the entry from the text box. Such functionality could be used to change the case of the input or to make certain that the entry is numeric or text before sending the data for processing on the back end.

```
<A HREF="http://home.netscape.com"
onClick='alert("Link got an event: " + event.type)'>Click for link
    event</A>
<br>
```

OnClick is the useful event that will trigger an action when the element is clicked. It can be used to dynamically set a URL, to validate input elements, or to perform calculations.

```
<INPUT TYPE="checkbox" NAME="check1" VALUE="check1"
onDblClick="return confirm('This purges all your files. Are you
    sure?')">
<br>
```

In this case, the onDblClick can be used to send a message to the user. Alternatively, another action can be taken, such as calling context-sensitive help windows or changing the state of an element that is already using the click event for something else.

```
<img name="imagebad" src="euni3.gif"
onError="alert('You didn\'t get to see the image euni3.gif!')">
<br>
```

OnError can be used as a provision for processing in the event of an error. In the illustration, if the image does not load correctly or is missing, the message indicates that the image has not been seen. Often the browsers are too tolerant of errors and end up not doing anything, ignoring the commands that cannot be performed. OnError provides a means for warning the user that something has been omitted.

```
<INPUT TYPE="textarea" VALUE="first" NAME="valueField1"
onFocus="document.bgColor='black'">
<br>
```

OnFocus takes an action when the element mentioned has been chosen.

```
<INPUT TYPE="textarea" VALUE="second"
    NAME="valueField2"
onKeyDown="document.bgColor='blue'">
<br>
```

OnKeyDown is an event that monitors the element for some new typing in the input field. When a key is pressed, the action is triggered. In this case, the background color is changed to blue. The OnKeyDown event applies to textarea and input elements.

```
<script>
sampleString="This is first item.\nThis is second item.\nThis is
    third item."
```

```
        sampleString2="This is fourth item.\nThis is fifth item.\nThis is
          sixth item."
      </script>
```

The code creates two string variables and assigns some text to them.

```
      <FORM NAME="form1">
      <INPUT TYPE="button" Value="Disappearing text in the
        textarea"
      onKeyPress="document.form1.textarea1.value=sampleString"
      onkeyUp="document.form1.textarea1.value="">
      <br>
```

The onKeyPress event is closely related to the keyDown and keyUp events. In the case of onKeyPress, both the keyDown and keyUp events have occurred, and in this case, the textarea is assigned the text previously defined. The event can be readily applicable to the TEXTAREA and INPUT elements.

```
      <TEXTAREA NAME="textarea1" ROWS=6
        COLS=55></TEXTAREA>
      </form>
      <br>
      <img name="imageB" src="euni2.gif" align="top"
      onLoad=displayAlert(this)
      onMouseDown="alert('image has been moused!')">
      <br>
```

When the document is loaded, the image is loaded as well. As the image is chosen by onMouseDown, the alert message is displayed.

```
      <A HREF="http://www.microsoft.com/"
      onMouseOver="window.status='Click this if you dare!'; return
        true"
      onMouseOut= "window.status='safe mode'; return true">
      Click me</A>
      <br>
```

As the mouse is brought over the hyperlink, the first message is written to the status line of the displayed window. As the mouse moves out of the link, the second message replaces the first on the status line.

```
      <INPUT TYPE="text" VALUE="select to change items"
        NAME="valueField"
      onSelect="document.form1.textarea1.value=sampleString2">
      <br>
```

When some text is selected, then the text defined in sampleString2 is written to the textrarea1.

```
<form name="myForm" onSubmit= "return submitting()">
<b>Enter 3 characters:</b>
<INPUT TYPE="text" NAME="threeChar" SIZE=3>
<br>
<INPUT TYPE="submit" VALUE="Done" NAME="button1"
    onClick="checkData()">
</form>
</body>
</html>
```

The input box will accept text, which will be validated by the function checkdata(). If the text is composed of three characters, then the form will be submitted; otherwise the error message will appear.

DHTML is a powerful tool that, when sparingly used, can bring some life to a website. DHTML code has the ability of polling the user for the current configuration (e.g., IE Explorer or Netscape browser). Many of the otherwise annoying incompatibilities can be avoided by customizing the path based on the detected configuration. With advanced tools, it will be possible to customize the site and generate parallel implementations offering the optimal experience to most visitors.

PDF

Adobe Systems developed the **portable document format (PDF).** The Adobe Acrobat software includes a PDF writer and distiller that transforms documents from a variety of desktop publishing applications into a format readable on multiple computer platforms. It makes it possible to send formatted documents and have them appear on the recipient's monitor or printer with all the attributes intended. The PDF file saved in a single format can be opened, viewed, browsed, and printed on any of the major desktop computing platforms (e.g., DOS, Macintosh, Windows, and UNIX).

Viewers

Adobe distributes Acrobat Reader free, the software necessary to view and print PDF files. When configured on a workstation with the proper add-in, a Web browser launches Acrobat whenever a PDF file is encountered.

Three methods can be adopted to display a PDF document:

- Download the file and open it from within the Acrobat application.
- Configure the browser to launch Adobe™ Acrobat Reader automatically when a PDF file is encountered.

- Load the Adobe PDF Viewer plug-in that will launch the Acrobat Reader software within the browser when a PDF file is encountered.

The latest versions of Illustrator and FrameMaker are able to write PDF format. Other software firms, such as Corel with WordPerfect, have licensed the technology and can export to the native PDF format but cannot modify existing documents.

CSS

Cascading style sheets (CSS) have been added to HTML to provide both website developers and users more control over how pages are displayed. They offer a powerful and flexible way of specifying formatting information for Web pages. Users can design a consistent look throughout the site with standardized font sizes, background and foreground colors, margins, and layout schemes. With CSS, designers and users can create style sheets that define how various elements, such as headers and links, appear. These style sheets can then be applied to any Web page. CSSs provide developers with the tools to define their own classes, enabling the authors to define new HTML elements.

CSS Fundamentals

Style sheets are derived from multiple sources, with a defined order of precedence when the definitions of any style element conflict. Therefore, the formatting rules are applied in a hierarchical manner, with default rules from the browser merged with overriding rules from the style sheet. The cascading style sheet, level 1 (CSS1) recommendations from the World Wide Web Consortium (W3C), which are implemented in the latest versions of the Netscape and Microsoft Web browsers, specify the possible style sheets or statements that may determine how a given element is presented in a Web page.

CSS allows authors and readers to attach style to HTML documents. It uses common desktop publishing terminology, which makes it easy for professionals as well as untrained designers to use its features. Visual design issues such as page layout can thus be addressed separately from the Web page logical structure.

HTML has been notoriously inadequate at representing layout. To resolve the difficulties of using HTML to create pages, developers used all possible tricks and side effects of the language. Some of these techniques worked with the intended browsers, but often the pages were broken in subsequent release of the browsers or did not work across platforms. CSS instituted a welcome cure for some of these afflictions.

The safest action for developers is to use HTML tags for their original purpose and use style sheets to respond to the presentation issues. The common use of HTML tags for their side effects may lead to confusion and unmaintainable code. But some developers still question style sheet usage, preferring to use FONT elements and BGCOLOR attributes with HTML. Important effects, such as leading (the space between lines) and text shadow, are not available with HTML. The use of CSS facilitates better consistency, more flexibility, and greater productivity. For example, if users want all their main headings to be "yellow Helvetica," one statement is sufficient with a style sheet, whereas every heading would have to be adjusted with HTML. Repeated operations can save a lot of space on a typical website. If only 40 bytes are saved on one heading and this page is retrieved 50,000 times per month, this can save considerable bandwidth.

Style sheets are patterns that are very similar to templates in desktop publishing applications. They contain a collection of rules that specify the rendering of various HTML elements. By attaching style sheets to structured documents on the Web (e.g., HTML), authors and readers can influence the presentation of the documents without sacrificing device independence or adding new HTML tags.

CSSs bring the following decisive assets to the Web developer's toolbox:

- Separate the style and layout of HTML files from their informational content. They can be referenced from multiple documents, providing a uniform style to a website.
- Provide relative measurements so that users can present documents that look good on any monitor at any resolution.
- Avoid breaking existing pages because older browsers simply ignore style sheets.
- Allow readers to influence the presentation of HTML documents.
- Enable companies to implement a house look and feel on their site, thus facilitating consistent branding.
- Improve the printing of Web documents instead of having unpredictable HTML transfer to paper.
- Enable access to the Web for people with disabilities. Visually impaired Web users need increased font sizes or variation of colors and are among the first to benefit from style sheets.

While not all browsers support CSS1 adequately, W3C has released the CSS2 (cascading style sheets, level 2) specification, which represents a cross-industry agreement on a wide range of features for richer and more accessible Web pages. CSS2 includes all the capabilities of CSS1 and adds improved typographic control, including dynamically downloadable fonts. New positioning properties to control layout, for example, produce sidebars and navigation areas. Images and text can be layered and over-lapped and can be dynamically moved around the screen with scripts. CSS2 also adds control over table layout, which is particularly useful for XML documents, and allows the automatic numbering of headings and lists. The CSS2 recommendation is supported by the W3C CSS2 package, consisting of the CSS2 validation service, a set of W3C core style sheets, and the CSS test suite. The CSS2 package helps document authors use CSS2, and it also helps developers create CSS2-compliant software.

Display Customization

Style sheets have a number of useful functions as follows:

- Style sheets help control the display through the use of two types of measurements: absolute and relative. Absolute values are fixed; for example, the font size can be defined as 12 point. Relative values are measures that are compared with others such as larger, bolder, smaller.

- Style sheets allow for control of the color within the browser. Colors can be defined in a number of ways, including a standard color name, a hexadecimal value, an RGB percentage, or a decimal value from 0 to 255; for example, P {color: green}; P {color: rgb(60%, 10%, 30%)}; P {color: rgb(180, 0, 60)}. Other color commands include background-color, background-image, background-repeat, background-attachment, and background-position.

- Fonts and text can be formatted with attributes for font, color, font-size, font-family, font-style, font-weight, line-height, text-indent, text-align, text-decoration, and text-transform.

- Position and visibility can be similarly controlled with a set of powerful commands. The position property permits users to set a box's position in the layout of a page with choices of normal, relative, and absolute. The left property allows users to set the distance between the element box and the left edge of the containing block. The top property lets users set the distance between the element box and the top edge of the containing block. The display property is a fundamental function for hiding or showing an element. This function is often used in Dynamic HTML to hide and display elements based on user choice. It can take values of NONE, BLOCK, INLINE, and LIST-ITEM. Visibility has two values, visible or hidden.

- The most comprehensive set of commands addresses spacing and areas. It is also the most inconsistently supported feature set among browsers. To be safe while developing e-commerce websites, it is important to use the commonly supported tags and to test under various browsers. The attributes covered encompass (1) borders, (2) margins, (3) padding, (4) width, (5) height, (6) the float property for placing an element, such as an image, to the left or right of the container, and allowing other elements, such as text, to flow around it, and (7) the clear property, which lets users specify whether to float the element or to have it clear below other elements.

A simple style would be as follows.

```
<html>
<head>
<title>Style sheet</title>
        <style type="text/css">
        <!--
        body {background: #FFFFFF}
        A:link {color: #80FF00}
        A:visited {color: #FF00FF}
        H1 {font-size: 24pt; font-family: arial; color: blue}
        H2 {font-size: 18pt; font-family: braggadocio}
        H3 {font size:14pt; font-family: desdemona}
        -->
        </style>
</head>
<body>
<h1>this is heading 1</h1>
<h2>heading 2</h2>
<h3>heading 3</h3>
</body>
</html>
```

A style sheet allows the developer to create a Web page with a distinctive and consistent look.

Tools Supporting DHTML and Style Sheets

Some of the major HTML editors have evolved to support DHTML and CSS, of which GoLive, Dreamweaver, and Netobjects Fusion are among the most popular. Tools that are specifically designed to support the construction of style sheets have become available. Shareware can also provide inexpensive utilities for facilitating the creation of style sheets. Among them, TopStyle, CoffeeCup StyleSheet Maker++, Prime Style, and Style Master have received good reviews.

Links to Resources about DHTML

As style sheets become more popular, a number of sites offer numerous examples and tutorials:

- http://wdvl.internet.com/Authoring/DHTML/Intro/ offers a good introduction to DHTML.
- http://builder.cnet.com/Authoring/Dhtml/ tries to address some of the issues of incompatibilities among browsers.
- http://www.webreference.com/dhtml/ publishes a number of articles about DHTML and provides useful sample code.
- http://webreview.com/wr/pub/98/06/26/feature/index.html demonstrates smart layout and dynamic positioning.
- http://www.dhtmlzone.com/tutorials/index.html has tutorials, articles, and more.

XML

While DHTML addressed many of the issues raised by HTML, some still considered the solution lacking. HTML was at an indecisive development stage, and DHTML had difficulty breaching the differences in implementation. This left the door open for a new approach to emerge, the **eXtensible Markup Language (XML).**

What Is XML?

Developed by the World Wide Web Consortium, XML is compatible with SGML. While HTML is a markup language with a fixed set of tags that allows users to specify the appearance of a document, XML allows the user to create new tags to provide a document structure appropriate to the task at hand.

A document has three aspects—structure, appearance, and content. For instance, this chapter has a structure that it shares with all other chapters. It starts with an outline, lists learning objectives, and presents the content in various sections and subsections. Similarly, the chapters share a uniform appearance in terms of fonts, line spacing, arrangement of images, and page size. The content differs from one chapter to another.

In the case of HTML, the same document carries information relating to appearance, content, and visual structure, such as lists and tables. In the case of XML, these functions are separated, with different means employed for defining the structure, the appearance, and the content (see Figure 7–3). Usually, the document type definition (**DTD**) file describes the structure of a document; the appearance is specified by an eXtensible (**XSL**) style sheet; and the content is provided in the XML document.

FIGURE 7–3

*HTML and XML
document systems*

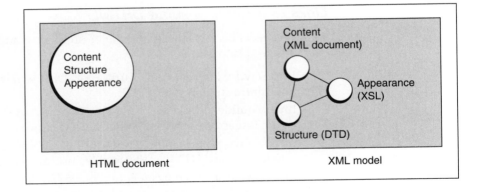

In the case of XML, the Web server does not send an HTML document but rather sends the XML and the XSL documents, and the client must have XML/XSL processors to display the document.

HTML is designed primarily for specifying the appearance of a document. The document may have a visual structure, such as lists and tables, but this structure is not available to a program that may be processing the document. For example, a user cannot merge lists from two different documents in the user's browser to provide a single integrated list.

In contrast, XML allows users to define a structure much as it is done for databases. For example, with XML, users can define a proper structure for price quotations to present product descriptions and prices over the Web even if coming from various vendors. Given two such documents, users not only can merge them, but also can rank them according to decreasing prices or group them by description.

This ability is referred to as semantics; that is, the structural elements have a certain meaning for the document processor, which the processor can now employ to sort, merge, and modify them according to certain business rules (see Figure 7–4). For example, in the case of an HTML document, the source code for a small office memo would appear as follows:

```
<html>
<head> <title> A Simple Example </title> </head>
<body>
<P> From: Aby</P>
<P> To: Jean-Pierre </P>
<P> Date: December 12, 2001 </P>
<P> This is a small memo example </P>
</body>
</html>
```

FIGURE 7–4

*Semantic data
processing in XML*

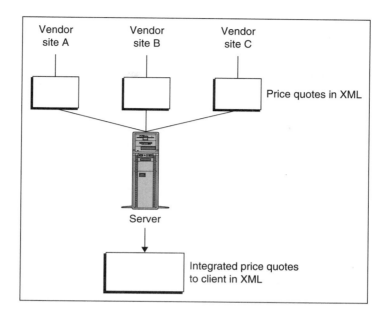

In the case of XML, instead of the formatting tags, there would be tags that define the structure. The code in XML would be as follows.

```
<!DOCTYPE Office_Memo [
<!ELEMENT From (#PCDATA)>
<!ELEMENT To (#PCDATA)>
<!ELEMENT Date (#PCDATA)>
<!ELEMENT Content (#PCDATA)>
]>
<Office_Memo>
<From> Aby </From>
<To> Jean-Pierre </To>
<Date> December 12, 2000 </Date>
<Content> This is a small memo example </Content>
</Office_Memo>
```

The above snippet of XML code does not define what the appearance would be, but defines the structure. The structure of Office Memo consists of four elements: From, To, Date, and Content (see Figure 7–5). A computer program that is processing the XML code can treat each part of the structure differently. If there were many such memos, the code could sort the memos according to date, and it could divert them to different folders according to the name of the sender or the receiver.

FIGURE 7–5
A simple document structure in XML

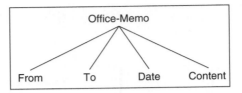

Unlike HTML, XML allows for the separation of appearance issues from the content through an eXtensible style sheet. The focus of an XSL sheet is on formatting, and XSL processors are required to process XSL documents. Different media, such as printers, monitors, browser displays, and displays on handheld devices, require different XSL processors, each suitable for the specific medium. For the same information to be displayed over different media, users can define different XSL documents for different media or define a single XSL document, but where the different XSL processors format the document differently depending on the media (see Figure 7–6). An example of use for XSL is news display. The user needs to download the XSL sheet only once, and thereafter, the same sheet is used every day to arrange the news display. This saves formatting tags from being transported to the user's browser every time the user wants to read the news. Not only is it no longer necessary to send formatting that is specific to the media, but it also is enough to send it once. With fresh delivery of news, only the fresh content needs to be sent.

FIGURE 7–6
News delivery in XML

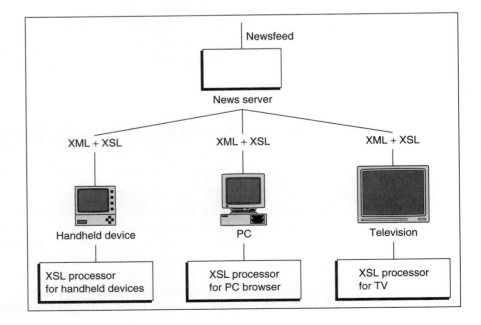

For the example on page 270 of the office memo, anXSL sheet could define the appearance as follows.

```
<style>
.From, To {
font-family: Garamond;
font-weight: bold;
font-size: 12;}
.Content {
font-family: Ariel;
font-style: italic;
font-size: 12; }
</style>
```

XML Tools

Current browsers are not very adept at interpreting XML directly, other than IE 5.x. Any XML document requires two qualities to be processed correctly: it must be well-formed and valid. An XML document is well-formed when the document conforms to the syntactic requirements of XML. For instance, the following is not a well-formed document because it violates the requirement of having end tags (i.e., the end tag for the elements "To" and "Date" are missing).

```
<Office_Memo>
<From> Aby </From>
<To> Jean-Pierre
<Date> December 12, 2000
<Content> This is a small example </Content>
</Office_Memo>
```

An XML document is said to be valid when it confirms to the structural definition. For example, the following is not a valid document because it has an element, Cc, not defined in the structure for Office_Memo.

```
<Office_Memo>
<From> Aby </From>
<To> Jean-Pierre </To>
<Cc> Noushin </Cc>
<Date> December 12, 2000 </Date>
<Content> This is a small example </Content>
</Office_Memo>
```

Parsers are available on the Internet to check both of these attributes. A document that does not comply with XML format would not be processed.

While most parsers check for being well-formed, not all of them verify the validity of the XML document. Parsers are available from

- IBM at http://alphaworks.ibm.com/tech/xml4j.
- Java project X at Sun http://developer.java.sun.com/developer/products/xml/.
- Oracle at http://technet.oracle.com/tech/xml.
- Microsoft at http://msdn.microsoft.com/downloads/webtechnology/xml/ msxml.asp.
- James Clark at http://www.jclark.com/xml/xp/index.html.

While XML is still in its infancy, a number of specialized editors have already been developed and commercially released, including

- BladeRunner Composer/Styler (Interleaf, a pioneer of the SGML area).
- X-metal (Softquad).
- Xeena (IBM) (this is a free experimental tool).
- XML notepad (Microsoft).
- XML writer (Wattle Software).
- Stylus (eXcelon Corp.).
- XML Authority (Extensibility).
- XML Spy (Altova).

A number of editors available in all ranges of functionality and prices are listed at www.xmlsoftware.com/editors/.

Writing Simple XML Documents

Simple XML documents can be developed using only Windows Notepad and Internet Explorer V5.0. The documents are all text type and need to be saved as "FileName.XML." The quotes marks are necessary; otherwise the file would be saved as FileName.XML.txt. The concepts behind XML involve the following steps:

1. Creating an XML document that uses a simple cascading style sheet. The document structure is defined within the XML file.
2. Developing an XML document in which the structure is defined using document type declaration within the XML file. The formatting details are obtained from the style sheet.
3. Creating an XML document that uses an external document, document type definition (DTD) to specify the structure.
4. Learning to use an XSL style sheet to specify the formatting requirements.

Consider the program provided in the file SALUTATION.XML, given below:

SALUTATION.XML

```
<?xml version="1.0" standalone="yes"?>
<?xml-stylesheet type="text/css" href="SALUTATION.css"?>
<SALUTATION>
Hello Readers!

Hope you are enjoying the book.
</SALUTATION>
```

It is a text file developed using the Notepad. The line <?xml version="1.0" standalone="yes"?> refers to the XML version. The standalone feature says the document is complete by itself and does not need to import any other file. Any line that is enclosed within <?..?> is processed as a program code by the XML processor.

The next line, <?xml-stylesheet type="text/css" href="SALUTATION.css"?>, refers to the type of style sheet used and the name of the file. In this case, a CSS type sheet is used and bears the name SALUTATION.CSS. The structure of the XML file is simple. It has only one element, SALUTATION. XML is case-sensitive and the element SALUTATION is different from Salutation, which, in turn, is different from salutation. Also, except for few exceptions, tags come in pairs (i.e., an end tag must follow a beginning tag). The SALUTATION element has the value "Hello Readers. Hope you are enjoying the book."

The file SALUTATION.CSS specifies the font and font size for display. Figure 7–7 shows the display when the file SALUTATION.XML is loaded in the browser, Internet Explorer.

SALUTATION.CSS
SALUTATION {display: block; font-size: 18pt; font-weight: bold;}

FIGURE 7–7

A simple XML document on display

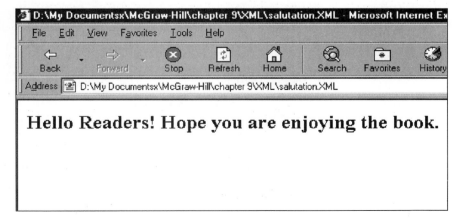

XML with Document Structure and Style Sheet

This section displays the use of document type definition (DTD) for specifying the structure of the XML file. Consider the file SALUTATION1.XML presented below. The declaration is part of the XML file and is provided in the lines:

```
<!DOCTYPE SALUTATION [
<!ELEMENT SALUTATION (#PCDATA)>
]>
```

It begins with, <!DOCTYPE followed by the name of the structure and then the elements of which it consists. The name of the structure is SALUTATION and there is a single element here called SALUTATION. The type of the element is #PCDATA, which stands for parsed computer data, and in this case, it is text data.

As before, the file SALUTATION.CSS specifies the format and when the file is loaded in the Internet Explorer, the display is shown as in Figure 7–8.

```
SALUTATION1.XML
<?xml version="1.0" standalone="yes"?>
<?xml-stylesheet type="text/css" href="salutation.css"?>
<!DOCTYPE SALUTATION [
<!ELEMENT SALUTATION (#PCDATA)>
]>
<SALUTATION>
Hello Readers! This is an XML document on view
</SALUTATION>
```

FIGURE 7–8

Display of XML with document type definition

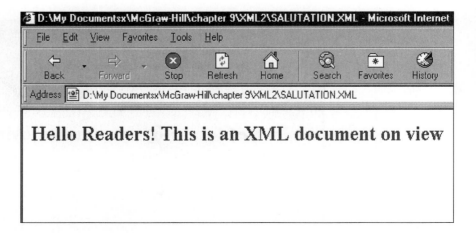

SALUTATION.CSS

SALUTATION {display: block; font-size: 18pt; font-weight: bold; color:blue;}

The next example has a more complex structure. Consider the file SALUTATION2.XML, as shown below. The SALUTATION structure has two elements: TO and MESSAGE, and both are of the #PCDATA type. The XML file contains the value for both the elements. The value of the TO element is "Hello Readers" and the value of the MESSAGE element is "Enjoy this XML document." The style sheet specifies the format of both the elements, TO and MESSAGE. Figure 7–9 presents the display as the file is loaded in the Internet Explorer.

SALUTATION2.XML

```
<?xml version="1.0" standalone="yes"?>
<?xml-stylesheet type="text/css" href="SALUTATION2.css"?>
<!DOCTYPE SALUTATION [
    <!ELEMENT TO (#PCDATA)>
    <!ELEMENT MESSAGE (#PCDATA)>
]>
<SALUTATION>
    <TO>Hello Readers!</TO>
    <MESSAGE> Enjoy this XML document</MESSAGE>
</SALUTATION>
```

SALUTATION2.CSS

TO {display: block; font-size: 18pt; font-weight: bold; color:blue;}
MESSAGE {display: block; font-size: 12pt; font-weight: bold; color:red;}

FIGURE 7–9
Display of XML with a complex document type definition

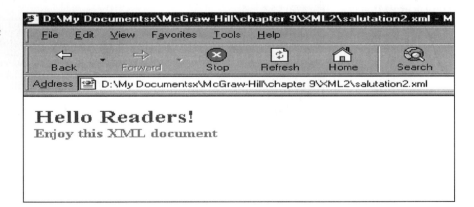

XML with DTD and Style Sheet

This section discusses the use of external **document type definition (DTD)** files along with the style sheet. The DTD file prescribes the structure and the style sheet specifies the formatting requirements. Consider the XML document SALUTATION3.XML. As usual, it begins with the standard preamble referring to the version of XML being used as well as the reference to the style sheet being used. The next line provides the linkage to the document type definition file, SALUTATION3.DTD:

<!DOCTYPE SALUTATION SYSTEM "SALUTATION3.DTD">

The DTD file, SALUTATION3.DTD, defines the structure through two lines:

<!ELEMENT TO (#PCDATA)>
<!ELEMENT MESSAGE (#PCDATA)>

The three files, SALUTATION3.XML, SALUTATION3.CSS, and SALUTATION3.DTD, are shown below. When loaded, the XML file displays as shown in Figure 7–10.

SALUTATION3.XML
<?xml version="1.0" standalone="yes"?>
<?xml-stylesheet type="text/css" href="SALUTATION3.css"?>
<!DOCTYPE SALUTATION SYSTEM "SALUTATION3.DTD">
<SALUTATION>
<TO>Hello Readers!</TO>
<MESSAGE> This XML document uses an external DTD
</MESSAGE>
</SALUTATION>

FIGURE 7–10

Display of XML document with external document type file

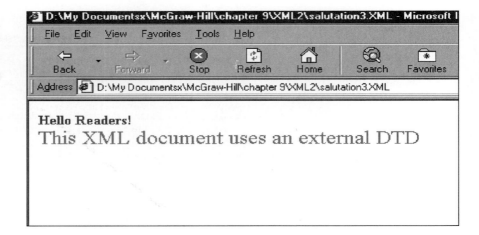

SALUTATION3.CSS

TO {display: block; font-size: 12pt; font-weight: bold; color:blue;}

MESSAGE {display: block; font-size: 18pt; font-weight: normal; color:red;}

SALUTATION3.DTD

```
<!ELEMENT TO (#PCDATA)>
<!ELEMENT MESSAGE (#PCDATA)>
```

Formatting XML Using XSL

An **eXtensible style sheet (XSL)** document describes how the content provided in an XML file is to be formatted. Consider the XML file CAFE.XML, which provides the structure and the content. At the root is a structure called CAFES. This structure at the next level has a repeated number of child structures called CAFE. In turn, the structure CAFE has one attribute, CAFE_TYPE, and it has five elements:

- CAFE_NAME
- FOOD_QUALITY
- ENVIRON
- COST_RATING
- COMMENTS

Five CAFE elements are described within the CAFES structure. Besides the standard preamble referring to XML, reference to the associated XSL file is made through the statement:

```
<?xml-stylesheet type="text/xsl" href="cafe.xsl"?>
```

Brief Examples

The content and structure of a CAFE is described by the following code:

```
<CAFE CAFE_TYPE="Primarily Take-Out">
  <CAFE_NAME>New Mexico</CAFE_NAME>
  <FOOD_QUALITY>Average</FOOD_QUALITY>
  <ENVIRON>Great!</ENVIRON>
  <COST_RATING>$3.50 per meal</COST_RATING>
  <COMMENTS>Should order well in time.</COMMENTS>
</CAFE>
```

The code for the entire file CAFE.XML is:

```xml
<?xml version = "1.0" ?>
<?xml-stylesheet type="text/xsl" href="cafe.xsl"?>
<!-- Define the XSL stylesheet to be used with the XML
  Document -->
<CAFES>
  <CAFE CAFE_TYPE5"Primarily Take-Out">
  <CAFE_NAME>New Mexico</CAFE_NAME>
  <FOOD_QUALITY>Average</FOOD_QUALITY>
  <ENVIRON>Great!</ENVIRON>
  <COST_RATING>$3.50 per meal</COST_RATING>
  <COMMENTS>Should order well in time.</COMMENTS>
  </CAFE>
  <CAFE CAFE_TYPE="Brunch">
  <CAFE_NAME>Moscow</CAFE_NAME>
  <FOOD_QUALITY>Outstanding</FOOD_QUALITY>
  <ENVIRON>Average</ENVIRON>
  <COST_RATING>$8 per person</COST_RATING>
  <COMMENTS>A good place for weekend
    brunch</COMMENTS>
  </CAFE>
  <CAFE CAFE_TYPE="Formal Dinner">
  <CAFE_NAME>Spring in Paris</CAFE_NAME>
  <FOOD_QUALITY>Excellent</FOOD_QUALITY>
  <ENVIRON>Fantastic</ENVIRON>
  <COST_RATING>$19 per plate</COST_RATING>
  <COMMENTS>Got to be rich to go there</COMMENTS>
  </CAFE>
  <CAFE CAFE_TYPE="Asian Grill">
  <CAFE_NAME>Big Saigon</CAFE_NAME>
  <FOOD_QUALITY>Good</FOOD_QUALITY>
  <ENVIRON>OK</ENVIRON>
  <COST_RATING>$7 per plate</COST_RATING>
  <COMMENTS>Good for quick lunch</COMMENTS>
  </CAFE>
  <CAFE CAFE_TYPE="Take-Out">
  <CAFE_NAME>Aby's Diner</CAFE_NAME>
  <FOOD_QUALITY>Fantastic</FOOD_QUALITY>
  <ENVIRON>Splendid</ENVIRON>
```

```
<COST_RATING>$7 per plate</COST_RATING>
<COMMENTS>Always eat out at Aby's Diner</COMMENTS>
</CAFE>
</CAFES>
```

Now consider the XSL file, CAFE.XSL. The file accomplishes several tasks:

1. The XSL file generates the HTML code that eventually runs on the browser. The XSL file has to create the necessary HTML tags for that purpose.
2. As part of the above, the XSL code creates a table that has the tabular headings in the first row.
3. Looping constructs allowed in XSL are used to read individual elements of CAFE in the associated XML file and then to output the values in the HTML table.

Preamble.   The file begins with a preamble that defines the location of the XSL specification by the following line:

```
<xsl:stylesheet xmlns:xsl="http://www.w3.org/TR/WD-xsl">
```

Template Match.   The line: `<xsl:template match="/">` instructs the system to match the XSL template right from the root stage of the structure described in the XML file (i.e., the entire structure of CAFES/CAFE is to be processed as per the XSL file).

HTML Tags.   The HTML tags for the file and for defining the table are achieved by the code:

```
<HTML>
  <BODY>
  <P><B> This is an XML Document on View! </B> </P>
  <P><EM> It uses XSL Sheet </EM> </P>
  <P> These XML documents have been produced </P>
  <P> using only NotePad and Internet Explorer v5.0 </P>
  <TABLE BORDER="1">
```

The header row of the table is defined by the code:

```
<TR>
<TD><b>Cafe </b></TD>
<TD><b>Cafe Type</b></TD>
<TD><b>Food </b></TD>
<TD><b>Environment </b></TD>
```

```
<TD><b>Meal Cost</b></TD>
<TD><b>Comments</b></TD>
</TR>
```

Extracting the Values of Each CAFE Structure.   The XML file defines the overall structure of CAFES, which consists of multiple repeated child structure elements CAFE. The file CAFE.XML has five CAFE child structures. XSL provides the necessary language constructs to extract these values and puts them in an HTML format with the appropriate formatting.

The "for-each select" looping construct of XSL is used to loop through the CAFES structure, and the XSL construct "value-of select" is used to fetch the values of the individual CAFE elements, such as CAFE_NAME and FOOD_QUALITY, and includes them in the table. The looping construct, such as a WHILE loop, is fixed in length, irrespective of how many CAFE child structures are involved. The looping code is as follows:

```
<xsl:for-each select="CAFES/CAFE">
<TR>
  <TD><xsl:value-of select="CAFE_NAME"/></TD>
<TD><xsl:value-of select="@CAFE_TYPE"/></TD>
      <!--use the @ symbol to pull values of attributes -->
  <TD><xsl:value-of select="FOOD_QUALITY"/></TD>
  <TD><xsl:value-of select="ENVIRON"/></TD>
  <TD><xsl:value-of select="COST_RATING"/></TD>
  <TD><xsl:value-of select="COMMENTS"/></TD>
</TR>
</xsl:for-each>
<--! .....End of the loop construct ---->
```

The complete code for CAFE.XSL follows and the display is shown in Figure 7–11.

CAFE.XSL

```
<?xml version='1.0'?>
<!--XML Declaration -->
<xsl:stylesheet xmlns:xsl="http://www.w3.org/TR/WD-xsl">
<!--declaration that the document is a stylesheet -->
<xsl:template match="/">
<!--Apply template from the root node-->
  <HTML>
    <BODY>
      <P><B> This is an XML Document on View! </B> </P>
```

FIGURE 7–11
Display of an XML document using XSL sheet

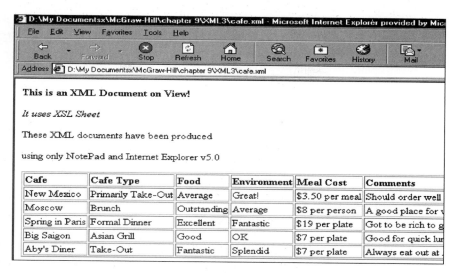

```
<P><EM> It uses XSL Sheet </EM> </P>
<P> These XML documents have been produced </P>
<P> using only NotePad and Internet Explorer v5.0 </P>
<TABLE BORDER="1">
<!--Set up the first, that is, the header row -->
<TR>
<TD><b>Cafe </b></TD>
<TD><b>Cafe Type</b></TD>
<TD><b>Food </b></TD>
<TD><b>Environment </b></TD>
<TD><b>Meal Cost</b></TD>
<TD><b>Comments</b></TD>
</TR>
<xsl:for-each select="CAFES/CAFE">
<!--set up a loop where for each occurrence of the form defined
in the "select", execute the following steps-->
<TR>
<TD><xsl:value-of select="CAFE_NAME"/></TD>
<!--"value-of" pulls the value of the contents specified in the
"select" attribute -->
<TD><xsl:value-of select="@ CAFE_TYPE"/></TD>
<!--use the @ symbol to pull values of attributes -->
<TD><xsl:value-of select="FOOD_QUALITY"/></TD>
```

```
        <TD><xsl:value-of select="ENVIRON"/></TD>
        <TD><xsl:value-of select="COST_RATING"/></TD>
        <TD><xsl:value-of select="COMMENTS"/></TD>
      </TR>
      </xsl:for-each>
  <!-- close for-each loop -->
        </TABLE>
        </BODY>
        </HTML>
      </xsl:template>
      <!-- close template tag -->
      </xsl:stylesheet>
      <!-- close stylesheet tag-->
```

Tools and Resources

In addition to a growing number of XML editors, validators, and parsers, the Internet is providing numerous informative documents and tutorials allowing developers to track the rapid advances in XML. Two XML document processing methods are in common use. The **document object model (DOM)** is more comprehensive, while the **Simple API for XML (SAX)** provides a faster and simpler solution.

DOM

The **document object model** is a platform and a language-neutral interface that allows programs and scripts to dynamically access and update the content, structure, and style of documents. The document can be further processed and the results of that processing can be incorporated into the presented page. It is also the specification for how objects in a Web page (text, images, headers, and links) are represented. The DOM defines what attributes are associated with each object and how the objects and attributes can be manipulated. Dynamic HTML (DHTML) relies on the DOM to dynamically change the appearance of Web pages after they have been downloaded to a user's browser. Users can create pages with content, style, and absolute positioning that can be modified on the fly, based on a variety of inputs, without requiring additional server requests. For example, by changing the absolute positioning coordinates of an object, users can achieve immediate animated effects without downloading a new applet or control. The DOM also reduces server load and network traffic as it moves these defined objects locally without a roundtrip back to the server.

Currently, there are three different document object models, but unfortunately, they are not compatible. The Netscape Navigator model is quite different from its Internet Explorer counterpart. The third model is the WWW consortium model. Netscape 6, Internet Explorer 5 (for Macintosh), and Opera solutions are close to the WWW proposal.

The DOM offers two levels of interface implementation: (1) DOM Core, which supports XML and is the base for the next level, and (2) DOM HTML, which extends the model to HTML documents. The functionality specified in the core specification is sufficient for basic passing, access, and manipulation of HTML and XML.

- Most HTML or XML elements are individually addressable by programming.
- The specification is language-independent, and when available it is described using the interface definition language (IDL) from the industry open standard group, CORBA.
- The interface is described in terms of the Java programming language and ECMAScript, an industry-standard scripting language based on JavaScript and JScript. DOM is not to be confused with Microsoft's Component Object Model (COM) or Distributed Component Object Model (DCOM). COM and CORBA are language-independent ways to specify objects and can be used to create DOM objects (documents) just as specific languages such as Java can.

DOM successive developments have been released by the W3C DOM working group. Several working drafts have been issued, and software producers have been working in parallel with the advances in this technology. The first working draft to be published was the requirements document. Its level 0 functionality definition is equivalent to that in Netscape Navigator 3.0 and Microsoft Internet Explorer 3.0. Level 1 specification contains additional functionality for document navigation and manipulation of the content and structure of HTML and XML documents. The DOM level 1 specification has been reviewed by W3C members and other interested parties and was endorsed by the director as a W3C recommendation on October 1, 1998. The DOM level 2 specification is at the candidate recommendation phase, which means implementation feedback is being solicited. The next phase involves the standardization as a proposed recommendation, where member organizations will review the specification. The full text of the level 2 recommendation can be found at www.w3.org/TR/2000/CR-DOM-Level-2-20000510/. The draft provides detailed information about:

- What is a DOM?
- How does the core interface work?
- DOM HTML.
- DOM views.

- DOM style sheets.
- DOM CSS.
- DOM events.
- DOM traversals.
- DOM ranges.

The W3C recently released the requirements for the DOM level 3. While it is developed in the same spirit as its predecessor, the level 3 draft will include a number of new features. It is more comprehensive and encompasses the following general requirements.

- The object model is language neutral and platform independent.
- There will be a core DOM that is applicable to HTML, CSS, and XML documents.
- The object model can be used to construct and deconstruct the document.
- The object model will not preclude use by either agents external to the document content or scripts embedded within the document.
- Consistent naming conventions must be used through all levels of the object model.
- A visual user interface component will not be required for a conforming implementation of the object model.
- The specific HTML, CSS, and XML document object models will be driven by the underlying constructs of those languages.
- It must be possible to read in a document and write out a structurally isomorphic document.
- The object model will not expose the user to problems with security, validity, and privacy.
- The object model will not preclude other mechanisms for manipulating documents.

The document object model is so powerful that one can do almost anything with the XML document once it has been parsed in memory. Some applications do not require the functionality that imposes burdens on server memory and slows document loading.

The Simple API for XML (SAX)

The Simple API for XML is a response to the growing complexity of the document object model. It provides an application programming interface (API) that allows programmers to interpret a Web file that uses XML. SAX is an alternative to using the DOM and is appropriate where many or very large files are to be processed, but it contains fewer capabilities for manipulating data content.

TABLE 7–2   SAX Definitions

SAX Name	Type
AttributeList	Interface
DTDHandler	Interface
DocumentHandler	Interface
EntityResolver	Interface
ErrorHandler	Interface
Locator	Interface
Parser	Interface
HandlerBase	Class
InputSource	Class
SAXException	Exception
SAXParseException	Exception

SAX was developed by the XML-DEV mailing list. The goal was to produce an event-driven interface to allow plug-and-play between the actual parser and the application that used the data. Details of the standard and a Java implementation are available at www. megginson.com/SAX.

SAX defines seven interfaces, two classes, and two exceptions (see Table 7–2). There are four handler interfaces, one each for resolving entities (EntityResolver), handling entities and notations (DTDHandler), dealing with the document structure and content (DocumentHandler), and fielding any errors (ErrorHandler). These handlers are brought together in the parser, described by its own interface (Parser). The parser steps through the actual XML document and calls the appropriate methods in the handlers as necessary.

The other two interfaces define how to specify the attributes for a tag (AttributeList) and the location of the parser in the source document (Locator). The latter allows for better error reporting if something goes wrong.

Two helper classes are also included, HandlerBase and InputSource. HandlerBase is a default implementation for all the handler interfaces. The parser uses an object of this type if no other handler is specified. Typically, these default methods do nothing. By deriving the handler from this base, the users need only to override those methods that they want to do something useful. The InputSource class defines an input stream containing the XML document and can load that stream from local storage or across the Internet. It also contains details as to where the document came from and how it was encoded.

For error reporting, two exceptions are defined, SAXException and SAXParseException. SAXException, the parent of all SAX exceptions, includes a property allowing for embedding any other exception within it. Thus, a normal exception can be wrapped to make it appear as a SAXException. SAXParseException, which is derived from SAXException, adds properties to identify the originating document and the position within it that caused the error.

For more information on the SAX specification, visit www.megginson. com/SAX. While SAX may appear complicated to an HTML user not familiar with all these new functions, many of the dimensions have default value and can be used as the developer becomes more familiar with the new technology.

SAX implementation for Java and C++ have been around for a while and Microsoft has made available a SAX parser for Visual Basic. SAX has much better performance than DOM both in terms of memory usage and document loading time.

XML Applications, Standards, and Frameworks

Over the past two years, a number of initiatives have emerged that are centered on the XML technology. Figure 7–12 illustrates some of the influential activities coming under the umbrella of the W3C.

FIGURE 7–12
Use of XHTML with other tag sets

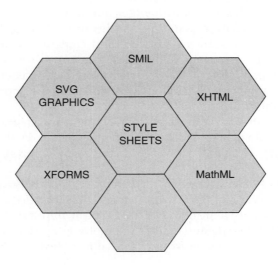

As industry groups perceive the potential of XML to streamline their business, they have launched a number of projects. Many organizations join multiple projects to hedge their bets. Often these initiatives recognize that XML provides an extraordinarily flexible set of structures that can hold many different types of information, but that guidelines need to be developed to harvest its potential. An early test (MathML), an XML application applied to mathematics, provided the experience upon which to build more advanced models. Another initiative was to recast the latest HTML standard in terms of an XML template leading to XHTML.

XHTML

The XHTML 1.0 recommendation maps closely to HTML 4. A proper XHTML document requires few steps:

- Make tags case-sensitive. XHTML uses lowercase. This is a good transition measure to start using lowercase for all HTML coding.
- Include end tags for the HTML tags that are ordinarily singleton (e.g., </p>, </li>).
- Add a / to empty tags (e.g., <br/>, <hr/>).
- Quote all attributes (e.g., <img src="tiger.gif" Border="1">).

Following these simple rules will make a site more maintainable in the future.

SMIL

The **Synchronized Multimedia Integration Language (SMIL)** describes interactive synchronized multimedia distributed on the Web. It is an easy-to-author XML-compliant format similar in syntax to HTML. SMIL 1.0 became an official W3C recommendation in 1998. A new version, SMIL-Boston, is under review. SMIL 1.0 provides Web users with the following benefits:

- Easily defined basic timing relationships.
- Fine-tuned synchronization.
- Spatial layout.
- Direct inclusion of nontext and nonimage media.
- Hyperlink support for time-based media.
- Adaptive to varying user and system characteristics.

SMIL is written as an XML application and is currently a W3C recommendation. SMIL enables authors to specify what should be presented and when, enabling them to control the precise time when a sentence is spoken. It may synchronize the display of a given image appearing on the screen with related vocal comments.

Named media components for text, images, audio, and video with URLs will be called by SMIL script and scheduled in parallel or in sequence. A typical SMIL presentation has the following characteristics:

- The presentation is composed of several components that are accessible via URLs, (e.g., files stored on a Web server).
- The components have different media types, such as audio, video, image, and text. The beginning and ending times of various components are specified relative to events in other media components. For example, in a slide show, a particular slide is displayed when the narrator in the audio begins talking about it.
- Familiar looking control buttons, such as stop, fast-forward, and rewind, allow users to interrupt the presentation and to move forward or backward to another point in the presentation.
- Additional functions include random access, which enables the presentation to be started anywhere, and slow motion.
- The user can follow hyperlinks embedded in the presentation.

SMIL has been designed to be easy to author simple presentations with a text editor. The key to success for HTML was that attractive hypertext content could be created without requiring a sophisticated authoring tool. Similarly, SMIL achieves this goal for synchronized hypermedia.

SMIL-Boston will be supported in IE 5.5. Microsoft Internet Explorer 5.5 Developer Preview release includes support for several of the SMIL-Boston modules, including Animation, Timing and Synchronization, and Media Object. The SMIL-Boston working draft proposes XML tags for controlling presentation of multimedia components in sequence and in parallel, as well as on an exclusive basis. The draft also defines a number of new elements and attributes useful for controlling presentation, synchronization, and interactivity. Originally advocated by Microsoft, SMIL is now embraced by a number of companies.

An excerpt from the W3C illustrates the concept:

```
<par>
  <a href="#Story"> <img src="button1.jpg" /> </a>
  <a href="#Weather"> <img src="button2.jpg" /></a>
  <excl>
    <par id="Story" begin="0s">
    <video src="video1.mpg" />
    <text src="captions.html" />
</par>
    <par id="Weather">
    <img src="weather.jpg" />
```

```
        <audio src="weather_rpt.mp3"/>
        </par>
      </excl>
    </par>
```

The <par> tag indicates that captions for the story will run in parallel to the video and a spoken weather report in parallel to the picture of the weather.

RosettaNet

RosettaNet is a nonprofit organization (www.rosettanet.org) that seeks to implement standards for supply chain (manager–supplier) transactions on the Internet. The group, which includes American Express, Microsoft, Netscape, and IBM, is working to standardize labels for elements such as product descriptions, part numbers, pricing data, and inventory status. RosettaNet anticipates implementing the framework for data and process interchange with e-business through XML.

Figure 7–13 depicts the parallel between a human-to-human business exchange and a server-to-server electronic business exchange. To communicate in a human-to-human business exchange, humans must be able to produce and hear sound. Further, they must then agree on a common alphabet for creating individual words. Grammatical rules are then applied to the words to create a dialog. That dialog forms the business process, which is conducted or transmitted through an instrument such as a telephone.

XML/EDI

Open electronic data interchange (EDI) standards such as ANSI X12 and UN/EDIFACT provide the basis for unambiguous business-to-business data exchanges. XML enables a Web-based alternative for dynamic relations

FIGURE 7–13
The RosettaNet schema

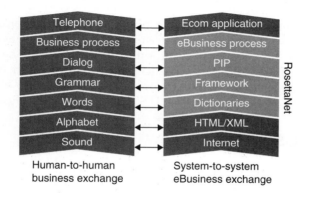

Human-to-human
business exchange

System-to-system
eBusiness exchange

for small and medium size companies. **XML/EDI** provides a standard framework/format to describe various types of data (e.g., an invoice, a health care claim, and project status) so that the information, whether a transaction, a catalog, or a document in a workflow, can be searched, decoded, manipulated, and displayed consistently and correctly by implementing EDI dictionaries. Thus, combining XML and EDI forged a new powerful paradigm.

XML and EDI are very different. The creators of EDI were mainly concerned about the size of their messages. Bandwidth for EDI networks is very expensive, even today. EDI messages are thus very compressed and use codes to represent complex values. All of the metadata is stripped from an EDI message, which makes the message difficult to read and debug. The complexity of EDI makes it difficult to train EDI programmers and expensive to keep them, which, in turn, makes EDI applications expensive to buy and maintain. Complexity drives cost.

BizTalk

BizTalk is an industry initiative started by Microsoft and supported by a range of organizations, from technology vendors such as SAP and CommerceOne to technology users like Boeing and BP/Amoco. BizTalk is not a standards body; instead, it is a community of standards users, with the goal of driving the rapid, consistent adoption of XML to enable electronic commerce and application integration.

The BizTalk Framework™ is a set of guidelines for publishing schemas in XML and for using XML messages to easily integrate software programs. The design emphasis is on leveraging the existing data models, solutions, and application infrastructure and to adapt them for electronic commerce through the use of XML.

XBRL

Extensible Business Reporting Language (**XBRL**), formerly code-named XFRML, is an open specification that uses XML-based data tags to describe financial statements for both public and private companies. The international XBRL project committee developed XBRL with assistance from firms representing the financial information supply chain. The American Institute of Certified Public Accountants sponsored the project. XBRL has an active working group at www.xbrl.org dedicating efforts to XBRL financial statements specification and the U.S. commercial and industrial taxonomy.

XML Schemas

XML can be used to define applications for different organizations in industrial sectors. A number of schemas are being developed for a variety of subjects.

- The open application group (OAG) is developing a full set of XML, DTD files that define interoperability APIs for financials, human resources, manufacturing, logistics, and supply chain components.

- The open financial exchange specification enables financial institutions and brokerage firms to implement online connectivity for both personal financial management software products, such as Microsoft Money and Intuit's Quicken, and to build dynamic websites. Open financial exchange supports transactions for banking, credit, brokerage, and mutual fund markets.

- Open trading protocol (OTP) is used for the development of software products that will permit product interoperability for electronic purchases that are independent of the chosen payment mechanism. OTP encapsulates the payment with the offers, invoice, receipts for payment, and delivery.

- IMS Global Learning Consortium, Inc., is developing and promoting open specifications for facilitating online distributed learning activities such as locating and using educational content, tracking learner progress, reporting learner performance, and exchanging student records between administrative systems. Sun has made available to the distributed learning community a developers' toolkit for the creation of XML documents that conform to the IMS meta-data specification standard (www.imsproject.org/tools/sun.html). Similarly, Microsoft is providing a Learning Resource Interchange toolkit for creating IMS-compatible online learning content for Web-based training solutions (www.microsoft.com/eLearn/).

- VML is an application of XML 1.0. It defines a format for the encoding of vector information, together with additional markups to describe how that information may be displayed and edited.

- The Java Speech Markup Language (JSML) is used by applications to annotate text input to API speech synthesizers. The JSML elements provide a speech synthesizer with detailed information on how to specify the text. JSML includes elements that describe the structure of a document, provide pronunciations of words and phrases, and place markers in the text. JSML also provides prosodic elements that control phrasing, emphasis, pitch, and speaking rate. Appropriate markup of text improves the quality and naturalness of the synthesized voice. Since JSML uses the unicode character set, JSML can be used to mark up text in most languages of the world.

- This project addresses how the Unified Modeling Language (UML) models can be interchanged. It proposes an application-neutral format called UXF (UML eXchange Format), which is an exchange format for UML models based on XML. UXF is a format powerful enough to express, publish, access, and exchange UML models and a natural extension from the existing Internet environment. It serves as a communication vehicle for developers and as a well-structured data format for development tools. With UXF, UML models can be distributed universally.

With XML becoming more popular, XML schemas will be developed for a wide range of applications.

XML Query

XML-QL, a query language for XML data, will respond to some of the above questions related to the manipulation of data through XML. XML-QL can express queries, which extract pieces of data from XML documents, as well as transformations, which, for example, can map XML data between DTDs and can integrate XML data from various sources.

XSLT

As more content publishers and commercial interests deliver rich data in XML, the need for presentation technology increases in both scale and functionality. XSL will meet the more complex, structural formatting demands of XML document authors.

Extensible style language transformation (XSLT) makes it possible for one XML document to be transformed into another according to an XSL style sheet. As part of the document transformation, XSLT uses XPath to address parts of an XML document that an author wants to transform. XPath models an XML document as a tree of nodes. There are different types of nodes, including element nodes, attribute nodes, and text nodes. XPath defines a way to compute a string value for each type of node. Some types of nodes also have names.

XPath fully supports XML Namespaces [XML Names]. Thus, the name of a node is modeled as a pair consisting of a local part and a possibly null name space universal resources identifier (URI). This is called an expanded name. XPath is also used by another XML technology, XPointer, to specify locations in an XML document.

XFORMS

Smart forms will address the lack of features in HTML forms. Where documents are passed from application to application, XFORMS associates the structure to fields, making the form more portable.

These initiatives represent only a few examples of the projects under construction. Businesses should be aware of the germane dominant projects and follow their progress closely to hedge their opportunities and to avoid being sidetracked if any of them becomes widely adopted. Any of these schemas will have increased usefulness when a larger number of partners agree on their use as a derivative to the Metcalf law (the value of a network is a function of the number of nodes connected to that network; value grows exponentially with each node).

SOAP

The **simple object access protocol (SOAP)** was developed by Microsoft as a means for a program running in one type of operating system, such as Windows NT, to communicate with a program in the same or another kind of an operating system, such as Linux, through the World Wide Web's hypertext transfer protocol (HTTP). It uses XML as the mechanism for information exchange. Since Web protocols are readily available for all major operating system platforms, HTTP and XML provide a simple solution to the problem of how programs running under different operating systems in a network can communicate with each other. SOAP specifies precisely how to encode an HTTP header and an XML file so that a program in one computer can call a program in another computer and pass it information. It also specifies how the called program can return a response.

SOAP consists of three parts:

- The SOAP envelope construct defines an overall framework for expressing what is in a message; who should deal with it; and whether it is mandatory or optional.
- The SOAP encoding rules define a serialization mechanism that can be used to exchange instances of application-defined data types.
- The SOAP RPC representation defines a convention that can be used to represent remote procedure calls and responses.

In addition to the SOAP envelope, the SOAP encoding rules, and the SOAP RPC conventions, this specification defines two protocol bindings that describe how a SOAP message can be carried in HTTP messages either with or without the HTTP extension framework.

Scripting Languages

As the Web evolved, another weakness of HTML became apparent. As a language, HTML is nonprocedural. This deficiency comes from its inability to process structured information along with a lack of interactive qualities. To remedy these limitations, the capability to embed procedural code was devised through scripting languages. Two camps developed their own languages. On the one hand, Microsoft advocated the use of VBScript derived from the firm's Visual Basic, a widely understood programming language, making the use of VBScript a logical step for PC users desiring a Microsoft solution.

The other option advocated by a group of vendors led by Netscape developed a language called LiveWire, later renamed JavaScript. Often misrepresented by its name, the language is not a relative of the Java language. Rather, it emerged from a Netscape effort at having a scripting language when it dominated the browser market. Microsoft supports the language as a viable alternative to VBScript, with its own dialect, JScript. The language has been standardized and normalized by ECMA, a European standard body. As ECMAScript, it is similar in form to JavaScript and is more multiplatform than VBScript, which runs only on MS Windows.

In addition to JavaScript and VBScript, a number of programming languages have been adapted for use on the Web. They provide the glue between the displayed interface and the back-end processing of the numerous existing legacy systems. A Web page can either collect data from the user and pass it to the back office or extract data from back-end systems and dynamically offer it to the Web user. These scripting languages offer a set of tags inserted within the Web page documents. Scripting commands are used on both the client side and server side to facilitate Web transactions.

CGI

The **common gateway interface (CGI)** is the oldest means of adding server side functionality to a website. CGI is not a language but an approach to adding interactivity use scripts in PERL, PHP, or C. CGI is not very scalable, as each new request to a CGI script requires the server to start a new process in the kernel, which uses both CPU time and memory. With a high transactions rate, CGI scripts are rapidly reaching unacceptable speed as multiple concurrent CGI scripts run very slowly.

JavaScript

JavaScript is a major scripting language developed by Netscape. Often mistaken as a relative to Sun's Java, JavaScript does not have much in common with Java, apart from the marketing gimmick of name association. JavaScript enables Web authors to design interactive sites. Although it shares some of the philosophy and structures of the Java language, JavaScript was developed separately and is purely an interpreted language. Its code is embedded and can interact with HTML source code, enabling Web authors to animate their sites with dynamic content.

Endorsed by a number of software companies on multiple platforms, JavaScript is an open language that anyone can use without purchasing a license. Recent browsers from Netscape and Microsoft support it, though

Internet Explorer supports only a variant, which Microsoft calls **JScript.** Microsoft JScript is a scripting language targeted specifically at the Internet that fully conforms to ECMAScript, the Web's only standard scripting language. ECMAScript, the European version of JavaScript, has received the endorsement of the European Computer Manufacturers Association (ECMA) standardization agency.

VBScript

Visual Basic Scripting Edition, a scripting language developed by Microsoft and supported by Microsoft's Internet Explorer Web browser, is based on the Visual Basic programming language, with the same syntax, but it is much simpler. In many ways, **VBScript** mimics the functionality of JavaScript, but it is not multiplatform. It enables Web authors to include interactive controls, such as buttons and scroll bars, on their Web pages in a pure Microsoft environment. Microsoft has promoted the solution quite timidly, making it difficult to recommend this alternative, apart from an intranet where the software environment can be controlled.

ColdFusion

Developed by Allaire, **ColdFusion** consists of a server component that supports proprietary tags in Web pages. ColdFusion Web pages include tags written in ColdFusion Markup Language (CFML) that simplify integration with databases and avoid the use of more complex languages such as C++ to create translating programs.

Developing applications with ColdFusion does not require coding in a traditional programming language. Instead, applications are built by combining standard HTML with a straightforward server side markup language, CFML. ColdFusion provides tags, expressions, and functions. CFML provides a number of proprietary tags that can be used to interact with databases, send e-mail, build HTML output, and manage files. CFML tags look like HTML, but they are preprocessed on the server, not in the browser. Expressions combine data, variables, operators, and functions to manipulate data and return a result. Expressions are used for mathematical calculations, string manipulation, date-time operations, and formatting results.

ColdFusion functions are predefined operations that can be used to manipulate data. Functions can be used in expressions in a variety of places in templates. CFML supports over 130 functions in the following categories:

1. Mathematical and trigonometric functions.
2. Bit manipulation functions.
3. Decision functions.

4. String functions.
5. Date and time functions.
6. Administrative functions.
7. System-level functions.
8. Date, time, and number formatting functions.
9. List functions.

Since Macromedia, which controls a large segment of the Web content development, is buying Allaire its solutions should benefit from the new market synergy.

PERL

Practical Extraction and Report Language (PERL) is a programming language, especially designed for processing text. Because of its strong text processing abilities, it has become one of the most popular languages for writing CGI scripts. PERL is an interpretive language, which makes it easy to build and test simple programs. It evolved in recent years to become a powerful tool used on the server side of many UNIX-based e-commerce sites. While the language interpreter has been ported to other operating systems and Microsoft Windows, in particular, PERL is still dominant on the UNIX server side.

PERL is a fairly straightforward, comprehensive, widely known in the UNIX community, and well-respected scripting language. It is used for a variety of tasks, including the equivalent of DOS batch files and C shell scripts. One advantage of PERL is the community of dedicated and talented developers who have contributed scripts to the public domain. This offers the opportunity to learn PERL by example. Users can also download and modify thousands of PERL scripts for their own use. One of the disadvantages of PERL is that much of this free code is impossible to understand, a problem somewhat alleviated by a number of publications on the topic. A number of sources exist online, including:

- Webopedia (webopedia.internet.com/TERM/P/Perl.html)
- PERL reference site (www.perl.com/pub)
- About.com (http://perl.miningco.com/compute/perl/)
- For MS WIN32 users (www.ActiveState.com/)

PHP

Personal Home Page (PHP) is a programming language created by Rasmus Lerdorf. During the past five years, it has attracted a solid group of followers and new contributors to the language. Some very talented developers, Zeev Suraski and Andi Gutmans, rewrote the parser for the interpreter. PHP version 4 (PHP4) is shipping with a number of Web servers, including RedHat Linux. Since most of the existing documentation exists only for version 3, the diffusion of the newest version could take some time. The strong points of the language include its stability, ease of use, and the fact that PHP can perform any task a more complex CGI program would do. An additional strength is its compatibility with many types of databases. PHP is one of the Internet's hottest and fastest growing server side programming languages, attracting more than a million developers. In early 2001, PHP was being used on more than 250,000 Apache Web servers on the Internet. PHP solved one of the crucial performance problems with CGI by becoming a part of the Web server, saving the end user a considerable amount of load time.

PHP tags are embedded within the documents on the server side. The author can move between HTML and PHP and reach functionality matching active server pages, Java server pages, and proprietary ColdFusion tags instead of having to rely on heavy amounts of code to output HTML. Since PHP is executed on the server, the client is not bothered by the PHP code and security is enhanced as well.

Another reason for PHP's growing popularity is that it is free and an open source project (i.e., users can download both the source code and executables for PHP and install them and use them at will). PHP has been ported and is currently available for all major platforms. It is supported on the Internet on a number of websites and user groups, among the most popular being:

- The official PHP site (www.php.net/)
- PHP Builder (www.phpbuilder.com/)
- PHP Wizard (www.phpwizard.net)
- Developer Shed (www.devshed.com/Server_Side/PHP/)

In addition to adding interactivity to page content, PHP can also send HTTP headers. Users can set cookies, manage authentication, and redirect users. It offers excellent connectivity to many databases through ODBC, as well as integration with various external libraries that let users do everything from generate PDF documents to interact and parse forthcoming XML documents.

ASP

Active server page (ASP) is a specification for a dynamically created Web page with an ASP extension that utilizes ActiveX scripting. Usually implemented with VBScript or JScript, the code is interpreted when a browser requests an ASP. The Web server generates a page with HTML code and then sends it back to the browser. Thus, ASPs are similar to CGI scripts, but they enable Visual Basic programmers to work with familiar tools. As CGI scripts, they suffer from some performance degradation when multiple concurrent requests hit the Web server. Once limited to the Microsoft Windows platform, small companies such as Chili-Soft and Halcyon have recently ported the ASP solution to others (UNIX, Linux).

Java

Java is an ever-present component of the e-commerce landscape. Introduced as a way to spruce up Web pages with moving applets, it has evolved to be more of a server side development feature. Java brings Web browsers to a new level, which is very important to companies that use them to conduct business. Web browsers retrieve information over the Internet or an internal company network, determine the format, and display it for the user.

Software vendors are constantly developing applications that will most likely require a new or updated browser to view information in a meaningful format. For a single user, this is not a problem, since browsers can usually be downloaded in minutes. However, for a large corporation, upgrading browsers on thousands of computers can become a nightmare. This is where Java plays a major role in business. With Java compatibility, a browser becomes more like a computer that can execute programs and communicate with other computers, saving companies a lot of time and money. While the capabilities of Java were oversold and hyped at its inception, the language has matured and is now replacing C++ as the most ubiquitous business language when speed is not critical. As a programming tool, Java is easier to learn than C++ and has the additional advantage of being widely available. Java 2 Platform Enterprise Edition is more than a programming language; it is a complete development environment that allows the developer to build complete networked systems.

As the Web evolves, Java is gaining more presence in the multiple components of e-commerce. Excellent Java tutorials are available on the Internet from some of the main e-commerce stakeholders (e.g., http://java.sun.com/docs/books/tutorial/ or http://www 105.ibm.com/ developerworks/education.nsf/dw/java-onlinecourse-bytitle). Java technology is also used in conjunction with two of the previously mentioned e-commerce components. The two most popular XML parsers (DOM and SAX) are often implemented as Java classes that can be integrated into business solutions. Many of the application servers (replacing legacy transaction servers) mentioned in Chapter 6 are increasingly implemented entirely in Java as servlets or JavaBeans.

Summary

Since its inception, Web page development has moved from being purely static to involving a rather complex design. This chapter discussed some fundamental instruments used in page construction. While HTML remains the building block for most site design, more sites are using Dynamic HTML, style sheets, and a host of scripting languages. In addition, XML, while only a recent addition to the Web designer toolbox, has made rapid inroads in industry. As e-commerce becomes more prevalent, XML, with its ability to manipulate structured information, will evolve into the prevalent approach. A number of initiatives have sprouted as a result of XML adoption. Some of the most notable, such as Biztalk, RosettaNet, and XML/EDI, were presented.

Key Terms

Active server pages (ASP)   297
BizTalk   290
Common gateway interface
  (CGI)   294
ColdFusion   295
Cascading style sheet (CSS)   263
Dynamic HTML(DHTML)   254
Document object model
  (DOM)   282
Document type definition
  (DTD)   276
Hypertext markup language
  (HTML)   246
Java   298
JavaScript   294
Jscript   295
Portable document format
  (PDF)   262

Practical Extraction and Report
  Language (PERL)   296
RosettaNet   289
Simple API for XML   284
Standard Generalized Markup
  Language (SGML)   245
Simple Object Access Protocol
  (SOAP)   293
Synchronized Multimedia
  Integration Language
  (SMIL)   287
VBScript   295
XBRL   290
XML/EDI   289
eXtensible Markup Language
  (XML)   267
eXtensible style sheet (XSL)   277

Review Questions

1. What are the differences between HTML and DHTML?
2. Why was XHTML developed? Do you think this addresses most of the HTML weaknesses?
3. What are the similarities between JavaScript and VBScript?
4. What are the similarities and differences between ASP and JSP?
5. What are the differences between the various approaches to scripting?
6. List some commercial products used for page design. Should a developer rely on one tool or use various tools? What are the pros and cons?
7. List some of the shareware or freely available tools for Web design. In addition to a good HTML editor, what utilities could be very handy to the developer?

8. Given that XML is a moving target, why do you think that its adoption by the business community is being so prompt?

9. XML has triggered the development of many related applications. As a business manager, would you choose one of these instead of developing your own framework?

10. List five or six tags common to most versions of HTML and illustrate each of them with a particular use.

11. Conduct Internet research to find out what tools can be used to parse an XML document to be well-formed and valid.

12. XML schema is a forthcoming development of the technology. Visit the W3C website and search for information on schema. What are the benefits of adopting a schema standardized for a business sector?

13. What are DOMs and why were they developed? Why are some developers using SAX instead of DOM for document processing?

14. SMIL is an application of XML. What is the purpose of this technology? Where does it apply?

15. The current recommendation of W3C is to use XHTML as an alternative to HTML. Do you think adopting XHTML is a wise move?

Projects

1. Write the HTML code that would produce the following Web page.

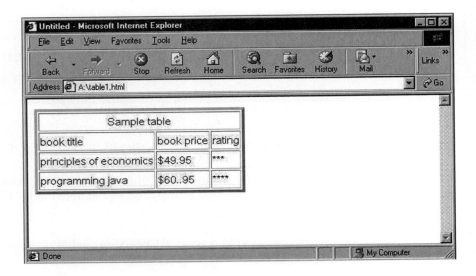

2. Write the XHTML code that would produce the following page.

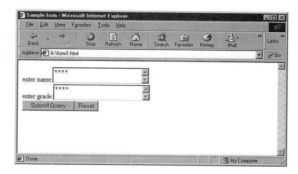

3. Write the HTML code to produce a three-pane frame page.

4. Access a shareware site (e.g., www.tucows.com) or a commercial site and download a trial of an HTML editor. Design a simple page using HTML. What attribute of the product did you like and which one could, in your opinion, be improved? What online help was available in the product? What version of the product did you try and when was it released to the market?

5. Find an online tutorial of DHTML. Did the tutorial warn the user about incompatibilities between browsers? Design a sample page and try to display it with two different browsers. Did they display the same output? Can a commerce website rely on luck when using DHTML?

6. Find a current review or article about scripting language. Which one seems to be gaining market share? Find an online article about a scripting language not mentioned in the chapter (e.g., Python, Rexx). What attributes did it claim that is missing from mainstream scripting language? Would you consider using it for a mainstream project? What are the issues?

7. Use the examples in the chapter to develop an XML project applicable to e-mails. An e-mail document should have the following structure: From, To, CC, Subject, Content, and Attachment. Write for these three alternatives:

    a. XML document with document type definition specifying the structure of an e-mail document, accompanied by a CSS style sheet.

    b. XML with an external document type definition file specifying the structure of an e-mail document, accompanied by a CSS style sheet.

    c. XML with an external document type definition file specifying the structure of an e-mail document, accompanied by an XSL sheet.

    (Use the programs in the chapter as a template to begin with. Note that XML is case-sensitive and tags come in pairs.)

References, Readings, and Hyperlinks

1. Ceponkus, Alex, and Faraz Hoodbhoy. *Applied XML.* New York: John Wiley & Sons, 1999.
2. Hall, Marty. *Core Web Programming.* Upper Saddle River, NJ: Prentice Hall PTR, 1998.
3. Harold, Eliotte Rusty. *XML: Bible.* Chicago: IDG Books Worldwide, Inc., 1999.
4. Holzner, S. *Inside XML.* Indianapolis: New Riders, 2001.
5. Lowery, Joseph. *Dreamweaver 3 Bible.* Foster City, CA: IDG Books Worldwide, Inc., 2000.
6. Marchal, B. *XML by Example.* Indianapolis: Que, 2000.
7. Negrino, T., and D. Smith. *JavaScript for the World Wide Web.* Berkeley, CA: Peach Pit Press Atlanta: Peachtree Publishers, 1999.
8. Pardi, William J. *XML in Action Web Technology.* Redmond, WA: Microsoft Press, 1999.
9. Stanek, W. *HTML, Java, CGI, VRML, SGML Web Publishing Unleashed.* Indianapolis: Sams Publishing, 1996.
10. While some of the links may disappear as the Web evolves, many more can be found using the Internet and search engine with keywords such as "XML tutorial" or "HTML tutorial."
11. www.htmlprimer.com/index.html Simple HTML primer with some JavaScript.
12. www.segment7.net/tutorial/HTML4.html Short HTML4 tutorial.
13. www.w3.org/TR/1999/REC-html401-19991224/ Current recommendation for HTML 4.01.
14. www.w3.org/TR/2000/REC-xhtml-basic-20001219/ XHTML basic.
15. www.w3.org/Style/CSS/ The W3.org Cascading Style Sheet resource page, CSS1 to 3.
16. www.dynamicdeezign.com/htmltutorial/ Another HTML4 tutorial.
17. http://all-html.com Another HTML tutorial.
18. www.w3schools.com/xhtml/ XHTML tutorial.
19. www.w3schools.com/soap/ SOAP tutorial.
20. http://msdn.microsoft.com/workshop/XML/general/soapspec.asp Microsoft SOAP specification.

21. http://xml.apache.org/soap/index.html The Apache Open Source SOAP project.
22. www.xml101.com:8081/ Tutorial and various resources about XML.
23. www.xmlmag.com A new magazine dedicated to the advances in XML.
24. www.webreview.com/authors.shtml Web author resources on Web review site.

Appendix 7.A
A Brief HTML Tutorial

Introduction

```
<html>
<head>
<title> New Page 1 </title>
<body>
<p> Welcome Readers ! </p>
</body>
</html>
```

Display with Netscape Communicator.

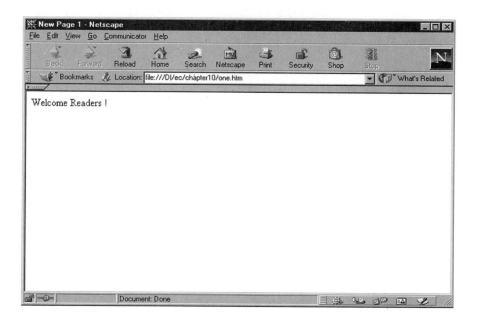

HTML controls the appearance of the document.

```
<html>
<head>
```

```
<title>New Page 2 </title>
</head>
<body>
<h3><big><big>This is a big and bold heading! </big></big>
   </h3>
<h4><em>><big><big>This is smaller but with emphasis>
   </big> </big></em></h4>
<h5 align="center"><u>underlined and </u></h5>
<h5 align="center"><u>centered </u></h5>
</body>
</html>
```

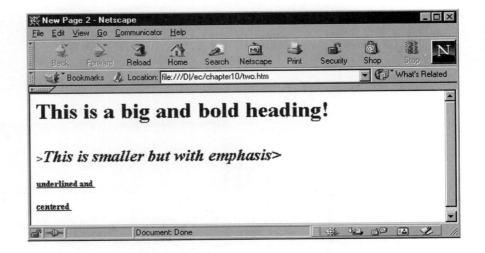

Display illustrates bold, underlined, and emphasis in the rendering. HTML also allows for the definition of visual structures.

```
<html>
<head>
<title>New Page 3 </title>
</head>
<body>
<p> Welcome Readers !</p>
<p>This is a numbered list:
<ol>
   <li>First item of the list </li>
   <li>Second item of the list </li>
   <li>Third item of the list </li>
```

```
</ol>
</p>
<p> </p>
<p>This is an ordinary list
<ul>
   <li>First item of the list </li>
   <li>Second item of the list </li>
</ul>
</body>
</html>
```

This will display:

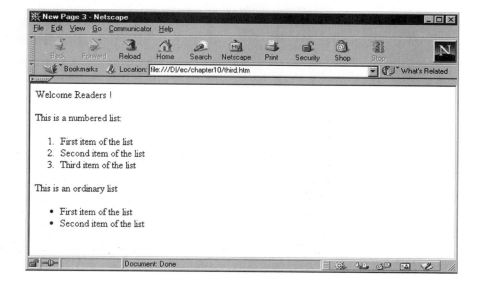

HTML can define interactivity on a Web page.

```
<html>
<head>
<title>New Page 4 </title>
</head>
<body>
<p> Welcome Readers !</p>
<p> </p>
<form method="POST" action="--WEBBOT-SELF--">
<p>Last Name
<input type="text" name="T1" size="20"></p>
```

```
<p> Please Provide your comments</p>
<p> </p>
<p><textarea row="2" name="S1"
  cols="20"></textarea></p>
<p> </p>
<p><input type="submit" value="submit" name="B2"></p>
</form>
</body>
</html>
```

This will display as:

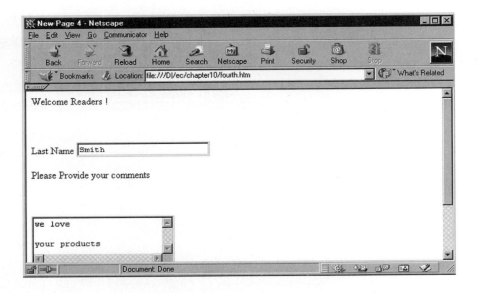

The host site would then receive a Form Confirmation. Thank you for submitting the following information:

T1: Smith
B1: Submit
S1
We love your products
<u>Return to the Form</u>

HTML visual structure—Table

```
<html>
<head>
<body>
```

```
<table border="1" width="66%"
  <tr>
    <td width="33%">Cell A1</td>
    <td width="33%">Cell A2</td>
    <td width="34%">Cell A3</td>
  </tr>
  <tr>
    <td width="33%">Cell B1</td>
    <td width="33%">Cell B2</td>
    <td width="33%">Cell B3</td>
  </tr>
  <tr>
    <td width="66%" colspan="2">A merged Cell C1</td>
    <td width="34%"> Cell C2</td>
  </tr>
  <tr>
    <td width="33%" rowspan="2">A merged Cell E1</td>
    <td width="67%" colspan="2"> Cell E2</td>
  </tr>
  <tr>
    <td width="67%" colspan="2"> Cell F1</td>
  </tr>
</table>
<body>
<html>
```

This will display:

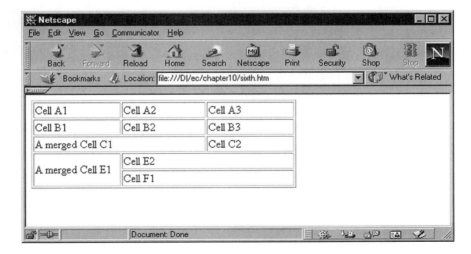

More elaborate designs include the use of HTML style sheets.

```
<html>
<head>
<title>Favorites</title>
<style>
<!--
H1.red{ font-family: Arial; font-size: 18pt }
H1.blue{ font-family: cursive; font-size: 16pt }
P.main{ font-family: Courier; font-size: 12pt }
P.special{ font-family: fantasy; font-size: 10pt }
-->
</style>
</head>
<body>

<h1 class="red">This is a red heading</h1>
<h1 class="blue">This is a blue heading</h1>
<p class="main">This is a normal main paragraph</p>
<p class="special">This is a special type of paragraph </p>
</body>
</html>
```

This will display:

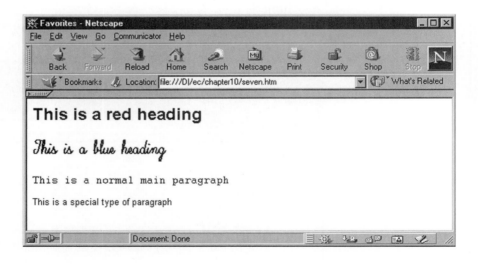

With the following additions, the H1 section will appear in color:

```
<style>
<!--
H1.red{ font-family: Arial; font-size: 18pt ; color: rgb(255,0,0) }
H1.blue{ font-family: cursive; font-size: 16pt ; color: rgb(0,0,255) }
P.main{ font-family: Courier; font-size: 12pt }
P.special{ font-family: fantasy; font-size: 10pt }
-->
<style>
```

SEARCHING MECHANISMS

Chapter Outline

Learning Objectives

By the end of this chapter, you should be able to:

- Explain how search engines work.
- Describe the use of search engines in intranet and extranet environments.
- Identify the important features of popular search engines such as Yahoo!, Alta Vista, and Excite.
- Describe a flexible search strategy for use on the Web.
- Identify various information sources such as the Web, specialized databases, and usenet groups.

Chapter Overview

This chapter focuses on search engines, their various types, and how they operate. Company websites, such as www.microsoft.com and www.oracle.com, often have millions of pages. Current and prospective customers need search engines to access information from these sites. Search engines also play an important role in intranets. As companies transfer more internal data to their websites for access by employees, search engines help make these websites usable.

The chapter begins with a consideration of search mechanisms on the Internet such as Archie and Veronica. These search tools were developed for use on files, directories, and documents listed on the Internet. Early search engines used software that roamed the Web collecting information from URL names, meta-tags, and document titles. This software was variously termed *spiders*, *crawlers*, *agents*, and *softbots*. Subject and topic directories such as Yahoo! and full-text search mechanisms such as Alta Vista are described. The concepts of relevance and precision are also discussed in the context of evaluating search engines. Finally, the distinctive features of search engines such as Excite, Lycos, and HotBot are considered.

A Technical Vignette

Since the advent of e-commerce, the Web has been increasing in size at a phenomenal rate. By some estimates, about a million documents (at a few kilobytes each) are being added every day. These documents include unstructured material such as research papers, tables, indexes, video and audio clips, advertisements, and regulations. The content of the Web changes continuously with the addition of material that is often temporary, making it difficult to catalog the Web as one can catalog a library. Libraries carry mostly books. The search for books is facilitated by a catalog system that contains meta-data about books such as authors, titles, and subject. No such meta-data exists for the content on the Web.

Search engines help make the Web usable. When a query is submitted to a search engine, it lists all Web documents where the query words occur. The search engines also provide a **relevance ranking** of the returned results, with the most relevant items listed first. The relevance-ranking mechanism considers how often the search items occur in a document and where they occur. Unfortunately, the relevance-ranking mechanism often fails to perform, and the user is left to deal with a deluge of responses.

Search engines do not ascribe importance to documents in the same manner that people do. Automated programs have difficulty judging the overall characteristics of a document such as its theme or its genre (e.g., whether it is an advertisement or a research document). If searching for information about computers, IBM may be an important site for the user, but it does not often use the word *computer* in its website, and thus IBM is unlikely to rank high on a search engine list. The relevance-ranking system also is open to manipulation. Website designers abuse the system to improve their site ranking by repeatedly using popular words such as sex, Microsoft, and computers.

Many solutions are being attempted to solve the relevance-ranking problem. For example, researchers at several centers are trying to adopt a method called citation index, a metric for judging the quality of journals. The method depends on the fact that high-quality journals are more likely to be cited than their lesser counterparts. Citation indexing computes the total number of citations that a journal receives and makes quality judgments based on that. There are many variations to citation indexing; for example, citations from higher-quality journals carry more weight than citations from lower-quality ones. Investigators at Stanford University have developed a search engine called Google (www.google.com) that ranks Web documents according to principles of citation indexing. For a given Web page, Google calculates a score by identifying all documents that point their links to that page and then summing their individual scores. Highly visited sites are often sites that have many links pointing to them. With Google, such sites have high rankings.

Clever, a project of the IBM Almaden Research Center in San Jose, follows a principle of assigning Web pages as either hubs or authorities. Authority pages are those that have authoritative contents, while a hub page is one that points to authority pages. Clever takes advantage of the social phenomenon that humans create hublike structures around experts and authority figures. Clever operates over a standard text-indexing engine such as Alta Vista. It runs a query on Alta Vista and finds the pages that contain the query terms. Clever initially assigns some authority figures to the Web pages. Then it seeks out other pages that point to it and assigns initial hub figures to them. It goes through many iterations of score assignments before the hub and authority values stabilize. While Google is fast, Clever provides a superior relevance ranking.

Other solutions are looking at humans working in close concert with machines, with humans assigning scores manually to important sites dealing with popular topics. Machines then take over and help propagate the values to other sites based on hub and authority relationships.

Need for Search Engines

Search engines play an important role in the context of public portals, intranets, and extranets. Important search sites such as Yahoo! and Alta Vista have emerged as popular websites that act as portals to other sites. Searching is one of the most popular activities for Web users. The popular search engine companies also sell their software for incorporation in other company's websites.

The size of websites is daunting (e.g., Compaq, IBM, and Microsoft have websites with more than a million documents each, spread over a few thousand servers). This information has to be accessible to employees, customers, and suppliers. Companies, therefore, have become major users of search engines on their websites. On intranets, search engines help company employees learn about regulations, company information, and many discussion topics. On extranets, search engines help customers find products and inform suppliers about production plans and deliveries.

History of Search Mechanisms

The Internet was created to allow researchers at laboratories and universities to share information. This sharing is promoted through the exchange of files residing on various computers located throughout the country. Files are posted on servers, where they are accessible to users having access to the Internet. The popular method for storing and retrieving files from the Internet is file transfer protocol (FTP). The system works on the basis of FTP clients requesting files from FTP servers. One who wants to share files makes them available on FTP servers. "Anonymous" FTP sites are a popular means for sharing files with collaborators. On such FTP sites, user names and passwords are not necessary for access; users log onto the server using the name "anonymous." FTP is popular even on the Web. It is used to distribute software and files among Web users. To use FTP through a browser, the URL takes the form: ftp://domain-name/directory/file-name.

Archie

As the number and volume of files on FTP sites grew significantly, "word of mouth" for letting people know what files resided where became impractical. Archie, a system for searching FTP sites, was developed. Archie collects the site listings of FTP archives into a database, and users can then query the database. Archie provides a means for matching text expressions in user-requested file names with the file listings in the database. When a match is found, the user is given the full file name, the size, and the address.

Veronica and Wanderer

Gopher is a system of text documents on the Internet. The documents contain no images and can be retrieved through the Gopher system. Researchers make their documents available to Gopher for other users to download. Veronica is a search system for documents on Gopher. It searches text documents for the query or search strings.

Archie and Veronica were the inspiration for the first search engine for the World Wide Web. Called Wanderer, it created a database of URLs. Wanderer led to more sophisticated programs called **spiders.** A spider starts on a popular site at a starter page and then moves on to other pages following the hyperlinks. While at a site, it sends back information about the title and header of the Web pages; the information is then compiled into a database that could be searched through query strings.

How Do Search Engines Work?

A Web search engine studies a database at the search site that contains information about the Web. This database is built up by software programs, variously called spiders, **crawlers,** or **agents.** These programs bring back information about the websites visited (see Figure 8–1). This

FIGURE 8–1

Search engines

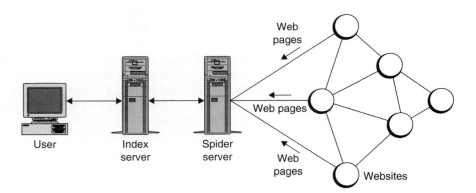

information is then processed and incorporated into a database. When a user submits a query, the database is searched according to the search terms specified in the query. In summary, there are three major functions of a search engine: gathering information, developing a database, and searching the database.

Gathering

There are two factors to consider in this phase: which sites to visit and what information to collect from each site. In the early 1990s, spiders were developed that would start at a popular site and go visiting following the hyperlinks. The software program would revisit sites at some interval, say a month. As Web pages changed, the change would eventually be reflected in the search database. Search engines often untruthfully claim to visit the entire Web. Even the largest of the Web search databases, such as Northern Lights, have at best 30 percent of the Web indexed at any time. The choice of websites depends on factors such as popularity, focus of the search engines, and submissions from Web administrators. Some search engines give primacy to certain topics such as computers or medicine, while some give preference to geographical location of the website. Web administrators can influence site selection by submitting details about their websites to individual search engines.

As for data collection, earlier versions of search programs collected the URLs, the titles, and the headings of the Web documents. In 1995, search engines began collecting entire Web documents. Alta Vista retrieves the first hundred kilobytes of the document. Since most pages are below this size limit, they are collected in their entirety. Now most search engines, including HotBot, Northern Lights, and Alta Vista, collect almost the entire Web document and transport it to their sites for further processing.

Indexing

Once the Web pages are brought to the search engine site, the pages are processed. The search engines store the processed information in a database called an **index.** The search engine usually collects all the words and phrases occurring in the document (see Figure 8–2). For instance, Alta Vista has an automatic phrase-searching mechanism that uses linguistic patterns to recognize phrases. For each word and phrase, the database contains the URL address of the page as well as the location in the document.

Searching

The third function of a search engine is searching the index. When a user inputs words and phrases, the search engine shifts through the index and

FIGURE 8–2
Search engine indexing

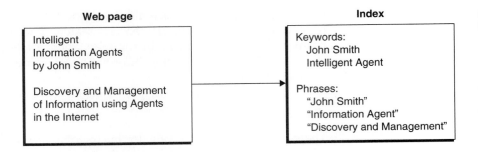

retrieves the URLs where these words and phrases occur. Once the list of URLs is built, the search engine orders them according to relevance. More relevant URLs are exhibited higher in the listing. Relevance ranking is a major issue in the use of search engines. It is not unusual to get a few million hits for the submission of a query. No user can wade through such a large list, and thus inspection is limited to just the first few entries.

Common Search Features

Most search engines share common features, including the use of Boolean operators, phrase searching, proximity searching, wild card searching, and concept searching.

Boolean Searching

Boolean searching is common with most search engines. The Boolean operators used are AND, OR, and NOT. The AND operator is used when all the keywords are required to be in the document. If searching for pages that relate to businesses as well as e-commerce at the same time, the search expression "e-commerce AND business" may be used. Figure 8–3 indicates that use of AND narrows the response to only pages that contain both the terms *e-commerce* and *business*. Pages that contain only the term

FIGURE 8–3
Boolean operators

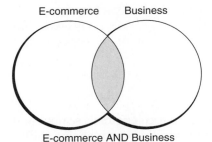

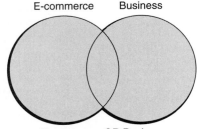

e-commerce and pages that have only the term *business* are kept off the list. The use of AND makes the search much more focused and stringent. In some search engines, the + sign is used in place of AND. In such systems, the search criteria would be: + e-commerce + business.

A search expression such as "e-commerce OR business" would return pages that contain the term *business* only, pages that had the term *e-commerce* only, and pages that contain both the terms (see Figure 8–3). The OR operator casts a much broader net and may result in a huge response set. It is useful when a single concept may be referred to in multiple ways. For example, an automobile may also be referred to as a car or auto.

The use of the operator NOT is used in case of polysemy (i.e., when the same word carries different meanings). If a user is interested, for example, in astronomical stars but wants to avoid movie stars from Hollywood, the user can phrase the search as "stars AND NOT (Hollywood)". Some search engines allow the use of the NOT operator to stand for the combination of AND NOT. Similarly, some allow the use of - in place of NOT.

Phrase Searching

A phrase is a string of words that appear next to each other. For example, many concepts are represented as phrases, such as "acid rain." Most search engines require that a phrase be placed in double quote marks for a **phrase search.** Search engines employ phrase recognition systems to aid in collecting all phrases from a document and then to include them in their indexes.

Proximity Searching

Sometimes ideas and concepts do not come neatly packaged in a phrase. For instance, in a search for information about the warming of the American continent, the terms *America* and *warming* will likely occur close to each other but not be a phrase. Search engines such as Alta Vista and Lycos allow **proximity searching.** The operator NEAR is used to specify proximity. The search expression would be "America NEAR warming." Alta Vista defines NEAR as words that appear within 10 words of each other, while Lycos defines it as 25 words.

Wild Card Searching

Use of wild card characters such as * allow words to be represented that have most of the characters in common. For instance, men and man could both be represented as m*n. Wild cards can also be used to take care of a concept and its plural such as animal and animals, by writing the query as animal*.

Concept Searching

With **concept searching,** a search engine seeks Web pages that have synonyms for or similar terms to the query words. For instance, if a user searches for the word *war*, the search engine would also look for words such as *conflict* and *aggression*. The search engine Excite supports this feature. The system uses statistical methods to extract concepts from documents. The concepts are used for indexing the documents.

Natural Language Searching

Many search engines support expressing queries in plain English (e.g., "Where can I find information about black holes?"). In research laboratories, search engines have been equipped with natural language processing systems on the front-end to process such queries. At this point, the technology is not sufficiently mature to have successful applications. The search engine Ask Jeeves responds to a query by providing a set of questions in plain English from which the user chooses. Its services are used with other search engines such as Alta Vista, so when a plain English search expression is put to Alta Vista, the search is redirected to Ask Jeeves.

Common Display Features

Relevance Ranking

Relevance ranking is currently the major technical challenge to developers of search engines. Every search engine follows its own algorithm for arranging the response list in the order of relevance. Some factors used by the search engines to determine relevance are:

- The location of the words. The heading and title are usually considered to be more important than the body. In the body, words occurring in the first few paragraphs are assigned greater weight.
- The frequency with which the words occur. Word frequency is a common factor for computing the relevance ranking of a Web page. The more often the search words occur, the higher the document is ranked.
- The popularity of the sites. Some search engines, including Alta Vista, rank different sites with different weights (i.e., popular sites are ranked higher than less popular sites).

• The currency and connectivity of the pages. Pages with many links pointing to them are taken as more important than pages that have fewer links pointing to them. Likewise, new pages are ranked higher than old pages by some search engines.

Summaries

Some search engines include short descriptions of each Web page that they return. These summaries help users to assess the relevance of the page. Often, these summaries are automatically generated by software systems. Some systems simply select the first few sentences on each page as an indicator of what the page is about. Others provide a collection of important phrases from the page that are available in the index.

Subject Directories and Specialized Databases

Some search engines do not directly search websites. Instead, these sites maintain a searchable subject or a topic directory. The most popular site of this type is **Yahoo!,** which is a directory-based Web search tool. When a user searches Yahoo!, the search system examines the site's topic categories and the brief description it carries for the sites. The system does not employ spiders or crawlers to search the Web. Instead, it depends on Web administrators to submit their URLs to Yahoo!. All submissions are reviewed by Yahoo!, and they are included in the appropriate topic category. Yahoo! maintains the equivalent of a telephone Yellow Pages directory.

Since the entry process is manual, Yahoo! cannot afford to index the entire Web. But it can afford to impose a strict regimen of quality control. Yahoo! has a large hierarchical topic system. For instance, all business-related sites are included in "Business & Economy." A Yahoo! search can be conducted by browsing the topics to find appropriate URL listings. The search can also be conducted using keywords, and the system searches for the keywords in the site descriptions that Yahoo! carries for each site. Since Yahoo! does not actually visit a site and collect page data, the listing is unaffected by changes that may be implemented on the site.

Virtual libraries are subject directories that are maintained by professionals such as librarians. They provide access to reference sources such as handbooks, dictionaries, and encyclopedias. A popular virtual library is the Librarian's Index to the Internet (http://sunsite.berkeley.edu/internetindex). It contains over 3,000 evaluated resources, and it allows browsing on topics as well as phrase searching. The library is maintained by the California State Library System.

Specialized databases maintain subject directories on certain topics. In contrast to general-purpose subject directories, databases do not maintain just links; they also contain the actual content or a summary of the content. Often, these sources, which are available on a payment basis, are maintained by for-profit companies. Free databases are maintained by government departments and universities. These electronic databases deal with specialized topics such as medicine, law, and academic research. Popular specialized databases include FirstSearch, DIALOG, MEDLINE, and Lexis-Nexis.

Meta-Search Engines

Meta-search engines simultaneously farm out the search query to several search engines. They collect the results received from these search engines, arrange them, and then provide them to the user. These search engines allow the user to select the search engines and also the search area. For instance, Dogpile (www.dogpile.com) permits the user to specify the search scope in terms of Web, FTP sites, Usenet, or news services. It submits the search query to three search engines. If the response received is less than 10, then it goes out to three more search engines.

Metacrawler (www.metacrawler.com) is another popular meta-search engine that uses, for example, the services of Alta Vista, Excite, Lycos, and Yahoo!. It takes the top 10 results from each search engine and provides them to the user, eliminating the duplicates and displaying the results according to relevance.

Evaluation of Search Engines

Search engines are often evaluated based on two criteria: **recall** and **precision,** both of which are expressed as ratios. Recall involves the ratio of pages returned to the total volume of pages on the Web that are related somehow to the query. Precision measures the quality of the recall, and it is expressed as a ratio of highly relevant pages returned to the total number of pages returned by the search engines.

Precision and recall are often conflicting. Search engines that are good at recall are usually poor at precision and vice versa. Full text-based search engines such as Alta Vista and Northern Lights are very good at recall. They are able to identify many Web pages that relate to a query, but because automated systems are poor at measuring the relevance of documents to the query, the precision is poor. Most pages returned have little relevance. It is the reverse case with searchable directories such as Yahoo!. Since the entries in Yahoo! are evaluated by humans and they are organized according to a logical hierarchy, the precision is high. Because there are only so many entries on the Web that can be manually checked and entered in a database, the recall is poor.

The requirement for precision or recall varies over the life cycle of a search process. At the beginning of the search process, users usually are certain of what they are seeking. They are said to be in the exploration mode. Search engines with high recall serve this exploration phase better. Toward the end of the search process, the user's requirements become more precise. This is called the exploitation phase, and at this point a search system with high precision serves user needs better. The two phases, exploration and exploitation, sometimes alternate in a complex search activity. Exploration generates ideas that are exploited through further search activity. During the exploitation phase, when the search needs are more sharply defined, users are typically more interested in the efficiency of the search process, spending less time and effort to locate what they already know they are looking for.

Search Engine Listing

Consumer surveys indicate that few users want to review more than the 10 top listings of a search. An e-commerce business's survival may depend on winding up in the top 10 listings. All search engines have a process by which sites are listed. With search engines such as Yahoo!, it is not guaranteed that a particular site will be included in its directory. Search sites also indicate the time that they take to include a site in their indexes, the number of pages that can be submitted at one time, and the number of times they can be submitted. Some search engines give preferential treatment in ranking to sites that have registered with them. GoTo (www.goto.com) allows Web administrators to bid against each other to get a high ranking.

Many commercial sites, for a small payment, will arrange to have sites listed with several popular search engines. How well a site will be ranked depends on how skillfully the administrator can exploit the ranking methodologies used by the search engines. Generally, the first step is to identify all the keywords and phrases that relate to a site. These are the words that the users are likely to use during their query. Since ranking algorithms use location and frequency of these words to develop rankings, the next step for site developers is to ensure that these keywords and phrases appear in the title, in meta-tags, in headings, and frequently in the first few paragraphs of the introductory Web pages. However, these techniques should be used judiciously. Software is now becoming clever in spotting **spamming** (i.e., repeated use of popular phrases). If keywords occur more than a threshold frequency, the software identifies the site as a spammer and rejects it.

Popular Search Engines

The popular search engines, such as Yahoo!, Alta Vista, Lycos, Excite, and HotBot (which is now part of Lycos), have important distinguishing features.

Yahoo!

Yahoo! (see Figure 8–4) is not strictly a search engine; it is a database of Web addresses in the manner of the Yellow Pages. Most search engine sites, such as Alta Vista, offer such a feature, but Yahoo! continues to have the most detailed subject or topic hierarchy. Where other database directories have subjects that are at best two levels deep, Yahoo!'s directory structure is usually four to five levels deep in terms of topics and subtopics. Because the Yahoo! database structure is maintained manually, the quality of its entries is assured. The database contains topic categories, Web titles, and brief descriptions of the websites. On the Yahoo! site, users can also search Usenet news groups and e-mail addresses.

While using Yahoo!, users search not only the topic categories but also the individual site descriptions. The results returned include both the topics and the individual sites that match the query. Users can further refine a search by choosing Yahoo! categories or websites. Yahoo! permits use

FIGURE 8–4
Yahoo's directory listing on electronic commerce

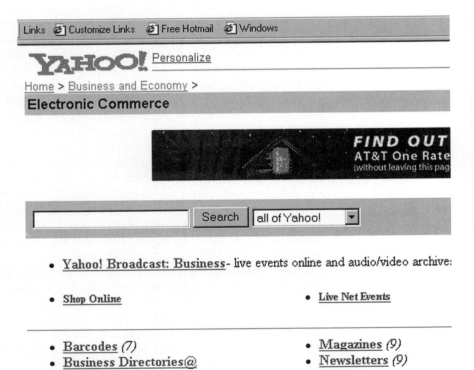

of Boolean operators such as AND and OR as well as phrase searching. It is important to have some knowledge about the topic or subject structure of Yahoo! in order to use the system efficiently. For example, all commercial and business sites are found under the "Business and Economy" section in the Yahoo! directory. Knowing this can save time.

Alta Vista

Alta Vista (see Figure 8–5) continues to maintain one of the largest copies of the Web for searching, almost 300 gigabytes in size. The database is created by a spider, called **scooter,** that roams the Web once every month to update the Alta Vista database. It also has a topic directory similar to Yahoo! but smaller. The topic or subject directory is supplied by LookSmart. Users can also search Usenet news groups at the Alta Vista site.

Alta Vista provides two different interfaces for the user to input a query. The basic search form is better used when one has a few unique words to drive the search process. The advanced search page is used to input complex Boolean statements using operators such as AND, OR, and NEAR. To narrow the search, Alta Vista permits the use of field search, where particular values of the field can be specified; for example, one can specify the title of the Web page to have the term *computer*. The search results can be further refined by use of a "refine" button, which analyzes the words that the sites contain and suggests likely topics and keywords to further tighten the search criteria.

FIGURE 8–5
Alta Vista's interface for advanced search

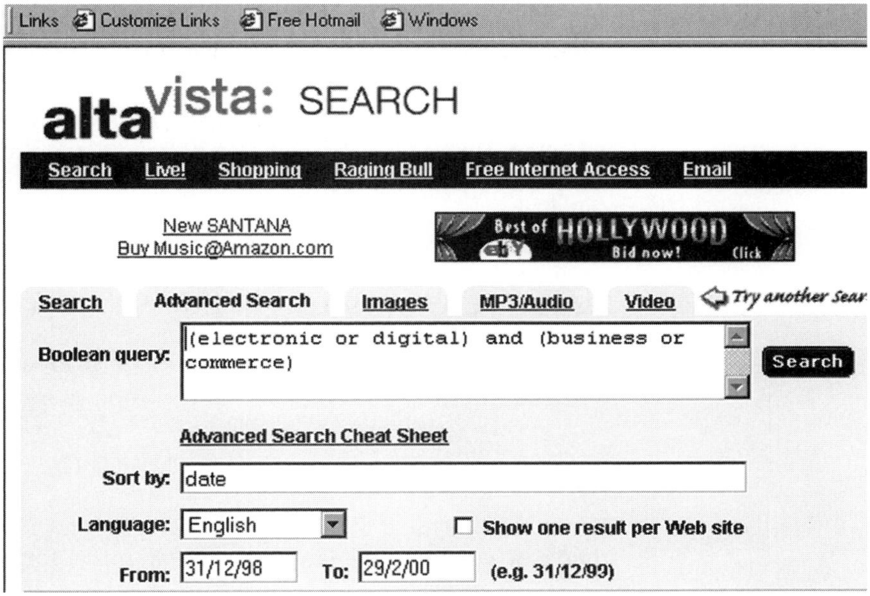

FIGURE 8–6

*Directory-based search
at Lycos*

Lycos

Lycos is popular for its "Lycos Top 5%" websites, which are indexed for a variety of topics and subtopics, called Web guides (see Figure 8–6). These listings are created manually on the basis of site popularity and content quality. A limited number of sites are presented on any one topic. The site selection process is considered to be reliable and authoritative. Lycos attempts to marry the advantages of a site such as Yahoo! with a general full-text search engine. The top 5 percent listings improve the precision of the searches and the full-text searching promotes high recall.

Lycos is also popular for providing access to multimedia Web content. It maintains a vast directory of pictures, clip art, fonts, video clips, and sound and music clips in various formats. Lycos also offers a number of other specific search tools on topics such as news, postal addresses and e-mail addresses, books, music, and company information.

Excite

Excite (see Figure 8–7) uses a concept-based approach to searching rather than keyword-based searching. For example, for the query, "adolescent

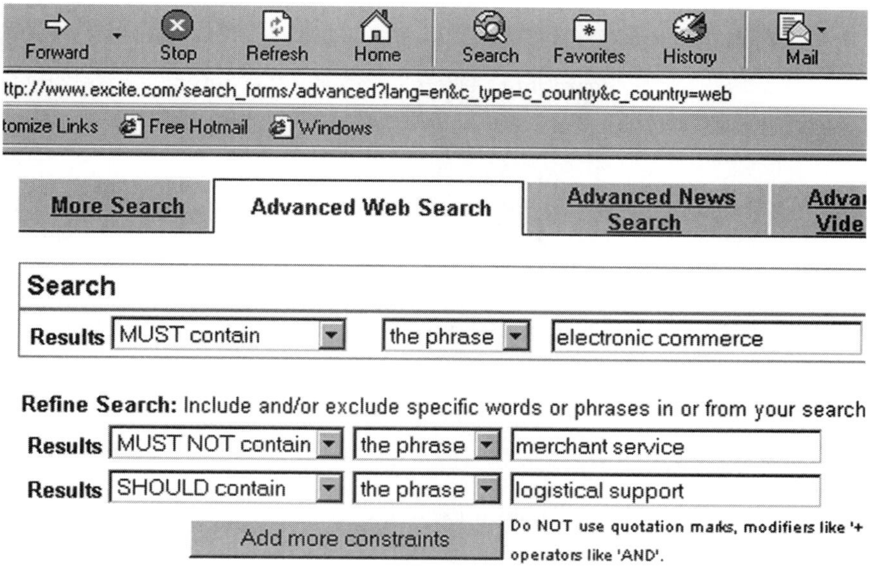

FIGURE 8–7

Advanced search interface at Excite

diseases," the search engine would also look for "young adult sickness" (i.e., it looks for Web pages that have related ideas and concepts). Excite searches a much smaller portion of the Web compared to other search engines such as Alta Vista, but it analyzes the sites visited not only in terms of words but also based on the underlying concepts to which the site relates. Websites are indexed according to these concepts. To achieve this, Excite uses a technique called intelligent concept extraction.

Excite allows successive refinements to search results. Users can select one of the entries from the results and ask for "more like this." This process of search refinement is called "query by example." The search engine also suggests keywords along with the search results, which may be used to refine the search. Excite also permits users to input queries in plain English.

In addition, Excite also maintains a topic structure similar to Yahoo!'s, although there are fewer topics. The topics in Excite are called channels and cover areas such as sports, shopping, investing, and money. About 150,000 sites are listed in these channels and they are tagged with reviews and ratings supplied by Excite.

HotBot

HotBot is powered by the search engine Inktomi. The word comes from a Lakota Indian legend about a powerful spider that is known for defeating its enemies through cunning and intelligence. HotBot has often done very well in search engine contests. It accepts Boolean operators and has a window that permits inexperienced users to construct the Boolean query by clicking on a menu. It allows search refinement through set searching. Users can use the returned websites to do more specific searches. Also, users can search on the basis of domain names, media types, and the depth of a website.

As with all other search engines, HotBot provides a searchable directory as well. It uses the same LookSmart directory system as Alta Vista. LookSmart has some 16,000 categories that users can search. LookSmart supplies the URLs under each category, along with a brief description of each site written by LookSmart. In its shopping category, HotBot employs a searching agent to give users access to merchants who offer the particular merchandise being sought.

Search Strategy

Search engines work best if users follow a strategy. The first step is to determine the stage of the search process. At the beginning of the process, users usually do not know the specifics of what they are searching for. On the other hand, toward the end of search process, users become clear as to what they need to know more about. This helps to determine the specificity of the search.

The second step is to choose a suitable search engine. If the search is highly specific, users should search databases such as Yahoo!, which has high precision. In the exploration phase, users should search text databases such as Alta Vista or concept-based sites such as Excite. In the exploratory phase, a meta-search engine such as MetaCrawler should also be considered. The meta-search engine often allows users to select the search engines the meta-engine will use.

The third step is to build the search query. In searching a database, it is important to be as specific as possible. Users should identify all the important concepts and keywords that stand for the concepts being sought. For example, if searching for manufacturing businesses, terms such as *company*, *business*, *engineering*, and *manufacturing* can be used. The Boolean statement for the search discussed could be comprised of four phrases: "engineering company" OR "manufacturing business" OR "engineering business" OR "manufacturing company."

Many search sites also offer topic lists and popular sites. Searching these is sometimes a good alternative to query-based searches.

Once the response set is listed, the high-ranking returns should be consulted. The search process should then be refined. Concepts need to be narrowed. If the search engine allows further search on the returned set, the facility should be used to narrow the search requirement. The fourth step is the revision of the search query by considering the search results. The process iterates through the above steps until satisfactory results are obtained.

Project: Searching to Develop an E-Business Plan

Assume that Nancy Aldridge, who has a bachelor's degree in mechanical engineering, wants to start a small company that will help manufacturing companies in and around New England develop e-commerce applications. Nancy is currently enrolled in an MBA program where she is taking various courses dealing with e-commerce. To launch her business, Nancy needs to develop some expertise in business planning, finance, and developing a marketing plan. She also needs to develop a list of prospective customers in her trading area and determine what e-commerce services they require.

We will follow Nancy as she identifies sites that provide her with guidance in developing a small business and creating a list of prospective customers. Because Nancy has a good idea what she is looking for, she begins with a specialized database or a virtual library instead of a general purpose search site such as Yahoo! or Excite. She goes to the Librarians' Index to the Internet at http://sunsite.berkeley.edu/internetindex (see Figure 8–8). Her query is simple. In the search box,

FIGURE 8–8

The first page of Librarians' Index to the Internet

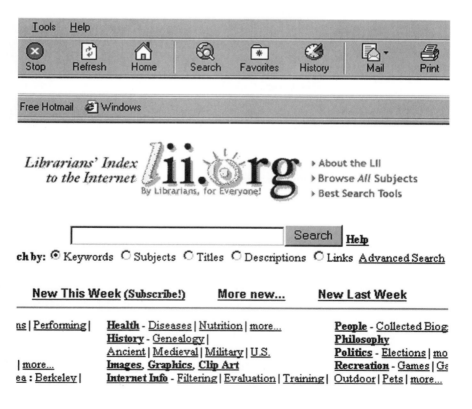

FIGURE 8–9

Response to the search query "small business"

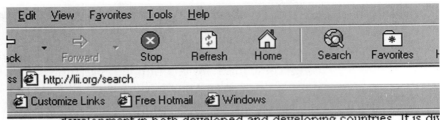

development in both developed and developing countries. It is div
entrepreneurship, incubators, microfinance, marketing, cyberbusin
geographically or via an alphabetical index. The close to 500 reso
listed first. Sites are also listed geographically and alphabetically. :
Subjects: Small business | Entrepreneurship | Economic development

Small Business Development Center - http://sbdcnet.utsa.edu/
The National SBDC National Information Clearinghouse provide
Development Centers throughout the United States, Puerto Rico
several sections of interest to the small business planner. *Informa*
business, research companies, and a Spanigh language guide to se
links in more than twenty categories, from start-ups and buying/se
and tax information. - cl
Subject: Small business

she types "small business." The search yields the window shown in
Figure 8–9.

Nancy then clicks on the entry database, which takes her to a site
that provides a great deal of information about small business (see
Figure 8–10). At the site, she selects the icon labeled "Business Basics"
and chooses "Accounting." That brings her to a site (see Figure 8–11) that
provides a link to the *Business Week* site on Small Office and Home Office
(SOHO). At the SOHO site (see Figure 8–12), Nancy finds a series of
primers on small business.

Having read the material on starting a small business on the
Internet, Nancy now wants to obtain a list of prospective customers in
the New England area. Again her needs are well known and specific.
Therefore, she goes to a specialized site that provides a listing of companies according to various categories, which may or may not have
websites. Nancy needs to know the company names, their locations,
and their areas of operations. She goes to the site www.zip2.com (see
Figure 8–13). In the search area, she selects the button "near my home,"
she provides her address, and selects the business category "engineering-
manufacturing." The listing of companies in the Boston area is depicted
in Figure 8–14. This finishes Nancy's search process for now.

FIGURE 8–10

Site on small businesses

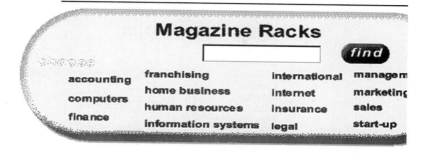

FIGURE 8–11

Site that links to SOHO Guidebook

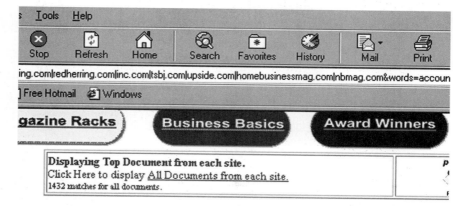

Publication 538, Accounting Periods and Methods; Accounting Metho
01/04/00

> , ; [Click for Text Only Version] ACCOUNTING METHODS An
> method is a set of rules used to determine when and how income and
> reported. The term "**accounting** method" includes ...
> *Go to this article at **www.irs.ustreas.gov***

The SOHO Guidebook | Accounting Basics | 53% | 16 kb |

> | SOHO GUIDEBOOK: Managing Your Business Finances **Account**

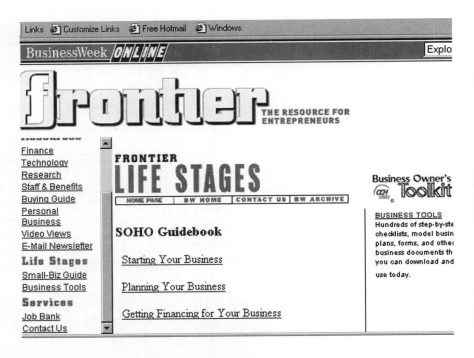

FIGURE 8–12
Business Week site on small businesses

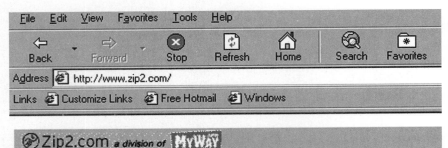

FIGURE 8–13
First page on www.zip2.com

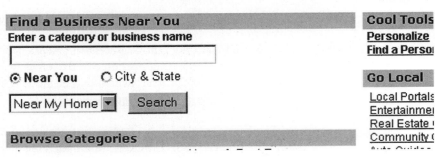

Case: The Alta Vista Group[1]

Digital (now Compaq) has always been a research powerhouse in the field of computing. According to Bob Supnik, former vice president of research at Digital, its approach has been to "gather very bright people, give them the best possible environment, then sit back and wait for magic to happen." While Digital's research philosophy later evolved to account for more practical realizations, the company could still bank on such "magic" to happen occasionally. The Alta Vista project is a good example of this process, where a propitious mix of brilliant people, corporate support, and a practical focus led to a superlative product in only six months.

The development of the Alta Vista search engine took place at Digital's Palo Alto research laboratory in 1995. The key figures on the team were Louis Monier, a researcher from Digital's western research lab; Joella Paquette, a marketing specialist; and Paul Flaherty from Digital's network systems laboratory. The idea of a search engine originated during a lunch meeting attended by these key individuals in the spring of 1995.

Flaherty was eager to use the latest version of Digital's Alpha server, Alpha 8400, which was reputed to be a hundred times faster than any other machine, for database processing. He wanted to develop a database of the Web and test the awesome power of the new machine. Monier made the bold suggestion that the entire World Wide Web be copied on to Digital servers. The challenges were many, including how to copy the entire Web on servers and then how to index that gigantic database.

As previously noted, the software for searching the Web is variously known as "spiders" or "crawlers." But Monier needed a super spider that could bring the entire Web on to Digital's site, say, every few weeks. He subsequently led an experienced team of computer scientists in developing the spider that came to be known as scooter.

The next key challenge was to record every word of every document on every website in the world in the database. Digital had already developed a high-speed, full-text searching mechanism that created an index of all words and their location in a document database. This software was called indexer. Digital was using the indexer to manage its e-mail libraries on research projects. The indexer was put to use in this project.

In the first few trials with the scooter and the indexer, the team was surprised to find that the Web, in its totality, was quite manageable. The total Web in 1995 had 80,000 servers containing about 30 million documents, with an average size of 5 kilobytes each. While the Web has grown significantly, it is still not monstrous. Even in January 2001, the Web was estimated to be less than 35 terabytes in size, with a million hosts, that is, devices with IP addresses and 3.3 billion Web pages of an average size of 10 kilobytes each. In other words, their bold idea of copying the entire Web in an indexed form on their servers was feasible.

On September 29, 1995, Monier presented the Alta Vista search program to corporate management. He revealed the "ultimate" Web search mechanism—the Alta Vista system could find and fetch each page from each server on the Web, read the contents of each page, find all the words, and then add them to an index. The index could be available for search by anyone who had access to the Internet. In 1995, Alta Vista was the first search engine that dared to take on this monumental task and achieve it.

The hardware platform on which the search engine ran is, even by today's standards, very impressive. The query interface, the interface seen when logging onto http://altavista.digital.com, ran on three Digital Alpha stations, each with 256 megabytes of RAM and 4 gigabytes of hard disk space. The queries from these machines were sent to the index servers. The indexes resided on the index servers and the query ran on them. Seven Alpha machines served as index servers, each with 10 Alpha processors, and with 6 gigabytes of RAM and 210 gigabytes of hard disk space on each server. Each index server held the entire copy of the Web's index and could provide a response time of less than a second. The scooter itself ran on a single Alpha server with 1 gigabyte of RAM and 48 gigabytes of hard disk space. The scooter roamed the Web, retrieved information from websites, and then sent it to another server that compiled the index. The indexing was done on a machine that had two processors, 256 megabytes of RAM, and 1 gigabyte of hard disk space that actually built the index and passed it on to the index servers.

Since Alta Vista achieved the task of indexing the Web, several search engines based on full-text searching have been developed. Engines such as HotBot, Lycos, and Northern Lights have now achieved almost equal popularity as Alta Vista.

Summary

This chapter focused on search engines, their variety, and how they operate. We began with the precedents of search engines on the Web, such as Archie and Veronica. These were search tools developed for use on files and texts available on the Internet. They were followed by the development of software designed to collect information from URL names, meta-tags on the Web documents, and document titles. These software were variously termed spiders, crawlers, agents, or softbots. We described subject databases such as Yahoo! and full-text searches such as Alta Vista. The concepts of recall and precision were discussed in the evaluation of search engines. We also covered the important features of search engines such as Excite, Lycos, and HotBot.

Key Terms

Agents   314

Boolean   316

Concept searching   318

Crawlers   314

Directories   319

Excite   324

HotBot   325

Index   315

Lycos   324

Meta-search engines   320

Precision   320

Phrase search   317

Proximity searching   317

Recall   320

Relevance ranking   312

Scooter   323

Spamming   321

Spiders   314

Yahoo!   319

Review Questions

1. How do search engines such as Alta Vista differ from information directories?
2. What is a spider? What does it do?
3. What is the problem of relevance ranking?
4. What is meant by the term *precision?*
5. What is recall and how does it relate to precision?
6. Describe a search situation where the requirement for recall is high.
7. What is a meta-search engine? Provide some examples.
8. What is spamming?
9. How can you get your site listed at major search sites and how could you improve your site ranking?

Projects

1. Use the Web-based search system to write a short note on optical transmission and optical routers.
2. Write a short note on availability of multimedia content and associated searching mechanisms on the Web.
3. Visit sites such as www.cyveillance.com and www.netsize.com and write a short note about the current size of the World Wide Web.

References, Readings, and Hyperlinks

1. Seltzer, Richard, Deborah S. Ray, and Eric J. Ray. *The Alta Vista Search Revolution*. Berkeley: Osborne McGraw-Hill, 1997.
2. Chakravarti, Soumen, Byron Dom, S. Ravi Kumar, Prabhakaran Raghavan, Sridhar Rajagopalan, and Andrew Tomins. "Hypersearching the Web." *Scientific American*, June 1999, pp. 54–60.
3. Glossbrenner, Alfred, and Emily Glossbrenner. *Search Engines for the World Wide Web*. Berkeley: Peachpit Press, 1999.
4. Lynch, Clifford. "The Internet: Bringing Order from Chaos." *Scientific American*, March 1977, pp. 50–56.
5. Sonnenreich, Wes, and Tim Macinta. *Guide to Search Engines*. New York: John Wiley & Sons, 1998.
6. www.altavista.com
7. www.cyveillance.com
8. www.excite.com
9. www.google.com
10. www.hotbot.com
11. www.infoseek.com
12. www.infospace.com
13. www.lycos.com
14. www.metacrawler.com
15. www.netsize.com
16. www.northernlights.com
17. http://searchenginewatch.internet.com
18. http://sunsite.berkeley.edu
19. www.telecordia.com
20. www.yahoo.com
21. www.zip2.com

SOFTWARE AGENTS FOR E-COMMERCE

Chapter Outline

Learning Objectives

By the end of this chapter, you should be able to:

- Describe what software agents are.
- Differentiate various classes of software agents.
- Understand how techniques such as artificial intelligence and statistical reasoning are used in software agents.
- Describe the range of agents available to aid consumers in the buying process.
- Identify various activities in e-commerce where software agents are being used.

Chapter Overview

In the last chapter, we covered the use of software objects, such as spiders and crawlers, by search engines. In the world of software agents, they are known as information search agents. Software entities that operate autonomously on behalf of humans and machines are called agents. In this chapter, we develop an understanding about software agents in general and in the field of e-commerce. We consider basic technologies such as artificial intelligence and statistical methods used in building software agents. Various types of software agents are reviewed. A variety of agents actually in use in e-commerce activities are considered.

A Technical Vignette

The dream of the artificial intelligence (AI) community is to develop computers that are able to reason like people do. Although impressive advances have been made in the area of reasoning and learning, general intelligent behavior has not been achieved because of a knowledge bottleneck. Humans have the capacity to learn and retain a vast amount of information, and that has been difficult to replicate in computers. The process of eliciting knowledge from humans and transferring that knowledge manually to a database is the critical bottleneck in this pursuit.

With the advent of the Web, a vast body of material is suddenly available in a machine-readable format. If computers could make sense of this material, the knowledge bottleneck would be resolved. While the Web holds vast amounts of data, there is no consistent structure among all the documents. The World Wide Web Consortium is working on developing a semantic Web, where all the data would make sense to computers. The computers could then communicate among themselves to accomplish routine tasks, freeing humans to perform those tasks that call for creativity and inspiration.

If and when the semantic Web becomes a reality, Web users could, for example, ask software to suggest places for a family vacation. The software would present a list that was personalized in terms of the user's budget and preferences. That would be possible only if the software could figure out the kind of vacation places that are reasonable, given the season; find a spending limit from past behavior; and make an ordered listing of places from types of vacation sites that the user has previously visited. Before it could reason, the software needs to be able to read the documents on the Web and place relevant information into appropriate categories such as weather, costs, and time to travel. Currently, this is not possible. This is where the concept of a semantic Web comes into play.

Semantics of data is not a new concept in the world of computers. In relational databases, columns or fields of information relate to each other, and the relationship between columns is referred to as the semantics of the data. In a database relating to human resources, the data dictionary clearly defines what is meant by terms such as *wages* and *retirement benefits*. All records conform to this single set of definitions. Unfortunately, that is not the case on the Web. A search engine looks only for phrases and words that are queried and is insensitive to what is actually meant by those words. In the case of shopping agents that fetch comparative prices from multiple sites, a program needs to be manually coded to read the price from a particular location on the document. If the document is changed, the program ceases to work. This process is known as scraping, that is, scraping data from documents that are meant for humans.

The first step in building a semantic Web is for documents on the Web to have predefined structures. A language called resource description format (RDF), which is based on Extensible Markup Language (XML), is being developed by the World Wide Web Consortium to provide this structure. Once documents follow a well-defined structure, a program will be able to access the required data without the need for scraping.

The next step is for software programs or agents to have logic capability. In the vacation example, the agent needs to be able to deduce from local weather the season that might be attractive to a vacationer and use logic to work on historical spending patterns and current earnings to derive spending limits. Finally, a semantic Web requires software objects, such as agents, to be able to develop meaning as to how a concept is associated with other concepts and the way it is used. For instance, concepts such as *vacation* and *holiday* are related, as are terms such as *costs* and *expenses*. The software agent must be able to understand the same word used in different ways, as well as different words used in a similar fashion. Once the semantic Web becomes a reality, then the immense amount of information and expertise that is available on the Web will be accessible through computers. Retrieval of such knowledge and expertise will become routine for computer agents, and humans will be left to do what they do best—creative work and forming social networks.

What Are Software Agents?

There have been many definitions of a software **agent.** Riecken defines software agents as "systems which engage and help all types of end users."[1] Moses Ma is more specific and relies on the concept underlying a human agent to define software agents as "atomic software entities operating through autonomous actions on behalf of the users—machines and humans—without constant human intervention."[2]

We use human agents in business dealings involving, for example, real estate and travel. A human agent relieves us of the necessity of doing the work on our own and provides the expertise and information sources that we may lack. To be successful, an agent needs to be conversant with the needs and preferences of its principal and be expert in the domain in which it is operating. Consider what makes a successful agent:

- Autonomy. Agents operate without detailed and direct commands from the principals.
- Social and mobility skills. Agents travel around to interact with other individuals to acquire the information they need to conduct the transaction.
- Purposeful. Agents are goal-driven. They are proactive, and they take initiatives to fulfill their principals' goals. To do so, agents need to be sensitive to their principals' goals and their idiosyncratic needs.
- Reactive. Agents react to changes in the environment when they occur and are capable of learning to adapt to new circumstances.

Software agents have one or more of the above characteristics of a human agent. Patti Maes[3] of MIT's Media Laboratory identifies software agents, unlike traditional software objects, as programs that are semiautonomous, run continuously, and can be personalized for each user. According to Negroponte[4] of MIT's Media Laboratory, a software agent is like a digital relative that combines domain expertise with deep knowledge about the user. That is, personalization capability is an essential characteristic of a software agent.

IBM describes software agents in terms of three dimensions—agency, intelligence, and mobility (see Figure 9–1). Agency is the degree of autonomy and authority vested in agents; intelligence is the degree of reasoning and learning that agents exhibits in their behavior to achieve the tasks delegated to them; and mobility is the degree to which agents travel around the network.

In terms of agency, software requires increasing autonomy as it moves along from data to application to services (see Figure 9–1). Along this dimension are database agents that can query a variety of relational databases; Lotus Notes, which can deal with unstructured data; and Web

FIGURE 9–1

Scope of intelligent agents

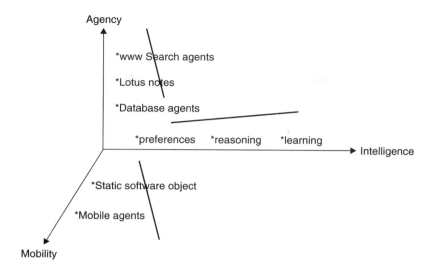

search agents, such as Entrypoint (www.entrypoint.com discussed later in this chapter), that provide a variety of personalized news delivery services. The site www.artificial-life.com introduces many software agents that provide comparative information about consumer products available on the website. For instance, Alife-WebGuide, at that site, engages customers in a natural language conversation to help refine the search so that customers can precisely locate desired products.

In terms of intelligence ability, software exists that can deduce a user's preferences; reason, as exhibited by expert systems; and learning, by neural networks. For example, DataBots from Imagination Engines Inc. (www.imagination-engines.com) use ordinary Microsoft Excel spreadsheets to create advanced neural networks for adaptive artificial organisms and knowledge agents. These DataBots can "(1) exercise their own independent judgments in perusing databases, (2) choose their own perspective on or physically move through the data, (3) automatically learn hidden data patterns, and (4) cooperatively build compound cascade structures capable of autonomous discovery and invention,"[5] according to Dr. Stephen Thaler, the founder and CEO of the company. In the same vein, visit www.moviecritic.com and experience how a software agent learns to provide personalized movie rankings based on a viewer's previous movie ratings.

Along the mobility dimension, static software can be attached to objects that travel around the network collecting information. Research into developing mobile agents is still in its infancy.

While agents that can exhibit impressive behavior along any two of these dimensions simultaneously are still many years away, a visit to www.botspot.com shows evidence of increasing sophistication of commercially available software agents.

Logic of Agent Behavior

Technologies used in software agents originate in widely disparate sources such as artificial intelligence, statistical techniques, pattern recognition, and machine learning methods. Agents are not so much a separate piece of software as an additional capability that is added to existing software programs. This additional capability can be obtained in several ways. In this section, we survey some of the important methodologies such as symbolic reasoning, statistical reasoning, multiattribute utility theory, constraint satisfaction approaches, and auction protocols.

Symbolic Reasoning

Symbolic reasoning uses rule-based representation, as is used in expert systems. The rules, known as production rules, have the form:

IF <condition> THEN <action>

The action part is also called conclusion or consequent. The system continuously checks if the condition part of any rule in the rule set is true. When the condition part of a rule is satisfied, the rule is set to "fire," that is, the action part is executed. As actions execute, the condition part of other rules get satisfied, leading to these rules firing. Rule-based systems are used in messaging as in BeyondMail (Fig. 9–2).

Symbolic rules are used in the agent system Frontmind (discussed later in this chapter), which is marketed by Manna. Frontmind allows for

FIGURE 9–2

Rule-based messaging in BeyondMail

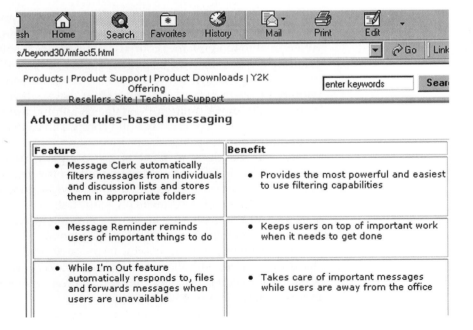

Feature	Benefit
• Message Clerk automatically filters messages from individuals and discussion lists and stores them in appropriate folders	• Provides the most powerful and easiest to use filtering capabilities
• Message Reminder reminds users of important things to do	• Keeps users on top of important work when it needs to get done
• While I'm Out feature automatically responds to, files and forwards messages when users are unavailable	• Takes care of important messages while users are away from the office

symbolic rules that guide a Web visitor on a site. Depending on the actions by the visitor, the system may offer advice on what to buy and discounts on a variety of products. A customer buying several books in the crime/thriller category, for example, would be advised about new arrivals in that particular category and offered discounts.

Statistical Reasoning

Statistical reasoning methods are used in market segmentation. Segmentation involves breaking the total market into segments that are homogeneous according to some characteristic of the customer, such as demographic factors or buying or usage patterns. Behavior of customers in each segment is sufficiently alike for them to be treated similarly. For instance, the publishing industry recognizes separate segments such as technical, crime, poetry, and history. Each of these segments is characterized by differing emotional needs of readers, their lifestyles, and demographic characteristics such as age and income. To segment the world of consumers, data about usage, attitudes, and demography are obtained. Based on the data, classification functions are developed that can help in predicting group membership. The greater the volume of data, the more accurate are the classification functions. Based on the prediction of group membership, promotion and discount offers can be targeted to individuals specific to that group.

In the world of agent technology, segmentation techniques are called **collaborative filtering.** Such techniques were first used by the product Firefly, which was developed at MIT in 1995. The technology was subsequently incorporated at popular sites such as www.Amazon.com. Firefly is discussed later in this chapter.

Multiattribute Utility Theory

Multiattribute utility theory can be used to rank different choices (e.g., items to buy, movies to watch, and sports events to attend). Currently, agents are used to obtain competitive prices for the same kind of product from different auction and selling sites. Obtaining price data for the same or similar products from different sites is called content-based filtering. Content-based filtering is one of the most popular usages of agent technology. Lycos uses Jango (discussed later in this chapter) for this at its portal site. Another popular content-based filtering agent, Junglee, is used by shopetheweb.amazon.com. Other sites that use this technology include MySimon.com and www.neuromedia.com.

However, agents such as Jango and Junglee are not appropriate where products differ considerably along dimensions of quality, brand appeal, and warranty. Currently, at sites such as MySimon.com, products are listed according to price. But consumers have different utilities along each of these separate dimensions of price and quality with possible trade-offs. Multiattribute utility theory helps to derive a single number that is indicative of joint utility based on different product characteristics. Given this single utility number, products can be ranked and the user advised accordingly.

There are various functions to represent utility as a real number; some of the popular utility functions being:

$$U(x) = \log(x + b)$$
$$U(x) = a + bx + cx^2$$
$$U(x) = (1/k)(1 - e^{-kx})$$

where U is the utility and x is the measure of the attribute. In the case of an automobile, x could be price, quality, or fuel economy.

In case of multiple attributes, various additive and nonadditive functions are used to obtain the joint utility. In the case of an automobile, for example, such a function might appear as follows:

$$U(\text{car}) = k_1 U_1(\text{comfort}) + k_2 U_2 (\text{price}) + k_3 U_3(\text{quality})$$

where the ks are constants and the Us are utility functions.

The ks and the Us are estimated from data sets, and the function obtained can be used to get a single utility number for a particular model of a car.

Tete-a-Tete, a purchasing agent developed at MIT's Media Laboratory, uses multiattribute utility theory to advise buyers. The technology is sold by Frictionless.com and the agent is discussed later in this chapter.

Constraint Satisfaction Approach

Like multiattribute utility theory, the constraint satisfaction approach (CSA) helps in making a selection where a wide choice is possible. In retail marketing on the Web, CSA can be used to prioritize various available options. Whereas multiattribute utility theory generates a number for each choice, CSA is a qualitative method. The problem here is formulated in terms of variables or features that need to satisfy some constraints, which can be hard or soft. Hard constraints cannot be violated, whereas soft constraints can be. An example of a hard constraint would be: "Price needs to be less than $1,500." "Delivery preferable within three days" is a soft constraint.

Choices that fail to satisfy the hard constraints are eliminated from further consideration. Other choices are ranked according to how much they violate the various soft constraints. The constraint satisfaction approach can provide justification as to why a certain product was recommended. The justification is provided in terms of constraints to which the users themselves had input and this leads the users to have more trust in the decision-making process. PersonaLogic is an agent that uses constraint satisfaction approach, and it is discussed later in this chapter.

Auction Protocols

Like markets, auctions help to determine prices. Markets work when the item in question is like a commodity, with many buyers and sellers.

Auctions are valuable when the item is one of a kind or when supply and demand are in flux. Auctions are used, for example, in determining prices for antiques and art objects, as well as for items such as flowers, tea, and coffee.

There are many kinds of **auctions;** four well-known types are:

- English auction, where the bidding starts at a low value and then increases as bidders offer higher prices. The auction ends when it reaches a price that is not superseded by another higher bid.
- Dutch auction, which works in reverse order to the English auction. It starts at a high value and the price is progressively reduced until a bidder accepts it.
- Sealed-bid auction, where offers are made in sealed envelopes. The envelopes are all opened at the same time and the highest bid is accepted.
- Vickrey auction, where sealed bids are used and the winner is the bidder with the highest bid but pays the second highest value that has been bid.

The nature of an auction is called its protocol. Various protocols lead to differing prices. Agents have been developed that participate in the different types of auctions. Companies such as Fairmarket.com (see Figure 9–3) develop auction engines that run on their Web servers and

FIGURE 9–3

An auction engine on the Web

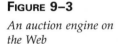

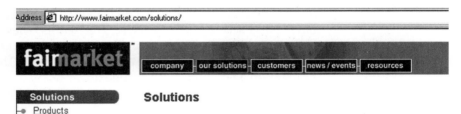

Address 🔁 http://www.fairmarket.com/solutions/

| company | our solutions | customers | news / events | resources |

Solutions

- Products
- Services
- Benefits
- FairMarket Network[sm]
- Technology
- Request Information

Solutions

What is the FairMarket[sm] Solution?
E-commerce and Internet community leaders choose the FairMarket solution sell surplus goods, help build communities and run effective customer acquisi programs.

FairMarket provides <u>dynamic pricing products</u> such as AuctionPlace[sm] and AutoMarkdown[sm]. AuctionPlace incorporates auction pricing formats including English, Dutch, Reserve and Quick Win[sm], in addition to key selling features as mass product upload tools, the BizPartner Toolkit[sm], and auction services account management. And our AutoMarkdown[sm] clearance solution enables reduce prices over time.

In addition to providing a proven technology and infrastructure for dynamic pric FairMarket works with our clients very closely throughout the entire process o designing and launching client sites, providing consulting services to impart be practices on how to run successful auctions, and managing the day-to-day customer and IT support <u>services</u>.

allow visitors to participate in auctions held on the site. Many Web retailers have adopted the auction model for pricing, including eBay and
www.uBid.com. Research is being conducted at several universities, including the MIT Media Laboratory and the University of Michigan, on
the development of agents that participate in auctions using a variety of
strategies. Later in this chapter, we discuss auction-agent systems such as
AuctionBot from the University of Michigan and Kasbah from MIT.

Types of Agents

For the purpose of e-commerce, agents can be categorized into various types:

- Information agents that help users cope with the vast array of
information available on the Web.
- E-commerce agents that help in obtaining the best deal from Web
retailers and from auction sites.
- Mobile agents that travel around the Web executing operations
specified by the user. Information and e-commerce agents, in
contrast, execute at one server and exchange data with programs
running at other servers.

Information Agents

Information agents are programs that access information from the Web,
usenet groups, and information news feeds such as Reuters and provide
it to the user according to the user's preferences. They perform the service
of brokers (i.e., they act as mediators between information suppliers
and the user, who is the information consumer). The various types of
information agents are discussed next.

Information Search Agents

Search agents roam the World Wide Web looking for documents that contain the query words or phrases indicated by the user. They are used by
popular search engines such as Alta Vista and HotBot, and they employ
software objects called spiders or crawlers. Search engines were considered in the previous chapter.

Information Filtering Agents

In contrast to search agents, **filtering agents** not only identify documents
that are of interest to users but also produce the content of the document
as well. Unlike search agents, which search the entire Web, filtering agents
look up only a small set of information sources such as a few specific websites and news feeds. The filtering is done not on the basis of a few phrases

or words but rather on preferences that have been specified on a form-based interface. The filtering systems do not limit only to the Web or use-net news groups, as is common with ~~gines~~; they also consult news feeds and other sources such as Reuters and Associated Press.

Filtering agents help users avoid information overload by reducing the information stream available to them. The filtering is accomplished in accordance with the users' interests. The filtered information from various sources is presented to the user as an e-mail or as a Web document that serves as a personalized newspaper. Several information services on the Web use information filtering agents, including NewsHound and NewsPage Direct. Most Web-based subscriptions to newspapers also provide a similar service (see Figure 9–4).

The logic of the filtering process (see Figure 9–5) is as follows: A user profile is created based on input from the user on a form-type interface. In the profile, the user may describe interests such as sports and business and provide further refinements in terms of which sports teams and companies the user is interested in. The filtering agent resides on the company's server. The agent collects information as it comes in on the live news feeds and other sources. Depending on the words in the document, the document is rated as to its relevance to the user. All documents that have a relevance factor beyond a threshold level are sent to the user in the form of an e-mail or as a Web document.

FIGURE 9–4

News delivery by The Economist

From: The Economist **To:** chaudhury@umbsky.cc.umb.edu
Subject: Business This Week March 4th - March 10th 2000

The Economist

Business this week

German empire

Deutsche Bank and **Dresdner Bank** announced that will create the world's second largest bank with $1.2 trillion, but at the cost of as many as 16,000 job a German insurance company that
See article: Europe's banking blues   SUBSCRIBERS ON

New America, same old politics
Democrats and Republicans have voted

European banking continued to consolidate on a le: **MeritaNordbanken**, a Nordic banking group, agre acquire **Unidanmark**, a Danish bank, for around e

FIGURE 9–5

Logic of filtering agents

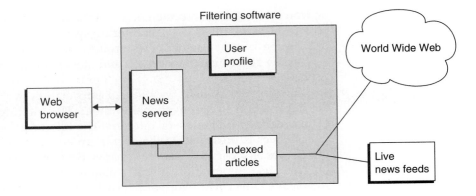

Information Delivery Agents

In off-line information filtering and delivery agents a client is installed on the user's computer that connects to a server to download information, as prescribed by the user (see Figure 9–6). Several such off-line delivery systems are available on the Web today, including Entrypoint (previously

FIGURE 9–6

Entrypoint, an information delivery system

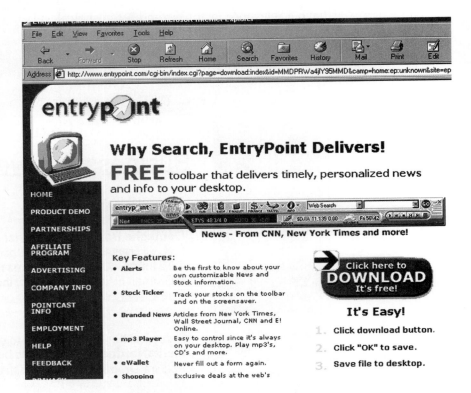

known as Pointcast), Freeloader, and V-Cast. Subscription to these services requires the installation of desktop software that works as a Web browser plug-in. The client works in the background and at specified intervals contacts the company's server to download financial, weather, and sports news from news feeds and popular newspapers from throughout the country.

This type of information delivery is known as a push-delivery system, in contrast to a pull-delivery system, where users take the initiative to log in and obtain news on their own. In the push-delivery services, information seems to arrives on its own to the user. This is achieved by the client software on the user's machine asking the server at periodic intervals for information, which creates the illusion that the server is taking the initiative to deliver the news.

Information Notification Agents

Notification agents track changes on websites indicated by the user and notify the user via e-mail of the content changes that have occurred. The software continuously monitors the websites that are of interest to the user for the kinds of changes in which the user is interested. The changes are monitored in terms of keywords and selected phrases. Such monitoring and notification is useful to lawyers, for instance, who want to be notified of changes in legislation, to investment professionals who need to know about stock and investment news such as IPO announcements, and to managers who are interested in competitor information such as press releases and new product announcements.

NetMind (www.netmind.com) provides a free personalized tracking service called Mind-it (see Figure 9–7). It does not require specialized software on the user's computer. All the user needs is an e-mail account to receive the notification.

Information Reconnaissance Agents

Letizia, which is under development at MIT, is an example of an information reconnaissance agent. It assists users by bringing to their attention interesting pages that are within a few links from the Web page under view. The agent builds up an interest profile for the user, depending on the pages the user has browsed. The agent then visits neighboring pages that are within a few links of the existing pages. Given the user profile, it ranks the pages according to the user's interest and provides the ranking to the user.

The process depends on the principle of term frequency inverse document frequency (TfIDF), which represents the discriminating power of a word in a document. It is the product of two factors: (1) how frequently

FIGURE 9-7

*NetMind, an
information
notification system*

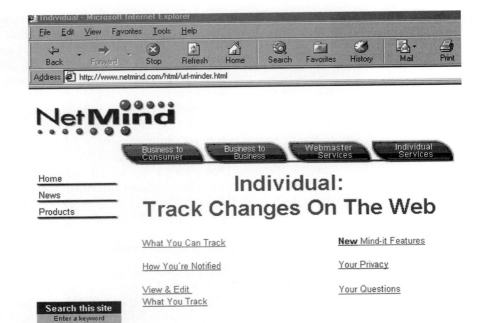

the term occurs in a document and (2) how infrequently documents with that term occur on the Web, as follows:

TfIDF of a word X in a document K = frequency of the word X
in the document K * 1/frequency of documents with the word X
appearing on the Web

For example, the word *is* will occur frequently on any page, but such pages occur very frequently and therefore the TfIDF product is low and so is the discriminating power of the word *is.* On the other hand, documents with the word *metastasize,* a cancer-related word, occur infrequently, and in a document that has repeated use of that word, the TfIDF product will be high, indicating that the discriminating power of the word in that document is high as well. If a user is consulting pages on the topic of cancer, then documents with frequent occurrence of the word *metastasize* will be highlighted by Letizia for the user to consult.

Letizia outperforms a search engine because, unlike the search engine, the user does not have to input words of interest; the agent does that. Also, the agent searches only in the neighborhood of the current document in use and, therefore, provides continuous guidance to the user as the user is browsing.

E-Commerce Agents

Pattie Maes of MIT Media Laboratory uses a framework based on consumer behavior research to classify agents used in e-commerce. Consumer behavior research provides models of the decision-making process used by consumers. According to these models, the consumer decision-making process has six stages:

- Needs identification stage, where the consumer becomes aware of an unmet need. At this stage, a consumer is open to suggestions and stimulation. Firefly, for example, is used by Amazon.com to offer appropriate suggestions to visitors about books and CDs.
- **Product brokering** stage, where information is retrieved about alternative products that satisfy a defined need, and various alternatives are evaluated to make a choice. Agents such as BargainFinder and Jango help identify several alternatives from the Web.
- **Merchant brokering** stage, where the choice is made as to the merchant from which the product is to be obtained. In this stage, details about merchants are obtained and a selection is made. Agents such as BargainFinder and Jango assist a consumer at this stage.
- Negotiation stage, where the details of the deal are forged. The details relate to factors such as price, quality, delivery, and warranty. Alternative deals are considered and a choice is made. Agent systems such as Kasbah and AuctionBot have the potential of helping consumers negotiate the best deal.
- Purchase and delivery stage, which signals the end of the negotiation stage and where the act of placing an order, making payment, and receiving delivery transpire.
- Service and evaluation stage, which is the postpurchase phase where an overall evaluation of the purchase experience occurs.

Table 9–1 lists e-commerce agents and the role they play in various stages of the consumer behavior cycle. The agents are discussed in detail in the next sections.

Jango

Jango was one of the earliest commercial products on the Web to do comparative price shopping. It is used by the portal and search site Excite

TABLE 9–1   Examples of Agent Systems in E-Commerce

	Personal Logic	Firefly	Bargain Finder	Jango	Kasbah	Auction Bot	Tete-a-Tete
Need identification	Agents such as Firefly and FrontMind help anticipate consumer needs based on evaluation of past buying and click behavior.						
Product brokering	Yes	Yes		Yes			Yes
Merchant brokering			Yes	Yes	Yes		Yes
Negotiation			Yes	Yes	Yes		
Purchase and delivery	Agents systems such as Kasbah are making provisions for collecting feedback from consumers concerning various merchants to develop an agent-based trust and reputation system in e-commerce.						
Product service and evaluation							

(see Figure 9–8). Jango followed the experimental product BargainFinder, developed by Andersen Consulting. As with BargainFinder, Jango visits several sites for product queries and obtains prices.

FIGURE 9–8

Jango agent at work at Excite portal

Programs called wrappers read these prices. Because prices are indicated in varying places on Web documents, wrappers differ and need to be hand-coded. When the site format changes, the wrappers need to be changed as well. But Jango developed a partly automated process of developing a wrapper for a particular site. The process entails performing several queries on the system and generalizing from the responses. BargainFinder and Jango faced the problem of retailers blocking access to their sites when they did not want to compete solely on prices. To combat this, Jango uses a mechanism in which the queries are raised from consumers' browsers, thus preventing merchants from knowing the source of the queries.

AdOne

The AdOne technology, used at www.classifiedwarehouse.com, is a descendant of an experimental product, Infomaster, developed at Stanford University. Originally, Infomaster was used to search classified advertisements to help university students find things such as apartments, furniture, and used cars. AdOne also is designed to search classified advertisements. ClassifiedWarehouse.com (see Figure 9–9), which is partly owned by 11 major newspaper chains, connects the user to ads from over 800 newspapers from around the country. It uses a content-based approach to search the classifieds of the member newspapers against information provided on a form-based interface.

PersonaLogic

PersonaLogic, (www.personalogic.com), is an example of a search tool based on the principle of constraint-satisfaction. It classifies constraints

FIGURE 9–9

Content-based search on classified advertisements

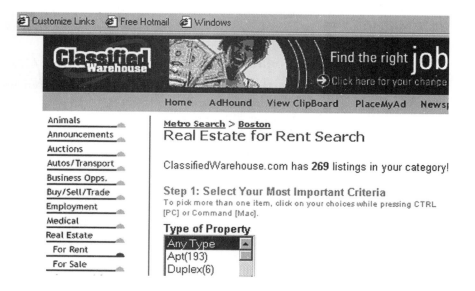

FIGURE 9–10

Constraint satisfaction approach to decision making on the Web

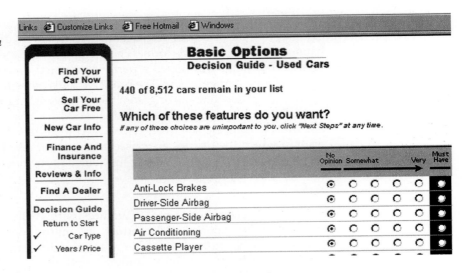

into hard and soft constraints, where hard constraints have to be satisfied and the violation of soft constraints reduces the attractiveness of an option. Using a form (Figure 9–10), users are prompted to provide their hard and soft constraints. The hard constraints are used to prune the space of possibilities. For instance, the site may have an inventory of 500 cars. As users indicate their price limits, the number of cars that could be of interest would be reduced. Similarly, with more information about model and age, the possibilities would be reduced even further. The soft constraints are used to rank-order all the possibilities that have met the hard constraints.

AuctionBot

AuctionBot (www.eecs.umich.edu) is a general-purpose auction server for the Internet. The site allows users to create new auctions to sell products by choosing different auction types and specifications (see Figure 9–11). The specifications relate to factors such as time to clear, number of individuals who can participate, and the type of auction, as discussed earlier in this chapter.

AuctionBot provides an application programming interface that can be used by programmers to develop buying and selling software agents that can be plugged into the system. At the University of Michigan, the site is used to study the results of various types of auction behavior, as programmed into buyer and seller software agents, which encode various bidding strategies.

FIGURE 9–11

Auction-based agent system

How can I use the Michigan AuctionBot?

There are two main operations you can perform with the AuctionBot. You can start a new auction, or bid AuctionBot account. The AuctionBot also provides facilities for examining ongoing auctions, and inspecting are free of charge.

Further information is available on the pages invoking these operations, and in the AuctionBot glossary.

Create an Account

Anybody can create an account. Registration comprises the following steps

Kasbah

Kasbah (Figure 9–12) is a multi-agent platform developed at MIT that allows several buyer and seller agents to interact, thus giving rise to an electronic marketplace. The agents, buyers and sellers, represent the interests of human buyers and sellers and the agents negotiate on their behalf.

The seller agents are given the description of the product that they have to sell. They then go to the electronic marketplace, Kasbah, to seek buyer agents with whom to negotiate. The seller agents are autonomous and do not require any intervention by the sellers they represent. The human seller programs the seller agents with basic information such as:

- Desired time to sell by (i.e., the deadline by which the item has to be disposed of).
- Desired price (i.e., the price the seller would like to get for the item).
- Lowest acceptable price (i.e., the price below which the seller would prefer not to sell).
- How often the agent is to report back to the human user.
- Locations of the seller and the item on sale.

FIGURE 9–12

*The Kasbah electronic
market at MIT*

The above parameters can be modified as the market is in progress.
The parameters define the highest and lowest price and the time frame
in which the deal needs to be made.

The human sellers also program the agent to follow strategies to negotiate with the buyer agents. The strategies are in the nature of a decay
function on the demanded prices. The required prices decrease over time.
The nature of the decay in prices represents the selling strategy. Three
functions for price decay are popular: (1) linear, (2) quadratic, and (3) cubic (see Figure 9–13). The three functions can be respectively described
as anxious, coolheaded, and frugal.

A deal is made when the price offered by a seller agent coincides with
what is acceptable to a buyer agent. The seller agent also acts as the "eyes"
for the seller in the marketplace. It keeps the human seller informed about

FIGURE 9–13

*Three price decay
functions used in
Kasbah*

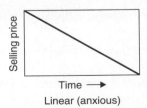

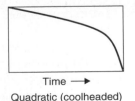

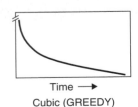

the items on sale and the current prices being demanded by the buyer agents. The human seller retains control of the seller agent and can change negotiation strategy. When a deal is struck, the seller agent may wait for the human seller to give a go-ahead or it may be programmed to close the deal on its own. When the deal is consummated, the seller agent sends an e-mail notification to the human seller.

The buyer agent has a similar relationship to the human buyer. It informs the human buyer of the items on sale and the price demanded. The parameters programmed by the buyer include:

- Desired price.
- Highest acceptable price.
- Time frame within which a deal, if possible, is to be made.
- How often the agent is to report back to the human buyer.
- Minimum reputation of the seller necessary for the buyer agent to proceed.
- Minimum acceptable quality of the product that the buyer is willing to buy.

Likewise, the human buyer programs the buyer agents with an appropriate negotiation strategy that is the inverse of the common seller strategy: linear, quadratic, and cubic. It starts low and goes up to a predetermined limit.

Kasbah is a prototype for electronic marketplaces that are emerging in the business-to-business markets. It goes beyond the auction mode, where there is usually a single seller and multiple possible buyers. Kasbah allows multiple buyers and sellers dealing in a wide variety of goods to interact simultaneously.

PDA@Shop

This comparative shopping agent is designed to work in an actual shopping environment. Running on a PDA, the shopper is expected to be physically present in a shopping environment such as a mall. With PDA@Shop, the buyer has the capability of comparing prices of similar offerings available at other sites.

PDA@Shop is an extension to the Kasbah multi-agent platform, with the PDA connected to the Kasbah server through a network. The PDA connects to the network through a code division multiple access (CDMA) radio modem or a serial modem that connects to a network media cable.

The buyer in a shopping mall does not have time to engage in long negotiations with multiple selling agents across the network. The functionality that is required here is for the buyer agent to contact other shopping agents that sell similar products and obtain prices for comparison. The buyer can use the PDA to launch multiple buying agents, which, in turn, connect to multiple seller agents and convey to the buyer the deals that are available on the network.

The comparative shopping process goes through four steps, each of which corresponds to four commands to the system: (1) ASK, (2) OFFER, (3) ACCEPT, and (4) COMMIT. The cycle begins with the shopper executing an ASK command, whereby buyer agents created at the remote Kasbah server search for agents that are selling items of interest. The seller agents make OFFERs. These offers are compared and evaluated by the PDA@Shop system, and the shopper is notified of the best offer. The shopper, if choosing to buy in response to the offer, executes an ACCEPT command. On receipt of this command, the buyer agent then executes a COMMIT command, thus consummating the deal.

Tete-a-Tete

While AuctionBot and Kasbah both focus on negotiation on the price dimension alone, Tete-a-Tete (see Figure 9–14) is an agent system that promotes negotiation on multiple dimensions. It is based on a retail sale scenario, in which a buyer is faced with offerings that differ not only on price but also on qualitative factors such as quality, warranty, and after-sales service. The agents exchange proposals that are XML documents and conform to a certain predetermined structure for making offers and counteroffers. Each proposal defines a product in terms of price and availability, as well as other characteristics.

FIGURE 9–14

Agent system for negotiation on multiple dimensions

fixing online shopping

Frictionless Commerce, Inc. is actively comparison shopping technologies be on this new venture, please visit us

overview

multi-agent systems

user interface design

retail electronic commerce

internal

retail consumer
Shopping online is convenient, but cumbersome.

I want to perform product comparisons, but I need more powerful tools to make sense of all of the available merchant offerings. What is the product that best meets my individual needs?

Price is not my only concern when making buying decisions. What

The buyer agent evaluates an offer on the basis of multiattribute utility theory. It uses the human buyer's utility function to evaluate proposals and rank them. Depending on this evaluation, a buyer agent may furnish a counterproposal that might trigger another proposal from the seller agent. The buyer agent includes not only product features in its consideration but also the reputation of the seller, so this product assists users in the product brokering phase and in the merchant brokering phase.

Tete-a-Tete, which is marketed by Frictionless.com (see Figure 9–15), is used at Lycos and Computer.com, among others.

Firefly

Firefly, an agent system that works in the background, provides Web visitors with customized and personalized information. It helps marketers develop demographic information about a market that is useful for segmentation. The software aids in segmenting a customer population into various groups, with each group consisting of members who have relatively homogenous tastes. New customers are allocated to one of the

FIGURE 9–15

Comparison shopping using multiattribute utility theory

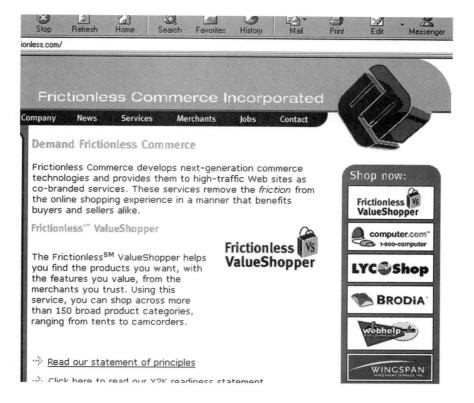

segments on the basis of their purchasing record. Customers are provided with information and leads for products that the customers are likely to enjoy.

Firefly began as an experimental system called RINGO at MIT in 1994. It used "social information filtering" to make music recommendations to users based on the user's history of music purchases. Users were asked to complete on-screen forms indicating their music tastes. The more information that was provided, the more reliable was the system in its predictions. It 1995, RINGO technology was taken over by Agents, Inc., and later by Firefly, Inc. Currently, Web-based retailers such as Amazon.com use this technology.

Extempo

The Web purchasing experience is currently mechanical in that users interact with lifeless forms such as Web documents. Interactive agents offer the possibility of enlivening that experience by using interesting personality characteristics similar to cartoon characters (see Figure 9–16). Extempo is in the forefront of this technology. Several popular websites, such as www.petopia.com (see Figure 9–17), www.jellybelly.com, and www.firstregistry.com, are employing interactive agents from Extempo to liven up visitors' experiences, on their websites.

These interactive interface agents, referred to as Imps, are semianimated graphical characters that can interact with users in natural language, with limited vocabulary, both in written and oral form. Because these characters exhibit a consistent personality, repeat visitors may develop an attachment to them. The Imps provide a socially engaged experience to visitors by acting as guides, spokespeople, and

FIGURE 9–16

Extempo's interactive Imp character gallery for websites

Figure 9–17

*Use of interactive
agent at Petopia
website*

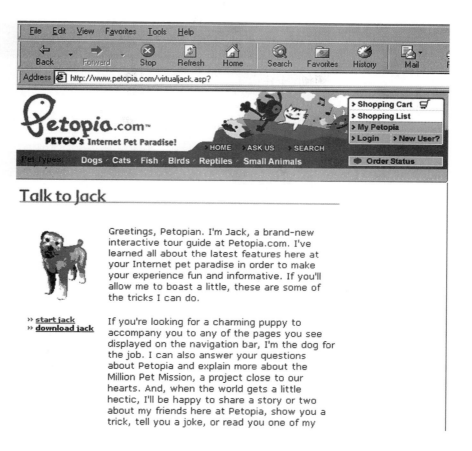

product experts. They also help develop a brand identity for the site
(see Figure 9–18).

Imp characters are based on intelligent agent research conducted at
Stanford University. Barbara Hayes-Roth, director of the Adaptive Agents
Project at Stanford, is the founder and CEO of Extempo Systems. The company provides a development environment where these cartoon-like interactive characters can be developed and an engine on the Web server
where these software characters execute.

Each Imp character has two characteristics: (1) a personality, (2) a role.
In turn, these characteristics have both a content part and a competence
part (see Figure 9–19). The content part is the equivalent of a database,
and the competence part is the counterpart of the processing that is done
on information stored in the database. For instance, on a university website, an Imp character may have the personality of a student counselor,
play the role of a major selection guide, and have the knowledge of ma-
jors offered at the university.

FIGURE 9–18

Use of interactive Imp character at Proctor & Gamble site

FIGURE 9–19

Architecture of the Imp system

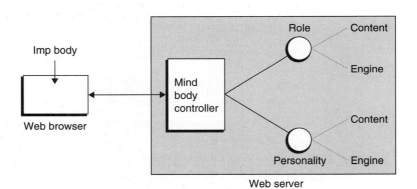

There are two parts to any Imp character. One part runs on the Web browsers and is called the body; the other part runs on the Imp engine on the Web server and is called the mind. The body is a software that needs to be downloaded. A mind-body controller mediates between the two-way communication between the character's mind running on the Imp engine and the body running on the user's browser.

Software developers and artists collaborate to develop an array of characters. Imp characters are interactive and have rudimentary understanding of natural language. They guide a visitor around a website according to the requests made by the visitor. Imp characters can sustain an interactive conversation with a visitor and are programmed to respond according to various keywords used by the visitor.

Frontmind

Frontmind, an online personalization tool offered by Manna (see Figure 9–20), provides a distributed system of agents that embody several methodologies. **Personalization** refers to techniques that help present Web content that is tailored to each visitor. Personalization is generally recognized as an important tool for Web-based retailing that aids in developing brand images and deeper customer relationships.

Personalized Web content is not developed in real time, but rather on the basis of information that may have been collected over an extended period. For instance, many websites will induce visitors to fill out detailed questionnaires, and the site content is designed accordingly. Some sites incorporate obvious business logic that offers customized discounts to repeat visitors. For example, if a visitor has been buying mystery books, she would be offered discounts on books that belong to that genre. Some sites categorize buyers into market segments and target promotions that are appropriate to those segments. For example, a buyer of multimedia software may also be offered suggestions and discounts on products such as digital cameras and DVD players.

The logic of personalization employs either rule-based business approaches or statistical reasoning methods that help in categorization. Rule-based approaches are appropriate for encoding business common sense, but they are static. The rules are applicable not just to a particular visitor

FIGURE 9–20

The Manna Inc. website

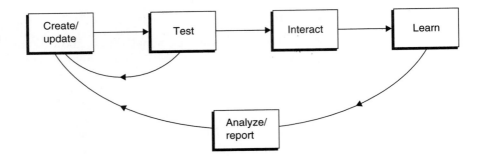

but to all visitors, and these rules cannot be changed dynamically. This approach does not consider data such as the current clicking behavior by the user and the current status of the shopping cart. On the other hand, statistical reasoning methods, while able to use customer-specific data such as purchasing history to predict buying preferences, require a great deal of data to work. The visitor has to supply sufficient data points to be categorized reliably.

The Frontmind solution combines both rule-based and statistical reasoning approaches. It also is adaptive in nature; that is, new rules can be incorporated temporarily in the system, their efficacy seen over time, and finally they can become part of the system. It provides for self-updating customer behavior models. There are several steps in this update procedure (see Figure 9–21):

- Create and update stage, where new business rules can be created and incorporated into the system. The system operator interacts through a business command center to change the existing rule set (see Figure 9–22).
- Test stage, where the consequences of the new rules are identified by simulating the operation of the new rule set.

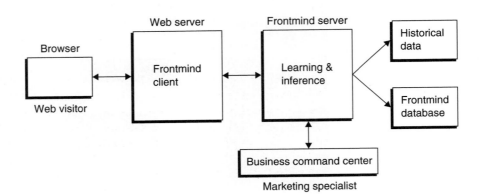

- Interaction stage, where the current behavior of the customer is used to update the behavior model of the customer on a click-by-click basis. The customer interacts with the system, and the clicking data are used to improve predictions related to the customer. As a customer moves from one page to another or clicks for more product information, the customer either confirms the behavior model or provides evidence against it. This provides the potential for continuous updating of the applicable model that Frontmind employs.
- Learning stage, where the updated model is applied to customers and new data are generated. The data are also used to suggest new rules and new behavior models that are applicable to various customers.

Frontmind offers a system of customer guidance based on the concept of the federation or community of agents; that is, there is not a single agent, but rather multiple agents that belong to different classes. All these agents collaborate to provide service to the user. The site at www.mamainc.com provides an interesting introduction to the technology. Currently, sites such as www.gourmetmarket.com and www.salesoutlet.com are using the Frontmind technology.

Frontmind employs four classes of agents:

- System agents
- Inference agents
- Prediction agents
- Messaging agents

System agents keep the system working. Inference agents use rules to arrive at decisions. Learning agents collect data through their interaction with the visitors and keep updating their statistical models. Messaging agents carry messages from one agent to another. The language that is used is derived from XML. The messages contain data about the sending agent, the recipient agent, and their states.

Mobile Agents

Mobile agents are software that actually travel over the Web, performing tasks specified by users. Agents such as search agents depend on a server-based program requesting other servers to do tasks on their behalf. Data are communicated between various programs residing on different servers. In the case of a mobile agent, not just the data moves, but also the program that is going to execute on different servers. Having programs move around with their own data reduces traffic over the network and reduces total computation.

FIGURE 9–23

*Remote procedure call
versus remote
programming*

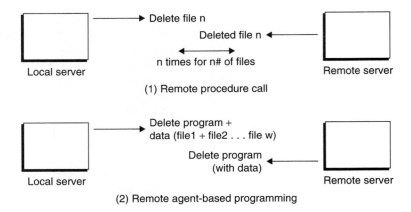

Local server → Delete file n

Deleted file n ←

← n times for n# of files →

Remote server

(1) Remote procedure call

Local server → Delete program +
data (file1 + file2 . . . file w)

Delete program
(with data) ←

Remote server

(2) Remote agent-based programming

A number of major companies including IBM and AT&T are particularly active in developing mobile agents. While commercial products are still a few years away, the basic architecture and platforms as well as the languages are now emerging.

A mobile agent is a new paradigm for computers to collaborate across distances (see Figure 9–23). The standard method of communication is called remote procedure call (RPC). With RPC, a computer calls on another computer and supplies the name of the program and the data that are required by the nonlocal program to operate. The remote computer accepts the data along with the program identification, executes the program, and sends back the result. A simple example involves deleting files from a remote computer. The local computer has to call a delete command and identify the parameter of the command, which is the name of the file that is to be deleted on the remote computer. For each deletion, the local computer must send a message and the remote computer must acknowledge the success or failure of the deletion operation.

General Magic is at the forefront of developing mobile agents for business applications. Its Telescript is intended to aid developers building electronic marketplaces that are populated by mobile buyer agents and seller agents.

A typical scenario of a platform using Telescript would be as follows: A user planning to visit another city on the weekend would instruct the buyer agent about the plan and preferences about price, seating location, and flight times, for example. The buyer agent would then visit several airline websites with the information specified by the user. At each site, the buyer agent would identify the best available deal and then move on to the next site and do the same thing. If the next airline site has a better offer, the buyer agent would carry the better offer to the next site for comparison. At all times, the agent is carrying only the information about the single best deal it has found. After visiting several sites, the agent would come back to the user with the best offer so far available. Depending on the user's instructions, it could then book the flight or continue the search.

There are several important differences between this scenario using mobile agents and the usual method of using shopping agents, such as at MySimon.com, to get multiple offers from various airlines. In the case of a shopping agent, requests are sent out to multiple airlines that answer with voluminous responses. All these responses arrive at the user's desktop for evaluation. In the case of mobile agent, little information is sent over the network. The processing involved in seeking the optimal deal is conducted over the remote servers that host the airline websites. Not only is information traffic limited, but the processing is distributed as well.

Logic of Mobile Agents

The above scenario is possible because Telescript is based on an agent architecture that involves the following basic concepts:

Mobile Agent Places.   Mobile agents move from one computing place to another. The network has to provide servers where the agent can come and perform its computation and information search. In the case of electronic marketplaces, the servers should make it possible for agents to request information, use a communication facility, and get local processing support. A shopping center website should provide a directory of facilities available to the agent and allow agents to order items and book tickets. It should also provide merchandising support for credit card processing and bank payments.

Mobile Agents.   Mobile agents are processing codes that move around with the requisite information. In the case of a mobile shopping agent, an agent should be able to carry comparative information about various offers and have the processing code necessary to compare offers, provide credit card details, and execute orders.

Mobility.   A mobile agent travels from an originating site, usually a user's desktop, to several sites that have the potential to serve the agent's informational and transactional needs. An agent should be able to locate the addresses of the remote servers and decide on a travel plan that is economical in terms of time and resources. The agent should further be able to negotiate a variety of networking media, protocols, and operating systems. The trip may succeed or fail due to network congestion, and the agent should have sufficient decision-making powers to respond appropriately.

Authority and Permit.   An agent, since it accesses the files and processing power of the host server, must carry the necessary permit because, for example, an agent could be malicious, such as a virus. There needs to be a system of permits that the host can consult before allowing access to the agent. On the other hand, the remote server should have the authority to grant or not to grant the agent access to local resources. The system of authorities and permits allows agents to interact with local hosts in a secure and a controlled environment.

Summary

This chapter reviewed general characteristics of software agents. A variety of agents were identified such as information search agents, retrieval agents, notification agents, and reconnaissance software agents. In the area of e-commerce, we covered the use of agents in product brokering and merchant brokering. We considered basic technologies such as artificial intelligence and statistical methods used in building software agents. A variety of agents actually in use in e-commerce activities were reviewed.

Key Terms

Agent 338	Multiattribute utility theory 341
Auction 343	Notification agent 347
Collaborative filtering 341	Personalization 361
Filtering agent 344	Product brokering 349
Merchant brokering 349	Symbolic reasoning 340

Review Questions

1. Describe what software agents are.
2. Differentiate the various types of software agents.
3. Describe how artificial intelligence and statistical techniques are used in software agents.
4. List popular software agents currently in use in the commercial world.
5. Identify various activities in e-commerce where software agents are currently in use.

Project

Visit www.botspot.com and list some software agents that can assist a buyer through the different stages of the purchasing process.

References, Readings, and Hyperlinks

1. Riecken, Doug. "Intelligent Agents." *Communications of the ACM,* July 1994, pp. 18–19.
2. Moses, Ma. "Agents in E-Commerce." *Communications of the ACM,* March 1999, pp. 79–80.
3. Maes, Pattie, Robert H. Guttman, and Alexandro G. Moukas. "Agents That Buy and Sell: Transforming Commerce as We Know It." *Communications of the ACM,* March 1999, vol 42, no 3, pp. 81–91.
4. Negroponte, Nicholas. "Agents: From Direct Manipulation to Delegation," in "Software Agents," ed. by Jeffrey M. Bradshaw, AAAI Press/MIT Press, Cambridge, 1999, pp. 57–66.
5. http://www.imagination-engines.com/databots.htm on 5/1/2001.
6. Chavez, Anthony, and Pattie Maes. "Kasbah: An Agent Marketplace for Buying and Selling Goods." MIT working paper, available at http://ecommerce.media.mit.edu.
7. "FrontMind." White paper, Manna Inc., February 2000.
8. Guttman, Robert H., and Pattie Maes. "Agents as Mediators in Electronic Commerce." In *Intelligent Information Agents: Agent-Based Information Discovery and Management on the Internet,* ed. Mathias Klusch. Berlin: Springer-Verlag, 1999.
9. Guttman, Robert H., and Pattie Maes. "Cooperative vs. Competitive Multi-Agent Negotiations in Retail Electronic Commerce." MIT working paper, available at http://ecommerce.media.mit.edu.
10. Guttman, Robert H., Alexandros G. Moukas, and Pattie Maes. "Agent-Mediated Electronic Commerce: A Survey." MIT working paper, available at http://ecommerce.media.mit.edu.
11. Guttman, Robert H., Alexandros G. Moukas, and Pattie Maes. "An Agent System for Comparative Shopping at the Point of Sale." MIT working paper, available at http://ecommerce.media.mit.edu.
12. Ionnis, S. Terpsidis, Alexander Moukis, Bill Pergioudakis, Geogios Doukidis, and Patti Maes. "The Potential of Electronic Commerce in Re-engineering Consumer-Retailer Relationships through Intelligent Agents." MIT working paper, available at http://ecommerce.media.mit.edu.
13. Lieberman, Henry. "Personal Assistants for the Web: MIT Perspective." In *Intelligent Information Agents: Agent-Based Information Discovery and Management on the Internet,* ed. Mathias Klusch. Berlin: Springer-Verlag, 1999.
14. Samson, Dawson. *Managerial Decision Analysis.* Homewood, IL: Irwin, 1988.
15. Sheth, Jagdish N., Banwari Mittal, and Bruce I. Newman. *Customer Behavior: Consumer Behavior and Beyond.* New York: The Dryden Press, 1999.
16. Williams, Joseph. *Bots and Other Internet Beasties.* Indianapolis: Sams Publishing, 1996.

17. White, James E. "Mobile Agents." In *Software Agents*, ed. Jeffrey M. Bradshaw. Menlo Park, CA: AAAI Press, 1997.

18. Zahedi, Fatemeh. *Intelligent Systems for Business: Expert Systems with Neural Network.* Belmont, WA: Wadsworth, 1993.

19. http://auction.eecs.umich.edu/

20. http://ecommerce.media.mit.edu/

21. http://ecommerce.mit.edu/kasbah

22. http://ecommerce.media.mit.edu/tete-@-tete

23. www.adone.com

24. www.artificial-life.com

25. www.botspot.com

26. www.classifiedwarehouse.com

27. www.frictionless.com

28. www.jango.com/xsh/index.dcg?

29. www.mannainc.com

30. www.moviecritic.com

31. "Online Personalization for E-Commerce." Manna Inc., February 2000.

MULTIMEDIA AND WEBCASTING ON THE WEB

Chapter Outline

Learning Objectives

By the end of this chapter, you should be able to:

- Find your way among the different multimedia techniques available for the Web.
- Use static graphics to illustrate Web pages without harming performance.
- Recognize how webcasting can generate interest for your site.

- Understand how using multimedia technology can supplement your Web presence.
- Scan the market for advances in new media technology.
- Evaluate the feasibility of the new media technology in your environment.

Chapter Overview

Improvements in hardware, software, and network infrastructure have alleviated some performance problems confronting the Web developer. Wider bandwidth encourages creativity and enables new choices and more dynamic graphics. Once a feature to be avoided, multimedia is slowly making inroads to many commercial sites. This chapter covers a range of techniques that can energize an e-commerce website. For example, webcasting enables the broadcast of audio or video through the Internet. It can be used to disseminate company news to inform and convince customers through an enhanced experience.

A Technical Vignette

Vcall, a service of Investor Broadcast Network, now offers its webcasting services for quarterly earnings calls for free after increased demand from publicly traded companies. Vcall (www.vcall.com) is a leading webcaster of corporate events, including earnings releases, shareholder meetings, press conferences, merger and acquisition announcements, introductory calls, and special announcements.

"Companies are quickly realizing the value that webcasting provides to a company's investor relations efforts," said David Bauman, president and CEO of Investor Broadcast Network. "The ability to reach an extremely broad audience of investors at relatively no cost is only one of the many benefits that companies derive. With a proposed ban from the U.S. Securities and Exchange Commission on selective disclosure, companies will be able to comply with these proposed changes without significantly changing the way they conduct their investor relations efforts."

Another benefit that audio webcasting can provide to companies is managing the rumor mill that emerges over the Internet. With a direct statement from the company, these rumors can be quelled relatively quickly.

References: Hedge call, a service of investor Broadcast Network Release Webcast, January 4, 2000.

Multimedia Graphics on the Web

Graphics Standards

World Wide Web publishers from novice to experts have discovered a lot of good reasons to include images in online documents. Pictures give Web pages more visual appeal and are often a good way to entice and encourage visits to a website.

Pictures can be used to overcome design limitations of Web publishing, specifically HTML codes. On printed material, the desktop publishing format instructions control the appearance of text, but HTML controls only slightly the appearance of the document. While many of the deficiencies are being addressed with style sheets, images are still a powerful tool to enhance pages.

Many effects require the developer to import pictures into HTML documents as inline elements. Inline graphics appear within the main browser window and are positioned in the text flow. Currently, inline graphics are restricted to a few file formats: the CompuServe Graphics Interchange Format (GIF), the Joint Photographic Expert Group format (JPEG), and the Portable Network Graphics (PNG).

In addition, pictures in a wide range of graphics file formats can be linked to pages. External graphics can be downloaded for off-line viewing or viewed online with the assistance of a player (or MIME) application.

Static Graphics

The most widely used graphic format is **GIF,** a proprietary bit-mapped graphics file format used by the World Wide Web, CompuServe, and many BBSs. GIF supports color and various resolutions. It also includes data compression, making it especially effective for scanned photos. A notable characteristic of GIF is that a variant of the format supports animation.

Another widely supported graphic format is **JPEG.** JPEG means Joint Photographic Experts Group. JPEG has a compression technique for color images that does not preserve all the original fine points of the image. Although it can reduce files sizes to about 5 percent of their normal size, some detail is lost in the compression.

JPEG is designed for compressing either full-color or gray-scale images of natural, real-world scenes. It works well on photographs, naturalistic artwork, and similar material; not so well on lettering, simple cartoons, or line drawings. JPEG handles only motionless images, but there is a related standard called Movies Photographic Expert Group (MPEG) for video.

It takes longer to decode and view a JPEG image than to view an image in a simpler format such as GIF. Thus using JPEG is essentially a time/space tradeoff. Given that bandwidth is still the most limiting factor in document transfer through the Internet and that workstations are becoming more powerful, the time savings from transferring a shorter file can be greater than the time needed to decompress the file. The advantage could be reversed if the client had large bandwidth but limited processing capabilities.

The last common standard format is **PNG,** a new bit-mapped graphics format similar to GIF but not proprietary. PNG was approved as a standard by the World Wide Web Consortium to replace GIF because GIF uses a patented data compression algorithm called LZW. The most recent versions of Netscape Navigator and Microsoft Internet Explorer support PNG.

For Web images, PNG has three main advantages over GIF:

1. Alpha channels (variable transparency).
2. Gamma correction (cross-platform control of image brightness).
3. Two-dimensional interlacing (a method of progressive display).

PNG also compresses better than GIF in almost every case, but the difference is generally only about 5 to 25 percent. One GIF feature that PNG does not try to reproduce is multiple-image support, especially animations; PNG was and is intended to be a single-image format only. A complementary format called Multiple-Image Network Graphics (MNG) is under development, but the major browsers do not yet support the format. MNGs and PNGs will have different file extensions and different purposes. MNG will also share a number of PNG's best features:

- Multiple cyclical redundancy checks (CRCs) so that file integrity can be checked without viewing.
- Ultra-clever magic signature that can detect the most common types of file corruption.
- Nonpatented compression, either completely lossless (PNG) or lossy (JPEG).
- Full alpha support (multilevel transparency) for all image objects.
- Gamma and color correction for cross-platform consistency.
- Ability to store copyright and other textual information, either compressed or uncompressed.

While supported by most leading image editors such as Adobe PhotoShop, CorelDraw, Macromedia Fireworks, Ulead PhotoImpact, and Microsoft Image Composer, the PNG format has been adopted at a slow pace. Many image libraries in various domains were composed with either GIF or JPEG and remain in use.

There are similarities between the various static image formats. GIF, JPEG, and PNG are raster (i.e., bit-mapped or paint) image formats. They can represent various image types (drawings, pictures of text, paintings, or photographs) with their own respective strength and can be viewed on multiple browser platforms from PCs, Macs, to UNIX machines.

Due to bandwidth limitations, the Web publisher needs to compress the image file size while preserving image quality. Three avenues are available to lessen the file size: reduce the number of pixels the image displays by using smaller images, limit the number of colors available, and utilize a compression scheme.

Publishing to the Web is different from publishing print media. The output is a monitor where definition could range from 640 by 480 to a high end of 1,600 by 1,200. Because the designer has little control over the type of monitor or browser utilized by the user interface on the client side, some compromises have to occur. Both Internet Explorer and Netscape Navigator do a great job downloading and displaying the two most popular graphics formats (i.e., GIF and JPEG). Monitors are low-resolution devices and limited in size, affecting the dimensions of pictures. Icons should be small or they will slow the loading of the page. Details, fine line drawings, or small originals are difficult to reproduce. Little images, bright colors, and solid backgrounds facilitate the rendering of pages.

The second avenue employed to increase graphics performance is reducing the number of colors and their depth. Simplifying the 16 million colors to a mere 256 acts as a miracle in improving downloading speed. GIF supports the limited 256 colors of an elementary color palette. Also, altering the resolution or bit depth dramatically changes the size of the file, the trade-off being a change in picture definition. A 4-bit depth is equivalent to 16 colors (2^4), while an 8-bit depth offers 256 colors (2^8). If the Web page rendering has to match the colors on an original, the palette choice has to be done cautiously.

Dithering is another way of reducing the number of colors used. Dithering is the method of mixing colors when the chosen color is not on the current palette. The system blends little dots of color to approximate the color chosen. A better alternative is to have the chosen color in the palette in the first place. Dithering is preferable to either solid colors or a regular pattern. Using solid areas of color usually results in posterization, and patterning creates a checkerboard of dots, which can be detrimental to image quality.

The last and often preferred model for performance improvement is compression. Graphics formats include a compression algorithm triggered by the opening of the file. GIF and JPEG differ in that the original GIF compression is lossless, while the JPEG uses a lossy method. GIF images are lossless and use the patented Lempel-Ziv-Welch (LZW) compression scheme. The algorithm safeguards the visual attributes of the original while achieving good compression. A compression of 2:1 is usually achievable.

In JPEG, the compressed file does not preserve all attributes of the original. The compression attained is much higher due to the discarded data. An image where quality is not essential can be compressed to a 20:1 ratio, thereby facilitating speedy transfer. While the files download much faster, the client has to decompress them before displaying them on the screen. The lengthy decompression may compensate for the gain in transfer time. In the present environment, the bottleneck is still the network bandwidth.

The secret of gaining and keeping the attention of Web visitors is to break the monotony of the site. Text and pictures can be complemented by the addition of effects.

In addition to raster graphics, vector graphics are gaining in popularity. Vector graphics are digital images created through a sequence of commands or mathematical statements that draw lines and shapes in a given two-dimensional or three-dimensional space. In mathematics, a vector is a representation of both a quantity and a direction at the same time. In vector graphics, the file that results from a designer's work is created and saved as a sequence of vector. Instead of containing bits in the file for each pixel of a line drawing, a vector graphic file describes a series of points to be connected. One result is a much smaller file. The vector image is converted into a bit-map only at the time it will be displayed, therefore saving bandwidth.

Most images created with tools such as Adobe Illustrator, Macromedia Flash, Microsoft Visio, and CorelDraw are in the form of vector image files. Vector image files are easier to modify than raster image files because a simple mathematical scale can easily manipulate them.

Animated Graphics and Rich Media

Rich media is a subspecialty in interactive advertising and entertainment and it is also several new technologies with advanced multimedia characteristics. Recent technological advancements in digital video creation, streaming, compression, caching, bandwidth, and content-delivery technologies are bringing video, audio, and the Internet together as rich media. The leading e-commerce sites spend millions of dollars on site design, but the latest animated graphics technology is available to all Web designers. The market is currently dominated by Flash technology.

Flash is a low-bandwidth, browser-independent vector-graphic animation technology developed by Macromedia. It is well supported by free plug-ins, available for the major browsers. Flash animations look the same on both browsers. With the Flash animation application, users can draw their own animations or import other vector-based images.

Flash is leading the pack in rich media in advertising. Jupiter Media reported it was deployed by over 50 percent of advertisers. The closest competitors, Enliven and RealAudio, were used by less than 25 percent of this market.

Shockwave, also from Macromedia, is another major animation player on the Web. Shockwave is a Web standard for entertaining, engaging, rich media playback. It allows users to view interactive Web content such as games, business presentations, entertainment, and advertisements from the Web browser. Top business and entertainment sites such as Disney.com, Intel.com, SharperImage.com, and Palm Computing use Shockwave extensively on their websites. Shockwave Players are free, easy to get, and available on multiple platforms. Shockwave Player ships with Windows 95, 98, NT, Mac OS, Internet Explorer, America Online, and Netscape Navigator.

Web Design Effects (WDE), a technique developed by Intel, provides a 3-D engine that can render high-quality, client-generated 3-D text. Licensed to RealNetworks under the name RealText 3D, WDE energizes text messages and adds excitement to RealPlayer G2 and SMIL content with scalable, low-bandwidth 3-D fonts and effects. Fonts generally dominate Web pages, yet typically they remain static on a printed page. WDE not only provides 3-D text, but it also provides a powerful animation tool for creating font presentations such as those seen in motion picture title sequences.

Multimedia Sounds on the Web

Digitized Radio

The Web is the site of a growing global market for radio. Many radio stations have added digitized broadcasts of their programs. With the RealPlayer interface, the user can search for a radio station according to the following criteria: format, speed, language, city, city if in the United States, state if in the United States, country, any city not in the United States. Surfing through the choices one can easily find news, music, or any other genre. The use of the radio feature only requires a connection to the Internet, a sound card, and a pair of speakers or earphones.

Sound Clips

Static Web pages often lack the bells and whistles expected from the demanding visitor. Adding the option of sound clips to a page helps teaching, public relations, and marketing personnel in the delivery of their message.

The sound clip can be repeated as desired. With a sound device installed, the user can utilize readily available accessories to record original sound.

The steps are simple on the Microsoft Windows platform:

1. From the "Programs" group select the "Accessories" subgroup then "Multimedia" or "Entertainment".
2. The program is named Sound Recorder.
3. With an attached microphone record the sound clip.
4. Once the sound clip is made, use the File "save as" option and store the result in the desired directory.
5. The sound clip can later be edited, playing it to the point to edit and clicking Edit. This will require some practice and it is advisable to save the new clip under an alternative name in case the process is not adequate.

Sound clips can be as long as needed, but shorter clips have better performance and typically take proportionately less time to download. Using a microphone from a headset usually provides good quality by reducing background noise.

Telephony

Computer and telephony integration enables people to use the Internet as the transmission medium for telephone calls. For users who have free or fixed-price Internet access, Internet telephony software essentially provides free telephone calls anywhere in the world. To date, however, Internet telephony does not offer the same quality of telephone service as direct telephone connections because of bandwidth limitations and the immaturity of current systems.

Many Internet telephony applications are available. These include CoolTalk and NetMeeting, which come bundled with the popular Web browsers. Other products, such as Callserve, DialPad, Netvoice, and Net2phone, are available as standalone devices and can be purchased inexpensively. Internet telephony products are sometimes called IP telephony, Voice over the Internet (VOI), or Voice over IP (VOIP) products.

Web plug-ins designed for Web-based communications applications can enable a live voice connection from any website to any regular telephone over the Internet. The IP telephony plug-in can be used on e-commerce sites to allow users to call the company to speak with the help desk. A multiservice standard-based platform for IP communications, for only the cost of an Internet connection, can allow customers to receive the personalized customer care of call centers from their computer.

While limited to computers or other devices with voice processing capabilities, this solution offers attractive features. After the plug-in is installed, website visitors use their multimedia computers to speak with a representative at a preset phone number. No callbacks or additional phone lines are necessary because a single connection is used for browsing and talking.

Best Effort Service

Telephony service through the Internet is still questionable. The Internet network layer provides service but without guarantee regarding end-to-end delay, packet loss, and packet jitter. For real-time applications such as multimedia, teleconferencing, and Internet phone, this causes serious problems. Mechanisms have been devised to attenuate these hurdles.

With an Internet telephony application, the voice is digitized and placed into chunks appended with a header and sent through the Internet. In the best of conditions, the packets travel end to end without loss and with rather constant acceptable delay. The receiver plays the chunks as they arrive and reach an intelligible communication. With a more inconsistent network, the chunks arrive irregularly, some are lost, and the receiver cannot comprehend the conversation. The problems are of two types: loss of packet or irregular delays.

- Loss of packet is a serious problem. The UDP datagrams encapsulating the digitized voice travel the Internet and are relayed by a number of routers. In case of congestion, a router stores the packets in buffers that can be full, resulting in datagrams being trashed. Because the packet does not arrive, the receiver is missing segments of the conversation. One remedy is to send the packets via TCP instead of UDP. The transmission control protocol retransmits packets that do not reach their destination. This alternative is not attractive, however, as the real-time nature of telephony applications does not bear such delays. In addition, the variable rate of the sender would render the conversation almost unintelligible. For these reasons, most Internet phone applications use UDP exclusively. To alleviate packet loss, forward error corrections techniques are used that conceal some of the loss.
- End-to-end delay depends on the distance traveled and the medium on transmitting segments. Below a threshold of 100 to 300 milliseconds, conversation quality is acceptable. Above 400 to 500 milliseconds, the packets are effectively lost.
- Jitter among packets can be depicted as unequal delays in a packet sequence. The packets can incur different path congestions as they compete for bandwidth with other applications, thus they can arrive either in a burst or be delayed. Jitter can be partly corrected by sequencing the packets and queuing the packets before replay. This compensates for bursts by buffering the burst and regulating the delay with the help of these buffered segments.

Two techniques are used to balance the jitter effect. In the first mechanism, fixed playout delay equalizes the delay. A packet generated at time t will play out at time $t + 200$ milliseconds for example. The subsequent packets will all play at their originating time plus 200 milliseconds. If a packet arrives at a time exceeding the delay, it will be discarded and a subsequent packet will be played as planned. In the adaptive playout delay, the delay is not considered fixed but is optimized for minimum loss of packet and minimum delay. The packets playback are either slowed or hurried depending on network conditions.

As mentioned above, the use of TCP instead of UDP is rarely considered because the retransmission of the packet is not feasible in a timely manner. Loss is commonly anticipated and preventive measures are taken by using either forward error correction or interleaving techniques in the flow of packets.

Multimedia Standards and Protocols

Video

As illustrated in Figure 10–1, the development of video for consumption on the Web includes hardware and software multiple components. These are the CPU of the computer, a capture card enabling the conversion of an analog signal into a digital video stream, a large mass storage device to hold the newly digitized content, and a video source deck, probably a VCR, VTR, video camera, or a laser-disc player.

Video Compression

Video compression is a core technology for DTV, HDTV, and DVD and is or will be a part of almost any video or audio storage or transmission. The efficient working of compression systems is an essential element of

Figure 10–1

A video capture system

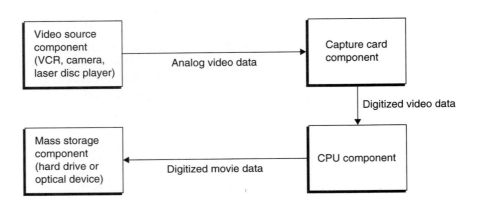

delivered quality. Digital compression methods fall into different camps. There are different forms, but there are just a few relevant standards. One predominant standard is MPEG and another one is Indeo. Each video compression standard serves a different purpose.

MPEG.   The Moving Picture Experts Group (MPEG) develops standards for digital video and digital audio compression. It operates under the auspices of the International Organization for Standardization (ISO). The use of MPEG video files requires a personal computer with sufficient processor speed, internal memory, and hard disk space to handle and play the typically large MPEG file. The computer needs some MPEG viewer or client software that plays MPEG files. While MPEG files can be decoded by special hardware or by software, as it often is a processing burden on the CPU, most multimedia personal computers require the installation of a MPEG co-processor to achieve acceptable performance. MPEG files are easily recognizable as they often use a file name suffix of .mpg. MPEG players are readily available on the Internet. MPEG should not be confused with the now popular MP3 format used to download music. MPEG reaches a high compression rate by storing only the variation from one frame to another, instead of each entire frame. The video information is then encoded using a technique called DCT. MPEG uses a type of lossy compression, since some data is removed. But the dilution of data is generally imperceptible to the human eye. MPEG generally produces better-quality video than competing formats, such as Video for Windows, Indeo, and QuickTime.

Since 1988, MPEG has issued a number of increasingly ambitious standards to accommodate the new audio and video demands. The MPEG standards are an evolving series, each designed for a different purpose. MPEG-1 is the first standard, adopted in 1991. When MPEG began its work to develop a standard for digital compression, its goal was to develop an algorithm that could compress a video signal and then be able to play it back off a CD-ROM or over telephone lines at a low bit rate. This rate was less than 1.5 mbits per second and the data rate of uncompressed audio CDs. The intention of the group was to achieve a quality level that could deliver full-motion, full-screen, VHS quality from a variety of sources. Its goal was not to achieve broadcast quality but to be good enough to display on a computer monitor or to play back from a consumer multimedia device.

MPEG 1 has potentially three layers with different use and increased complexity. Table 10–1 represents the relative complexities of the MPEG-1 layers. These will translate into more demand on computer resources or equivalent time lags.

Examples of products using MPEG-1 Layer I coding include:

- Solid-state audio (theme parks, traffic).
- Disk storage and editing.
- CD-I full motion video.

TABLE 10–1   MPEG—overview
of layer complexity

	Complexity	
Layer	Encoder	Decoder
I	1.5 to 3	1.0
II	2 to 4	1.25
III	> 7.5	2.5

Products using MPEG-1 Layer II coding in addition to the above are:

• Video CD.
• Digital audio broadcast.
• DVD.
• Cable and satellite radio, TV.
• Contribution, distribution, and emission links (ISDN).
• Movie sound tracks.

Layer III coding is used mostly for ISDN commentary.

The most common implementations of the MPEG-1 standard provide a video resolution of 352-by-240 at 30 frames per second (fps). This produces video quality slightly below the quality of conventional VCR videos. To stream a video from existing media into digital MPEG one can use a MPEG converter.

MPEG-2 was created by the ISO committee because the standard of MPEG-1 did not serve the requirements of the broadcast industry. The group developed a compression algorithm that processed video at full resolution that would match CCIR 601 video (704 x480 NTSC, 704 X 576 PAL). MPEG took advantage of the higher bandwidths available to deliver higher image resolution and picture resolution. It targets increased image quality, support of interlaced video formats, and provision for multi-resolution scalability. It allows compression at high resolution and higher bit rates than MPEG-1. MPEG-2 runs at a data rate of 6.0 mbps and is designed for broadcast-quality video that delivers better quality at a faster data rate. MPEG-2 allows for compression ratios that fit 6 to 10 digital channels into the bandwidth required for one analog channel.

MPEG-2 is like its predecessor in that the standard consists also of the three layers—video, audio, and system. The video quality of MPEG-2 technology is superior to MPEG-1; however, MPEG-1 is useful and still being used. The two standards are complementary technologies designed to address the needs of specific markets and data transfer rates. MPEG-1 operates on a much smaller bandwidth, which allows for a greater number of channels per given signal range. It is designed to provide higher-quality video output than MPEG-2 at single-speed CD data rates. For many broadcast uses, MPEG-1 provides cost-effective and more-than-adequate video quality. The different standards allow a system designer to pick the compression technology that is right for a particular application. Also, because MPEG-1 is a subset of MPEG-2, any MPEG-2 decoder will be able to decode MPEG-1 syntax video. The advantages of both MPEG video compression standards include significant overall system saving costs, higher quality, and greater programming choices.

In 1994, anticipating the rapid convergence of the telecommunications, computer, and television and movie industries, the MPEG embarked on a more ambitious project. The MPEG-4 mandate was to standardize algorithms and tools for coding and flexible representation of audiovisual data with a view to multimedia application. The MPEG-4 standard took effect in 1999. The new standard addressed the needs for universal accessibility and robustness in error-prone environments, high interactive functionality, coding of natural and synthetic data, and compression efficiency. MPEG-4 represents the convergence of two standards: the MPEG and the QuickTime file format.

Since the adoption of MPEG-4, the ISO body has been working on a new version of MPEG called MPEG-7. Information about the latest development is available at www.cselt.it/mpeg/standards.htm.

Indeo.   Indeo is a codec (compression/decompression technology) for computer video developed by Intel Corporation. Although it is a software codec, Indeo is based on the digital video interaction (DVI), which is a hardware codec. It is not widely used and has not been widely marketed by Intel, which is partnering with other firms on many related products and its offering of Intel® Easy Web Media. As with any video, the movement is obtained through a series of frames sequenced to achieve the animation.

Internet Video Products and Solutions

Some of the biggest changes of the past years have been the rapid increase in computer speed and power. Available memory and disk space have also made possible video storing and editing that could be considered only by the most advanced workstation in 1999.

Recent products are more powerful and easier to use and set up, and they have incredible features that make video editing much more productive. One of the most important of these is timeline playback, which allows users to bypass the 2GB file size limit and saves half the disk space. Before timeline playback, to create a 10-minute video required enough storage space for all the raw footage in addition to the new 10-minute avi file rendered. With timeline playback, only the transitions, filters, and effects are rendered. The original avi files are used, saving disk space and speeding the rendering of the final video.

Another change in the industry is the new video compressions used. Since the original MJPEG, the first compression revolution came as DV. It was very slow to take off because the early hardware FireWire capture cards, along with the Non Linear Editing (NLE) software, were not stable. Over the past year, DV/FireWire editing has dominated the marketplace with incredible video quality with a fixed throughput of only 3.6 megs per second.

While this initially required SCSI drives, today any high-end Pentium III with an Ultra DMA EIDE hard drive can easily handle it. DV/FireWire capture cards feature frame-accurate device control. This allows the user to use batch capture features that save disk space and make the overall editing process more productive because the DV cam can be controlled from within the editing application.

The video capture card market is divided into three segments—analog capture cards, DV/FireWire cards, and Hybrid DV systems.

- Analog capture cards have regular video and S-video inputs and outputs. They do not have FireWire. The more expensive cards in this category have audio built on to ensure perfect audio sync, even on very long projects. The less expensive boards without audio are susceptible to audio sync issues, especially when making video longer than five minutes.

- The DV/FireWire card market consists of three distinct marketplaces. Low-cost cards ($150 to $400) with very limited software bundles, midrange cards ($500 to $1,000), and analog/DV hybrid cards for more than $2,000. The most important thing to understand when comparing all these DV cards is this: DV in = DV out. As a result, all the DV/FireWire cards on the market deliver the identical video quality and all of them have the identical video specs—720 × 480 image size, 29.97 frames per second, and a data rate of 3.6 megs per second. With all of these cards, at least a gigabyte of storage is needed for each 4.5 minutes of DV video.

- The last category of video capture cards has one very important feature: They use hardware codecs, so they accept DV, S-video, and composite video. Whatever format is used as input, these boards can support it. Encoding is in real time, and the user can create projects from multiple source formats. These boards all also come with a breakout box to handle all the different jacks these formats require.

Getting moving images into a Web page or document is cheaper and easier than ever. A video capture board can take analog input from a camcorder or VCR and turn it into digital video clips that the user can edit on a computer. While there is no upper limit on the amount one can spend, with a low budget of $500 the user can get a respectable video capture card and the necessary software needed to create video vignettes.

Video on Demand

Video on demand describes a system of internetworking applications to serve the needs of digital video. With the help of mass-storage, high-performance networks and specialized software, the move to production video serving can support visualization efforts of many businesses.

This technology has high potential to provide asynchronous diffusion of information on the user's terms. This allows individuals to select videos from a central server and display them on either a television or a computer. The technology can be used for education, entertainment, or deferred videoconferencing. The hurdle of a lack of network infrastructure or bandwidth could be remedied by advances in the enabling technologies such as wide adoption of fiber optics.

In the personal computer universe, video on demand is often consumed as a clip that plays on a Web page. A mouse click on the icon starts a video after a few seconds of delay. Once connected to the video server site, the video is streamed through the Internet and buffering occurs when the transmission is of unequal quality. On the playing side, the video is smoothed and uninterrupted. Line quality affects the experience, but progress on high-speed connectivity and improved bandwidth will ease the current difficulties in the near future. On the production side RealNetworks is selling the RealProducer G2 Authoring Kit containing a SMIL wizard to help the developer quickly create multimedia layout presentations using data types such as RealAudio, RealVideo, RealPix, RealText, and Real G2 with Flash—as well as an SMIL Syntax Checker and more.

Players can easily be installed to play audio or display video in a friendly computing environment. Figure 10–2 illustrates the video streaming displayed with RealPlayer. RealPlayer is one of the most widely used display mechanisms for animated features on the Web, making it unlikely the user will have to load new software.

For example, RealNetworks' content-creation products make it easy to convert existing media (VHS tapes, live feeds, avi files, digital photos) into streaming media files for live events or on-demand content for the Internet and corporate intranets. Then a server or access to a server is needed to stream the content created. RealServers allow media content to be streamed from a website or intranet.

Apple is distributing a range of products aimed at the video production market. **QuickTime** Pro can work with 35 different file formats and provides easy-to-use authoring tools. QuickTime Pro supplies the

FIGURE 10–2

RealPlayer

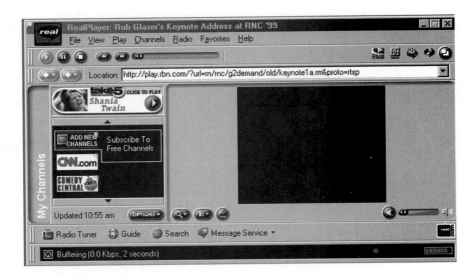

core capabilities needed to create professional-quality digital video, but the QuickTime free player has limited customization features and the displayed image is too small to be sufficiently visible. Figure 10–3 shows a QuickTime interface.

With the release of Windows Media Player 7, Microsoft attempts to redefine the audio and video experience with its first all-in-one experience including SRS WOW 3-D Audio Enhancement Technology. For the developer desiring to provide complex content, Microsoft has developed a support website (http://msdn.microsoft.com/windowsmedia) where software development kits can be downloaded. The Windows media format SDK 7 offers a number of improvements:

The improved video playback supports:

- Progressive download enabling applications to play a media file while simultaneously performing a progressive download of the file. This is critical when the Windows media format content is hosted on an HTTP server.
- Networked fast-forward and rewind enabling applications to fast-forward and fast-rewind on demand of local media content.
- User-specified maximum connection bandwidth enabling applications to specify the maximum delivery bit rate for media content delivered over the Internet. This facility is important when the playback bit rate (downstream) is different from the capture and encode bit rate (upstream).
- Seek-to marker enabling applications that support the format SDK 7 to "seek to" specific locations on Windows media format files with markers, similar to how DVD works today.

FIGURE 10–3

QuickTime

The content creation and authoring supports:

- Inverse Telecine enabling applications to deliver improved playback quality for film-sourced content. Video content that originates from 24 frames per second (fps) film is "padded" with extra frames for delivery at 30 fps. Applications that support the format SDK 7 are able to intelligently extract the original 24 fps and encode this out at 24 fps, eliminating artifacts. This results in improved quality at lower bandwidth.

- Deinterlacing enabling applications to deliver improved playback quality on progressive scan-line displays (computer monitors) for National Television Standards Committee (NTSC) and phase alternation system (PAL)-sourced content, which is interlaced. Deinterlacing eliminates flicker on interlaced content, resulting in better quality playback.

- Streaming and archiving of content separately enabling applications to read Windows media format content while simultaneously archiving the content.

- Compressed video enabling applications to view or monitor the compressed video as it is being archived (for on-demand video) or streamed live to the Web.

Figure 10–4

Microsoft Media Player

Figure 10–4 shows the newly redesigned interface of Microsoft Windows Media Player. While the interface presented is relatively similar to other competing players, the product is customizable with a number of what Microsoft calls skins.

Adobe has offered competitive products in the same area for some time. With Adobe Premiere, Adobe aims at the professional market. Adobe Premiere software spans the world of broadcast and online media. Supported by an elegant interface and excellent editing tools, the developer can work with efficiency, control, and flexibility to produce broadcast-quality movies for video, film, multimedia, and the Web.

Video Conferencing

Standards: The H Series

Most network telephony now uses H.323 as a standard protocol that includes videoconferencing as well as IP telephony. With H.323, the International Telecommunications Union (ITU) defined how audiovisual conferencing data are transmitted across networks. In theory, today's gateways are based on the H.323 standard but differ among vendors and are implemented in a slightly different way and many may not completely

FIGURE 10–5

H.323 architecture

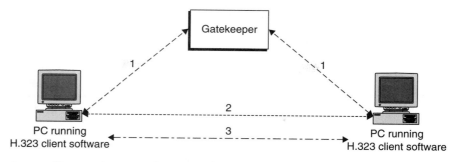

1 – – – – Query and response for new user's address
2 ········ Session established with H.225
3 ·—–— Feature negotiation with H.245

interoperate. This is especially true for supplementary services such as call forwarding and call transfer.

The current H.323 series has evolved from the earlier generations of the videoconferencing world and therefore includes most of the video protocols along with audio protocols and call control and setup protocols. The H standard has several drawbacks, including encompassing a large scope of protocols going well beyond what is required for a single application. It also provides opportunity for expansion but at the cost of added complexity, and the time needed to set up a call in H.323 limits the protocol. Figure 10–5 depicts how the components fit together. In practice two versions have been deployed, one for corporate networks (high quality and high bandwidth) and one for the Internet (optimized for low bandwidth 28.8/33.6 kilobits/second—G.723.1 and H.263).

In today's IP telephony products and services, companies are working to make the standards more interoperable and to streamline their communication protocols. H.323 terminals allow for built-in multipoint capability for ad hoc conferences and multicast (multi-unicast), allowing three to four people in a call without centralized mixing or switching. In today's environment, businesses are trying to find more streamlined solutions and are increasingly looking for convergent but simpler solutions to their IP telephony problems.

Session Initiation Protocol

SIP, the session initiation protocol, is a signaling protocol for Internet conferencing and telephony. It is seen by many as the successor to the H series and promises to overcome some of the scalability problems of H.323. SIP was developed within the IETF MMUSIC (Multiparty Multimedia Session Control) working group, with work proceeding in the IETF SIP working group. SIP is an application-layer control (signaling) protocol for

FIGURE **10–6**

Session initiation protocol

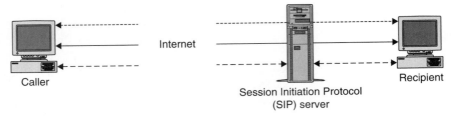

Caller

Internet

Session Initiation Protocol
(SIP) server

Recipient

◄------► Voice call established
◄– – –► Voice call request and response

creating, modifying, and terminating sessions with one or more participants. These sessions include Internet multimedia conferences, Internet
telephone calls, and multimedia distribution. Members in a session can
communicate via multicast or via a mesh of unicast relations or a combination of these. Figure 10–6 shows the streamlined use of SIP for an
Internet multimedia session. SIP speeds up call setup as the initial request
includes all configuration information. Requests sent to the recipient either directly or through a proxy server will initiate the session immediately when the recipient accepts the call.

While H.323 is still the dominant deployment method for delivering
multimedia traffic through the Internet, it was retrofitted from a non-Web
standard and is not a perfect fit for IP voice calls and other types of multimedia traffic. SIP was designed from the outset to match Web applications such as multimedia conferencing, feature-rich Internet telephony,
and distance learning.

SIP is based on HTTP. The protocol is easily understood and enables
developers to design Web applications accessible from a variety of devices.
With the rising importance of mobile IP phones and wireless handheld units,
the protocol is due to spread faster. Figure 10–6 illustrates a fundamental
difference over the H.323 setting—SIP does not require a centralized gateway to control calls, thus avoiding an important potential bottleneck.
Interoperability tests among a number of vendors including Cisco, 3Com,
MCIWorldCom, and Level 3 Communications have demonstrated the scalability and ubiquity of the SIP solution. Another uncommon advantage of
SIP is its interoperability with Domain Name System (DNS), the directory
technology that translates between domains and IP addresses.

Webcasting

What Is Webcasting?

Webcasting is a method of delivering the audio of video content across
the Internet based on the creation of Web channels that support interaction with subscribers. It is the Internet counterpart to traditional radio

and TV broadcasting. Webcasting has two distinct segments: first, it can be described by its ability to use the Web to deliver live or playback versions of sound or video broadcasts, and second, it is a synonym for **push** technology.

The webcasting server pushes information to the subscribers rather than waiting until the user specifically requests it (as in **pull** technology). In reality, most of the push is triggered by the users or the administrator and arrives only as the result of client requests triggered either by events or time. Webcasting is aimed at changing the user's experience from exploring the Web to one of harvesting predetermined subjects grown for the user's specific consumption. For example, a user can subscribe to channels specific to a particular stock, hockey team, and political party. For the corporation, webcasting offers an organized way to manage information for the intranet and focused news broadcast to stakeholders and potential customers.

"Net Talk Live" is the world's first interactive triplecast, reaching audiences worldwide via television, radio, and the Internet. The talk show, broadcast from Dallas, invites computer users to log-on and surf along while they listen and watch. Others offering sounds and video broadcasts through the Web include Audionet and CNET TV. Viewing webcasts requires having an appropriate video viewing application such as Windows Media Player, RealVideo, or VXtreme streaming video players; these can usually be downloaded from any site offering a webcast.

Other uses of webcasting include:

- A news organization can broadcast information to subscribers such as political and financial news about a particular country. Advertising can be attached with the news, providing revenue.

- Software publishers often look for an effective medium to distribute their software and the associated service releases. The software publisher can offer a fee-based channel, promising to keep an up-to-date stream of useful software and patches on a periodic basis. Such a practice may be essential in the domain of virus checking software, where the currency of the virus data file is essential to the protection of the user.

- An online employment agency can devise a channel to inform job seekers (subscribers) of opportunities that arise in their skill or chosen location. For the potential employer, the medium can be an efficient way to post vacancies.

- An auction house can propose to customers a channel aimed at information about forthcoming promotions and deadlines. Channels can also be appropriate for receiving updates on the status of multiday bidding.

- Digital goods can be delivered cost effectively on a dedicated channel. With improved bandwidth, users are increasingly finding that Internet delivery may be feasible. The webcasting approach will have varying benefits for different segments of e-commerce and will be increasingly used either for delivery of digital goods or to flag opportunities linked to priority news.

Webcasting is becoming a common feature used by home users and by corporations diffusing information through their intranets. The two segments are well differentiated. While home users tend to set channels customized to their taste, the corporate market uses webcasting to control directed proprietary information.

Webcasting, as a push technology, is the prearranged updating of news, weather, or other selected information on a computer user's desktop interface through periodic and generally unobtrusive transmission over the World Wide Web (including the use of the Web protocol on intranets). Webcasting can create bottlenecks on the network when the bandwidth is limited and users subscribe to multiple channels in unicast mode. In this environment, users at the same location may redundantly request the same information, which is then individually fetched multiple times from the Internet. One partial solution is to employ multicast or cache the content on a local server. Multicast is the communication between a single sender and multiple receivers on a network. A common use of multicast is the updating of mobile personnel from a home office and the periodic issuance of online newsletters. Combined with local caching, multicast can speed up the delivery of multimedia materials. Multicast is one packet type in the new IP Version 6, and its adoption should increase the diffusion of this new protocol. As new product lines hit the market, better support in the routers along the Internet will facilitate webcasting. The main Internet infrastructure providers will have an inherent interest in modernizing their backbone. Webcasting is also available through separate applications such as Entrypoint and Backweb that run on current desktop systems.

Software support will also facilitate adoption. Progress has been made in the past few years in both streaming technology and compression techniques.

Starting in 1995, webcasting generated a great deal of excitement. However, the enthusiasm has subsided considerably since 1997, leading to the demise of most of the pioneers. Xing Technology Corporation entered the arena in 1995 with the first streaming video product, Streamworks. It was based on the MPEG standard. VDONet was another early pioneer with a promising position in 1995. PC Magazine Online listed eight leading providers of video over the Internet in May 1995. Two companies supported true streaming video: VDONet Corp. with VDOLive and Xing Technology with Streamworks. From 1995 to 1997 other start-ups such as Vivo and Vxtreme joined the streaming landscape, but by May 2000 VDOnet stopped selling its products. VDOPhone users can keep making Internet calls by using the ICQ software and launching VDOPhone from ICQ, but no further development will occur on this product. This leads to an uncertain future as new operating systems will be unlikely to tolerate this older version. VivoActive can still be obtained from the RealNetworks site, but no development work has been done on the product since 1997. Vxtreme ceased independent operation after being acquired by Microsoft. Progressive Networks mutated to the now prominent RealNetworks and merged with Xing, its former rival in the streaming market segment. This industry consolidation is a symptom of the upcoming maturity of the technology.

Approaches to Webcasting

Various industry providers have implemented webcasting differently. Their solutions are not compatible, forcing the user to employ multiple viewers or concentrate on a single source. The current three dominant formats are Microsoft Windows Media, Apple Quick Time, and RealNetworks.

Microsoft is promoting **active channels,** which use HTML 4.0 with the addition of Microsoft implementation of dynamic HTML and a number of other ingredients. Channels are simply Web pages that are downloaded automatically. The channel definition format (CDF) was initially proposed by Microsoft to the W3C and is currently supported in the Microsoft browser. The CDF file points to the Web pages and subpages that the user sees after selecting a channel with the browser. Push technology such as Entrypoint or Backweb can be used as the substrate, but the solution also offers direct delivery without the complexity of a dedicated server. CDF is built from XML. To create a CDF file, the first step is to determine the hierarchy, or structure of the channel. The channel can be designed to map the structure of an existing website, or it can be a subset of a website's content with a different hierarchy.

Objects appear on the desktop as they are needed. The channel bar allows control over the delivery of the subscribed channels. CDF provides file information and an index of the downloadable content. Any site on the Internet can prepare a CDF file to offer pages through a Web channel. This is what most people identify as webcasting. While Microsoft encourages the use of CDF for efficient webcasting, three levels are supported.

1. Basic webcasting. It supports a webcast without any necessary CDF file. It is much less efficient as the program has to crawl through unindexed pages.
2. Managed webcasting. It provides organized webcasts through the use of a CDF file.

3. True webcasting. It facilitates multicasting through the use of more advanced technology. Mostly this is achieved through the use of third-party software such as Backweb or PointCast.

The resource description framework (RDF) is a general framework for how to describe any Internet resource such as a website and its content. RDF describes the resources on the network with the author's name, when and how the resource was created or modified, and a number of other metadata. With the addition of keywords, RDF can be instrumental in making the work of intelligent agents and search engines more relevant.

In general, the same design and production principles applied in any Web page authoring can be used for webcasting.

- Special attention has to be taken when an update occurs. Two types of sections may exist on an e-commerce site; for example, one can contain product information, news, and other special features. If adding a new feature, then a new channel is necessary, as the site will contain a new URL not included in the existing channel.
- Avoid elements in Web pages that would force users to be online if off-line browsing is desired. (Elements that require them to be online include Java applets and ActiveX Controls.)
- Active channels alert users when new material is added to the site, but only at the regular update intervals. To gain more exposure, update pages often and increase the channel update frequency but avoid being an annoyance to the user.
- Limit site crawling to avoid waste of bandwidth, disk space, and processing power retrieving unrelated links.

Microsoft presents a number of resources helpful to the channel developer. A Web workshop tutorial is available at http://msdn.microsoft.com/workshop/delivery/channel/tutorials/tutorials.asp.

Microsoft also produces the Windows Media Player and servers. These products have evolved from Microsoft Netshow and now compete with a number of technologies. In the audio market, the Windows media solution achieves CD-quality sound similar to the MP3 format but takes less storage space. In streaming audio and video content, it offers quality audio and video, flexible and easy-to-use content authoring tools, and a commerce-enabled streaming server. The Windows Media Player supports the broadest set of content formats, including ASF and QuickTime®, that the older RealSystem G2 players do not support. Microsoft has released Windows Media 7 with an improved player. Formatting tools, audio/video encoder, rights manager, and Windows Media Services are built in to Windows 2000 Server, offering a complete integration with a corporate infrastructure.

Figure 10–7

Microsoft Media Player

The Windows Media Player has a highly configurable interface that will take personalities (skins) adaptable to the audience. Figure 10–7 illustrates the classic interface.

Despite the long list of attractive features including (1) the extensible digital media format, (2) high-quality audio and video, (3) high-quality input processing, and (4) industrial-strength security, adopters should be aware of the platform's limitations. The new Windows Media Player is developed for Windows 2000 and Windows 98. Previous versions of the desktop operating system, such as Windows 95 or Windows NT, and alternative platforms such as Mac OS or any flavor of UNIX will not be able to execute these programs.

RealNetworks offers G2 that competes in the same sphere as the Microsoft Windows Media Player. G2 system capacity tops out at 1 mbps versus 5 mbps for Microsoft Media Player and relies on frame doubling to achieve 30 frames per second (fps) at low bandwidths. Figure 10–8 illustrates the RealPlayer interface. As with the other players, the RealPlayer interface is intuitive and easy to navigate.

Netscape's initiative in this market segment has been riddled with hurdles. The chosen name for its solution, "Netcaster," belonged to another business and a long lawsuit ensued. As a result, Netscape is presently a marginal player in the webcasting arena on the desktop. Netscape uses a navigation bar called Channel Finder. Channel Finder includes a built-in tuner for Marimba Castanet. Similarly to Microsoft's option, it offers features to control the delivery and appearance of the chosen channels.

FIGURE 10–8

RealPlayer

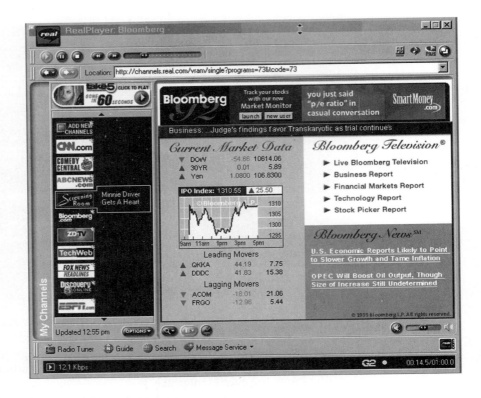

A useful and informative development guide is available on the Netscape site: http://developer.netscape.com/docs/manuals/netcast/ devguide/index.html. The guide explains channels from the concepts to in-depth samples illustrating floating palettes, full-screen immersion, drag and drop user customization, animation, automated refresh, context sensitive help, and persistence. The samples include high-quality scripts for dynamic HTML and JavaScript. The resulting Netcaster channels can be delivered in two ways: as standards-based Web server channels or Castanet transmitter channels.

Marimba Castanet channels are similar to Web server channels: They are collections of files that, from a user's point of view, automatically install and update themselves over the network. Web server channels are hosted on an HTTP server, while Castanet channels are hosted on a Castanet transmitter. Castanet is a Java-based push platform designed to deliver applications, services, and information. Delivering software and upgrades as well as website content make it particularly popular among IS managers. Castanet has the following advantages and disadvantages:

- Castanet uses bandwidth economically because it transmits updated content only, not an entire Web page, with each update.
- Castanet allows personalizing downloads for each subscriber.
- Castanet provides feedback to channel creators on user preferences, usage patterns, and so forth, to allow for customizing and product improvement.
- However, Castanet development requires Bongo, Java, and scripting or programming expertise to create sophisticated effects comparable to dynamic HTML.
- While it is a very scalable technology, it requires a large investment in proprietary servers.

Another interesting technology is IBM HotMedia. Its toolkit enables the developer easy access to cross-platform packaging of images, audio, and video, compressing them in the form of a Java applet that can be run anywhere. The solution provides a highly flexible multipurpose tool. While it does not allow for editing of the content, its packaging feature makes it a useful means of porting otherwise incompatible media. Figure 10–9 depicts the tool interface.

The channel programming tools mentioned above come with inherent limitations. One of the constraints to consider is the interaction between the

FIGURE 10–9

The IBM HotMedia tool

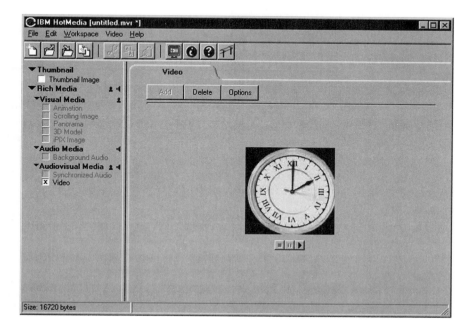

TABLE 10–2   **Matrix of Dynamic Scripting versus Channels**

	Netcaster	Active Channels	Pointcast	Castanet
JavaScript 1.1	√	√		
JavaScript 1.2	√			
Jscript 3.0		√		
Layers	√			
JavaScript accessible style sheets	√			
VBScript		√		
Cascading style sheets	√	√		
CSS positioning	√	√		
ActiveX Controls		√		
Document object model	√	√		
Java	√	√		√
CDF		√	√	
DTC utilities		√		
Dynamic fonts	√	√		
PointCast Studio			√	
Bongo				√

scripting language and the adopted channel development tool. Table 10–2 illustrates a compatibility matrix. Be aware that the combination of channels and dynamic scripting makes development far more complex.

Content Dynamism Update.   As important as the choice of technology is the ability of the site administrator using these dynamic imaging tools to keep the content up to date. Visitors will expect a fulfilling experience and great content will keep them coming back. The development of new multimedia material will always be a challenge, even for well-staffed sites.

News Publishers and Webcasting

EntryPoint/PointCast webcasting solutions include Connections channels that run on the PointCast network client. They can be viewed through a scrolling ticker, a PointCast window, or a PointCast screensaver. EntryPoint is the result of the combination of PointCast technology and Launchpad. EntryPoint delivers customized content and alerting functionality directly to the users' desktops without intruding on their daily computer tasks. Users can retrieve news, monitor stock activity, get sports scores, shop at their favorite online stores, view personal financial information; make travel plans, and much more. But in the lightning-fast life cycle of Internet business trends, PointCast and its programs to automatically send data to computer desktops have been lagging. The new company is betting that focusing its business and designing navigation tools for the superfast and supremely confusing future landscape of broadband Internet can rescue the company. PointCast was an early pioneer in push technology that succumbed from its initial success when it became the virtual enemy of many network administrators leery of lost bandwidth.

The main news agencies and media conglomerates are active in webcasting. Popular channels include ABCNEWS.com and CNNfn transmitted through Netcaster. CNNfn adopted JavaScript-based dynamic HTML with stock tickers, which individual users can personalize. ABCNEWS.com uses JavaScript-based dynamic HTML to display scrolling headlines. MSNBC and Disney use Microsoft active channels technology. MSNBC promotes cascading menus, personalization, and multimedia, while Disney takes advantage of the power of Flash and Shockwave animations in creating an attractive channel.

Specialized broadcasting outlets such as the *Wall Street Journal* Interactive edition and Bloomberg have bet their reputations on the new media channel. Webcasting is rapidly becoming a critical supplement to their traditional audience, enabling them to address a global audience. The *Wall Street Journal* Interactive edition offers the choice of three localized versions: one targeted to the U.S. market, one for the European market, and one for the Asian market. Figure 10–10 illustrates the *Wall Street Journal* portal.

Site Crawling and Smart Pull Technology

Webcasting uses site crawlers and smart pull technology. In **site crawling,** a browser proceeds through the following steps:

- Retrieves an HTML page.
- Stores that page locally on a user's computer.
- Finds the links (anchors) in the page.
- Repeats the process recursively from the first step for each link to an HTML page.
- Stops the above process when the browser has run out of links to follow or when the process has repeated enough times based on some criteria (for example link depth).
- Retrieves the actual content for each link to a non-HTML document, such as an image file or a text file.

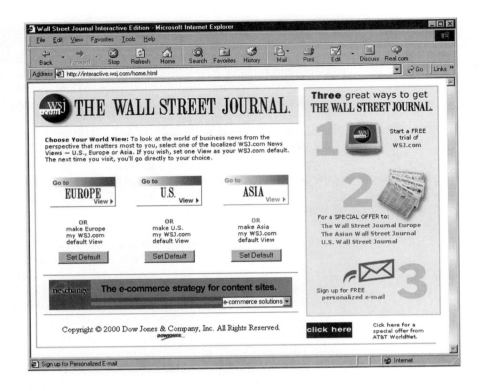

In practice this process duplicates the branch of the site accessed from the first HTML page for off-line viewing. Products such as WebZIP from www.spidersoft.com/ facilitate downloading in three easy steps: (1) enter the starting address (URL) of the Web content or site to download; (2) select a profile to tell WebZIP what, where, and how much to download, i.e., choosing 'Selected Directory (Text, Images)'; (3) click the download button to start the download.

Alternative products include Blackwidow at www.softbytelabs.com/, which is a website scanner, a site mapping tool, a site ripper, a site-mirroring tool, and an off-line browser program. It can be used to scan a site and create a complete profile of the site's structure, files, e-mail addresses, external links, and even link errors. Other alternatives are Offline Explorer from www.metaproducts.com/ or WebStripper from www. solentsoftware.com/. With the help of any of these tools, the downloaded website can then be browsed locally, thereby increasing performance.

The pull versus push dichotomy is a misnomer. In push, the activity is still pull but controlled and scheduled. Microsoft justifiably calls it "scheduled pull." Users' browsers are actually "pulling" the content from the Web. The difference between webcasting and the traditional way users pull content from the Web is that once they subscribe to the channel, they do not have to navigate back to the site to obtain updates.

Issues of Space and Bandwidth

The distinction between unicast broadcasting and multicasting is an important one. The adoption of multicasting relies on the support end-to-end by both hardware and software means. For example, with 1,000 receivers of a streamed channel, the burden on the network is significantly different:

Unicast: 1,000 live streams * 22k bits/sec = 22m bits/second (or 14 T-1s)

Multicast: 1,000 live streams * 22 bits/sec = 22k bits/second (a modem)

The feasibility of the first solution in terms of bandwidth and cost can easily jeopardize a project. The merits and challenges of using streaming technology to enhance the customer experience are still debated. Most traditional managers have little experience with the media and do not know how to measure presentment and reception. A demonstration of a clip run from a hard drive can convey a misleading good impression. Over the Internet, the transmission can be riddled with image blur, poor definition, and interrupting buffering sequences.

Statistics should be collected to benchmark performance. In this instance, the relevant parameters will be DNS lookup time; redirect time; initial buffer time; audio and video frames per second; dropped frames; late, lost, and dropped audio and video packets; bandwidth usage; and amount of encoded bandwidth. Given these factors the solutions can be evaluated in the real-world environment relevant to the business context. Often, the quality of the broadcast will have more to do with the network congestion than the broadcasting solution adopted.

Other Multimedia Technologies

Virtual Reality Technology

Virtual reality (VR) is an artificial environment created with computer hardware and software and used to simulate a scenario such that it appears and feels like a real world. The user wears special gloves, earphones, and goggles, all of which receive their input from the computer system. The reality impression is based on simultaneous coordination of input to multiple senses of the individual creating the illusion of a real situation. Virtual reality can be applied to e-commerce when the potential buyer cannot be physically present. For example, a real estate agency or a museum may develop a virtual tour of its premises either to initiate new sales or attract new patrons. The real estate company can set up a three-dimensional tour of a sample apartment in an apartment building illustrating the potential of the place.

VRML Versions and Basic Formats.   Chat and Internet relay chat (IRC) offer real-time online discussions. They do not provide the 3D reality of a virtual world but permit the interactive communication of individuals with common interests. IRC is still the largest chat forum with thousands of channels. Currently, IRC consists of numerous servers around the world divided into about two dozen separate networks. Each network is divided into channels, or rooms, which a user can attend, dedicated to some specific topic.

MUD and MOO.   A MUD (Multiple User Dimension, Multiple User Dungeon, or Multiple User Dialogue) is a computer program users can log into and explore. Each user takes control of a computerized persona/avatar/incarnation/character and can then walk around, chat with other characters, explore dangerous monster-infested areas, solve puzzles, and even create rooms, descriptions, and items. MOO stands for MUD, Object Oriented.

Virtual Worlds.   An example of a virtual world is Window on World Systems (WoW). In 1965, Ivan Sutherland laid out a research program for computer graphics in a paper called "The Ultimate Display" that has driven the field for more than 30 years. The challenge to computer graphics is to make the picture in the window look real, sound real, and act real. Many applications of this concept have appeared with the adoption of the graphical user interface, including video mapping, immersive systems, and telepresence. Telepresence is a variation on visualizing complete computer-generated worlds. This technology links remote sensors in the real world with the senses of a human operator. The remote sensors might be located on a robot. Firefighters or the bomb squad use remotely operated vehicles to handle dangerous conditions. Surgeons use very small instruments on cables to do surgery without cutting a major hole in their patients. The instruments have a small video camera that allows the doctors to see what they're doing. Robots equipped with telepresence systems have already changed the way deep sea and volcanic exploration is done, and NASA uses telerobotics for space exploration.

VR Applications in E-Commerce.   Diverse virtual reality capabilities can enhance consumer experience. Adoption of virtual reality on commercial websites has been slower than originally anticipated due to development difficulty or the need for specialized viewing devices. Development tools are becoming available and the rising competitive pressures could speed the adoption process, which could yield the following uses:

- Customers can examine an entire product with 3D virtual reality. Audio or closeups can be added to 3D images to show off special features and benefits of the products.

- Hotmedia or QuickTime virtual reality object images can let customers click on product features to hear what the product sounds like or hear a voice narration about the product or features.
- Multiple product image-map shows a set containing associated items. The selection of any product in the set displays its Hotmedia or QuickTime object image, and users then can select any or all items without ever needing the "Back" button of the browser.
- A flip-through catalog enables site visitors to find what they want faster and easier with a virtual catalog. The experience is similar to flipping through a magazine. There is no more back and forth use of the "Back" and "Forward" buttons.
- Even nonvirtual reality static images may come alive with interactivity. The combination of specialized commercial photography techniques with on-click or mouse-over may be used to make images come alive. This can include audio within still images for greater impact.

Virtual Reality Modeling Language.   Under the proposal for Web3D, **VRML** has a role to play in rendering more attractive websites. The term Web3D describes any programming or descriptive language that can be used to deliver interactive 3D objects and worlds across the Internet. This includes open languages, such as Virtual Reality Modeling Language (VRML), Java3D, and X3D (under development), and proprietary languages that have been developed for the same purpose.

Voice Synthesis and Voice Recognition

Voice-based Internet access looms in the near future and stands to revolutionize the way business is done over the Internet. This new technology may spark the growth of a new class of mega-billion dollar companies and diffuse the potential for wireless application protocol handheld devices. A few months ago the rage was on predicting handheld pen-based devices. For example, Nokia, still the industry leader in mobile phone production, was quietly developing pen-based mobile computer phones with Palm, Inc., the leader in the handheld market. These devices will use a touch-sensitive screen, and are reportedly going to use a supercharged version of the Palm operating system that already has a significant lead over Windows CE in the handheld market.

Now the predictions for innovative Web services are even more futuristic. At the core of these new services are voice recognition and text-to-speech technologies that have quietly been maturing during the past decade. Once a completely esoteric idea, voice recognition is making inroads into mainstream computing use. Without having to write any-thing down, Web surfers will be able to speak the name of the website or service they want to access, and the system will recognize the command and respond with spoken words.

The technology is aimed at multiple targets from the customer looking for items readily available in local stores to the impulse buyer enabled by a digital wallet. A number of businesses have prototyped voice-based por-tals. Among the pioneers, InternetSpeech.com, BeVocal.com, Tellme.com, and Talk2.com wish to make the use of a traditional computer obsolete. Tellme Studio leverages familiar Internet standards like VXML, JavaScript, SSL, and HTTP so developers can create rich phone sites that extend the power of the Web to anyone anywhere.

Microsoft has acquired Entropic and sees voice-activated technology as playing an increasingly important role in e-commerce as mobile broad-band grows and access to the Internet becomes common in cars and in other wireless devices. The merging of voice technology and telephony is critical to the development of Internet devices without keyboards. E-Commerce Times predicts that soon there should be a flood of voice-based e-commerce announcements from e-tailers.

Under the umbrella of the W3C, a consortium with high-profile mem-bers such as IBM, Lucent, Motorola, and AT&T has submitted a proposal for the standardization of VoiceXML that aims to:

- Simplify creation and delivery of Web-based, personalized interactive voice-response services.
- Enable phone and voice access to integrated call center databases, information and services on websites, and company intranets.
- Enable new voice-capable devices and appliances.

The VoiceXML forum will continue its activities to support and promote VoiceXML as a standard method for providing voice access to Internet con-tent and services. While other initiatives have been launched, this proposal has the backing of the market leaders and should be watched closely.

VoxML

Motorola has recognized the need to provide an easier way to produce voice applications and so created **VoxML.** As mobile phone and hybrid comput-ing appliances enter the market, the importance of such initiatives will be-come more critical to e-business. The main goal of Motorola's VoxML is to offer a common approach and broadly supported platform for voice applications just as HTML provides for Web-based applications. VoxML technology enables the application interface to be in the form of dialogs: Navigation and input are produced via speech recognition of the end user's voice and output is produced via text-to-speech technology or recorded au-dio samples. VoxML is based on the W3C eXtensible Markup Language

(XML) standard. As such, the language follows all of the syntactic rules of XML with semantics that support the creation of interactive speech applications.

A number of links to Motorola resources and other developers' information can be found at www.oasis-open.org/cover/voxML.html.

Summary

From a text-based information deployment tool, the Web has grown to a multimedia channel. This chapter covered a range of technologies aimed at broadening the reach of e-commerce. We covered a number of graphics technologies, from the static raster images of GIF, JPEG, and PNG to their vector graphics competitors such as Flash. Techniques known as webcasting enable the diffusion of live or asynchronous audiovisual messages through intranets and the Internet. Aimed at informing or convincing its target, webcasting is a powerful medium.

Key Terms

Active channel 391	QuickTime 383
GIF 371	RealPlayer 384
JPEG 371	RealProducer G2 384
MPEG 379	Site crawling 397
PNG 372	VoxML 402
Pull 389	VRML 401
Push 389	Webcasting 388

Review Questions

1. What are the main formats for static graphics?
2. What is the main difference between a raster graphic and a vector-based graphic?
3. What is a channel? What are the steps in setting up an active channel in IE?

Projects

1. If you are using Microsoft Windows, what steps are necessary to add a new channel to your active desktop? If you are not using the product, visit the Microsoft site and search for the instructions.
2. How do you add a new channel to Netscape Communicator? Find instructions on the Netscape website.

3. What are some dominant graphics packages available today? What are the costs? Do they support the preferred graphics formats?

4. Visit the sites of Microsoft, RealNetworks, and Apple and compare the features of the latest version of their media players.

5. Search the Web for image designing and editing tools. Download one of the tools you found (e.g., Paint Shop Pro, Ulead Cool 3d, or Xara 3D). Prototype a logo for your business and save it in various formats. Which provides the best aesthetic? Which provides the smaller file? How easy is it to modify the graphics with the tool you tried?

6. Search the Web for a development toolkit for Microsoft Windows Media Player, QuickTime, and RealPlayer. Is there any third party among your discoveries? As a business Web developer, which one seems to be the most appropriate? Why?

7. Download IBM HotMedia and package some static images into an animation applet. What are the advantages and disadvantages of this technology?

8. Visit the W3C website and find the status of the VoiceXML project. When do you think it will affect business on the Web and what will its impact be?

9. Develop a project that encompasses the use of backgrounds, layered imaging, and text layered over images (material needed: scanner and image editing software).

   What you are expected to do:
   - Create or download an image.
   - Edit, resize, and retouch the image.
   - Add text to the image.
   - Create a business card that encompasses a background, layered imaging, and text layered on the images.

10. Develop a project that encompasses the use of backgrounds, layered imaging, and text layered over images (material needed: scanner and image editing software).

    What you are expected to do:
    - Create a unique imaging project.
    - When complete make a GIF file.

Mini term paper topics

- Audio production and telephone companies. How are telco-services used in radio and audio production?

- Creating the appearance of three dimensions in a two-dimensional medium. How do graphic artists do it?

- Legal restrictions and the use of fonts. You mean I have to pay for the use of fonts? A history of typesetting and the legalities involved in using fonts.

- Video strategies on the World Wide Web. What's available to me and how does it all work?
- The Gif construction set. What is it and how does it work?
- Video fileservers. What are they, what are their potential uses, and why is everybody so excited about them?
- Cascading style sheets. What are they, how are they used, and what benefit are they to website developers?
- What's all the fuss about ActiveX? How can it be used to deliver audio or video effects?
- VRML. What is it? Is it important to the Web?
- Real Audio. What is it? What is its competition and what's involved with it?
- Bit-mapped or vector-based computer graphics. Why should I care about the difference?
- Java. What is it? How does it relate to multimedia on the Internet?

References, Readings, and Hyperlinks

1. Bhaskaran, Vasudev, and Konstantinos Konstantinides. *Image and Video Compression Standards Algorithms and Architectures.* Boston: Kluwer Academic Publishers, 1998.
2. Haskell, B. G., A. Puri, and A. N. Netravali. *Digital Video: An Introduction to MPEG-2.* Boca Raton, FL: Chapman & Hall, 1997.
3. Johnson, N. *Web Developer's Guide to Multicasting.* Scottsdale, AZ: Coriolis Group, 1997.
4. Pannebaker, William B., and Didier J. Le Gall. *MPEG Digital Video Compression Standard.* New York: John Wiley & Sons, 1995.
5. Purcell, L. *Guide to Creating Web Channels.* New York: John Wiley & Sons, 1998.
6. Symes, Peter D. *Video Compression.* New York: McGraw-Hill, 1998.

PACKAGED SOLUTIONS FOR E-BUSINESS

Chapter Outline

Learning Objectives

By the end of this chapter, you will be able to:

- Use a coordination theory framework to specify the role of IT in e-business.
- Explain the nature of enterprise resource planning (ERP) systems.
- Appreciate the role of ERP in e-business as a platform for efficient order execution.

- Understand interenterprise systems such as business-to-business procurement systems and supply chain management (SCM) software.
- Describe the functionality of customer relationship management software.

Chapter Overview

This chapter focuses on software packages that help implement e-business. E-business requires a platform that enables integration among business applications within a single company and across different companies. The technological challenge in e-commerce is not limited to front-end systems such as websites that display catalogs and take orders. It also includes back-end systems that are necessary to execute the orders received, which is the core of e-business. Efficient order execution is possible only when an appropriate platform is developed that integrates Web-based order processing with associated business processes such as payment systems, customer support, and shipment.

These back-end systems are frequently based on enterprise resource planning (ERP) software. ERP systems allow businesses to run efficient business processes that link multiple functional activities such as accounting, order processing, manufacturing, procurement, and shipment. New bolt-on systems on ERP have appeared that tie in the information systems of a firm with its suppliers and customers. These new systems, which run either independently of, or as an add-on to, existing ERP systems, focus on coordination with the customer and the suppliers. They are called supply chain management (SCM) systems. This chapter explains the nature of the SCM software and the role it plays in business-to-consumer and business-to-business e-commerce. It also covers the functionality of customer relationship management (CRM) software. The chapter introduces the use of a coordination theory framework to delineate the scope and functionality of software packaged solutions such as ERP, CRM, and SCM.

A Technical Vignette

The concept of Internet time has invaded the world of manufacturing. In Internet time, consumers want not only products customized to their personal needs, but they also want them immediately or at some specific date. In a process known as **"available to promise" (ATP),** customers log onto a website to determine the amount of widgets they can purchase at some future date. These widgets may be in finished goods storage and can be allocated to the customer or they may not even be at the raw material stage, but the customers still want definite predictions of whether the suppliers can satisfy the delivery dates. They do not want to spend time and money negotiating deliveries with multiple suppliers when the information is available over the Web. Customers do not want a mere promise from sales representatives; they expect a commitment for certain delivery. Manufacturers that do not provide ATP service to their customers find themselves at a competitive disadvantage.

The requirements of ATP represent a major challenge to manufacturers serving their customers on the Web. It is not only necessary for customers to be able to view the current state of the manufacturing system, but also to be able to predict future deliveries for the order under review. ATP systems require that the manufacturing data be made available to business information systems and that the future state of the system be amenable to simulation in order to predict deliveries. The major obstacle is not that manufacturing equipment and plants are not generating computer data, but that these data are not able to be shared with business information systems running in the same company.

ATP capability requires integration between manufacturing systems that control and run shop floors and the business information systems. Manufacturing information systems are geared to engineering requirements related to quality, scheduling, and material control. They are built around the basic logic of manufacturing employed, which could either be discrete (i.e., there are countable items such as toys and automobiles) or the process type, as in the case of petroleum and fertilizer. The objective of these systems is to minimize in-process inventory, resulting in systems referred to as lean manufacturing. They allow companies to build against actual orders in contrast to building to stock. Manufacturing against orders is possible when there is close synchronization between the various stages of the process chain. This synchronization requires significant exchange of data up and down the process chain.

Unfortunately, the shop floor information systems run on different standards and protocols than the business information systems. The data originate at microprocessors running on machine tools and conveyor belts. There are multiple suppliers of these microprocessor-based controls and these employ different communication and processing standards. Manufacturing information systems have been developed to take this heterogeneity into account, and the data are used to plan and control material flow along the process chain. Some large integrated manufacturing systems control manufacturing processes across multiple plants.

On the other hand, the integration of business information systems has led to a class of software called enterprise resource planning systems (ERP) that tie together various business processes such as order processing, invoicing, and accounts payable. None of the ERP packages currently has effective connectivity to integrated manufacturing information systems. The data stream that originates from shop floor systems cannot be plugged into ERP systems.

Firms that are planning to offer ATP facility to their customers are building one-off unique links to feed their manufacturing data streams into ERP packages. This is a laborious and expensive development process. Some ERP vendors have taken up the challenge. Informational integration between business systems such as ERP and manufacturing information systems will lead to achievement of the dual goals of responsiveness promised by ATP and manufacturing efficiency as provided by lean manufacturing information systems.

A Coordination Theory Framework

IBM defines e-business as the use of Internet technologies to transform key business processes. A key goal of such transformation is effective coordination within different functions in a company and across the company's boundaries with suppliers and customers. Coordination theory perspective provides a detailed view of what this coordination consists of and what the functionality of the information technology solution needs to be for effective coordination. E-business can be viewed as a coordination mechanism.

A coordination mechanism, such as e-business, consists of (1) an informational structure and (2) a set of decision functions. The informational structure describes who obtains what information from the environment, how that information is processed, and then how it is distributed among different members participating in the coordination mechanism. Decision functions describe how decisions are made by the organizational members, and they help to translate from the information provided to the decision maker (via the information structure) to the managerial and operational tasks that need to be performed. The coordination mechanism serves some organizational goals (see Figure 11–1). From the perspective of coordination theory, the organizational goals are efficiency and flexibility. Efficiency involves the productive use of assets such as manufacturing plants and inventories, and flexibility is concerned with the ability of the organization to cope with changes in the environment.

FIGURE 11–1

A coordination theory framework

Decision-making function	Efficiency
Informational structure	Flexibility
Coordination	Goal

TABLE 11–1   Reach and Range of Informational Structure for E-Business

Range of Informational Structure for E-Business					
Informational services such as e-mail and Web portals (a)	Database-dependent services such as human resource applications (b)	Transaction-oriented services such as order processing (c)	Work flow applications such as procurement (d)	Collaborative applications such as joint document development (e)	Decision support applications such as data mining (f)
Reach of Informational Structure for E-Business					
Within function of a single company (1)	Within a single department (2)	Within a single strategic business unit (3)	Link to immediate suppliers (4)	Link to customers (5)	Link to all members of the value chain (6)

In the context of a company that is assembling PCs, the information structure is the IT platform with its associated applications; the members are the managers who make the decisions that help run the company; the tasks are engineering, selling, and assembling; and the organizational goal is to assemble PCs and earn a profit. For the PC assembler, environmental changes are brought about by a rapidly evolving technology and changing consumer tastes.

The informational structure of an organization can be detailed in terms of its range and reach. The range refers to the type of applications that are supported and the reach is described by the stakeholders who are served. The range of an informational structure spans different types of applications, including (see Table 11–1):

- Informational services such as Web portals with static HTML pages.
- Database-dependent services such as websites that provide product prices and descriptions that are read from a database.
- Transaction services such as order processing. Transaction services differ from database services in that there is usually a much higher rate of read/write of databases that needs to coordinated with software applications such as transaction monitors.
- Work flow applications such as office procurement where there is a single business process that consists of many transactions that span a period of days and weeks and are also distributed over various organizational agents.
- Collaborative applications as are supported by Lotus Notes.
- Decision support applications such as data mining.

The range of an information structure, thus, defines a range of functionality of an IT platform required for e-business. The reach of an informational structure ranges over a single function within a department, a single department, a single business unit, and linkages to customers and immediate suppliers, as well as the entire process chain. The reach describes the different stakeholders that the IT platform tries to serve.

Packaged software applications and development methodologies exist to supply solutions for different combinations of range and reach. For instance, for ranges (a) to (c) and reach (1) to (3) in Table 11–1 tools such as Microsoft Visual InterDev, Visual Basic, and Oracle are used to develop the applications. ERP applications are also a strong contender in this same field of reach and range. Collaborative applications for product design that span the entire process chain use tools such as Retail.com's Design. Oracle's data warehouse is an example of a decision support application for a single company, and i2 Technologies' RHYTHM allows decision support applications to be built that support a company and its suppliers and that help in mutual supply chain optimization.

Table 11–2 describes the organizational goals of a coordination mechanism or an e-business platform. The efficiency aspects are further detailed

TABLE 11–2 Organizational Goals and E-Business Software Solutions Space

	Efficiency		Flexibility	
Manufacturing	*Inventory & Shipment*	*Procurement*	*Customer Relationship & Service*	*Competitive Advantage*
Actual production, costs of delays, cost of unit production, plant utilization	Days of supply, inventory accuracy, spoilage cost, unit shipment cost	Number of purchase orders, frequency of purchasing, unit purchase order cost	Orders % unfilled, days to respond to emergency orders, average days to ship, % of customers who return	Cycle of change, time to share information, collaborative decision making
	Packaged Software Solutions		*Packaged Software Solutions*	
Traditional ERP software such as from SAP or Oracle	Supply chain management such as i2 Technologies' RHYTHM software, Aspect's inbound supply chain management e-CSM, and Manugistics' NetWorks	Business-to-business and business-to-customer e-commerce solution supplied by Ariba and CommerceOne	Customer relationship management systems as supplied by Siebel Systems, Vantive, Clarify, and Remedy	Collaborative design and planning applications such as Yet2.com collaborative design portal, Retail.com's WebTrack and Design, and i2 Technologies' TradeMatrix

as manufacturing efficiency, inventory asset efficiency, and procurement efficiency. Similarly, flexibility aspects are specified in terms of customer relationship and support and competitive advantage. Table 11–2 also presents an array of packaged software solutions that have emerged to serve these organizational goals. There are three major families of software solutions:

- Enterprise resource planning (ERP) systems that help to integrate different business processes that span multiple functions on a single platform. It does this on the basis of an integrated database system that is shared by all business departments and an interlinked set of predefined business processes that are claimed to be the best-of-the-breed solution in the particular industry.
- Supply chain management (SCM) systems that help manage the flow of information and material between a company and its suppliers and distributors. Different companies are specializing in different aspects of SCM. The firm Aspect specializes on the supplier side and has merged with i2 Technologies, which specializes on the customer side. Associated with SCM are procurement systems that are business-to-business and allow suppliers and customers to interact on a single portal. The portal permits customers to post their inquiries, the vendors to submit their bids, and all members to exchange order, delivery, and product information. Important software vendors in this area are Ariba and CommerceOne.
- Customer relationship and service applications that assist in building long-term relationships with customers. These applications are also known as customer relationship management systems (CRM), with vendors such as Siebel, Clarify, and Vantive active in this area.

Cherry Tree & Co., a leading IT service firm, proposes a similar view of e-business. It is promoting a concept called e-enterprise or extended enterprise, which is able to coordinate its activities closely with its partners in the value chain. The extended enterprise, like e-business, is built on a distributed information systems architecture. At the core of this is the ERP backbone (see Figure 11–2) that implements core accounting, manufacturing, and human resource (HR) functions. These applications

FIGURE 11–2

Software solutions for e-business

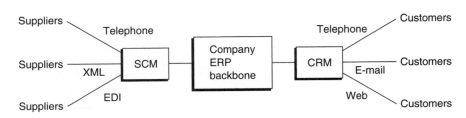

are primarily inward facing and track the internal flow of information. The enterprise starts to have e-business functionality when its information systems face outward by having connectivity with customers, suppliers, and distributors. The two main areas of connectivity are customer relationship management and supply chain management. The rest of the chapter focuses on packaged software solutions for implementing ERP, SCM, and CRM.

Evolution of ERP Systems

ERP systems have evolved from large software applications used in the manufacturing sector for inventory control. These packages ran on mainframes and were customized for each company. The software helped companies track and control ordering, consumption, and delivery of material. As with accounting systems, these systems focused on collecting historical data, but this was soon found to be limiting. The software did not help in estimating the when and how of the materials requirement issue. While it assisted in tracking history, it had limited use in planning.

This led to the rise of software systems called material requirements planning (MRP), which translated a master production plan into (1) detailed shipment plans for the finished goods and (2) a detailed production plan for each subassembly and item. The detailed plans for the items, in turn, helped in determining the procurement plans for raw material. MRP could represent not only historical data, but also compare them against plans and budgets. MRP systems were developed for a variety of manufacturing scenarios, from process manufacturing, as used in the petroleum sector, to discrete manufacturing, as done in the automobile industry. Different planning environments such as manufacturing-to-stock and manufacturing-to-order are covered.

In the 1980s, MRP systems graduated to MRP II systems that extended MRP into shop floor planning and control. MRP II helped large multiplant companies such as the automobile manufacturers to coordinate manufacturing across multiple plants all over the world. Subassemblies in these companies originated in plants across the world and got put together on assembly lines running on different continents. The manufacturers' suppliers, who numbered into thousands, were linked to these systems.

In the 1990s, MRP II systems were augmented to cover areas such as accounting, engineering, and project management. At this stage, the system produced a detailed plan that encompassed procurement, manufacturing, and shipment, as well as helped in planning for cash flow and receivables. The term *enterprise resource planning* was coined to better describe such a system. The world of ERP vendors is currently dominated by a handful of suppliers such as SAP, Oracle, PeopleSoft, Baan, and J.D. Edwards.

Why ERP Systems?

ERP systems are designed to solve the problem of lack of integration among different information systems running in a company. Historically, various departments in a firm had their own budgets and used them to develop information systems applications that were tuned to their own particular needs. But these requirements were often conflicting across different departments, resulting in systems that could not communicate with each other.

For instance, the sales department has one view of a customer and the accounting department has another. While the sales department is interested in the purchasing department of its customer, the accounting department usually interacts with the accounting department of its counterpart. The data for the same customer is input separately into two different systems. Over time, these data usually diverged. The customer address and the order references in one system ceased to be identical to another. This situation is often described as different applications operating within different "silos." (see Figure 11–3).

Moreover, the definition of basic business terms such as *costs* and *expenses* were often different in different systems. Different plants and departments would often follow different product identification schemes. If the purchasing department followed a six-character reference to product identification because that is what its suppliers followed, the sales or the accounting departments would follow a different identification scheme. This made integration of data between different systems problematic. Data from one system had to reformatted before being input to another system.

There was often no systems connection between two or more applications. The same data had to be input separately in different systems, and the output of one system could not become input to another system without human intervention. Data from the order processing system could not be fed directly into the invoicing system.

FIGURE 11–3

Unintegrated application systems in a company

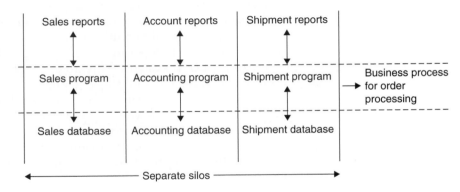

It is in the nature of many business processes that they span several business departments, and with different departments running their own systems, the same business process would span multiple applications that could not communicate among themselves. For example, order processing would involve several functional programs such as order input, accounting, and shipment (see Figure 11–3) and data would move only with human input from one business function such as accounting to another such as shipment. Business processes, therefore, took an inordinate amount of time to complete. This led to lack of responsiveness on the part of the company to its customers. Also, the company would not know why and where a certain order got delayed and this lack of process visibility damaged its relationship with customers.

Logic of ERP Systems

The basic logic of ERP systems revolves around a common and comprehensive database for the entire company and a system of standardized business processes. A data item such as product description or customer description occurs only once in the database (see Figure 11–4). This leads to minimization of data redundancy and the resultant lack of data integrity. All business processes within the firm read and write to the same database. Different elements of the same business process can now communicate because they are all feeding off the same database. There is no conflict of data definition nor of data value. Although these business processes may be spanning different departments and different business units and although they may be located at different places around the world, now they can communicate because of a common database.

The second important feature that makes ERP systems so powerful is that the business processes they incorporate are all standardized.

FIGURE 11–4

Logic of ERP systems

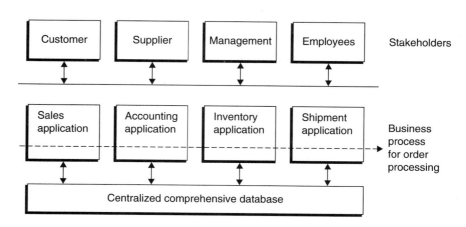

Usually an ERP vendor would offer best-of-the class business process for a particular industry. With the business processes standardized, the data input and output and their processing for each process is standardized as well. Now different processes can communicate among themselves because the data input and output requirement of each process is fixed and is not left to the idiosyncratic requirement of the department. Theoretically, it is now possible for an order to be placed on the Web and the ERP system to trigger an avalanche of related business processes whereby the customer's credit is approved, the order to the manufacturing plant is placed, the material is procured, and a shipment date is estimated and sent to the customer. These various business processes can act in concert only because the processes are standardized and their linkages are fixed beforehand.

An ERP system comes in the form of modules. For example, SAP's R/3 has modules relating to financials, human resources, operations and logistics, and sales and marketing. In turn, each module supports several functionalities. The human resource module, for example, would serve functions such as payroll, personnel planning, travel, and human resources time accounting. Similarly, the marketing module has functionalities such as order management, pricing, sales management, and planning.

The fully developed software system, in theory, can be up and running with little work. But in practice, these systems, which are vast and complex, need to be configured for each business. Businesses usually start implementation with one or more modules and after successful implementation move on to other modules. Because the modules are developed on the basis of preconfigured business processes, the businesses need to do a considerable amount of organizational restructuring and reengineering to be able to use the ERP software modules. The business needs to adopt a structure and an operation that conforms closely to what the modules require. The modules allow some flexibility, but they need to be configured for each business situation, which leads to expensive development processes.

Supply Chain Management

Supply chain management (SCM) is the management of information and flow of materials along the entire process chain. The value chain consists of procurement of inputs such as raw material, subassemblies, and consumables and delivery of finished goods to the distributor, retailer, and consumer (see Figure 11–5). The demand side of the process chain consists of the customers, retailers, and distributors while the supply side consists of the suppliers.

The full process chain for a product consists of not only the immediate supplier or the distributors but also the suppliers to the suppliers and

FIGURE 11–5

Two sides of a supply chain

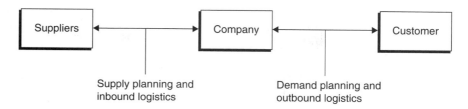

Supply planning and inbound logistics

Demand planning and outbound logistics

then their suppliers and so on. For example (see Figure 11–6), the full process chain of a PC assembler consists of its immediate suppliers such as the distributors for printers, monitors, and other subassemblies and then their suppliers such as printer manufacturers, CPU manufacturers, and the component suppliers and their suppliers and so forth.

The fundamental goal of SCM is to get the right product to the right customer at the right time at the right place and at the right price. To achieve this, SCM has to fulfill two objectives:

1. Minimize costs related to shipment, production, and storage.
2. Maximize business value to the firm by being able to respond quickly and flexibly to the changing market and competitive environment so as to supply the right product to the right customer at the right time. This is known as efficient consumer response (ECR).

In coordination theory, the first objective is identified as efficiency and the second is flexibility. Both efficiency and flexibility are required in both the supply and demand sides of SCM:

1. Supply side, where there is the management of inbound material and the associated information flow.
2. Demand side, where there is concern with the management of outbound material with its associated information flow.

As previously discussed, coordination theory differentiates between the information structure along which information is gathered, processed, and distributed and the pattern of decision making that this information structure supports. The decision-making part of SCM is often characterized

FIGURE 11–6

The full process chain of a PC assembler

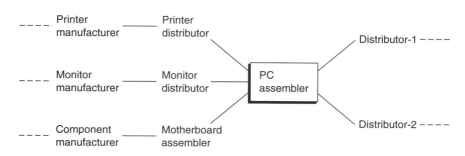

as the subject of logistics and the information aspects as the IT part. This differentiation helps to identify what each SCM software module from companies such Manugistics and i2 Technologies contributes to the SCM task. Some of the software focus on decision-making aspects of SCM, while others concentrate on IT aspects.

In logistics, efficiency is achieved with the use of optimization tools such as operations research and artificial intelligence tools such as constrained optimization. Products such as RHYTHM from i2 Technologies use constrained optimization techniques to develop efficient value chains. In the IT part of SCM, gains are obtained through the automation of data processing and communication activity. Flexibility is achieved through the sharing of information along the whole process chain. With the latest information available to all the participants of the value chain, all members can now respond immediately to changing customer needs.

SCM can be viewed from both strategic and operational perspectives. Strategic SCM focuses on designing the most efficient and flexible process chain, which can be seen as a network of nodes and links. The nodes are suppliers, warehouses, and distributors and the links can be viewed as transportation links. Strategic SCM is concerned with issues such as which suppliers to use, where to site plants, what capacity of plants to choose, and

TABLE 11–3   Strategic and Operational SCM

Informational Focus	*Decision-Making Focus*	
Select EDI-based and Web-based IT platform that permits close coordination between all members of the process chain.	Use operations research tools such as network design, transportation planning, and simulation to design the process chain. Decide on suppliers, warehouse locations, and transportation modes.	**Strategic SCM**
Follow traditional procure to pay transactions methods.	Demand forecasting using tools such as SAP's Advanced Planner and Optimizer (APO)	**Operational SCM**
Run scan-based trading (SCB) Implement vendor managed inventory (VMI)	Production planning using tools such as i2 Technologies' RHYTHM	
Operate collaborative planning, forecasting, and replenishment (CPFR) systems using tools such as Retail.com's WebTrack or SAP's APO	Transportation planning Replenishment policies	

what transportation modes to employ. Strategic SCM is also concerned with the IT platform that supports the manufacture and distribution of material.

In contrast, operational SCM involves day-to-day decision making such as when to order, from whom to order, what truckloads to ship, and the mode of shipment to use. As part of operational SCM, a firm has to prepare a demand forecast, develop a procurement and manufacturing plan, and finalize a shipment schedule. Table 11–3 highlights the informational and decision-making aspects of SCM, segmented according to whether they are strategic or operational in nature.

IT Aspects of Supply Chain Management

Traditional IT Platform for SCM

The information flow associated with material flow in the supply chain has traditionally been conducted on paper-based systems running over a delivery postal system. The sender and the receiver of each communication were employees who would then key the related data into their respective computer systems.

EDI instituted a major change to this communication system, enabling two different computers in two different companies to directly exchange messages without any human intervention. This enabled business processes in one firm to trigger a business process in another firm and to supply the data in a format that the other computer could understand. For instance, a shipment notice from the supplier could lead to the payment process to occur in the customer's system.

With EDI, computers could exchange textual data formatted to industry standards. The communication was one-to-one (i.e., a computer from one firm communicated with a computer from another firm). Based on such one-to-one linkages, a large network of computer communication among suppliers, transporters, bankers, and customers came into existence (see Figure 11–7). Third-party EDI providers came into being, and different parties could then contract out their services. These EDI providers

FIGURE 11–7

One-to-one EDI-based communication

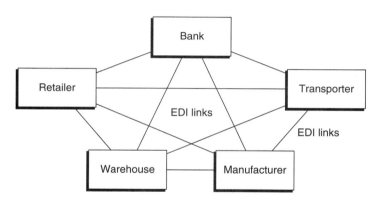

Figure 11–8

EDI-based hub communication

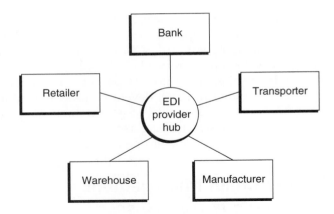

allowed different parties to communicate as the EDI provider acted as a hub. While the communication pattern became a hub or star-based (see Figure 11–8), communication still was limited to one party communicating to exactly one other party.

While this pattern of computer-to-computer communication was a major improvement on the paper-based postal system, EDI suffered from several limitations:

- Incompatible standards. This required EDI service providers to offer the translation service from one EDI format to another.
- Proprietary technology. Systems were expensive to install and run and depended on the vendor for the life of the system. Often suppliers and customers would have trouble deciding which proprietary system to adopt.
- Textual messages. EDI permits only characters to be exchanged between computers. This disallowed the use of richer media and content such as graphics and images for engineering drawings and catalogs.
- Little integration to back-end operations where ERP was absent. This led to delays in information flow from one link to another. These delays led to increased bullwhip effect in the supply chain. Bullwhip effect refers to the variability of demand increasing on the upstream side. Increased variability meant increased inventory.

Evolution of the IT Platform in SCM

The IT platform has evolved over the years as IT has been increasingly used for serving the dual objectives of SCM—efficiency and flexibility. This evolution can be viewed as transpiring in four phases (see Figure 11–9). In the first phase, information was shared between operating personnel

FIGURE 11–9

Phases in development of IT platform

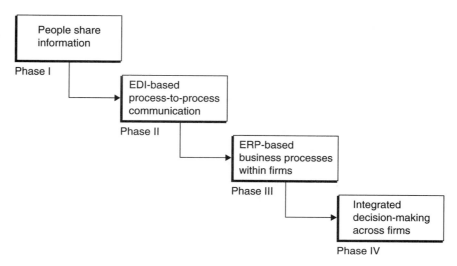

at one stage of processing with another. This was achieved in the pre-EDI days where information moved between the personnel of different companies based on paper moving through postal systems.

The next stage of the IT platform evolution occurred when computer processes in one firm began interacting with computer processes in another firm. EDI ushered in this era. In the third phase, with companies establishing ERP systems, processes were integrated within one firm and EDI provided the link to processes in another firm. This integration of process was facilitated if both the customer and the supplier employed ERP from the same vendor.

The current and the fourth phase of IT platform evolution is being ushered in by the Web and browser-based linkages between firms, replacing EDI. This facilitates alignment of decision making in one firm with decision making in another. For the first time, the effort here was not directed optimal response over a single stage of the supply chain but over the entire chain.

In terms of coordination, this could be described as increasing coordination span and coordination depth. Coordination span refers to connectivity among industry participants, while coordination depth involves integration from the stage of information, to processes, to decision making. Figure 11–10 describes how, in coordination theory, the state of SCM has been changing with the evolution of the IT platform.

The Promise of the New IT Platform

The new Web-based platform offers several qualitative changes to the SCM scenario. Web-based linkages now allow firms to move from

FIGURE 11–10

Span and depth of coordination

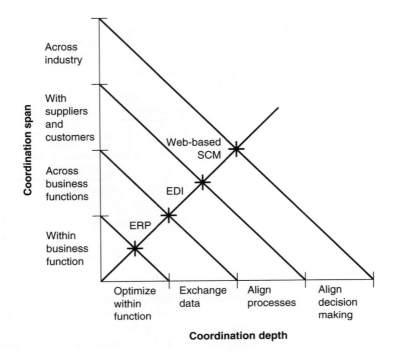

one-to-one communication to many-to-many communication. This is evident in business-to-business portals where customers can post their requirements and multiple suppliers can respond (see Figure 11–11).

The Web makes several different configurations of information exchange possible. There can be one supplier conducting an **auction** with multiple customers; one customer asking for bids from multiple suppliers (**reverse auction**); multiple customers and suppliers interacting simultaneously (market exchange); and the old pattern of a single customer dealing with a single vendor (negotiation) (see Figure 11–12).

The Web not only allows different patterns of interaction, but it also allows much richer messages to flow back and forth. Computers are no

FIGURE 11–11

Many-to-many communication in Web-based SCM

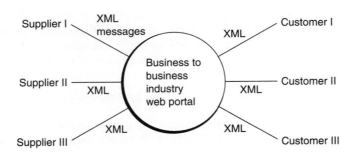

FIGURE 11–12

Multiple interaction patterns in Web-based SCM

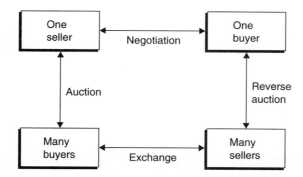

longer restricted to textual messages as in EDI. With XML, the messages can be structured but still have embedded in them graphics and sound so that richer information as available in the catalogs can now be made available to personnel.

The Web has other advantages. It is, for example, an open system. There is limited risk of incompatibility at the platform level. In fact, the standards are universal, thus permitting suppliers from all over the world to log into a business portal to undertake business exchanges.

Third-party vendors are helping in the integration of ERP systems with SCM software. The internal systems are now being made available to the world outside. Some of the exciting possibilities include:

- **Visibility,** which enables planners at different stages of a process chain to view from their desktops the logistics plans of each other and their point-of-sale (POS) and inventory data. This permits close coordination of activities across the process chain and alerts business partners to exceptions arising out of plant breakdowns and missed shipments.

- Availability to promise (ATP), whereby a supplier provides confirmed delivery dates on the Web for its available products. The supplier must not only have a system of stock reservations that is visible to prospective customers on the website, but it also must have a simulation capability. Customers should be able to do a "what-if" analysis relating to delivery dates and quantities ordered.

- **Synchronized supply chains** in which production and shipment plans across the entire process chain are coordinated. The business plans at every stage of the process chain relating to production, distribution, and procurement are concurrently developed and executed. Constraints due to capacity and material availability at any point in the process chain are considered while planning for the various stages of the supply chain.

- **Build-to-order** against **build-to-stock.** In build-to-stock, production plans are developed against a master plan that extends several weeks and months into the future. The master plan is built in response to a demand forecast. In contrast, build-to-order systems produce an item only against a confirmed order. Dell Computers, for instance, is one of the pioneers in developing this paradigm in the PC industry. Without a forecast, the challenge is to build sufficient flexibility into the process chain to take in stride continuously changing demand pattern on a real-time basis. Whereas in build-to-stock, inventories are developed to absorb the shocks due to exceptions arising in the system, in the build-to-order systems, extra capacity and responsiveness is used to cope with a continuously changing order stream.

- **Collaborative planning, forecasting, and replenishment (CPFR)** in which a joint business plan for the entire process chain is developed as a result of negotiation between various parties in the chain. Several steps are involved in CPFR. Business partners collaboratively develop a single time series forecast for demand. This time series is generated in a consensual manner based on actual point-of-sale data as well as other market conditions forecasted. Planning and shipment programs across all stages in the process chain are developed simultaneously to serve the consensual demand forecast. Forecast exceptions, such as changed consumer needs, are identified and resolved in a negotiated fashion. Sometimes new demand series are developed as a result of the exceptions, which, in turn, trigger new production and shipment plans across all stages in the process chain. CPFR is one of the tools used to synchronize operations across the entire process chain.

- **Vendor-managed inventory (VMI),** provided by a supplier for its customers in which the supplier tracks the consumption of the goods supplied at the customers' premises. The supplier does its own requirement and shipment planning to keep the customers' sites continuously replenished.

Customer Relationship Management

The impetus for the increasing popularity of **customer relationship management (CRM)** lies in intensifying competition. Factors such as globalization and deregulation fuel competition by dismantling entry barriers and enabling more firms to participate in any industry. Traditionally companies have differentiated themselves on the basis of products, prices, and place of distribution; however, the Web is weakening the differentiating ability of these factors. By allowing easy price comparisons across different vendors, products are becoming like commodities. Ordering over the Web renders the location of the company unimportant. Firms are, therefore, finding it increasingly difficult to charge premium margins based on product and placement features.

They are turning to customer relationship to differentiate themselves in the market. The goal is not only to satisfy the customer but also to provide a delightful experience—an experience that is achieved through personalization. The focus is on providing each individual customer with exactly what that customer wants. Firms are not just investing in brand equity but also in customer relationship equity. Brand equity provides a quality assurance to a large customer segment, and customer relationship equity assures an individual customer that specific needs will be taken care of.

Customer relationship management is an enterprisewide initiative that involves principally three functions: marketing, sales, and customer service. It enables the company to acquire new customers and to leverage existing customer relationships. CRM software facilitates the capture, analysis, and dissemination of data relating to existing and potential customers. The CRM software seeks to achieve the two goals of:

- Enabling the company to identify, contact, and help acquire new customers on a cost-effective basis. CRM applications help to automate the process of collecting potential customer lists, generating their profiles from existing data, and tracking the process of proposal and negotiation to the closing of the sale.
- Leveraging existing customer relationships so as to maximize the margins earned through each customer. Not all customers are equally profitable. CRM software helps to identify customers who are highly profitable and activities that help to generate these profits. By tracking and analyzing their sales patterns, CRM applications can generate suggestions for cross-selling of higher value-added services to these customers and ultimately improve both the quality and longevity of the customer relationship.

CRM Life Cycle

All CRM systems have at their root an activity cycle (see Figure 11–13). The **CRM life cycle** begins with data collection about the customer through a whole range of touch points such as mail, phone contact with salespeople, visits to company sites, faxes, e-mails, and interaction over the Web. The benefits of this stage include improved front-office productivity through the use of automated data gathering systems. In the second stage of the cycle, the data are stored and organized in a customer-centric database. A relational database and sometimes a data warehouse or a datamart product is used at this stage. In the third stage, the stored data are analyzed through special software to generate customer profiles and appropriate marketing and promotion strategies. This phase of analysis is critical

FIGURE 11–13

*Customer relationship
management cycle*

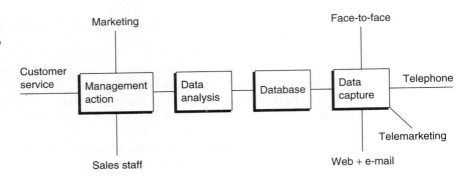

for the success of CRM. Analysis of customer interaction data leads to identifying behavior patterns and discovering causal relationships, which help to accurately model and predict customer satisfaction and behavior. In the final phase, strategic decisions are carried out. Business processes and structures are refined, and the organization is made more customer-centric as opposed to being product-centric. The heightened understanding derived in the analysis stage drives this process of transformation. Finally, customer data are made available to all company staff members who come into contact with the customer through any media. This helps the sales and service staff who interact with the customer to have a holistic view of the customer's interaction with the whole company.

The three major segments to the broad CRM software field are sales force automation, marketing automation, and customer service and support. Big CRM vendors such as Siebel and Vantive offer solutions that cover all the three segments. Smaller ones specialize in at least one segment.

Sales Force Automation

Historically, **sales force automation** has often been the first step in CRM initiatives. The sales force automation software increases sales force productivity by accelerating the process of converting leads to actual orders. These applications track the negotiation process, help generate proposals and preliminary quotes, and create complete sales packages based on a customer profile. They run on a platform that links the firm's external sales force with the CRM database, and they promote improved consultation between the field staff and the management. Goals of these applications include reduced sales cost, increased sales staff productivity, and enhanced order probability.

Marketing Automation

CRM software that serves **marketing automation** helps the firm distribute resources to target markets that have the highest potential value. These applications are based on data mining and data warehousing techniques. They seek out hidden patterns in customer buying behavior, help develop customer profiles, aid in planning marketing campaigns, identify target markets with high margins, and generate useful leads. They also help implement highly focused and targeted campaigns with the promise of better returns on the marketing investment and help track campaign effectiveness across different channels and market segments.

Customer Service and Support Applications

Customer service and support applications in CRM developed separately as automated help desk and call center systems. These systems are now being integrated as part of a complete CRM suite. The goal of these applications is to reduce the number of personnel in a firm's customer service and technical support departments. This is achieved by automating the order tracking and account status check activities and by responding to customer's difficulties with the product. These systems are a major source for collection of customer interaction data and a critical point for establishing and maintaining customer relationships. The objectives of service and support applications include helping organizations to not only please but also to delight their customers and to distinguish the firm in terms of the customer service and loyalty it generates.

Summary

This chapter focused on packaged software solutions that enable integration among business applications within a company and across the company boundary with its suppliers and customers. Integration occurs at two levels. There is an integration of applications within a firm and integration of applications across firms. Application integration within firms is often based on enterprise resource planning (ERP) systems. ERP systems allow businesses to run efficient business processes that link multiple functional activities such as accounting, order processing, manufacturing, procurement, and shipment. New bolt-on systems tie in the systems of one company with its suppliers and customers. These new systems that run either independently or as an add-on to existing ERP systems focus on coordination with the customer and the suppliers. Depending on its focus, these systems are known as customer relationship management, business-to-business e-commerce, or supply chain management systems. The chapter covered SCM and CRM in detail. A coordination theory framework was introduced. The framework helped in differentiating between different software classes such as CRM and SCM. It pinpointed the role such software plays in achieving the dual organizational goals of efficiency and flexibility.

Key Terms

Auction   422
Available to promise (ATP)   407
Build-to-order   423
Build-to-stock   423
Collaborative planning,
   forecasting, and
   replenishment (CPFR)   424
Customer relationship
   management (CRM)   424
CRM life cycle   425

Marketing automation   426
Reverse auction   422
Sales force automation   426
Supply chain management
   (SCM)   416
Synchronized supply chains   423
Vendor-managed inventory
   (VMI)   424
Visibility   423

Review Questions

1. Use the coordination theory framework to describe the contribution of ERP software to organizational goals such as efficiency and flexibility.
2. Describe the logic of ERP software.
3. Differentiate between software systems such as customer relationship management (CRM) software, enterprise resource planning (ERP), and supply chain management (SCM) software.
4. What are the limitations of the EDI platform? How does a Web-based platform for interenterprise communication rectify that?
5. What is visibility? Why is visibility good? Why is it difficult to deliver visibility to customers and suppliers?
6. Is CPFR related to the organizational goal of flexibility? What kind of range and reach of informational structure is needed to deliver CPFR?
7. Describe the CRM life cycle.
8. Describe the different segments of CRM software.

Project

1. Visit the websites of CommerceOne, Siebel, and i2 Technologies. Differentiate between their product offerings. Use the concepts of reach and range of informational structure to delineate these differences.

References, Readings, and Hyperlinks

1. Anderson, David L., and Hau L. Lee. "The Internet Supply Chain: From the First Click to the Last Mile in the New Internet Economy." In *Achieving Supply Chain Excellence Through Technology*, Vol. 2. San Francisco: Montgomery Research Inc., 2000.

2. Anderson, Gordon. "From Supply Chain to Collaborative Commerce Networks: The Next Step in Supply Chain Management." In *Achieving Supply Chain Excellence Through Technology*, Vol. 2. San Francisco: Montgomery Research Inc., 2000.

3. Anthony, Tom. "Supply Chain Collaboration: Success in the New Internet Economy." In *Achieving Supply Chain Excellence Through Technology*, Vol. 2. San Francisco: Montgomery Research Inc., 2000.

4. Appell, Kyle. "The Value Propositions of Business-to-Business Dynamic Commerce." In *Achieving Supply Chain Excellence Through Technology*, Vol. 2. San Francisco: Montgomery Research Inc., 2000.

5. Bancroft, Nancy H., Henning Seip, and Andrea Sprengel. *Implementing SAP R/3*. Greenwich: Manning, 1998.

6. Curran, Thomas, and Gerhard Keller. *SAP R/3 Business Blueprint: Understanding the Business Process Reference Model*. Englewood Cliffs, NJ: Prentice Hall PTR, 1998.

7. Davenport, Thomas H. "Putting the Enterprise into the Enterprise System." *Harvard Business Review*, July–August 1998, pp. 121–31.

8. Davenport, Thomas H. *Mission Critical: Realizing the Promise of Enterprise Systems*. Boston: Harvard Business School Press, 2000.

9. Fisher, M. "What Is the Right Supply Chain for Your Product?" *Harvard Business Review*, March–April 1997, pp. 105–16.

10. Fingar, Peter, Harsha Kumar, and Tarun Sharma. *Enterprise E-Commerce: The Software Component Breakthrough for Business-to-Business Commerce*. Tampa: Meghan-Kiffer Press, 2000.

11. Gattora, John L. "The E-Supply Chain Reaches Asian Shores." In *Achieving Supply Chain Excellence Through Technology*, Vol. 2. San Francisco: Montgomery Research Inc., 2000.

12. Hicks, Donald. "Next Generation Supply Chain Strategic Planning Technology and Applications." In *Achieving Supply Chain Excellence Through Technology*, Vol. 2. San Francisco: Montgomery Research Inc., 2000.

13. Kalakota, Ravi, and Marcia Robinson. *e-Business: Roadmap for Success*. Reading, MA: Addison-Wesley, 1999.

14. Kirkpatrick, David. "The E-Ware War Comes to Enterprise Software." *Fortune*, December 7, 1998, pp. 102–12.

15. Malone, Thomas W. "Modeling Coordination in Organizations and Markets." *Management Science*, October 1987, pp. 1317–32.

16. Marschak, J., and R. Radner. *Economic Theory of Teams*. New Haven, CT: Yale University Press, 1972.

17. Quinn, Chad. "Intelligent Commerce and the E-Business Revolution: The Story Continues." In *Achieving Supply Chain Excellence Through Technology*, Vol. 2. San Francisco: Montgomery Research Inc., 2000.

18. Stimson, Judith H. "Performance Simulation: Developing Your People to Build a World Class Supply Chain." In *Achieving Supply Chain Excellence Through Technology*, Vol. 2. San Francisco: Montgomery Research Inc., 2000.

19. www.ascet.com
20. www.ariba.com
21. www.commerceone.com
22. www.baan.com
23. www.cherrytreeco.com
24. www.i2.com
25. www.manugistics.com
26. www.oracle.com/products/applications
27. www.peoplesoft.com
28. www.sap.com/products/supchain/supe_hd.htm
29. www.siebel.com
30. www.vantive.com
31. www.yet2.com
32. http://berube.crmproject.com
33. http://crm.ittoolbox.com

INDEX